D1134603

EARLY MODERN HERBALS AND THE BOOK TRADE

Between 1525 and 1640, a remarkable phenomenon occurred in the world of print: England saw the production of more than two dozen editions identified by their imprints or by contemporaries as "herbals." Sarah Neville explains how this genre grew from a series of tiny anonymous octavos to authoritative folio tomes with thousands of woodcuts, and how these curious works quickly became valuable commodities within a competitive print marketplace. Designed to serve readers across the social spectrum, these rich material artifacts represented both a profitable investment for publishers and an opportunity for authors to establish their credibility as botanists. Highlighting the shifting contingencies and regulations surrounding herbals and English printing during the sixteenth and early seventeenth centuries, the book argues that the construction of scientific authority in Renaissance England was inextricably tied up with the circumstances governing print. This title is also available as Open Access on Cambridge Core at doi.org/ 10.1017/9781009031615.

Sarah Neville is Assistant Professor in the Department of English at Ohio State University. She is an assistant editor of the New Oxford Shakespeare and an associate coordinating editor of the Digital Renaissance Editions.

EARLY MODERN HERBALS AND THE BOOK TRADE

English Stationers and the Commodification of Botany

SARAH NEVILLE

Ohio State University

CAMBRIDGE
UNIVERSITY PRESS

CAMBRIDGE
UNIVERSITY PRESS

University Printing House, Cambridge CB2 8BS, United Kingdom

One Liberty Plaza, 20th Floor, New York, NY 10006, USA

477 Williamstown Road, Port Melbourne, VIC 3207, Australia

314–321, 3rd Floor, Plot 3, Splendor Forum, Jasola District Centre,
New Delhi – 110025, India

103 Penang Road, #05–06/07, Visioncrest Commercial, Singapore 238467

Cambridge University Press is part of the University of Cambridge.

It furthers the University's mission by disseminating knowledge in the pursuit of
education, learning, and research at the highest international levels of excellence.

www.cambridge.org
Information on this title: www.cambridge.org/9781316515990
DOI: 10.1017/9781009031615

This book is freely available in an open access edition thanks to TOME (Toward an Open Monograph
Ecosystem) – a collaboration of the Association of American Universities, the Association of University
Presses, and the Association of Research Libraries – and the generous support of The Ohio State University
Libraries. Learn more at the TOME website, available at: openmonographs.org.

First published 2022

A catalogue record for this publication is available from the British Library.

Library of Congress Cataloging-in-Publication Data
NAMES: Neville, Sarah (Assistant professor of English), author.
TITLE: Early modern herbals and the book trade : English stationers and the commodification of botany /
Sarah Neville.
DESCRIPTION: New York : Cambridge University Press, 2021. | Includes bibliographical references
and index.
IDENTIFIERS: LCCN 2021034746 (print) | LCCN 2021034747 (ebook) | ISBN 9781316515990 (hardback) |
ISBN 9781009031615 (ebook)
SUBJECTS: LCSH: Herbals – England – History and criticism. | Botany – England–History. | Publishers
and publishing – England – History.
CLASSIFICATION: LCC QK14.5 .N48 2021 (print) | LCC QK14.5 (ebook) | DDC 615.3/210942–dc23
LC record available at https://lccn.loc.gov/2021034746
LC ebook record available at https://lccn.loc.gov/2021034747

ISBN 978-1-316-51599-0 Hardback

For all my teachers who pointed,
then let me find my way

Contents

Figures

Acknowledgments

This project was born, as was I, on the northern shores of Lake Ontario, which are the traditional lands of the Huron-Wendat, the Mississaugas of the Credit River, and the Haudenosaunee Confederacy. It and I grew together on the banks of the Wolastoq, the traditional and unceded territory of the Wəlastəkokewiyik. Later, we moved south, where, beside Keenhongsheconsepung, we were nurtured and we thrived in the land of the Delaware, Miami, Shawnee and Wyandot Peoples. I am, and remain, grateful for the traditional caretakers of the lands on which I live and work.

Throughout my life, I have been fortunate to be often in the presence of teachers whose curiosity, empathy, and integrity have become a model for my own. My work on herbals is beholden to my undergraduate and graduate professors, without whom this work would neither have germinated nor have come to fruition. I am deeply obliged to Ian Lancashire, who, by sharing his enthusiasm for noncanonical books, planted the seed of this project in an undergraduate seminar long, long ago. David Galbraith has watched me sprout from a foolish undergraduate to a slightly less foolish professor, and his deep knowledge and deft kindness have always arrived just in time to save me from myself. I cannot express enough how grateful I am, both for his steadfast friendship and for the model of scholarship he provides.

My parents taught me to read, but Randall McLeod taught me to stop reading and to start appreciating that every book is foremost an object assembled by human hands. In Randy's world, a world he invites students to share with him, every book is different, and it is this difference that makes books wonderful to behold. If I have been able to show my readers any "strangeness" in the subjects – and the objects – they think they know, it is due to Randy's inimitable influence. David L. Gants showed me how to think quantitatively and critically about historical and bibliographic evidence, and how to move effortlessly between the general and the particular in both book history and the vicissitudes of academic life.

A spur-of-the-moment decision to change courses during my master's degree solidified my view that literature exists within an ecosystem of intertextuality. Peter W. M. Blayney's grip on the history of the London Stationers' Company created a gravitational pull so strong that it sucked me into its orbit, forever changing the nature of my scholarship and my approach to the early modern period. Blayney is to book history what Linnaeus is to natural history – the figure who brings precision to a mass of information, variously organized by his predecessors, with the design of explaining the relationships that govern how individuals are related to each other and to a larger pattern. His influence runs like an electric current throughout this project, for, once I saw early modern printed books as commodities produced in a shared community of physical and intellectual labor, my research was never the same.

My approach to scholarship also changed through discussions with friends and colleagues at meetings of the Society for the History of Authorship, Reading and Publishing, the Shakespeare Association of America, the Modern Language Association, the Medical Humanities Health Studies Seminar at Indiana University–Purdue University Indianapolis, the Renaissance Society of America, the International Shakespeare Conference, and the Society for Textual Scholarship, where, at various times and places during the past fifteen years, parts of this work were presented. For their encouragements, curiosity, and aid, I especially would like to thank Douglas Bruster, Ryan Claycomb, Jen Drouin, Lowell Duckert, Roger Gaskell, Geoff Georgi, Sara Georgi, Jean Howard, Dani Ghatta, Joshua Graham, David Scott Kastan, Sujata Iyengar, Laura Kolb, Peter Kuling, Zachary Lesser, Erin McCarthy, Kirk Melnikoff, Steve Mentz, Vin Nardizzi, Lorraine Nolan, Jason Woodman Simmonds, Gary Waite, and Erin Whitmore. My textual thinking improved immeasurably by spending half a decade sparring with Terri Bourus, Gary Taylor, John Jowett, Gabriel Egan, and, most especially, Francis X. Connor, my colleagues on the New Oxford Shakespeare.

My graduate students in a course on the Early Modern Medical Marketplace sharpened my investigations into herbals and healing in early modern English literature and culture. Amrita Dhar, Richard Dutton, Hannibal Hamlin, Jennifer Higginbotham, Chris Highley, Elizabeth Kolkovich, and Luke Wilson, my Renaissance area group colleagues at the Ohio State University (OSU), have offered sustained mentorship and provided me with a long-awaited community. Other OSU colleagues, particularly Sara Butler, Scott DeWitt, Molly Farrell, Harvey Graff, Richard Firth Green, Marcus Jackson, Mira Kafantaris, Erin

K. Kelly, Sandra Macpherson, Victoria Muñoz, Jacob Risinger, Jennifer Schlueter, Lauren Squires, Christa Teston, Lisa Voigt, Elissa Washuta, Nick White, and Robyn Warhol, raised my spirits, took me out, brought me snacks, read drafts, and gave me models for how to do the work. A chance meeting with Damon Jaggars over lunch made me aware of TOME: Towards an Open Monograph Ecosystem, a program that has made it possible for me to make this work widely accessible and freely available to all who wish to read it. A manuscript preparation grant from the Ohio State College of Arts and Sciences funded the cost of image permissions. At Cambridge University Press, I was lucky to have had this project marshaled through the press by Emily Hockley. The anonymous readers she found for me were exacting, generous, detailed, and very, very much appreciated. I thank them both wholeheartedly.

While I was a graduate student, my work was funded by the Social Sciences and Humanities Research Council of Canada, and my capacity for investigating the language of rare books is the result of a scholarship in Descriptive Bibliography at the Rare Book School at the University of Virginia. My investigations into the incredibly popular little *Herball* that started it all were supported by two blissful months of fellowship at the Huntington Library in San Marino, California. I owe a special obligation to the Huntington's dedicated staff, in particular Suzi Kraznoo, Catherine Wehrey-Miller, Meredith Berbée Jones, Juan Gomez, and Kadin Henningsen, who kept me out of trouble when the reading room was open and in the pub when it was not. My work on John Gerard was made demonstrably better through the assistance of Pamela Forde, archivist of the Royal College of Physicians in London. A 2018 weekend seminar on "Digging the Past" at the Folger Shakespeare Library, led by Frances Dolan, showed me the breadth of early moderns' interactions with nature and gave me a community of like-minded folks.

As a wayward and sometimes weird scholar, I cannot express emphatically enough my gratitude to the librarians everywhere who make imaging, document delivery, and interlibrary loans possible. To the reference, special collections, and circulation librarians of the Harriet Irving Library at the University of New Brunswick, the Wise and Downtown Libraries of West Virginia University, and the Thompson Library of OSU, the following bibliography is as much your work as it is mine. An especial thanks to Robin Rider of the University of Wisconsin–Madison Special Collections and to Eric Johnson of OSU's Rare Books and Manuscripts, both of whose stewardships have supplied images for this book. Aaron Pratt of the Harry Ransom Center at the University of Texas at Austin cannot be spoken of in anything but superlatives: his knowledge of bibliography is so vast and his generosity so limitless, and I am grateful to call him a friend.

The supportive presence of my friends and family has lasted even through the vicissitudes of time and distance. My parents and siblings have been my steadfast supporters from afar, and I remain grateful for the humor and love of Louise Paquette Neville, Bruce Neville, Désirée Arian-Neville, Ashley Neville Moate, Adam Neville, Matthew Neville, and Rea Godbold. (This is your official notice: you can now remove that copy of my dissertation from the coffee table.) My small dog posse of Lexicon Ignatius, Lucy Boethius, Tinkerbell Pericles, and Luna Erasmus made and make sure that, wherever I am, I always keep my heart close to the ground and my eyes on the ball. I have been held with loving care by many friends, whose advice and help were never more than a phone call or email away: Piers Brown, Glenn Clifton, Vicki Graff, Brett and Fen Greatley-Hirsch, Brecken Hancock, Janelle Jenstad, Merrill Kaplan, Tara Lyons, Rod Moody-Corbett, Pashmina Murthy, Emily Pawley, Hilary St. John, Steven Urkowitz, and Valerie Wayne. I cannot express enough what their fierce support and tireless love has meant to me. The labor and care of others also made it possible for me to finish this book during the devastating Covid-19 pandemic. I am particularly indebted to my in-laws, Sally Farmer, Elizabeth Linde, and Jens Linde, who have provided childcare, fancy cocktails, image corrections, and encouragement throughout the home stretch.

At long last: there are not enough thanks to spare for Alan Farmer, my perfect audience, my most exacting reader, and my best, most sympathetic friend. You are worth losing my Canadian accent for. Finally, thank you to Charlie, who taught me that "waiting is not easy" but who himself was worth every moment of the wait. Yes, we can play cars now.

Note on Transcription and Citation

When quoting early modern texts, I have retained the original spelling, including the use of *u/v* and *i/j*, with the exception of replacing the *long-s ʃ* with *s* and *vv* with *w*. I have expanded contractions (except for ampersands) with supplied letters in square brackets (as in "cōmon" → "co[m]mon"), and I have declined superscript letters (as in "M*ͬ*." to "Mr."). I also have retained original punctuation, including the now-obsolete virgule or / glyph. With the exception of ash (æ) and ethel (œ), all ligatures are silently separated where applicable to single graphemes corresponding to modern usage. I have shortened and standardized capitalization in titles throughout. The names of early modern figures are standardized using the preferred spellings of the STC or ODNB.

For the ease of my readers' ability to locate the particular editions I discuss, the first mention of a new title will be followed by its identification number in *STC*, Wing, and *USTC*. These numbers are also listed in the Bibliography.

Abbreviations

ODNB   *Oxford Dictionary of National Biography*, www.oxforddnb.com.
OED   *Oxford English Dictionary*, www.oed.com.
STC   A. W. Pollard and G. R. Redgrave, *A Short-Title Catalogue of Books Printed in England, Scotland, and Ireland and of English Books Printed Abroad 1475–1640*, 2nd ed., rev. W. A. Jackson, F. S. Ferguson, and Katherine F. Pantzer, 3 vols. (London: Bibliographical Society, 1976–1991).
USTC   *Universal Short Title Catalogue*, www.ustc.ac.uk.
Wing   Donald Wing, *Short-Title Catalogue of Books Printed in England, Scotland, Ireland, Wales, and British America, and of English Books Printed in Other Countries, 1641–1700*, 2nd ed., 3 vols. (New York: Modern Language Association of America, 1972–1998).

Prologue
Milton's Trees

After the pair eat of the Tree of Knowledge, Milton's Adam, mourning that their newly discovered nakedness leaves them vulnerable to reproach, admonishes Eve and counsels that they should cover their private parts. Adam notes the pair should

> devise
> What best may for the present serve to hide
> The parts of each from other, that seem most
> To shame obnoxious and unseemliest seen,
> Some tree whose broad smooth leaves, together sewed
> And girded on our loins, may cover round
> Those middle parts that this newcomer, shame,
> There sit not and reproach us as unclean. (9.1091–1098)[1]

The two cast about their woodland surroundings and settle on a fig tree, "not," Milton's narrator cautions, "that kind for fruit renowned" (9.1101) but another, one with branches that spread both so wide and so long that they bend down again towards the earth and root there, creating a forest of a single tree. These "bended twigs" (9.1105) create a "pillared shade / High overarched, and echoing walks between" (9.1106–1107), a living architecture like that which gives ease to the herdsman sheltering himself from the sun's oppressive heat and who "tends his pasturing herds / At loopholes cut through thickest shade" (9.1109–1110). This living copse thus offers the very kind of "glade / Obscured" (9.1085–1086) that Adam originally sought in order to hide himself from the dazzling, heavenly shapes of God and angels before he settled on the more solvable problem of the couple's nakedness.[2] Thus, instead of permanently secluding themselves within the fig tree's dark bower,

---

[1] Quotations from the poem are from John Milton, *Paradise Lost*, ed. David Scott Kastan (Indianapolis, IN: Hackett Publishing, 2005).

[2] On the means by which Eden's vegetation can both illuminate and obscure, see Joanna Picciotto, *Labors of Innocence in Early Modern England* (Cambridge, MA: Harvard University Press, 2010).

I

> Those leaves
> They gathered, broad as Amazonian targe,
> And with what skill they had, together sewed
> To gird their waist, vain covering if to hide
> Their guilt and dreaded shame.   (9.1110–1114)

Now recognized as a banyan tree, or *Ficus benghalensis*, commentators and literary critics have long noted that Milton's fig tree finds its source in the "arched Indian Fig tree" of John Gerard's *Herball or General Historie of Plantes*, which was first published in 1597 and republished twice in the 1630s.[3] In his description, Gerard comments on the way that the tree's branches offer

> the Indians . . . coverture against the extreme heate of the sunne, wherewith they are greeuously vexed: some likewise vse them for pleasure, cutting downe by a direct line a long walk, or as it were a vault, through the thickest part, from which also they cut certaine loope holes or windows in some places . . . that they may see their cattle that feedeth thereby.[4]

Critics have also located Milton's inspiration in the twelfth book of Pliny's *Naturalis historia* (*Natural History*), where Pliny describes trees;[5] of the Indian fig, Pliny notes that "the broad leaves of the tree have just the shape of an Amazonian buckler."[6] Other critics have searched elsewhere for the source of what Marissa Nicosia calls Milton's "sartorially useful Edenic tree" and found evidence of Milton's borrowings from *Purchas His Pigrimes* and Walter Raleigh's *History of the World*.[7]

Identifying both the tree of forbidden fruit and the tree with which Adam and Eve cover themselves has been seen as crucial for correctly deciphering Milton's allegorical and exegetical goals in *Paradise Lost*.[8] Yet, though the leaves of Milton's fig tree serve their

---

[3] John Gerard, *The Herball or Generall Historie of Plantes* (London: Edmund Bollifant for Bonham Norton and John Norton, 1597) (*STC* 11750). Gerard does not use the term "banyan"; besides the English name of "arched Fig tree," his alternative names for the tree include *Ficus Indica* and *Arbor Goa*.

[4] Gerard, *Herball* (1597), sigs. 4Q8r–4Q8v.

[5] Marissa Nicosia, "Milton's Banana: *Paradise Lost* and Colonial Botany," *Milton Studies* 58 (2017): 49–66.

[6] Pliny the Elder, *The Natural History*, trans. John Bostock and H. T. Riley (London: Taylor and Francis, 1855).

[7] Nicosia, "Milton's Banana," 49. S. Viswanathan, "Milton and Purchas' Linschoten: An Additional Source for Milton's Indian Figtree" *Milton Newsletter* 2 (1968): 43–45. See also Walter Raleigh, *The History of the World* (London: William Stansby for Walter Burre, 1614), 1.4.3.

[8] For a defense of Milton's appreciation of experiential approaches, see Karen L. Edwards, *Milton and the Natural World: Science and Poetry in Paradise Lost* (Cambridge: Cambridge University Press, 1999).

narrative purpose, they have proved a perennial problem for Milton's critics. Pliny's characterization of the banyan's leaves as broad and wide as a buckler, appropriate for the girding of Adam and Eve's loins, is botanically incorrect – the tree's leaves are much smaller, about the size of a hand. Because Gerard had not actually seen the tree himself (he notes in his account of its temperature and virtues that he has nothing "of our owne knowledge" to speak of), he is forced to repeat much of the substance of Pliny's account; however, Gerard differs from Pliny in his characterization of its leaves, suggesting that he is also following a different botanical resource. Gerard notes that the tree's leaves are "hard and wrinckled, in shape like those of the Quince tree, greene aboue, and of a whitish horie colour vnderneath, whereupon the Elephants delight to feed."[9] In making a simile of the leaves of the well-known English quince, Gerard assumes that his readers have a familiarity with English botany upon which he can base his botanical description of the novel Indian fig, hinting at the way that botanical knowledge in the period was more widespread than the popularity of large-format herbals may otherwise suggest. The descriptive science of natural classification was accretive and comparative, proceeding under the assumption that the reader of a botanical text had an existing knowledge or nomenclature upon which the herbal author could draw. The differing characteristics of Gerard's and Pliny's fig trees thus pose a thorny interpretive problem: while Pliny's leaves are broad as cloth, their size makes sewing somewhat redundant, while Gerard's "hard and wrinckled" leaves better conjure the effort involved in Adam and Eve's "first act of sweated labor ... Their loincloths are fig leaves transformed by their own manu-facture."[10] Thus, in querying the precise nature and emblematic significance of the leaves of the "sartorially useful fig tree," critics also raise questions about the accuracy of Milton's own botanical understanding as well as the botanical knowledge that Milton assumed was held by his readers.

Some commentators upon *Paradise Lost* have resolved these questions by asserting that Pliny, and Milton after him, simply conflated the banyan with another tree with broad leaves, namely the banana. John Bradshaw, in his nineteenth-century edition of *The Poetical Works of John Milton*, cites

---

[9] Gerard, *Herball* (1597), sig. 4Q8r.
[10] Ann Rosalind Jones and Peter Stallybrass, *Renaissance Clothing and the Materials of Memory* (Cambridge: Cambridge University Press, 2000), 269.

a passage where bananas are called "Indian figs" in Charles Dellon's *Voyage to the East Indies*, which was translated into English in 1698.[11] Bradshaw writes, "if, then, as appears, both the *banyan* and the *banana*, or plantain, were known as the Indian 'figs', we have the explanation of the banyan being described as 'renowned for fruit' and with 'leaves broad as Amazonian targe,' so true of the banana or plantain."[12] Supporting this account, Marissa Nicosia finds Horace Walpole transcribing into a printed copy of Milton's poem a portion of Griffith Hughes's *Natural History of Barbados* (1750) where Hughes too surmises that Milton's fig tree was actually a banana tree. Hughes finds his evidence through a close reading of Milton alongside Pliny, and Nicosia notes that Pliny's account of the banana tree immediately follows that of the banyan.[13]

For Nicosia, Walpole's endorsement of Hughes's banana theory indicates the uses to which Milton's poem, much like seventeenth-century books of natural history more generally, could be put in service of a colonialist enterprise "to authorize imperial knowledge and occupation."[14] I am just as interested, however, in the remarkable and recursive accretion of textual material that Nicosia describes: Walpole transcribing Hughes's account of Pliny's influence on Milton's choice of tree into Walpole's own printed copy of *Paradise Lost*, just as Hughes himself incorporated Milton's *Paradise Lost* into his *Natural History of Barbados* as a means of justifying his extensive attention to the plant.[15] I am also struck by the way that Nicosia herself uses the structure of Pliny's *Natural History* to lend additional support to Hughes's claim: knowing that Milton read (or had read to him) Pliny's account of the fig tree, Nicosia supposes that Milton kept reading to discover in the following chapter a tree whose leaf morphology better suited his sartorial ends. While it remains unclear whether Milton's conflation of the banyan and the banana within *Paradise Lost*'s fig tree was accidental or deliberate, scholarly attempts to elucidate and classify Milton's botanical intentions reveal the way that books of natural history were inherently intertextual, looping

---

[11] John Bradshaw, ed., *The Poetical Works of John Milton* (London: William Allen, 1878), 614.

[12] Bradshaw, *Poetical Works*, 614. A similar claim is made in the notes of A. W. Verity's Cambridge University Press edition of *Paradise Lost* (1929).

[13] Nicosia, "Milton's Banana," 53.

[14] Nicosia, "Milton's Banana," 54. For an explanation of the ways that books of natural history shaped British views of colonial possessions, see Jefferson Dillman, *Colonizing Paradise: Landscape and Empire in the British West Indies* (Tuscaloosa: University of Alabama Press, 2015).

[15] Nicosia suggests that Walpole may have been writing in a copy of *Paradise Lost* that was owned by someone else ("Milton's Banana," 63n17). The volume containing Walpole's annotations is held in the New York Public Library.

back upon each other to clarify, substantiate, and authorize particular knowledge claims about the natural world. The marginalia left behind in individual copies of all kinds of books, including poetry, reveal the ways that readers of texts of natural history engaged with these works selectively, approaching them with diverse strategies for gathering information and with various degrees of credulity. Alongside the authorial claims in these texts to direct observation or firsthand experience, the individual copies of books like Gerard's *Herball* or Milton's *Paradise Lost* were the property of individual users who, like Walpole, left evidence of their reading behind in idiosyncratic and sometimes reiterating ways.

Early Modern Herbals and the Book Trade reveals how printed books of botany functioned as exchangeable material artifacts within an emerging trade of ideas about the natural world. As artifacts, herbals enabled would-be authors to gather the descriptive botanical information of others and to refine it in accordance with their own experience. Once acquired by readers, printed books of botany thus provided opportunities for additional botanical writing by those who could surmise, conflate, correct, and comment upon the texts – and literally, in the form of marginalia, often upon the material books themselves – that preceded them. Booksellers concerned themselves with such issues because it was clear that Renaissance readers responded to the affordances that printed books offered almost as much as they did to the texts that those books contained. Organizational materials such as glossarial notes, indexes, and tables were selling points, and early modern readers deprived of such resources in books of natural history would regularly provide their own. The following pages reveal the ways that booksellers and printers responsible for the manufacture of books variously conceived of the material form of their herbals as they assessed the dynamics of English and continental print marketplaces throughout the sixteenth and early seventeenth centuries. Chief among booksellers' concerns was the salability of a particular title; and as they considered what to publish, booksellers were invested in details such as an author's current fame, professional status, or authority to speak over a particular knowledge domain. Booksellers also were concerned about practical issues like the size or format of a volume, its need for illustrations, and any similar books already in the marketplace with which their proposed new title would compete.

An attention to herbals' material forms enables us to recognize that, in composing the fig tree of *Paradise Lost*, Milton may have been as influenced by the organization of John Gerard's chapters as he was by Pliny's. Immediately below the woodcut of the arched Indian fig (banyan) tree in

Gerard's *Herball* of 1597 is the chapter heading "Of Adams Apple tree," a "herbie" tree "the bignesse of a mans thigh."[16] Gerard's descriptions of the tree's leaves and fruit make clear to modern readers that he is describing a banana tree. It has "diuers great leaues, of the length of three cubits and a halfe, sometimes more, according to the soile where it growth, and of a cubite and more broad, of bignes sufficient to wrape a childe in of two yeeres old."[17] The word "bananas" eventually emerges in Gerard's account as a title that is common "in that part of Africa which we call Ginny [Guinea]."[18] Nonetheless, in English the tree is known as "Adams Apple tree" because "[t]he Iewes also suppose it to be the tree of which Adam did taste; which others thinke to be a ridiculous fable," and so *this* name, despite Gerard's reservation of judgment, becomes the heading of his 130th chapter (see Figure 0.1).[19]

Gerard's description of the tree's leaves as being of sufficient size to use as a swaddling cloth lends credence to Hughes's theory that Milton's "Indian fig" was a banana, yet Gerard's Adam's Apple tree may have stuck in Milton's mind for more emblematic reasons. In his description of the Adam's Apple fruit, Gerard notes that it is "in forme like a small Cucumber, and of the same bignes ... in taste not greatly perceived at the first, but presently after it pleaseth, and intiseth a man to eate liberally thereof, by a secret intising sweetnes which it yeeldeth."[20] Gerard's repetition of the banana's subtle but "enticing" flavor is echoed in Milton's poem, suggesting Milton's familiarity with this chapter of Gerard when Eve offers Adam "that fair enticing fruit / With liberal hand" (9.996–997). Further testifying to Milton's close botanical reading as he characterized the forbidden fruit's allure, his Eve continues to liberally partake of the fruit "while Adam took no thought, / Eating his fill, nor Eve to iterate / Her former trespass feared" (9.1004–1006). The pair's shared transgression soon inflames their carnal desire, and after casting his "lascivious eyes" (9.1014) upon Eve, Adam seduces her via *comprobatio.* Despite the initial subtlety of the flavor of Adam's Apple, which, as Gerard notes, is "not greatly perceived at the first," such flavors in *Paradise Lost* likewise necessitate a refined appetite. Milton's seductive Adam carefully credits Eve's "judicious" palate, which is responsible for bringing them both to "true relish, tasting" (9.1024). The pair soon disport in "amorous play" as a result of the "force of that fallacious fruit" (9.1046), echoing Gerard's description of the virtues of a fruit that "yeeldeth but little nourishment"

---

[16] Gerard, *Herball* (1597), sig. 4Q8r.   [17] Gerard, *Herball* (1597), sig. 4Q8v.
[18] Gerard, *Herball* (1597), sig. 4R1r.   [19] Gerard, *Herball* (1597), sig. 4R1r.
[20] Gerard, *Herball* (1597), sig. 4Q8v.

HISTORIE OF PLANTS. 1331

through the thickeſt part, from which alſo they cut certaine loope holes or windowes in ſome places, to the end to receiue thereby the freſh coole aire that entereth therat; as alſo for light, that they may ſee their cattle that feedeth thereby, to auoid any danger that might happen vnto them, either by the enimie or wilde beaſts : from which vault or cloſe walke, doth rebound ſuch an admirable eccho, or anſwering voice(if one of them ſpeake vnto another with a lowde voice)that it doth reſound or anſwer againe ſower or fiue times, according to the height of the voice, to which it doth anſwere, and that ſo planly, that it cannot be knowne from the voice it ſelfe : the firſt or mother of this wood or deſart of trees, is hard to be knowne from the children, but by the greatnes of the bodie, which three men can ſcarſely fathom about : vpon the braunches whereof growe leaues, hard and wrinckled, in ſhape like thoſe of the Quince tree, greene aboue, and of a whitiſh horie colour vnderneath, whereupon the Elephants delight to feed : among which leaues come foorth the fruit, of the bignes of a mans thombe, in ſhape like a ſmall Fig, but of a ſanguine or bloudie colour, and of a ſweete raſte, but not ſo pleaſant as the Figs of Spaine : notwithſtanding they are good to be eaten, and withall very holeſom̄e.

Arbor Goa. ſiue Indica.
The arched Indian Fig tree.

※ *The place.*

This wonderous tree groweth in diuers places of the eaſt Indies, eſpecially neere vnto Goa, and alſo in Malaca, it is a ſtranger in the moſt parts of the world.

※ *The time.*

This tree keepeth his leaues greene winter and ſommer.

※ *The names.*

This tree is called of thoſe that haue trauelled *Ficus Indica*, the Indian Fig, and *Arbor Goa*, of the place where it groweth in greateſt plentie : wee may call it in Engliſh the arched Fig tree.

※ *The temperature and vertues.*

We haue nothing to write of the temperature or vertues of this tree, of our owne knowledge : neither haue we receiued from others, more then that the fruit heereof is generally eaten, and that without any hurt at all, but rather good and alſo nouriſhing.

Of Adams Apple tree. Chap. 130.

※ *The deſcription.*

1 WHether this plant may be reckoned for a tree properly, or for an herbie tree, it is diſputable, conſidering the ſoft and herbie ſubſtance whereof it is made, (that is to ſaie) when it hath attained to the height of ſixe or ſeauen cubits, and of the bigneſſe of a mans thigh : notwithſtanding it may be cut downe at one ſtroke with a ſword ; or two or three cuts with

Figure 0.1 John Gerard, *The Herball or General Historie of Plants* (1597), sig. 4Q8r. Image reproduced courtesy of the Ohio State University Libraries' Rare Books & Manuscripts Library (QK 41 .G34).

yet "stirreth to generation."[21] Milton's reading of Adam's Apple tree in Gerard generates both the fruit that leads to man's fall and the leaves that cover his shame. The two woodcuts that accompany the chapter (Figure 0.2) further serve to highlight these two characteristics of the plant.

Milton may have found the evocative characteristics of Gerard's description of the Adam's Apple fruit especially appropriate for a poem built around the theme of *felix culpa*: when cut open the fruit supposedly reveals the imprint of a crucified man.[22] As with his description of the virtues of the arched Indian fig, which he admits is limited by his lack of personal experience of the tree, Gerard is again forced to rely on the written accounts of others in his chapter on the banana: "if it be cut according to the length, saith mine author, oblique, transuers, or any other way whatsoeuer, may be seene the shape and forme of a crosse, with a man fastened thereto."[23] The identity of this "author" remains obscure, but Gerard's curiosity about the emblematic fruit eventually enabled him to confirm part of his account through firsthand investigation: "my selfe haue seene the fruit, and cut it in peeces, which was brought me from Alepo in pickle; the crosse I might perceiue, as the forme of a Spread Egle in the roote of Ferne, but the man I leaue to be sought for by those that have better eies and iudgement then my selfe."[24] If it is a banana, Gerard's Adam's Apple, which is forbidden and later eaten by Milton's Adam and Eve, Gerard's uncertainty about the fruit's religious connotations leads critics to an ambivalent end: Gerard neither confirms nor denies the presence of a man on a cross.[25]

The organization and *mise-en-page* of Gerard's *Herball* of 1597 seem to argue in favor of Griffith Hughes's (and Horace Walpole's) insistence on Milton's arboreal conflation of the banyan and the banana trees, one that is again supported by assuming Milton's sequential reading practice. However, it is not entirely clear to scholars precisely *which* edition of Gerard's *Herball* it was that Milton was reading, and a later edition resolves the banana's exegetical question. The second edition of the book, which was reprinted thirty-six years later in 1633, updated many of Gerard's entries to offer supplemental information on the basis of its new editor's botanical scholarship and his own personal experience.[26] The editor, the apothecary

[21] Gerard, *Herball* (1597), sig. 4R1r.
[22] Arthur O. Lovejoy, "Milton and the Paradox of the Fortunate Fall," *ELH* 4 (1937): 161–179.
[23] Gerard, *Herball* (1597), sig. 4Q8v.   [24] Gerard, *Herball* (1597), sig. 4Q8v.
[25] On Milton's strategies of botanical "naming and not naming," see Edwards, *Milton and the Natural World*, 143–153.
[26] John Gerard, *The Herball or Generall Historie of Plantes*, ed. Thomas Johnson (London: Adam Islip for Joyce Norton and Richard Whitaker, 1633) (*STC* 11751).

THE THIRD BOOKE OF THE

1332

with a knife, euen with as much eafe as the roote of a Radifh or Carrot of the like bignes: from a thicke, fat, threadie roote, rife immediately diuers great leaues, of the length of three cubits and a halfe, fometimes more, according to the foile where it groweth, and of a cubite and more broad, of bignes fufficient to wrap a childe in of two yeeres old, in fhape like thofe of Mandrake, of an ouerworne greene colour, hauing a broad rib or finewe running through the middle thereof: which leaues, whether by reafon of the extreme hot fcorching funne, or of their owne nature, in September are fo dry and withered that there is nothing therof left or to be feene, but onely the middle rib. From the middle of thefe leaues rifeth vp a thick trunke, whereon do grow the like leaues which the people do cut off, as alfo thofe next the ground, by which meanes it rifeth vp to the height of a tree, which otherwife would remaine a lowe and bafe plant: this manner of cutting they vfe from time to time, vntill it come to a certaine height, aboue the reach of the Elephant, which greedily feeketh after the fruit. In the midft of the top among the leaues commeth foorth a foft and fungus ftumpe, whereon do grow diuers apples in forme like a fmall Cucumber, and of the fame bignes, couered with a thin rinde like that of the Fig, of a yellow colour when they be ripe: the pulpe or fubftance of the meate, is like that of the Pompion, without either feedes, ftones, or kernels. in tafte not greatly perceiued at the firft, but prefently after it pleafeth, and intifeth a man to eate libe-rally thereof, by a fecret intifing fweetnes which it yeeldeth: in which fruit if it be cut according to the length, faith mine author, oblique, tranfuers, or any other way whatfoeuer, may be feene the fhape and forme of a croffe, with a man faftned thereto: my felfe haue feene the fruit, and cut it in peeces, which was brought me from Alepo in pickle; the croffe I might perceiue, as the forme of a Spread Egle in the roote of Ferne, but the man I leaue to be fought for by thofe that haue better eies and iudgement then my felfe.

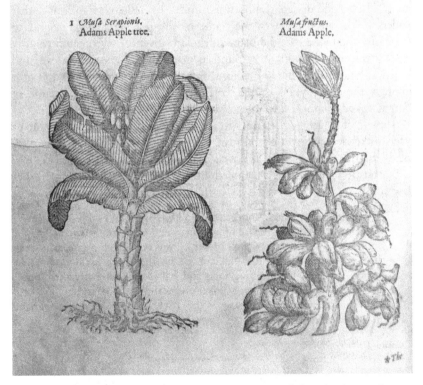

1 *Mufa Serapionis.*
Adams Apple tree.

Mufa fructus.
Adams Apple.

Figure 0.2 John Gerard, *The Herball or General Historie of Plants* (1597), sig. 4Q8v. Image reproduced courtesy of the Ohio State University Libraries' Rare Books & Manuscripts Library (QK 41 .G34).

Thomas Johnson, was supplied by the publishers with different woodcut illustrations, but he reproduced most of Gerard's verbal text and augmented it with his own writing. What in 1597 was known as "Adam's Apple tree" becomes, by 1633, "Adams Apple tree, or the West-Indian Plantaine."

Johnson's additions to the *Herball* are marked by double crosses, a typographical feature designed to enable readers of the 1633 edition to identify shifts in the identity of the authorial voice speaking of its own firsthand experience with the plants being described. Because he is functioning as the editor of the text of an esteemed, and now deceased, English authority, when Johnson refers to "our author" in one of his marked sections, he inevitably means Gerard, and he uses this designation to refute or to confirm Gerard's previous findings. Johnson quotes Gerard's chapter of the Adam's Apple tree verbatim, including Gerard's account of those who "suppose it to be the tree of which Adam did taste," but in his supplement Johnson notes that "some (as our Author hath said) haue iudged it the forbidden fruit; other-some, the Grapes brought to *Moses* out of the Holy-land."[27] In his glib update, Johnson minimizes any religious significance that readers might associate with the name of the tree, preferring instead to emphasize the name that the plant is regularly given in seventeenth-century travel literature: "This Plant is found in many places of Asia, Africke, and America, especially in the hot regions: you may find frequent mention of it amongst the sea voyages to the East and West Indies, by the name of Plantaines, or *Platanus, Bannanas, Bonnanas, Bouanas, Dananas, Poco, &c.*"[28]

Because of others' sea voyages to the West Indies, Johnson was able to offer his readers a better account of the status of the crucified little man inside the banana. Gerard's fruit was pickled, brought to him via Aleppo, but Johnson's connections enabled him to offer his readers a fresher description:

> April 10.1633. my much honored friend Dr. Argent (now President of the Colledge of Physitions of London) gaue me a plant he receiued from the Bermuda's: ... The fruit which I receiued was not ripe, but greene, each of them was about the bignesse of a large Beane; the length of them some fiue inches, and the bredth some inch and halfe: they all hang their heads downewards, haue rough or vneuen ends, and are fiue cornered; and if you turne the vpper side downward, they somewhat resemble a boat, as you

---

[27] Gerard, *Herball* (1633), sig. 6L6v.

[28] Gerard, *Herball* (1633), sig. 6L6v. For an examination of the way that publisher Thomas Hacket's promotion of travel literature "helped prepare the way for what would be a burgeoning idiom of colonial imagery" (97), see Kirk Melnikoff, *Elizabethan Publishing and the Makings of Literary Culture* (Toronto: University of Toronto Press, 2018).

may see by one of them exprest by it selfe: the huske is as thicke as a Beanes, and will easily shell off it: the pulpe is white and soft: the stalke whereby it is fastned to the knot is verie short, and almost as thicke as ones little finger. The stalke with the fruit thereon I hanged vp in my shop, were it became ripe about the beginning of May, and lasted vntil Iune: the pulp or meat was very soft and tender, and it did eat somewhat like a Muske-Melon.[29]

Johnson's detailed observations and comprehensive description of the bunch of Bermudan bananas that he was given is in keeping with what Brian W. Ogilvie has identified as "a final stage of a long condensation of observation, memory, and experience."[30] As Ogilvie remarks, the ambivalent nature of Renaissance description needed to distinguish between species while not misleading readers with the particular features of individual specimens: "[Renaissance naturalists] walked a tightrope between descriptions that were too vague, and allowed for the confusion of species, and those that were too precise, and took accidental differences to be essential."[31] Though Johnson's ripening bunch is more complete than Gerard's mere pickle, Johnson's singular experience means that he is unable to distinguish fully between the accidental and the essential features of his more impressive sample. To remedy this problem, Johnson adds an invaluable resource: a woodcut illustration commissioned to better share the particular characteristics of his specimen (Figure 0.3).

The earlier part of Johnson's 1633 chapter offers readers copies of the same two woodcuts of banana tree and bunch that were featured in Gerard's 1597 edition, but Johnson's annotated version supplements the verbal text with a four part "*Musa fructus exaction Icon* / An exacter figure of the Plantaine fruit," which Johnson sketched himself and then had made into a woodcut. He explains that his new image shows "1. The figure 2. Sheweth the shape of one particular fruit, with the lower side vpwards. 3. The same cut through the middle long wayes. 4. The same cut side wayes."[32]

While readers of the 1597 edition of Gerard's *Herball* are invited to accept Gerard's verbal account of the crosses visible in both "oblique" and "transuers" cuts of the banana fruit, readers of the 1633 edition are able to see at a glance that Gerard's "cross" is of minimum religious significance. Visible only in one of Johnson's two cross sections, the dark spokes in the banana's center split the fruit into thirds, leaving readers with little doubt that there is no image of a crucified man to be found.

---

[29] Gerard, *Herball* (1633), sig. 6L6r.
[30] Brian W. Ogilvie, *The Science of Describing: Natural History in Renaissance Europe* (Chicago: University of Chicago Press, 2006), 181.
[31] Ogilvie, *Science of Describing*, 181.   [32] Gerard, *Herball* (1633), sig. 6L6v.

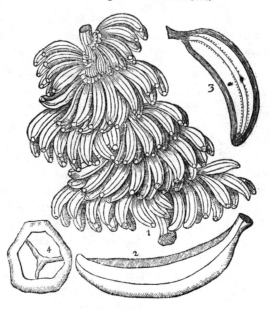

Musæ fructus exactior Icon.
An exacter figure of the Plantaine fruit.

Figure 0.3 John Gerard, *The Herball or General Historie of Plants* (1633), detail of sig.
6L6r. Image reproduced courtesy of the Ohio State University Libraries' Rare Books
& Manuscripts Library (QK 41 .G35).

Johnson's ability to speak authoritatively of his experiences with the
Adam's Apple fruit mitigates Gerard's ambivalence about the banana's religious symbolism, but Johnson's authority was made possible only through
the affordances, and the contingencies, of print. If Milton's Edenic botaniz-
ing was inspired by the close conjunction of the Arched Indian fig and
Adam's Apple tree in Gerard's original text, Johnson's later efforts to elucidate the plant seem to have provided Milton with the cover he needed to
engage in a "representational strategy that seeks to wed experimentalist
restraint with imaginative freedom."[33] A botanical specimen identified in
1597 as "Adam's Apple tree" whose fruit supplied New Testament imagery
may initially have been too heavy-handed to serve Milton's more subtle
hermeneutic, but Johnson's carefully recorded woodcut illustration of 1633
later undermined Gerard's account, thereby making space for Adam's Apple

[33] Edwards, *Milton and the Natural World*, 144.

to be evoked in Milton's Eden. Milton's refusal to identify explicitly his forbidden fruit was enabled by the editorial shift between one edition of a herbal and the next, while Johnson's interpretive and empirical acts as a natural historian and as an editor allowed Milton to take advantage of botanical ambiguity in his epic poem.

Milton's complex botanical strategy in *Paradise Lost* was facilitated not just by Johnson's additions to Gerard's account of the Adam's Apple tree but by the efforts of the publishers Joyce Norton and Richard Whitaker, who owned the rights to print Gerard's *Herball* and hired Johnson to edit Gerard's work in anticipation of bringing out a new edition after more than three decades. Norton and Whitaker took a calculated risk that readers in 1633 would want a second edition of an old yet authoritative herbal, updated to reflect new experiential theories of localized plant-gathering. It was a risk that paid off: the volume quickly sold out, and the publishers soon had cause to reprint a third edition of the massive folio *Herball* only three years later in 1636. Milton's opportunity to be inspired by the first printed English illustration of a banana therefore stemmed less from an apothecary's desire to describe a botanical specimen more precisely than had previously appeared in print than from a Caroline publisher's belief that there continued to be a lucrative market for an expensive Elizabethan tome about plants, updated from a working apothecary's firsthand experience.

By attending to the varied and material text of herbals, *Early Modern Herbals and the Book Trade* shifts critical attention away from authors as the primary generative force of natural history and towards the craftsmen and women whose capital enabled herbal texts to circulate within the marketplace of printed books. My focus upon the economic motivations of Norton and Whitaker as they commissioned Thomas Johnson to update Gerard's *Herball* illustrates how publishers, rather than authors, were the figures whose finances were ultimately at stake if a herbal failed to find its readers. The updated second and third editions of Gerard's *Herball* still elevated Gerard's status as an author despite Johnson's expert corrections because, for early modern English booksellers, the text's accuracy was seen as less important than the commercial impact of a popular figure's existing authority over a knowledge domain. In other words, for the London stationers who published works of natural history, the appearance of an author's name on a title page was less about originality and credit than it was a deliberate choice designed to generate a particular commercial effect. Attending to the choices of Norton and Whitaker enables us to understand that, in 1633, John Gerard's name was a "vendible commodity," while Thomas Johnson's was not.[34]

In asserting the primacy of book publishers, *Early Modern Herbals and the Book Trade* bridges two notoriously interdisciplinary fields, book history and the history of science, and uses the material form of printed English herbals to place the two subjects in sustained dialogue. Herbals – texts that list, order, and describe plants alongside their benefits – are an ancient genre that even predates the development of the codex, or book form. Long before the Scientific Revolution and the founding of the Royal Society, herbals, in scroll and codex, manuscript and print, illustrated and unillustrated, provided their readers with descriptions of individual plants as well as their medicinal value and applied usage. For book historians eager to chart developments in textual transmission over the *longue durée*, the genre of the herbal can provide an ideal case study. Yet historians of science more familiar with the genre can also benefit from a greater attention to the way herbals and other books of natural history circulated as material artifacts. As Agnes Arber has noted, herbals' dual purpose, both explanatory and utilitarian, has caused these texts to be studied in various and sometimes conflicting ways: as they were produced by classical authorities such as Theophrastus and Dioscorides, herbals were a product of natural history, but they were also foundational for the fields of agriculture and medicine.[35] These fields' emphasis on the varied purposes or categorization of knowledge that individual herbals could serve benefits from an additional examination of the perennially popular genre as a whole as well as the ways that methods of textual transmission influenced how early modern botanical authors approached their methods of study.[36] After the advent of printing in Western Europe led to an increase in the number of books produced for retail speculation, publishers soon realized that the printed herbal had a broad appeal to physicians, natural historians,

---

[34] I borrow the phrase "vendible commodity" from Adam G. Hooks, who uses the term to explain Shakespeare's dependence on the agents of the London book trade and argues that "[t]o think about Shakespeare and the book trade thus requires that we attend to how the stationers of early modern London employed his texts to further their own economic ends. To understand the relationship between these two corporate entities, we must focus on how the interests of the individuals and institutions of the book trade shaped Shakespeare, rather than on how Shakespeare may have used the technology of the trade to fulfil the literary ambition sometimes attributed to him." See Adam G. Hooks, "Book Trade," in Arthur F. Kinney (ed.), *The Oxford Handbook of Shakespeare* (Oxford: Oxford University Press, 2012), 126–142, esp. 127.

[35] Agnes Arber, *Herbals, Their Origin and Evolution: A Chapter in the History of Botany 1470–1670*, 3rd ed. (Cambridge: Cambridge University Press, 1986).

[36] Sachiko Kusukawa, *Picturing the Book of Nature: Image, Text, and Argument in Sixteenth-Century Human Anatomy and Medical Botany* (Chicago: University of Chicago Press, 2012).

gardeners, farmers, and any literate folks who regularly engaged with plants. Stationers ably responded to these customer demands.

As the genre developed in print throughout the sixteenth and seventeenth centuries, herbals came to offer ever more detailed information about plant morphology and habitat and about raising, harvesting, or treating plants to obtain specific effects. Dioscorides' *De materia medica* (*On Medicinal Material*), authored in the first century CE, catalogued about 500 plants; by 1623, the Swiss botanist Caspar Bauhin had described more than 6,000.[37] Perhaps more than any other Renaissance discipline, botanical science quickly encountered the three circumstances that led to what Ann M. Blair has called "information overload": "the discovery of new worlds, the recovery of ancient texts, and the proliferation of printed books."[38] As opportunities for gathering and synthesizing information about plants increased, the technologies of textual transmission improved to better accommodate this swelling dataset; herbals' material incarnations as books consequently make them particularly suitable for the study of how textual forms both create and affect meaning. Whether of plant identification or of medical exigency, herbals by their very nature assume that their audience of readers comes to them with specific real-world problems to solve. As books explicitly designed to supplement readers' material experience, herbals are a nexus where the fields of the history of science and book history intersect; they are texts deeply attentive to readers' needs and desires as users search for specific information about the natural world.

Herbals are thus books predicated on what William H. Sherman, citing Karl Marx, describes as having "use value," a capacity for satisfying human need.[39] As Sherman (and Marx) also notes, however, objects like books also have an "exchange value" whereby things become negotiable commodities in a larger economic system, a system that (by design) often elides human labor. The labor of bookmaking and bookselling is further elided when scholars suggest that authors somehow "published" or "printed" their own books, disregarding the historical agents who enabled an author's name to appear in print and made their works available for sale. By expressly attending to stationers, those figures who produced, distributed, and sold printed books in early modern England, this project links herbals' use value as texts with their exchange value as commodities to show how these expert

---

[37] Ogilvie, *Science of Describing*, 139.
[38] Ann M. Blair, *Too Much to Know: Managing Scholarly Information before the Modern Age* (New Haven, CT: Yale University Press, 2010), 11.
[39] William H. Sherman, *Used Books: Marking Readers in Renaissance England* (Philadelphia: University of Pennsylvania Press, 2008), 177.

and professional readers helped to create the conditions in which herbal authorship could itself become a valuable and vendible commodity. Stationers were not simply reproducers of texts but those whose expertise depended upon knowing what sorts of texts the book market demanded – or could be taught to demand. It was publishers who looked to medieval manuscripts and contemporary continental publications for books that would appeal to an English reading public, and it was publishers who sought local authors to revise, translate, edit, or supplement works in order to tailor them to particular niche markets. Book producers, in other words, were the agents that made Renaissance natural history possible.

Because the decision to commission authors to produce herbals often began in the bookshop, this project stresses the importance of stationers rather than authors, and authority rather than originality. One of my goals is to change the way historians of science think about the early history of proto-scientific fields like botany. By reframing the narratives of herbals to focus not on authors but on publishers, I account more fully for how the smaller-format, anonymous herbals of the 1520s through the 1550s later enabled the production of larger works like Gerard's *Herball*. Such scholarship also benefits book and literary historians of the Renaissance who, in focusing their studies on the latter half of the sixteenth century, have largely underappreciated the role of the Tudor book trade in setting up the circumstances for the "golden age" of Elizabethan and Jacobean literature. Once they see how grander, authored volumes like herbals were financially dependent upon the "proof-of-concept" laid out by smaller, anonymous books, scholars are better positioned to understand how early modern booksellers negotiated competing claims to authority through books' title pages, paratexts, and affordances.

Whitaker and Norton's decision to commission Johnson not to write his own herbal but to add material to a preexisting and well-regarded one upends the assumption that herbalists had control over their texts in print. Throughout his edition, Johnson's commission as an editor meant that he was forced to maintain Gerard in the role of "our Author," even as Johnson struggled to assert his own superior knowledge and experience. The stationers' choices in marketing their updated version suggest that they believed their readers would recognize Gerard's authorship instead of Johnson's, and the terms of Johnson's commission depended on his willingness to subject himself to a subordinate position. This arrangement indicates that the publishers were less interested in either author's relative scientific authority than in the careful deployment of an author's name to serve a specific commercial function. The history of English printed herbals shows that authorship often functioned in precisely this way, with names of botanical and medical authorities appearing on title pages as advertisements and endorsements. The addition of an author's name to herbals published in the second half of the sixteenth century was a strategic choice made by booksellers as they considered what would appeal to their customers.

Early Modern Herbals and the Book Trade illustrates how attention to the choices made by publishers and booksellers as they navigated the material, regulatory, and economic practices of the early English book trade influenced the trade in English herbals from the early decades of printing through to the English Civil War. Those effects also have value for historians of science. The vagaries of the competitive print marketplace led to important differences between one edition of a text and another, and the commercial context in which a book appeared offers a more comprehensive explanation of the cultural impact that books of botany had during the English Renaissance.[40] The case of Milton's banana illustrated in this Prologue shows how early modern English readers engaged not only with the botanical texts of authors but also with the products of publishers who wanted to market (or remarket) particular books at particular historical moments. The engagement of early English readers is in evidence from the early stages of printed herbals, an interest that stationers quickly seized upon and later satisfied by bringing out more capacious and more complicated texts. The first printed English herbals were created by booksellers invested in anonymous works, and it was only after the genre proved extremely popular with early modern readers that later botanical authors sought to assert their authority over this newly lucrative knowledge domain. The construction of botanical, and indeed scientific, authority in Renaissance England, I argue, was thus inextricably tied up in the circumstances that governed print.

My exploration of the publication of herbals as vendible wares exposes the ways that members of the book trade were at the very center of Renaissance natural history. So, too, were Renaissance readers. The reception of herbals accounts for the ways that printed natural history was experienced by those who purchased these books. I consider herbals' value to publishers as well as evidence of how readers engaged with these

---

[40] Anne Secord has noted similar developments in the popularization of works of illustrated botany in the nineteenth century: "[l]ecturers and writers . . . did not in this period regard popular botany as diffused knowledge for passive consumers" (55). See Anne Secord, "Botany on a Plate: Pleasure and the Power of Pictures in Promoting Early Nineteenth-Century Scientific Knowledge," *Isis* 93 (2002): 28–57.

volumes. This form of bibliographic and materialist analysis elucidates how the field of natural history crossed class, gender, and nationalistic boundaries – Johnson's additions to Gerard's *Herball* were of interest not just to other botanists but also to many types of readers, including poets like Milton. Plants were easily accessed and ubiquitous resources even for urban dwellers, and printed herbals appealed to booksellers who were ever on the lookout for profitable new titles that might interest broad swaths of the English public. While law books and medical tracts were often intended for a specialized, expert clientele, books like herbals attracted a wide range of customers eager to supplement their localized experience. Such readers made anonymous herbals in the first half of the sixteenth century remarkably popular. This popularity led to herbals becoming, in the second half of the century, contested sites for medical professionals wanting to exert political and social influence, transforming herbals into a knowledge domain that could be both authorized and author-ized. As the following pages will show, it was stationers who made it possible for herbalists to become authors.

Introduction
Authorizing English Botany

For almost a century before it was an adjective, the word "herbal" was a noun. As objects, individual copies of early English herbals were not only read and consulted but also inscribed and illuminated, purchased and bequeathed. Written forms for herb lore extended back long before the English language, and those lists of plant descriptions and medical remedies, or "book[s] containing the names and descriptions of herbs, or of plants in general, with their properties and virtues" (*OED* n.1), became a popular genre in Renaissance England within a few decades of William Caxton's importation of printing to Westminster. By that time, printed editions of classical works had already been increasing rapidly on the continent, including texts that contained accounts of plants: Pliny the Elder's *Natural History*, with its chapters on plants in books 4–6, was first printed in Venice in 1469 and was regularly reprinted thereafter. Theophrastus, Aristotle's pupil and Lyceum contemporary whose *Enquiry into Plants* influenced Pliny, initially found his way into print in Treviso in 1483. Peter Schoeffer published the first expressly vernacular herbal, *Der Gart der Gesundheit* (*The Garden of Good Health*), in 1485, and it was quickly reprinted and translated into other languages, its numerous pirated editions readily demonstrating that there was a lucrative market for vernacular books about plants.[1]

Given the genre's popularity on the continent, it is unsurprising, then, that the first examples of the word "herbal" cited in the *Oxford English Dictionary* (*OED*) stem from the titles of two sixteenth-century London publications: the anonymous *Grete Herbal* of 1526 (*STC* 13176) and William Turner's *A New Herball* of 1551 (*STC* 24365). The word "herbal," however, had first appeared in printed English a year earlier than the *OED* currently records in the title of an anonymous book of 1525 published by

---

[1] Anna Pavord, *The Naming of Names: The Search for Order in the World of Plants* (London: Bloomsbury, 2005), 160.

the London stationer and printer Richard Bankes, who copied his text from a popular medieval herbal manuscript known as *Agnus castus*.[2] Like many early printed works derived from medieval manuscripts, Bankes's title page used an incipit, a rhetorical convention of conspicuously delineating a text's beginning by offering a description of the nature of the work: *Here begynnyth a newe mater / the whiche sheweth and treateth of [the] vertues & proprytes of herbes / the whiche is called an Herball (STC* 13175.1). Through the efforts and investment of Richard Bankes, the era of the printed English herbal had officially begun.

When several discrete texts were copied and bound together within a single manuscript volume, titles starting with phrases like "here begynnyth" signified to readers the change from one text to another despite their seeming continuance on the handwritten page. In this context, Bankes's "newe mater" thus begun can be interpreted as signifying the verbal material that would follow the text's (now-printed) title page, the intellectual fabric "whiche sheweth and treateth of [the] vertues & proprytes of herbes." Such a reading might posit that which "is called an Herball" was not the book object itself but the book's content, and the word "herbal" would be an identifying characteristic not of the "matter's" material *medium* but of its verbal *meaning*. This reading might be used to support an argument that Bankes's 1525 book is a progenitor not to the first use of "herbal" as a noun but to the adjectival form of the word that the *OED* credits to 1612: the substance of the text of the verbal work that Bankes prints may be understood to refer to "belonging to, consisting of, or made from herbs."[3]

[2] For an account of the circulation of *Agnus castus* in manuscript, see *Agnus castus*, ed. Gösta Brodin (Cambridge, MA: Harvard University Press, 1950). On the popularity of *Agnus castus*, see George R. Keiser, "Vernacular Herbals: A Growth Industry in Late Medieval England," in Margaret Connolly and Linne R. Mooney (eds.), *Design and Distribution of Late Medieval Manuscripts in England* (York: York Medieval Press, 2008), 292–307.

[3] The initial identification of this text as "Banckes' [*sic*] Herbal" appears to be Agnes Arber's in her *Herbals: Their Origin and Evolution*. Though she acknowledges that "Dr. Payne suggests that it is probably an abridgement of some medieval English manuscript on herbs," Arber is content to identify publisher Bankes as the agent who should be responsible for serving in the place of the would-be author (*Herbals*, 38–40). A decade later, Eleanour Sinclair Rohde reinforces this ascription by repeating "*Banckes's Herbal*" as the proper title of the volume in *The Old English Herbals* (London: Longmans, Green and Co., 1922), 55; as does H. S. Bennett ("Bankes' Herbal") in *English Books and Readers, 1475–1557*, 2nd ed. (Cambridge: Cambridge University Press, 1969), 98–99; and Blanche Henrey ("Banckes's herbal") in *British Botanical and Horticultural Literature before 1800* (Oxford: Oxford University Press, 1975), 1:12. I follow the *Short Title Catalogue (STC)* in regularizing the spelling of Richard Bankes's name, but because Bankes did not own the rights to the text during the period of the text's immense popularity with Tudor printers, I do not use the name "Bankes's Herbal" to describe the many editions of this text. Instead, throughout this volume I use the name given to the text by printer John King when he licensed it in 1561: "the little *Herball*."

Such a reading of the word "herbal" is not possible, however, in one of the first of the many reprinted editions of Bankes's text. The stationer and printer Robert Redman, who set forth the work from his shop at the sign of St. George in Fleet Street around 1539, rechristened the volume as *A boke of the propertyes of herbes the whiche is called an Herbal* (*STC* 13175.5).[4] For Redman, the ambiguity of the medieval phrase "Here begynnyth a new mater" was easily eliminated to focus explicitly on the physical manifestation of the text that most concerned its producer: the book. While its title remains dependent on its work's verbal content in its delineation of the characteristics or "virtues" of plants, Redman's herbal is inseparable from its status as a material object able to be commodified. Over the next thirty years, as the little *Herball* was printed in various forms by at least thirteen other publishers, all but one chose to confirm on their volumes' title pages that "an herbal" is first and foremost a type of *book*. The word was also used to describe books by contemporaries: in the inventories of the Cambridge probate court, the word "herball" or "harball" appears as a generic marker to note an otherwise unnamed book artifact six times between 1545 and 1583.[5] It was the turn of the century before the cognate "herbalist" appeared to describe "a collector or writer on plants," as John Dee used in his diaries to characterize the barber-surgeon John Gerard in 1594.[6] Attention to the publication history of an extremely popular, anonymous herbal, as well as to the *OED*, illustrates how English stationers identified herbals as books well before those who composed botanical texts were ever identified as herbalists. The word "herbalist" entered the English language only after *other* figures made it possible for herbal texts to reach their readers.

The present book is an account of how stationers helped to create the position of the Renaissance English herbalist. *Early Modern Herbals and the Book Trade: English Stationers and the Commodification of Botany* argues that scholars need to consider botanical texts not just as the verbal works of authors but also as the products of the craftsmen and craftswomen who made printed books for profit. Tracking the development of botanical science through authors' original works provides a method for identifying the moments when particular descriptions or classification systems entered

---

[4] Like many of the books bibliographers credit to him, the Redman volume is undated, and the date provided by the *STC* is inferred and marked with a query that signifies "a range of up to two or three years on either side" of the date provided (1:xxxviii). Redman died in 1540.

[5] E. S. Leedham-Green, *Books in Cambridge Inventories: Book-lists from Vice Chancellor's Court Probate Inventories in the Tudor and Stuart Periods*, 2 vols. (Cambridge: Cambridge University Press, 1986).

[6] "Aug. 26th, Mr. Gherardt, the chirurgion and herbalist, [cam to me]." John Dee, *The Private Diary of Dr. John Dee*, ed. J. O. Halliwell-Phillipps (London: Camden Society, 1842), 50.

the broader discourse, but it tells a very narrow story that ignores the many in favor of a mostly elite few. By examining the motivations not just of authors but of the publishers who commissioned and wholesaled herbals, the printers who manufactured herbals, the booksellers who retailed herbals, and the customers who purchased and read herbals, scholars can better apprehend Renaissance English attitudes towards natural history. Authors may have sometimes been the originators of verbal works of botany, but stationers were the gate through which all would-be authors had to pass if their works were to reach the reading public. In many cases, a publisher's desire to publish a herbal even preceded an author's desire to write a book, such that herbal authors were regularly commissioned by publishers to compile herbals. In these cases, a stationer's desire to publish and sell a printed herbal actually spurred herbalists to create such texts.

The originating agency for a given herbal volume therefore does not necessarily begin with the figure whose name appeared in large letters on the title page. Indeed, throughout the sixteenth and seventeenth centuries, the names that most frequently appeared on title pages were those who manufactured printed books, not those who authored them. To be financially successful, English stationers needed to have a sophisticated understanding of the marketplace of readers, and it was stationers' judgments that determined what books, including what books of natural history, would be available for sale in Renaissance London. Stationers' agency, therefore, is central to understanding how and why authors were able to present themselves as authoritative in print. Their economic and commercial concerns took precedence over authors' botanical labor.

Investigations of the material texts produced by stationers also reveal that the study of plants not only was of interest to the social and intellectual elites of the Royal Society in the later seventeenth century but was popular with a wide swath of the English population early in the sixteenth century. This project's investment in the critical capacity of nonspecialist readers finds support from assessments that reconsider the ways that early modern vernacular science and related epistemologies were formed and maintained by artisans and women throughout the period.[7] Approaching herbals not simply as the verbal products of authors but as the artifacts of printers and booksellers enables us to see Renaissance readers, particularly those of the

---

[7] Wendy Wall, *Recipes for Thought: Knowledge and Taste in the Early Modern English Kitchen* (Philadelphia: University of Pennsylvania Press, 2016); Pamela Smith, *The Body of the Artisan: Art and Experience in the Scientific Revolution* (Chicago: University of Chicago Press, 2004); Antonio Pérez-Ramos, *Francis Bacon's Idea of Science and the Maker's Knowledge Tradition* (Oxford: Oxford University Press, 1988).

middling sort, as sophisticated thinkers capable of evaluating claims of authorial knowledge with skeptical and judicious eyes. Early modern stationers were deeply attuned to such readers' needs and desires because the purchasing power of readers determined the success or failure of publishers' own commercial ventures. The booksellers' attitudes towards the texts they sold could facilitate an author's success in print.

Close reading of the botanical texts in question reveals that herbal authors often responded to their dependency upon publishers. Authors were often frustrated by the limitations that publishers placed upon the material presentation of their works: they regularly complained that publishers were unwilling or unable to accommodate their demands for illustrations or corrections and were stymied by their necessary reliance on booksellers to disseminate their botanical scholarship. Yet those who wished to generate the authority that came from maintaining a large audience had no alternative but to seek print publication. Print's capacity for producing easy and seemingly unlimited repetition of heterodox ideas has long been recognized as leading to the success of the Protestant revolution, and reformers were especially attuned to the ways that print, coupled with shifting religious mores, could make people socially and politically vulnerable. As the Protestant and humanist veneration of individual study gained momentum, however, the vulnerability inherent in print also extended to naturalists who used others' printed books as a form of research alongside their own botanical experience. As the sixteenth century made way to the seventeenth, herbal authors began to downplay their reliance on the other printed books that they used both to conduct and to disseminate their research. Mimicking the strategies deployed by reformers in their religious tracts, authors began to use the paratexts of their herbals strategically to signal their superiority to other books in the marketplace as well as to the artisans who marketed books for commercial gain. Thus it was that the figure of the authoritative Renaissance herbalist emerged as a deliberate construct: a persona that authors could use to elevate their works above the material means that distributed their botanical texts to a reading public.

My project began with a desire to understand how a seventeenth-century apothecary like Thomas Johnson could so easily control later critical discourse about his professional rival, the Elizabethan barber-surgeon John Gerard. In the 1633 edition of Gerard's text that he was commissioned to edit, Johnson suggests that Gerard copied a dead associate's manuscript translation of Dodoens and then attempted to cover up his offense by reorganizing the material and adding details from other books he had read. Botanical historians have largely taken Johnson at his word, finding that Gerard did use others' books to supplement his own accounts of plants, and many scholars have condemned Gerard as a plagiarist or a fraud as a result. Yet, as I investigated this narrative further, I became unsatisfied with a conclusion that relied on an implicit veneration of authorial originality to demarcate scientific expertise. Renaissance authors of books of natural history, whether in England or on the continent, regularly declaimed their superior authority by denigrating their predecessors in their fields, and I recognized such claims as rhetorical appeals designed to position the authorial self within an emergent botanical discourse.[8] Likewise, my work on the history of English printing had taught me that the stationers who produced and sold books had a vested interest in positioning older volumes on similar topics as inferior to the new commercial products that they wanted to sell.

As I continued to investigate accounts of Gerard's *Herball*, I realized that it was important to keep the motivations of the two agents of publisher and author distinct: a publisher is primarily concerned with the economic ramifications of claiming that a book is superior, while an author is invested in the intellectual rewards that result from others recognizing that superiority. A single edition of a book required a sizable investment of publishers' capital, and stationers' concerns about profit were compounded when the volumes in question were large, illustrated, and complexly formatted, as Renaissance herbals eventually grew to be. In the case of these massive, expensive tomes, an author's disparagement of earlier texts could make both economic and rhetorical sense. Criticism of a previous volume made less sense, however, when the established earlier book was produced by the same publishing house. What's more, the material, regulatory, and economic concerns of printed books, particularly large ones, were different when a book was reprinted in 1633 rather than printed for the first time in 1597. A suggestion that a previous edition of a book was flawed could cast aspersions upon the quality of a publisher's other books and undermine the sales of the new, improved volume. The publisher and the editor of the 1633 second edition of Gerard's 1597 *Herball* therefore were motivated by two different sets of concerns. While it may have suited Thomas Johnson's interests as a botanist to denigrate the quality of Gerard's 1597 text, it had been published by Joyce Norton's late husband

---

[8] Surveying what she calls Gerard's "anthological" approach from the perspective of literary historians' scholarship into commonplacing, Leah Knight has come to a similar conclusion. See Knight, *Of Books and Botany in Early Modern England: Sixteenth-Century Plants and Print Culture* (Burlington, VT: Ashgate, 2009), esp. chap. 4.

John Norton, and her profits would be harmed by such open disparage-ment. Instead, the publishers of the 1633 edition used their governing role in the communications circuit to limit the authority that Thomas Johnson was permitted to display.[9]

Printed books may be the means through which a herbalist's success or failure could be measured by posterity, but the medium of print includes other figures who influenced how (and if) Gerard and Johnson ultimately met their audiences. As I explained in this book's Prologue, editing someone else's book rather than authoring his own placed Thomas Johnson in a subordinate position that made him intellectually defensive. The success of an author's ideas thus had much to do with the success of the bookseller who published his works. Hence, I realized that, if I was to understand how Johnson was offered the opportunity to malign Gerard in print, I needed to investigate the motivations of Norton and Whitaker, too. I soon found other questions that I wanted to answer: How did accusations of plagiarism function in the period as a means for a seventeenth-century author to discredit a sixteenth-century one? To what extent were those accusations modeled on the accusations of piracy that were sometimes leveled against early modern stationers? How did shifting regulatory constraints upon the ownership of textual works change with the incorporation of the London Stationers' Company in 1557? When did status-seeking authors begin to try to mitigate the social and intellec-tual ramifications of their dependency upon publishers? Why would publishers risk so much capital in the production of large illustrated books that could easily leave them bankrupt? How did booksellers use features like authorship or professionalization as marketing strategies to sell more books? As I sought answers to these questions, it became clear that there was room in the history of herbals for a more sophisticated under-standing of the relationship between works as the products of authors and the printed documents that were the products of artisans in the book trade.

Traditional scholarship into early modern English botany has examined authors' production of herbal works in order to highlight important nuances in their botanical discoveries, development of classification schemes, and methods of plant description. This research has primarily sought to credit authors' original contributions to scientific study or the history of ideas. In many cases, scholars have asserted that some authors plagiarized or otherwise copied others' work and have therefore sought to

---

[9] On the communications circuit, see Robert Darnton, "What Is the History of Books?" *Daedalus* III (1982): 65–83.

remedy the corruptions that crept into the historical record. Yet these studies often take authorial claims of originality at face value, missing the authors' need to position themselves as producers of valuable commodities within a competitive print marketplace. By shifting the focus away from authors to the forms their books ultimately took in bookstalls, I offer a fuller picture of the environment in and for which such authors wrote. In attending to herbals as commodities, I demonstrate how Renaissance natural history was understood to appeal, like the 1623 folio of Shakespeare, to a "great variety of readers." The production of a printed book required booksellers to risk large amounts of capital in the hopes of a future return; as a result, successful booksellers needed to be attentive to the tastes of their anticipated customers and were unlikely to produce books simply because authors desired them to do so. Because printers and booksellers often altered, and sometimes even commissioned, authors' works in order to suit their book buyers, *Early Modern Herbals and the Book Trade* argues that investigation into the contingencies of Renaissance printing can better clarify authorial behaviors in the cultural context of English botany. By focusing on publishers' *editions* rather than authors' *works*, this project uncovers the ways that bookmakers and booksellers shaped Renaissance natural history through print. Hence it is herbals' status *as books* that is the focus of this study.

Just as herbals themselves served a dual purpose, offering their readers herbal remedies as well as descriptions and sometimes depictions of plants, this book has two particular audiences in mind: those who are invested in herbals as texts and those who are interested in herbals as books. I hope that readers who enter from one category will gradually find themselves drifting towards the other as upcoming pages reveal how entangled medium and message were for both the early modern stationers who produced herbals and the authors who wrote for them. This study takes a deep dive into the ways that books were produced at the time that herbals were first printed in England. Historians of science will find in the following pages a broader context for understanding the texts they value through my attention to the structure of the Tudor and Stuart book trade. Likewise, book historians who specialize in the literature of the sixteenth and seventeenth centuries will also find that my history of the Stationers' Company of London both before and after its incorporation in 1557 clarifies the shape of the Elizabethan and Jacobean book trade. To understand how and why publishers invested in the books they did when they did, it helps to understand how their efforts were regulated and protected. These regulations fundamentally changed with the Stationers' incorporation and the introduction of a new, more equitable method of copyright than had been operating previously under the patent system. The new form of financial protection for publishers who were members of the Stationers' Company enabled them to take greater financial risks in ways that benefited would-be herbalists: stationers could invest in new works, make bigger books, and add more complicated paratexts. Put another way, the economic, material, and regulatory concerns of publishers provided herbalists with alternative opportunities to showcase the new specimens their botanical excursions had uncovered.

In seeking to illuminate the means by which herbals were understood by *all* of their textual progenitors, stationers and authors, as well as by the readers who used them, *Early Modern Herbals and the Book Trade* recognizes that the books under examination were, first and foremost, artifacts designed to be sold for profit.[10] Of course, it is also true that publishers' awareness of the political maneuvering of church and crown, as well as the social-climbing activities of civic groups, often determined what they printed, as did an awareness of continental trends gleaned during annual trips to the Frankfurt Book Fair. As I delineate the ways that publishers sought to distinguish their own editions of a botanical text, stationers' motivations for printing a particular work at a particular time figure heavily in my discussions. For example, prompted by the threat of John Parkinson's *Theatrum botanicum* reaching print before their second edition of Gerard's *Herball* could make it into London's bookstalls in 1633, the publishers Joyce Norton and Roger Whitaker seem to have given Thomas Johnson less than a year to edit the massive folio, leading him to grumble in his note to the reader that such forced haste should excuse any errors that remain in his text.[11] Similarly, the bookseller John Day may have published William Turner's *The Names of Herbes* (*STC* 24359) in 1548 specifically to pique the interest of his patron William Cecil, whose fascination with plants was widely known. For his part, Turner may have approached Day with his herbal manuscript after being introduced to him by their mutual acquaintance Thomas Gibson, a printer-turned-physician who had published his own herbal a decade earlier. An investigation into the

[10] On twentieth- and twenty-first-century bibliographers' disquiet with the economic motivations of Renaissance book publishing, see Melnikoff, *Elizabethan Publishing*, 9–11.

[11] Johnson complains throughout his 1633 edition that he is forced to work quickly; the preface to an appendix written after the rest of the work was printed or in press explains that such haste led to inadvertent omissions: "I finde that I haue forgotten diuers which I intended to haue added in their fitting places: the occasion hereof hath beene, my many businesses, the troublesomenesse, and aboue all, the great expectation and hast of the Worke, whereby I was forced to performe this task within the compasse of a yeare" (sig. 6S2r). See also Henrey, *British Botanical*, 1:48.

biographical histories of all three men reveals considerable overlap in both religious and social spheres that strongly suggests they were acquainted with one another. Such evidence makes it clear that the circumstances and contingencies of early English publishing often influenced authorial behavior.

As the means by which texts of botany were disseminated, English herbals have received increased scholarly attention in recent years as researchers have sought to uncover, among other topics, changes in the science of description, women's resistance to medical authority, the "urban science" practiced in Renaissance London, and Elizabethan authors' easy and ubiquitous facility with botanical metaphors.[12] While public interest in the names, properties, and virtues of plants is of crucial importance in understanding the role herbals played in such developments, it is herbals' physical status as exchangeable and commercial artifacts that facilitated these changes. As Elizabeth Eisenstein and others have shown, the medium of print offered early moderns seeking to better understand the natural world a powerful vehicle of information transfer, one that not only brought to light the work of classical and medieval authorities but also made explicit the work of those contemporaries who were translating, commenting upon, and revising these earlier authorities.[13] The mass proliferation of printed copies of these competitively "authoritative" texts permitted an increase in personal and institutional library holdings, and as a result natural historians working in distinct regions, or across borders, could refer to the features of specific editions of herbals in their communications with one another.[14] Printed books functioned both as a garden from which old information might be gathered and as a valuable public battleground upon which new authors might stake new claims. They enabled local naturalists to gain a larger and sometimes international public, making their private labors known to a wide audience. Their increasing ubiquity as resources led printed books to multiply: once commentators no longer had to invest their time in copying texts, or in traveling long distances to access particular copies of others, the restructuring of old knowledge and the

---

[12] See Ogilvie, *Science of Describing*, Rebecca Laroche, *Medical Authority and Englishwomen's Herbal Texts, 1550–1650* (Burlington, VT: Ashgate, 2009), Deborah E. Harkness, *The Jewel House: Elizabethan London and the Scientific Revolution* (New Haven, CT: Yale University Press, 2007), and Knight, *Of Books and Botany*.

[13] Elizabeth Eisenstein, *The Printing Press As an Agent of Change* (Cambridge: Cambridge University Press, 1979).

[14] See R. J. Fehrenbach (ed.), *Private Libraries in Renaissance England: A Collection and Catalogue of Tudor and Early Stuart Book-Lists* (Binghamton, NY: Medieval and Renaissance Texts and Studies, 1992–2004).

gathering of new could occur with greater ease, making it possible both to debate and to advance what was known about the natural world.

Yet, as I have been arguing, industrious translators, innovative authors, and intrepid explorers were not the only ones facilitating this spread of natural history. These figures' emerging spirit of inquiry was enabled and encouraged by the efforts of the bookmakers and booksellers seeking to capitalize on that spirit. By supplying the product that early herbalists required both to conduct and to disseminate their research, book producers played a crucial role in the emergence of what would eventually become the discipline of botany. For example, Leonhart Fuchs's beautifully illustrated and tremendously influential work *De historia stirpium comentarii insignes* (*Notable Commentaries on the History of Plants*; Basel, 1542) outlined the characteristics of 497 European and imported plants in 344 chapters that were illustrated by 511 woodcuts, making it "one of the noblest achievements of the German Renaissance."[15] A bestseller by any measure, *De historia stirpium* went through thirty-nine editions before Fuchs's death in 1566 and remained in print long thereafter. Yet despite his status as a revered botanical authority and *De historia stirpium*'s regular reprinting in vernacular translations throughout Europe, Fuchs could not find a publisher willing to risk the capital necessary to publish his follow-up work.[16] The Vienna Codex, as Fuchs's proposed three-volume sequel is now known, which was to be triple the size of his earlier book, was too expensive a risk for Basel publishers like the widow of Michael Isingrin (the initial publisher of *De historia stirpium*) and like Johannes Oporinus, so it never appeared in print.[17] Otto Brunfels likewise complained that the structure of his illustrated herbal *Herbarum vivae eicones* (*Living Images of Plants*, Strasbourg, 1530–1536) suffered because he was forced to accommodate the publisher Johannes Schott's organization of the efforts of artists, woodblock cutters, compositors, and pressmen.[18] As the cases of Fuchs's Vienna Codex and Brunfels's *Herbarum* illustrate, the efforts and investments of publishers and printers limited what herbals' authors could and

---

[15] Frederick G. Meyer, Emily Emmart Trueblood, and John L. Heller, eds., *The Great Herbal of Leonhart Fuchs*, 2 vols. (Stanford, CA: Stanford University Press, 1999), 1:15, 65.

[16] Meyer et al., *Great Herbal*, 1:45.

[17] In a letter to Joachim Camerarius dated April 3, 1563, Fuchs wrote in complaint: "I have long since finished my Commentaries on the History of Plants, arranged in three massive volumes. Isingrin's widow and her son-in-law have broken faith with me, notwithstanding that she is bound in her own handwriting. So my dear Joachim, no one anywhere can be trusted. I have much more material, which I completed earlier, in the hands of Oporinus. But he, too, has so far duped me with false hope." Quoted in Meyer et al., *Great Herbal*, 1:152

[18] Kusukawa, *Picturing the Book of Nature*, 19.

could not make available to a Renaissance reading public. To properly locate early modern knowledge of natural history, the increasing production of herbals over the course of the sixteenth century needs to be understood not only in terms of a developing scientific movement but also in terms of a robust but limited economic demand for a specific kind of commodity.

In England between the first appearance of the little *Herball* in 1525 and the release of John Parkinson's *Theatrum botanicum* (*STC* 19302) in 1640, the book trade saw the production of more than two dozen editions of books identified on their title pages or by contemporaries as herbals. These texts included translations of French texts such as the anonymous *Grete Herball* (trans. Laurence Andrewe, first edition 1526, *STC* 13176) and Rembert Dodoens's *A Niewe Herball, Or History of Plants* (trans. Henry Lyte, first edition 1578, *STC* 6984); books written for an English market but printed on the continent such as William Turner's three-part *A New Herball* (1551, *STC* 24365; 1562, *STC* 24366; and 1568, *STC* 24367); Latin books written and published in London that were authored by foreigners such as Pierre Pena and Matthias de L'Obel's *Stirpium aduersaria noua* (first edition 1570–1571, *STC* 19595); and interpretive or exegetical works that combined translation with a translator's creative additions, such as Thomas Newton's translation of Levinus Lemnius's *An Herbal for the Bible* (1587, *STC* 15454). These texts range from pocket-sized, unillustrated octavos to huge folios filled with costly woodcuts. They appear variously in black-letter, roman, and italic typefaces, all three occasionally used on the same page of text. The woodcuts used in one book reappear in others, sometimes appended to the same plants and sometimes to different ones.[19] Their verbal contents range from the descriptions of plants to accounts of their medicinal value or practical usage, to plants' emblematic significance to the Christian reader of "the book of Nature,"[20] or to the emphatic patriot seeking to demonstrate England's superior natural blessings over those of foreign climes.[21] Herbals contain indexes, tables of

---

[19] The woodcuts in Parkinson's *Theatrum botanicum*, for example, were copied from the second edition of John Gerard's *Herball, or General Historie of Plantes*, edited by Thomas Johnson (Henrey, *British Botanical*, 1:80).

[20] The full title of Newton's translation is *An Herbal for the Bible. Containing a plaine and familiar exposition of such Similitudes, Parables, and Metaphors, both in the olde Testament and the Newe, as are borrowed and taken from Herbs, Plants, Trees, Fruits and Simples, by obseruation of their Vertues, qualities, natures, properties, operations and effects: And by Holie Prophets, Sacred Writers, Christ himselfe, and his blessed Apostles usually alledged, and into their heauenly Oracles, for the better beautifieng and plainer opening of the same, profitably inserted.*

[21] From Thomas Johnson's "An Aduertisement to the Readers," in his 1636 edition of Gerard: "For I iudge it requisite that we should labour to know those Plants which are, and euer are like to be Inhabitants of this Isle; for I verily beleeue that the diuine Prouidence had a care in bestowing Plants

contents, equivalency listings of plant names across regional and national linguistic barriers, marginal notations, in-text citations, and ornamental types functioning as organizational and annotation markers; they are prefaced by their authors, their publishers, and their commenders; they contain addresses to the reader, to patrons, and to civic and royal authorities.[22] They were sold and resold for great and small sums of money and presented as bequests in wills; and they appear in the booklists of medical practitioners and in the portraits of gentry, identified both by their individual titles and by their generic marker of "herbal."[23] The herbals still extant were hand-colored by their producers or by later owners; they were corrected, annotated, and added to by later readers, and the pages of their copies can demonstrate both heavy use and none at all.[24] Herbals were mined for ideas by later authors writing advice books as well as by would-be ladies and gentlemen on husbandry and housekeeping.[25] They refer to other books currently offered for sale by the same publisher that might also interest readers, books that may or may not have anything to do with plants.[26] Indeed, the story of herbals *as books* can be seen as the story of nearly all early modern English books in microcosm, one that encompasses more investigations than have been appreciated by the traditional crediting of individual botanical discoveries. These studies are

in each part of the Earth, fitting and convenient to the foreknowne necessities of the future Inhabitants; and if wee throughly knew the Vertues of these, we needed no Indian nor American Drugges" (sig. 7B4v). On the phenomenon of local projects in early modern natural history, see Alix Cooper, *Inventing the Indigenous: Local Knowledge and Natural History in Early Modern Europe* (Cambridge: Cambridge University Press, 2007).

22 The title page of Turner's *A New Herball* of 1551 carries the royal arms for King Edward, while Pena and L'Obel's *Stirpium aduersaria noua* carries Elizabeth's arms. John Gerard's two catalogues of plants in his Holborn garden printed in 1596 and 1599 were dedicated to William Cecil and Walter Raleigh respectively.

23 For example, the Southwell-Sibthorpe Commonplace Book lists a copy of Gerard's *Herbal* in its inventory. Cited in Laroche, *Medical Authority*, 122.

24 Ann Blair, "Errata Lists and the Reader As Corrector," in Sabrina Alcorn Baron, Eric N. Lindquist, and Eleanor F. Shevlin (eds.), *Agent of Change: Print Culture Studies After Elizabeth L. Eisenstein* (Boston: University of Massachusetts Press, 2007), 21–41; 41.

25 Michael R. Best has demonstrated that Gervase Markham depended heavily on information contained in a late edition of the little *Herball* in his compiling of *The English Housewife*, reorganizing its information on remedies around illnesses rather than around plants and adding specific quantities to perfect remedies for healing simples. See Best, "Medical Use of a Sixteenth-Century Herbal: Gervase Markham and the Bankes Herbal," *Bulletin of the History of Medicine* 53 (1979): 449–458.

26 The full title of Peter Treveris's 1526 work is *The grete herball whiche geueth parfyt knowlege and vnderstandyng of all maner of herbes & there gracyous vertues whiche god hath ordeyned for our prosperous welfare and helth/for they hele & cure all maner of dyseases and sekenesses that fall or mysfortune to all maner of creatoures of god created/practysed by many expert and wyse maysters/as Auicenna & other.&c. Also it geueth full parfyte vnderstandyng of the booke lately prentyed by me (Peter treueris) named the noble experiens of the vertuous handwarke of surgery* (STC 13176). Treveris had printed Hieronymus' *The vertuous handwarke of surgery* (STC 13434) in 1525.

important in understanding the significance of herbals to early modern English readers, but they convey only a part of what is an interdisciplinary tale. To fully understand how herbals came to be and how they mattered for early modern natural history, we need also to appreciate why they were books.

Publishers

In previous pages, I have often used the word *publisher* in a manner that would be anachronistic in the sixteenth and seventeenth centuries, and it is one that requires some explanation. In the twenty-first century, a book publisher is the corporate agent that owns the right to distribute and wholesale a book and provides the capital to enable its manufacture. As a result of this right and these activities, publishers either earn a profit generated from the sale of the books to retail outlets or they suffer a loss if they are unable to sell a sufficient quantity of their product in order to break even. Some publishers also own and control the actual process of the manufacture of their books, but others contract out that process to agents who print and bind books on their behalf. Thanks to modern colophons, readers are easily able to distinguish those who front the money for a publication from those who are physically responsible for a book's manufacture. In early modern England, however, the term *publisher* simply meant "a person who declares or proclaims something publicly" (*OED n.*1.) and could refer as readily to a preacher or a ballad singer as to an agent responsible for the creation of a book. The equivalent early modern English term to the modern *publisher* was *printer*, a word that could, unhelpfully, refer both to the agent whose entrepreneurial initiative caused a book to be printed and to the contracted agent responsible for actually printing it. Though sometimes these roles overlapped (if, say, printers decided to risk their own capital to publish books for themselves), the concerns and priorities of each role are sufficiently distinct that, without an appreciation of the role of publishers as the "prime movers" of the book trade, historians are unable to fully comprehend the ways that books in the period were conceived of as products to be sold. As Peter W. M. Blayney notes, "it was the publisher, not the printer, who decided that the text should be made public and who would eventually make a profit if it sold well enough during his lifetime. And by the same token, it was the publisher whose investment was at risk if the public declined to buy the book."[27] Though the term *publisher* in this modern

---

[27] Peter W. M. Blayney, "The Publication of Playbooks," in David Scott Kastan and John D. Cox (eds.), *A New History of Early English Drama* (New York: Columbia University Press, 1997), 384–422; 391. The term "prime movers," used in the previous sentence in reference to publishers, is also Blayney's.

sense was not contemporaneous in the period under discussion, the word's utility in clarifying the arguments of this book is too significant to disregard.[28]

In focusing on the ways that herbals were the products of publishers, *Early Modern Herbals and the Book Trade* is of a piece with what is sometimes called the "New Textualism," a term popularized by the work of Margreta de Grazia and Peter Stallybrass, which describes a form of historicist literary criticism that distinguishes between physical documents and the texts transmitted by those documents.[29] Since the 1990s, literary scholars of Renaissance England, particularly those focused on the works of Shakespeare and his contemporaries, have begun to consider the behaviors of publishers more seriously as a means of understanding contemporary attitudes towards literature. By "thinking of plays as publishers thought of them, as commodities," Zachary Lesser writes, we can "change the ways in which we read the plays themselves."[30] More recently, Kirk Melnikoff has demonstrated that Elizabethan publishers "made substantial interventions in what were developing literary forms" to shape their would-be readers' sense of genres like travel narratives, lyric poetry, literary anthologies, and erotic verse.[31] In turning authors' texts into the commodities of books, Renaissance publishers anticipated the desires of customers whose preferred reading acts were satisfied or frustrated by the publisher's formatting choices or affordances, as well as by the ways that Renaissance printers presented these features in the printed books themselves. As Ann Blair has urged, "[c]loser attention to the people involved in the production of a book, from front matter and illustrations to indexes and errata lists, can bring to light the role of historical actors other than the author in shaping how a work was read, by whom, and for what purposes."[32] These concerns are precisely what *Early Modern Herbals and the Book Trade* is designed to uncover.

---

[28] Peter W. M. Blayney, *The Stationers' Company and the Printers of London, 1501–1557*, 2 vols. (Cambridge: Cambridge University Press, 2013), 30–33.

[29] Though it was initially common in legal terminology, the phrase was first used in a literary context in Margreta de Grazia and Peter Stallybrass, "The Materiality of the Shakespearean Text," *Shakespeare Quarterly* 44 (1993): 255–283. See also G. Thomas Tanselle, *A Rationale of Textual Criticism* (Philadelphia: University of Pennsylvania Press, 1989) and Alan B. Farmer, "Shakespeare and the New Textualism," in W. R. Elton and John M. Mucciolo (eds.), *The Shakespearean International Yearbook 2: Where Are We Now in Shakespearean Studies?* (Burlington, VT: Ashgate, 2002), 158–179.

[30] Zachary Lesser, *Renaissance Drama and the Politics of Publication: Readings in the English Book Trade* (Cambridge: Cambridge University Press, 2004), 4.

[31] Melnikoff, *Elizabethan Publishing*, 7.

[32] Ann Blair, "An Early Modernist's Perspective," *Isis* 95 (2004): 420–430; 428.

Richard Bankes's Little *Herball*

In 1525, Richard Bankes printed and published a small quarto herbal of 207 short chapters.[33] In all editions subsequent to his quarto reprint of 1526, the herbal was printed in octavo, with nine to ten sheets of paper folded thrice to make up the volume. In the absence of documentary records testifying to the activities within a particular bookshop or printing house, it is difficult for a modern scholar to determine a Renaissance publisher's success in anticipating the attractiveness of any given edition to their readers; however, the extant evidence of reprinting the same or similar titles strongly suggests that an earlier edition had sold out. Bankes's immediate reprinting of his 1525 edition the following year indicates that his sense of the little *Herball*'s probable appeal to Tudor readers was correct. The book that he chose to publish *was* a sufficiently desired textual commodity among London customers that he not only profited from its manufacture but did so quickly. What might have accounted for the little *Herball*'s popular appeal in print in London in 1525?

It may have had something to do with the affordances of the text he printed, the *Agnus castus* text, which survives in more than three dozen medieval manuscript copies.[34] Late medieval English manuscript texts had recently begun to include finding aids such as tables, and this feature, coupled with *Agnus castus*'s alphabetized chapters, helped to speed up readers' ability to locate desired information about plants and remedies, novel conveniences that were intensified by the standardization afforded by the new medium of print. In searching for a popular work in which to invest, Bankes seems to have realized that the well-liked *Agnus castus* had not yet appeared in print, and he set about to remedy the gap, mirroring the user-based conveniences that had lately accompanied the work in manuscript.

Many of the remedies and folk accounts of plants that were first outlined in the little *Herball* of 1525 later made their way into the massive botanical tomes of William Turner, Rembert Dodoens, and John Gerard in the second half of the sixteenth century. Before these large authorized volumes of botanical knowledge became available, however, Tudor readers clamored for smaller printed herbals, and booksellers resoundingly

---

[33] Subsequent reprints of the *Herball* vary in their number of individual chapters; the 1525 edition has 207, but only 206 are listed in the table that follows the text.

[34] George R. Keiser, "Vernacular Herbals: A Growth Industry in Late Medieval England," in Margaret Connolly and Linne R. Mooney (eds.), *Design and Distribution of Late Medieval Manuscripts in England* (York: York Medieval Press, 2008), 292–308; 300.

obliged: Bankes's anonymous herbal was reprinted at least eighteen times by 1567, more than a dozen times before the appearance of Turner's folio *A New Herball* of 1551 demonstrated that England too could produce a herbalist of its own to rival natural historians on the continent such as Brunfels and Fuchs.[35] Because extant medieval manuscripts confirm that there was nothing particularly new or original about the textual content of the little printed herbal of Bankes and his successors that could account for its widespread appeal, its extraordinary popularity must have been due, at least in part, to its increased availability within the new medium, demonstrating its first publisher's skill as a reader of the dynamic marketplace for English books.[36] Of course, modern historians considering Bankes's ability to evaluate the texts that would best sell in Tudor London are left with only the positive evidence of his selections (we don't have a means of knowing those texts that he considered and rejected), but we can judge from the multitude of subsequent editions that Bankes's initial decision to publish was widely and rapidly copied by his fellow booksellers, and these many reprint editions suggest that the economic benefits the little *Herball* offered to its first publisher were amply evident to others in the book trade.

Other features of the little *Herball* raise additional questions about the relationship between texts and the books that contain them. While Fuchs's *De historia stirpium* was celebrated throughout Europe for its naturalistic woodcuts that indicated the shape and features of plants, all the editions of the little *Herball* were unillustrated, and the text's descriptions of plant morphology are often too vague to be useful as a finding aid in the field. More curiously, its plant descriptions depend on readers having a preexisting acquaintance with the subject: "This herbe Auetum that men call Auete / otherwyse Dyll. This herbe hathe leues lyke to

---

[35] As several of the reprinted editions of Bankes's *Herball* exist in only single copies, it is reasonable to assume that there may have been additional editions that are no longer extant. Though his dataset examines books published more than a decade after the last edition of the little *Herball* was printed, Alan B. Farmer has demonstrated that edition loss rates decrease as the number of sheets of paper needed to print a copy of the edition increase (this unit is known as an "edition-sheet"). Assuming that herbals fall into a "low-loss genre," a book of similar length to the little *Herball* with nine edition-sheets would have a minimal loss rate of 9.7 percent; given the eighteen editions of the text that are extant, even a conservative estimate may posit the complete loss of one or two additional editions. See Alan B. Farmer, "Playbooks and the Question of Ephemerality," in Heidi Brayman, Jesse M. Lander, and Zachary Lesser (eds.), *The Book in History, The Book As History: New Intersections of the Material Text: Essays in Honor of David Scott Kastan* (New Haven, CT: Beinecke Rare Book & Manuscript Library and Yale University, 2016), 87–125.

[36] As Bankes was still a relatively inexperienced publisher in 1525, it should also be noted that his decision to publish the *Herball* in 1525 may simply have been a lucky guess, or the fortunate happenstance of a copy of what turned out to be a particularly appealing manuscript text somehow finding its way into his hands.

Fenell / but the Sede is Somdele brode as the Orage [orange] Sede is."[37]
Cominum (cumin) leaves are "moche lyke to Colynadre (coriander),"
Dragantia (*dracontium*) has leaves "lyke to Rew / but it hathe whyte
Speckes," while gout-curing woodbind (woodbine) "bereth lyke to the
Hoppe."[38] In order to use the little *Herball*, in other words, a reader must
already be familiar with the bulk of its subject matter – the work therefore
complements the plant knowledge that an early modern reader would
bring to the text but offers very little to the botanically illiterate.

There are other examples of this phenomenon. In her analysis of Fuchs's
De historia stirpium, Sachiko Kusukawa explains that Fuchs's descriptive
strategy in matching ancient signifiers to contemporary signifiers likewise
assumes foreknowledge on behalf of his readers.[39] By using images to
provoke readers' recall of the subjective features of known plants (like
taste and smell), Fuchs reveals that he anticipated a botanically literate
audience for his book. Yet, unlike the large illustrated and authorized
herbals with which it shares a genre, the herbals printed by Bankes and
those who followed him were not compendia of the best and latest
botanical information gathered by informed readers, and their medical
receipts seem to offer their readers little in the way of new morphological or
phytological information. To gain any practical import from these little
herbals, readers were required to be critically active and to bring as much
knowledge to the text as they could take away.[40] It was familiarity with
local plants, rather than the novelty of exotic ones, that provided much of
the book's appeal to readers in Tudor London, a response readily

---

[37] Sig. A2r. In Bankes's 1525 index or table, as well as in Wyer's versions of the herbal, this plant is
identified as "Anetum," or anise, which suggests that Bankes (or his compositor) experienced minim
confusion as they set type from their manuscript copy.

[38] Sigs. C1r, C2v, and I2v. As Larkey and Pyles note, Wyer's editions of the herbal have "more
descriptions of the plants, with characteristics of their growth" (*An Herbal [1525]* [Battleboro, VT:
New York Botanical Garden, 1941], xvi), a detail that suggests Wyer's supplementing Bankes's texts
with information of his own. In all editions of the little *Herball*, descriptions beginning with letters
located in the first half of the alphabet generally contain more information about morphological
characteristics of their plants than descriptions located in the latter half of the book. Such division is
likely the result of Bankes's (or his copy text's) use of two or more sources in the original
compilation, evident from internal evidence; from the midpoint of the text (after "Morell, or
Nyghtshadowe"), the text offers information about each plant's humeral characteristics, noting
whether the simple is hot, cold, moist, or dry and the degree of each. In Wyer's texts, these humeral
characteristics occur throughout.

[39] Kusukawa, *Picturing the Book of Nature*, 120.

[40] Even the modern editors of Fuchs's *De historia stirpium* find that their preexisting botanical
knowledge is called upon in a similar way: "Even with a knowledge of Latin, Fuchs's great herbal
cannot easily be understood without a knowledge of botany" (Meyer et al., *Great Herbal*, 1:xiii).

capitalized upon by Tudor publishers, whose livelihoods depended upon their knowing what readers wanted.

Such assumptions of a competent reader using a herbal not as a self-sufficient authority but as a guide to individual memory or to refresh experience is consistent with what Brian W. Ogilvie finds was the norm for natural historians operating in the second half of the sixteenth century when the number of known plants increased rapidly. Ogilvie argues that the published descriptions and illustrations of plants provided by Renaissance botanists served as the "final stage in the condensation of experience," and these printed books enabled botanists to share their experience with others in the "Republic of Letters."[41] The evidence of the eighteen surviving editions of the little *Herball*, however, suggests that use of printed herbals as a guide to experiential memory was occurring even in the simple botanical books that were designed for a less sophisticated reading public. The answer to the question of the little *Herball*'s popularity with Tudor readers may be found not in its novelty but in the way that the text of the book reinforces its readers' existing botanical knowledge.

Small herbals' lack of botanical originality and their initial failure to proclaim recognized (or recognizable) authorities may be the reason that, despite their unmistakable popularity with early modern readers, many scholarly works of botanical history have either dismissed them or disregarded them entirely.[42] Rather than seeing their regular appearance in the historical record as demonstrating the marketability of botanical knowledge to a paying public, the anonymous vernacular herbals of the fifteenth and sixteenth centuries, in both print and manuscript, have been denounced for their lack of sophistication.[43] As earlier English herbals lack both authorship and originality, histories of the English herbal regularly begin with the works of William Turner, whose three-volume *A New Herball* (1551–1561) led to his celebration as the "Father of British Botany."[44] Those histories ascend through the volumes of Henry Lyte, John Gerard, and John Parkinson to explore how the labors of these men led to the creation of a uniquely English genre of a scientific book. Yet, as the products of both late medieval scriptoria and early Tudor stationers

[41] Ogilvie, *Science of Describing*, 181.

[42] A. G. Morton, *History of Botanical Science: An Account of the Development of Botany from its Ancient Times to the Present Day* (London: Academic Press, 1981), 123.

[43] Jerry Stannard, "Dioscorides and Renaissance Material Medica," in *Materia Medica in the XVI Century: Proceedings of a Symposium at the International Academy of the History of Medicine* (London: Pergamon Press, 1966), 1–21; 8.

[44] Rebecca Laroche traces this celebratory phrase to Benjamin Daydon Jackson. See *Medical Authority*, 23n5.

ably demonstrate, the genre of the printed herbal in English preceded the efforts of these named authors. In the words of Wendy Wall, "authorship bears the mark of things unauthorized."[45]

By prioritizing authors and their botanical works over stationers and their editions, scholars of herbals have largely overlooked one of the most popular English books of the sixteenth century and missed the fact that thousands of early modern readers between 1520 and 1560 were eager to access botanical information however they could find it. Despite its quaint readability, abdicated authority, and ambivalent functionality, the eighteen-plus editions of the little *Herball* (as well as the marginalia that appear in surviving copies of these editions) testify to the existence of a robust popular reading culture for natural history in the first half of the sixteenth century. This is the context that would enable more "authoritative" English herbals by William Turner and John Gerard to appear in print, as these smaller volumes had demonstrated an eager market. Without considering the practical means by which ideas spread, a scholarly focus on the presentation and transmission of ideas can lose a great deal of important context. While the texts of printed herbals are of crucial importance in understanding the development of early modern descriptive science, the physical status of these books as marketable commodities facilitated such developments. Seemingly insignificant works such as the little *Herball*, together with its multiple reprints published by Robert Redman, Elizabeth Redman, Robert Wyer, William Powell, and others, demonstrate that the English public, like its continental brethren, was eager to own botanical works printed in the vernacular – and was willing to pay for them.

Expanding the agents of the production of knowledge to include the publishers, printers, and booksellers of herbals reminds us that the potential audience for herbals included those who did not necessarily have a vested interest in contributing to the creation of scientific knowledge on a grand scale. As one of the products offered in the burgeoning trade in books in early modern London, herbals were purchased by a wide variety of readers with an equally varied suite of attitudes towards the function of books in their daily lives. Because they contained "the names and descriptions of herbs, or of plants in general, with their properties and virtues," herbals could serve as authorities for plant knowledge. Their status as physical objects also allowed readers to use them as personal repositories

---

[45] Wendy Wall, *The Imprint of Gender: Authorship and Publication in the English Renaissance* (Ithaca, NY: Cornell University Press, 1993), 346.

to record their own experience, supplementing the printed page with marginal annotations detailing their own knowledge. The conjunction of a sixteenth-century hand with a printed book serves, in Monique Hulvey's words, as "one of the many invaluable testimonies of the active relationship between Renaissance readers and their books."[46] Like other books, herbals were objects that could be personalized by their owners, and individual readers could as easily have seen a herbal as an occasion for record-keeping and a supplement to experience, just as they could have used the text of a book as an authoritative source of information.

Several of the copies of the later editions of the little *Herball* held in the Huntington Library contain marginalia demonstrating a user's identification of crucial parts of the text or clarification of detail. A 1552 edition of the text printed by Robert Wyer has readers' marks explaining that "Emerodes" are also known as "piles," and that the important part of the chapter on "Saluia" is the *Herball*'s observation that "If ye haue an ytchynge on you wasshe it well with [the] ioyce of ths herbe & it Shall Slee ytchynge," which a reader saw fit to underline.[47] Neither of these manuscript annotations serves to say anything of the botanical import of the book in question, nor do they contribute anything especially useful to a different reader of the same copy of the book. What such marks in books do demonstrate, however, is evidence of their practical usage by readers who were engaging with these texts in both an intellectual and a *material* way. They serve as reminders that books are not only practical sources of information but also artifacts manipulated by people in real time and real space, and that the influences of such non-authorial actors on the reception and continued production of books for the marketplace are more complex than any account of their botanical authors alone could accommodate.

Traditional Accounts of Herbals

I argue throughout this volume that the significant economic consequences of the mass production of books in England that print made possible had lasting repercussions for those who wished to be recognized as experts within emerging disciplines like botany. Indeed, those early capitalists who invested in print technology created both opportunity and motive for herbalists to thrive. Stationers' facility with textual technologies was also

---

[46] Monique Hulvey, "Not So Marginal: Manuscript Annotations in the Folger Incunabula," *Papers of the Bibliographical Society of America* 92 (1998): 159–176; 174.

[47] Sig. A3r.

directly linked to English herbals' material features: as stationers' ability to print high-quality woodcut images improved over the sixteenth century, naturalists' long-standing debates over the utility of illustrations for descriptions gained increasing relevance. In Sachiko Kusukawa's words, "the fact that learned scholars envisaged their knowledge to be presented in printed books affected the way they devised text-image relations, and more crucially, the way they set up their arguments and even their methods of study."[48] My study adds to Kusukawa's observation by further shifting the agency of stationers to the forefront of studies of Renaissance natural history to delineate how a second, third, or fourth edition of a popular herbal differed from the one preceding it, or to explain how the popularity of early modern books might reasonably be determined in the first place.[49]

Compounding the difficulties of assessing Renaissance herbals in their original contexts is an anachronistic tendency to evaluate early works of natural history by later scientific standards. A preference for recognizing authors, particularly those who claimed to write from the basis of their own hands-on experience with plants, has sometimes led to studies of herbals that promote the role of authorial primacy and originality in an age that, by contrast, also placed a high value on comprehensive anthologizing (or, as early modern herbalists themselves termed it, "gathering"). These modern histories have provided somewhat arbitrary judgments of botanical reputations: early empirical herbalists are fêted for their modern outlooks, while those authors whose work was heavily composed of book-based research are considered derivative at best and plagiarists at worst. In one of the most popular narratives about English herbals, Thomas Johnson is credited for the ways that his plant-gathering expeditions into the wilds of Kent enabled him to edit the work of John Gerard. Despite Gerard's own ample botanical and medical experience, Gerard's open admission that he depended upon the books of others renders him, in the opinion of many historians, guilty of nearly all the crimes of which a modern man of science and letters can be accused. Once suspicious forms of textual production

---

[48] Kusukawa, *Picturing the Book of Nature*, 2.

[49] The present study recognizes its genesis in Agnes Arber, *Herbals: Their History and Evolution*, which was first published in 1912. The lasting impact of Arber's *Herbals* may be seen in the attitudes taken towards the volume in various journal reviews of its third edition, published in 1988. John M. Riddle calls *Herbals* a "classic" that remains "the best single volume in English on early printed herbals" ("[Untitled Review]," *Systemic Botany* 13 [1988]: 473); Karen Reeds sees it as "the single best work on herbals" ("[Untitled Review],"*Isis* 79 [1998]: 288); while Jeanne Goode's review in *Brittonia* asserts that "although Herbals have been studied extensively since [the 2nd edition of the text in 1938], this work of meticulous scholarship and lucid exposition has never been surpassed" ("[Untitled Review],"*Brittonia* 40 [1988]: 47).

have been detected, the villainy comes to be seen elsewhere, too, even in anonymous works well outside of authorial control; for example, the sixteenth-century printer Robert Wyer is considered a rogue and a plagiarist for reorganizing the text of the little *Herball* that was in the public domain and for adding his own modifications to it.

As Renaissance literary historians have turned towards the history of science, however, these assumptions about authorial originality, long the subject of literary study, can be seen to rest on precarious foundations. In particular, Leah Knight has shown that the large herbals of Turner and Gerard were often recursive and "anthological"; as she demonstrates, the extensive metaphors of gathering and planting found in these works signify how strongly linked authorial and botanical practices were in the English imagination. She writes:

> Like poems in a garden of verse, a period understanding of plants was always gathered from many sources: from anonymous and named poets, ancient and modern, as well as from both ancient and modern herbalists; from sometimes acknowledged but often unnamed women and husbandmen; from servants sent to collect plants from abroad, and from gardeners who sent plants and information by correspondence.[50]

This anthological thinking recasts what we may think of as "normative" botanical behavior, particularly during moments of composition. What's more, a recognition of the broader context in and for which early English books were authored, compiled, and offered for sale shows that herbals had a broad and diverse public-facing readership, and authors' own knowledge of these readers influenced the ways they wrote and read other books.[51]

Print's capacity for distributing complex packages of information in a relatively stable form granted early herbalists broad access not only to one another's work but also to the regularly translated works of classical botanical authorities like Theophrastus and Dioscorides.[52] It was through printed books that natural historians were eventually able to grasp that ancient authorities' understanding of plants was regionally contingent and therefore limited; it was only through fruitless attempts to identify

---

[50] Knight, *Of Books and Botany*, 108. Knight's *Books and Botany* is primarily focused on the relation of texts and plants in the early modern imagination, explaining how botany functioned as a readily understood and accessible metaphor of collection. She considers how readers and later authors used herbals, both how they manipulated the physical books themselves and how they mined them as sources of information. The present book is more concerned with how and why herbal books came to be written, printed, and published in the first place.

[51] Lorraine Daston makes a similar point in "Taking Note[s]," *Isis* 95 (2004): 443–448; 447.

[52] See Eisenstein, *Printing Press*. Statues of both figures appear on the frontispiece of Thomas Johnson's revised edition of Gerard's *Herball* of 1633; see Figure 8.2.

Mediterranean plants in other landscapes that the modern concept of biogeography gradually emerged. While the easy motility of geophytes like bulbs and tubers has long been understood as a major contributor to the infamous tulip craze in the seventeenth century (bulbs serve as food reserves that allow tulips to survive outside of soil and without light for long periods of time), the role of print in spreading knowledge about exotic and more fragile plants or about difficult-to-transport specimens like trees is far less appreciated.[53] In a sense, the ubiquity and familiarity of books have led to the printed medium being too often ignored by historians of botany, who, in searching for the forest, have largely neglected the trees.

Attending to material books often poses its own challenges, as book historians' interest in historical particularity often considers single copies or titles in isolation from a book's larger commercial context. Such studies discern some of the trees of the proverbial forest, but they may ignore the mutually beneficial relationship between their particular species of tree and the other growth sprouting from the forest floor. Book historians who organize their investigations around modern, rather than historical, notions of textual genre can sometimes suffer from the same narrow focus that can affect historians of science. As the verbal content of herbals often includes a combination of subjects such as medical remedies, discourses on gardening and agriculture, and systems of plant classification and description, the texts of herbals are often used indiscriminately in debates about emerging distinctions between the publication of works of husbandry, natural history, or medicine.[54] Depending on a book historian's particular purview, then, any individual herbal title might be slated into one generic category or another.

Commodifying Botany in the English Herbal

While literary scholars' interest in herbals is often piqued because the books can serve as resources for the interpretation of early modern botanical understanding, thereby answering questions about the significance of mad Ophelia's bouquets or King Lear's crown of weeds, ad hoc approaches that

---

[53] On the thefts to which tulip cultivators were subject as a result of their portability, see Anne Goldgar, *Tulipmaina: Money, Honor, and Knowledge in the Dutch Golden Age* (Chicago: University of Chicago Press, 2007), 57–58.

[54] For example, in John Barnard, D. F. McKenzie, and Maureen Bell, *The Cambridge History of the Book in Britain*, vol. 4 (Cambridge: Cambridge University Press, 2002), both Lynnette Hunter and Adrian Johns find reasons to discuss the herbals of John Gerard and John Parkinson in their retrospective chapters of "Books for Daily Life: Household, Husbandry, Behaviour" and "Science and the Book."

treat herbals as mere containers of botanical facts can sever the relationship between medium and message that allowed such botanical knowledge to spread.[55] Over the course of the sixteenth century, early modern English readers saw more than two dozen herbal editions appear in stationers' bookstalls, belying Cordelia's claim that plants are the "unpublished virtues of the Earth" (18.16).[56] By 1608, when the quarto text of *King Lear* appeared from the press of Nicholas Okes on behalf of its publisher Nathaniel Butter, a curious English reader eager to peruse a codex containing "the names, or descriptions of herbs, with their properties and virtues" had an impressive array of options from which to choose. If they were flush enough with coin, they could have purchased a copy of John Gerard's 1,400-page *Herball or History of Plantes* of 1597, a fashionable choice, no doubt, considering that Gerard had just been elected Master of the Barber-Surgeons' Company the previous August and had been "Surgeon and Herbalist" to James I since 1604.[57] If our hypothetical early modern reader desired an older work, but one with a continental pedigree, an English version of Rembert Dodoens's *Cruydeboeck* appeared in English bookstalls in 1578, translated from a French edition that had been circulating on the continent since 1557. The Englishman Henry Lyte had translated Dodoens's *Niewe Herball, or Historie of Plants* (*STC* 6984) from French for this 1578 edition, correcting and annotating the text against his own experience of plants and supplementing with new material supplied by Dodoens himself. Though *A Niewe Herball* was initially printed in Antwerp, it was distributed by Gerard Dewes at the Sign of the Swanne at his shop in Saint Paul's Churchyard, making this text readily available at the very heart of the English book trade. Three more editions followed in 1586, 1595, and 1619, while *Ram's Little Dodoeon* (*STC* 6988), an abridged "epitome," appeared in 1606. If our hypothetical reader instead preferred to read about plants in Latin, Pierre Pena and Matthias de L'Obel's *Stirpium aduersaria noua* (1570–1571; *STC* 19595), one of the earliest English books to feature an engraved copperplate title page, was considered both so elegant and so authoritative that the renowned

---

[55] Rebecca Laroche makes a similar point about the way that women engage with printed botanical books: "we should not think it enough to gloss any example as merely reflective of a general gendered material reality. Rather, each herbal reference should be taken on its own terms" (*Medical Authority*, 164).

[56] Quotations from Shakespeare are taken from the *New Oxford Shakespeare: The Complete Works, Modern Critical Edition*, ed. Gary Taylor, John Jowett, Terri Bourus, and Gabriel Egan (Oxford: Oxford University Press, 2016).

[57] Robert F. Jeffers, *The Friends of John Gerard (1545–1612), Surgeon and Botanist* (Falls Village, CT: The Herb Grower Press, 1967), 79–81.

Antwerp publisher Christopher Plantin purchased 800 copies of it to bind with his own editions of L'Obel.[58] And if new editions were too expensive for our reader in 1608, or simply could no longer be found in bookshops, secondhand copies were perhaps still available. The London secondhand market may likewise have featured copies of the extremely popular anonymous works like the illustrated *Grete Herbal* (*STC* 13176–13179; published 1526, 1529, 1539, and 1561) or the little *Herball* first published by Bankes and reprinted by many, many others. An awareness of the different herbals available for sale in Renaissance London makes it clear that selecting any one of them as a straightforward representative of Shakespeare's botanical knowledge is an arbitrary and questionable procedure.

Early Modern Herbals and the Book Trade functions both as a complement and as a corrective to accounts that examine herbals primarily as containers for botanical texts by contextualizing the provenance of the material artifact of herbals' bookish forms. In so doing, this work reveals the diversity of meanings that early English herbals could have for their earliest authors and audiences. My approach is in line with a particular theoretical development in the history of books, an approach that D. F. McKenzie has identified as the "sociology of texts."[59] Though McKenzie was not the first bibliographer to insist upon the importance of conducting historical and cultural investigations into the cir-cumstances surrounding textual production and reception, his work is con-sidered foundational in determining the ways in which material forms influence textual meaning.[60] McKenzie argues that the discipline of bibliog-raphy is well situated to include within its precincts not only the technical processes of printing but also the social processes that enabled written works to spread. By refusing to elevate the status of the verbal work over the printed object that mediates it, *Early Modern Herbals and the Book Trade* demonstrates the multiple subjectivities inherent in a term like Michel Foucault's "author-function," which should encompass the activities not only of writers but also of publishers, printers, and booksellers, agents whose identifiable acts define the boundaries of textual discourse. Foucault's assertion that the author-function is constrained by its context demands the establishment of that context for the unique circumstances of every would-be author: "[the author-function] is

---

[58] *STC* 2:225.

[59] D. F. McKenzie, *Bibliography and the Sociology of Texts: The Panizzi Lectures* (London: British Library, 1985).

[60] For a discussion of the influences of the New Bibliography upon McKenzie's "sociology," see Sarah Neville, "*Nihil biblicum a me alienem puto*: W.W. Greg, Bibliography, and the Sociology of Texts," *Variants* 11 (2014): 91–112.

a speech that must be received in a certain mode and that, in a given culture, must receive a certain status."[61] In the culture of sixteenth-century London, long before the legal establishment of a writer's right of ownership over their intellectual labors, the subject who was considered primarily responsible for a particular textual artifact was its publisher.

In his investigation of the author-function's more practical advantages, Foucault's "What Is an Author?" suggests that the discourse of authorship was largely prompted by an authoritarian need to adjudicate issues of censorship and punishment, particularly in response to the proliferation of subversive textual productions. Here, too, may be seen the import that early moderns ascribed to the producers of the material artifact: alongside the author of a given work, printers and publishers were subject to the same strictures of reward and punishment, and these risks determined what kinds of books stationers would produce. The penal function of authorship is why, in 1579, during the reign of Elizabeth I, it was not only John Stubbes who lost his right hand for authoring a treasonous pamphlet arguing against the queen's marriage negotiations with the Duke of Anjou; so too did his publisher, William Page. Had his sentence not been withdrawn out of compassion for his advanced age, the printer Hugh Singleton would have been subjected to the same harsh punishment as well.[62] A number of royal proclamations reveal that authorities through-out Europe viewed printers and publishers as critically responsible for book production and hence saw them as liable textual agents.

Early Modern Herbals and the Book Trade is divided into three sections that move from bibliographical and textual theory through the publishing and reception of particular herbals. The chapters of Part I are designed to show those unfamiliar with methods of analytic, critical, and historical bibliography how such scholarship reframes traditional debates over the nature of authors' works. These chapters consider the intellectual stakes of approaching herbals as documents as well as discursive products by examining how the early commercial practices of English printers shaped both popular reading habits and the development of scholarly and botanical authority. Because herbals were of demonstrable value to publishers prior to the appearance of authors on herbals' title pages, Part II of this book focuses on two popular anonymous works that have been less frequently considered by scholars. The chapters in this section argue that, in the case

---

[61] Michel Foucault, "What Is an Author?," in Paul Rabinow (ed.), *The Foucault Reader*, trans. Josué V. Harari (New York: Random House, 1984): 107.

[62] On Stubbes, see Cyndia Susan Clegg, *Press Censorship in Elizabethan England* (Cambridge: Cambridge University Press, 1997), 71–72.

of texts without authors, like the little *Herball* and the *Grete Herball*,
readers of natural history were unable to fall back upon authorship to
limit the scope of a book's authority. Instead, as my chapter on reference
books on the public stage (Chapter 6) shows, early moderns responded to
the physicality of the book form as a marker of a character's individual
credit, suggesting that readers were especially attuned to herbals' material
nature. The book's third and final section, Part III, returns to authors and
considers how authors' professional identities function to legitimize the
large-format herbals of William Turner and John Gerard, the authoritative
"English herbalists" whose books created the benchmarks for understanding early modern attitudes towards plants.

Chapter 1 begins with an expansion of Foucault's author-function to
include such figures as stationers, booksellers, and printers to show how an
author could attempt to establish their scholarly bona fides by denigrating
the publishing behaviors of others. To ground this approach in materials
that are familiar to those who study Renaissance natural history, I begin
with an examination of the way that Leonard Fuchs, the author of one of
the best-known herbals of the period, *De historia stirpium commentarii
insignes* (*Notable Commentaries on the History of plants*; Basel, 1542), orients
himself in relation to his publisher, Michael Isingrin. Throughout his
address to the reader, Fuchs tries to downplay his reliance on Isingrin (or
on any bookseller) to distribute his botanical knowledge among continental readers. Distribution of texts through print makes authors vulnerable in
other ways as well: Fuchs is so disquieted by the fear of losing control of his
text that he goes out of his way to condemn the Frankfurt printer Christian
Egenolff, a bookseller who had pirated the herbal of Otto Brunfels. This
example of Fuchs and Egenolff suggests that, to better understand how
herbalists themselves conceived of their authority in print (and how such
authority could easily be undermined), scholars of natural history need to
make a "bibliographic turn."

Chapter 2 addresses the regulatory constraints upon the printing of
herbals that are evident through examination of the records of the
Stationers' Company of London. This medieval bookmaking guild was
granted the legal status of a corporation in 1557 and given full authority
over the new technology of printing. Even before William Caxton brought
England's first handpress and movable type to Westminster in 1476, royal,
civic, and religious authorities had long struggled with containing the
spread of heretical and seditious material. Yet print's capacity for producing multiple copies of illicit work en masse was a far greater threat to
crown or ecclesiastical control than that posed by written manuscripts or

the singing of prohibited ballads. As the craft of printing spread, crown attempts to manage and censor the productions of various presses grew unwieldy, particularly as Protestant reformers took to using print as a vehicle for democratizing a Christian's relationship to God. It was Catholic Queen Mary I who attempted to solve the problem of press control by granting a single London company a monopoly over all printed material in exchange for monitoring potentially heretical output. All printed books, not just herbals, were affected by this event, but I argue that the development of the "author-ized" English herbal can be directly tied to the effects of the Stationers' Company's incorporation in 1557.

As a corporation, the Stationers' Company of London was legally able to own property in its own right, administer its own affairs, and police within the boundaries of its membership a standard of civic behavior in line with City customs. By registering with the Company the titles of works they published or wanted to publish, individual stationers were able to manage the high degree of short-term financial risk they undertook in the specula-tive process of bookmaking. The growth in the production of herbals shows that the Stationers' Company regulations helped to encourage larger and more elaborate books of natural history. Through establishing their legal ownership of a work prior to printing it, stationers could discourage others from copying or pirating their texts and undermining their invest-ments; by centralizing power over both the bookselling and the printing crafts, the incorporation of the Stationers' Company largely freed royal authorities from the minutiae of individual patent disputes that had previously plagued Chancery. In requiring all printed texts to declare the names of the publisher and printer who produced them, the authorities' comprehensive system of censorship and punishment ensured that the responsibility for what Foucault calls the "author-function" was shared among textual progenitors. Chapter 2 argues that, by enabling all stationers to protect their financial investments, the creation of the Stationers' Company licensing and entrance system had two significant effects on the early English book trade. First, licensing served to democratize the economic insurance that had previously been offered to a select few publishers under the Tudor patent system. Second, the ability to enter a title into the Stationers' Registers transformed what had been a temporary privilege protecting a publisher's right to recoup a past invest-ment (the ability to sell books that had already been printed) into a permanent and future one: the ability to reap benefits from a work in perpetuity. With the Stationers' Company system of entrance, therefore, came the ability to establish that verbal works have value within the book trade even before they were transformed into the commodity of printed books. Because of the Stationers' Company's attention to potential (but not yet existing) books, the products of authors were also able to become something that could be valued, bought, and sold.

Thinking bibliographically about herbals requires appreciating both the way that the printed medium affected how authors approached their works and the circumstances leading up to publication. To show how English stationers shifted their approach in marketing their wares between the first and second half of the sixteenth century, Chapter 3 reveals how the very *physicality* of the book form was understood to engage early modern consumers. What's more, by the seventeenth century, botanical illustrations, which were largely drawn from the continent, were seen as medicaments in their own right, able to soothe and comfort melancholic or agitated readers. By the beginning of King James I's reign, the age of the illustrated printed herbal had arrived, seemingly to stay. Customers' material preferences, however, had economic ramifications for the stationers who had to figure out how to produce – and to pay for – these ever larger and more complicated books. As the size of herbals increased, so too did the initial outlay of expense required to produce one, making the publication of illustrated herbals possible only after the regulatory systems of the sixteenth century had become sufficiently sophisticated to protect publishers' investments. Even so, illustrated herbal publishing was so expensive that it could be pursued only by the wealthiest stationers. The three chapters of Part I thus move from textual theory, to print history, to material practice.

Part II moves into a discussion of particular works: by examining the editions of the little *Herball* and *The Grete Herbal* (1526), the former unillustrated and the latter illustrated, Chapters 3 and 4 show that anonymous books of science reveal how early modern readers evaluated the texts – and not the authors – before them. These chapters demonstrate that figures other than authors were responsible for the extraordinary success of printed English herbals in the first half of the sixteenth century, and they paved the way for stationers' increased investment in larger, "author-ized" works of botany that are the subject of the book's third section. This deep dive into Tudor printing and publishing history demonstrates the value of investigating the separate provenance of each *edition* of a work to better account for stationers' anticipation of readers' market demands. Who was reading these early vernacular herbals in the 1530s and 1540s? Investigating the decisions of publishers as they promoted their bookish wares can help us to better answer that question.

In Chapter 4, I reexamine the publication of the little *Herball* in the context of the book trade of Tudor London. After charting the connections among its publishers, I ask whether crown attempts to control printing by the means of individual patents or copyrights issued to individual stationers may have inadvertently contributed to a culture of copying that modern scholars have since misinterpreted as piratical. In an era when the risk of ecclesiastical reprisal was very real, the *cum privilegio* privilege of the crown offered booksellers what appeared to be an implicit endorsement of a book's contents (though it explicitly was not one), indicating that such a book was unlikely to be flagged as seditious. Moreover, my attention to the sociology of the English print trade in the first half of the sixteenth century reveals that the default assumption of aggressive competition between rival booksellers may be overstated. A consideration of herbals *as books* reveals evidence that stationers also engaged in mutually beneficial social and economic relationships in order to minimize financial risk in their promotion of the commodification of the printed medium.

Chapter 5 continues this examination of books as artifacts by using contemporary readers' marks in anonymous English herbals to argue that Renaissance readers used printed texts as opportunities to record their own experiences of native plants and medical experiments, pushing back against a pervasive view of early herbal readers as credulous and unsophisticated. Former scholars have asserted that early modern readers were necessarily naïve and inclined to follow any recommendations communicated through the written word because they lacked an understanding of the value of scientific experimentation and expertise. Instead, I argue in favor of adopting Madeline Doran's more nuanced conception of early modern credulity, one which recognizes that sixteenth- and seventeenth-century readers were quite capable of critically evaluating the information they encountered in books.[63] Though botanical or medical historians with a vested interest in the accuracy of herbals' subject matter might scorn herbals' inclusion of folklore or medical practices that have little efficacy, a focus on the material book uncovers some of the processes by which early modern readers evaluated the texts in front of them. Commonplacing and the contemporary marginalia left in Renaissance books indicate that early modern readers, much like modern scholars, were capable of using books as authorities only inasmuch as it suited them to do so. A particularly pious reader of a copy of the 1529 edition of *The Grete Herbal* now held in the

---

[63] Madeline Doran, "On Elizabethan 'Credulity': With Some Questions Concerning the Use of the Marvelous in Literature," *Journal of the History of Ideas* 1 (1940): 151–176.

British Library, for example, even sought to replace that book's Catholic sentiments with her own preferred Protestant theology, striking out all references to "our Lady" and substituting the less inflammatory "God." If traditional religious pieties could be so easily supplanted by a reader's "truant pen," it is difficult to make a case that minor botanical details should offer greater resistance.

To illuminate the setting in which publishers, herbalists, and medical authors competed for readers, as well as to highlight the skepticism with which early modern audiences regarded the authority of books, Chapter 6 explores how books were used as properties on the English Renaissance stage to underwrite characters' affectations of medical and scientific expertise. Herbals and other books of natural history existed for early moderns not only as locations where information was stored but as objects that could be strategically deployed for professional or social effect. For attentive audiences, stage books served particularly *material* ends as recognizable resources that signified characters' social and intellectual pretentions. In plays by William Shakespeare and John Webster, the characters' medical acumen is signaled by book learning rather than by professional or formal training, and Thomas Heywood makes similar use of books in his innovative *Wise Woman of Hoxton*. Understanding how early moderns both thought about and performed with books is a crucial foundation for understanding how English herbalists conspicuously used others' books as they gathered materials for their own.

In the two chapters of Part III, I reveal the degree to which early modern herbalists *themselves* conceived of their works as printed books designed to be sold by publishers concerned about competition within a print marketplace. My chapter on William Turner (Chapter 7) discusses the ways that an author's "bibliographic ego" could surface even in a nonliterary text.[64] Turner is the first of the named English herbalists to identify his book as a uniquely valuable service that would benefit the Protestant English commonweal, and from this position he chastises his botanical contemporaries for declining to share their knowledge in print. Turner explains their refusals by claiming that cementing their expertise within a book would open these men up to critique or even force them to account for their opinions. He admits he is also concerned about such criticism, but he is more worried that some readers might interpret his research into continental herbals as little more than a compilation of other men's labors. His

---

[64] The phrase is Joseph Lowenstein's, who first used it to refer to Ben Jonson's attitude to print in "The Script in the Marketplace," *Representations* 12 (1985): 101–114.

preface describes how the continental herbals of his predecessors and contemporaries influenced his own investigations of plants and identifies which authors he used in his studies. Turner became a physician during his studies as a naturalist, and there is evidence that the shift in his professional status also changed his approach to his readership and his assumption of an authorial identity as a botanical expert.

Turner's careful attention to his printed botanical sources is well founded because it seems to have protected his long-term reputation with subsequent botanical scholars. In Chapter 8, I examine how Thomas Johnson employs a similar authorizing technique in his changes and additions to the 1633 edition of John Gerard's *Herball*. Early in the volume, Johnson makes a special point of highlighting the major players in the production of botanical knowledge from King Solomon through to his own time, with particular reference to continental printed works. Because he desired to distance his legitimate use of such materials from the sly thefts that he accuses Gerard of engaging in, Johnson's introductory matter explicitly refers his readers to other printed works in order to confirm his findings. Johnson's deference to printed authorities has accorded well with modern ideas of scholarly citation, and his use of other herbal works has served to elevate his reputation in botanical histories that regularly charge Gerard with plagiarism. My reexamination of the case of Gerard's *Herball* begins not with Johnson's accusations but with the perspective of John Norton, the publisher who first commissioned Gerard to produce the text that became Gerard's *Herball*. By centering the stationers who stood to make or lose money through the *Herball*'s three publications of 1597, 1633, and 1636, the chapter redeems Gerard's reputation and reframes the debate over his herbal.

This book thus employs a methodological strategy that recognizes the materiality of the books under examination and considers the circumstances that led to their production. Hence this project is a work of book history inasmuch as that discipline is modified by the word "book." Yet I recognize that there is a need for limitations in the scope of this study. The present work does not provide an exhaustive analysis of botanical texts printed in sixteenth-century England, nor is it an examination of the medical and botanical importance of herbal works, both of which have already been provided elsewhere.[65] The three parts of this book illuminate how herbals were variously understood by the diverse agents who produced and used them, from authors, publishers, printers, booksellers, and

[65] rey, *British Botanical*, and Arber, *Herbals*.

stationers to readers, annotators, players, editors, and compilers – all characters with a vested interest in the chapters that follow. By highlighting the shifting contingencies and regulations that characterized English printing in the sixteenth and early seventeenth centuries, *Early Modern Herbals and the Book Trade* is more than a history of a publishing trend. It is a history of artisan investors as they navigated the uncharted waters of economic speculation in printed books.

PART I

A History of Herbals

CHAPTER I

Authorship, Book History, and the Effects of Artifacts

Towards the end of the dedicatory epistle in his *De historia stirpium commentarii insignes* (Basel, 1542), Leonhart Fuchs turned his attention away from the study of plants to commend the person responsible for bringing his massive illustrated botanical text to fruition:

> At this point I should say more about the hard work and care in the printing of this book by Michael Isingrin, the most painstaking printer of Basel, except that we know that these qualities are sufficiently known and proved by the many works that have issued from his workshop for some years now. And surely this work speaks for itself well enough, as to how diligent he was in printing it. However, how great an expense he was put to can be estimated by anyone who cares to weigh the magnitude of the work and the pictures themselves for their quality. Students of herbal matters owe much to this man, who spared neither expense nor labor in order to serve their convenience and aid their pursuits.
>
> But the fact is that there are many today who, like drone bees, sneak into other people's labors and by their inept copying spoil and debase books that were set up in the best and most elegant type and adorned with superb pictures. This is done for no other reason than to profit at the expense of others. Since this is so, we must have a thought of Isingrin, too, who has incurred enormous expense in publishing this work; and to that end a prohibition has been issued by imperial decree, that no one else anywhere may print these our commentaries without penalty, as we warned at the very beginning of this book.[1]

Though his dedicatory epistle appears in the first pages of the printed book, Fuchs seems to suggest that he holds the remainder of the volume in his

---

[1] Meyer et al., *Great Herbal*, 1:215. The warning that Fuchs refers to appears on the book's title page: "Furthermore, by the decree of CHARLES INVINCIBLE EMPEROR, warning is given that no other person goes without punishment who anywhere in the world prints these commentaries on the history of plants, just as was said in the privilege previously made known to us" (1:49). Meyer et al. point out that the "flowery language" of the title page was likely determined by Isingrin rather than Fuchs (1:50).

hands as he writes – as indeed he very well may have done. *De historia stirpium*'s preliminaries (including a title page, full-length author portrait, dedicatory epistle, explanation of difficult terms, and tables of plant names in Greek, Latin, German, and in the contemporary jargon of apothecaries) were likely printed last, and Fuchs's epistle may have been written while he reviewed the bulk of Isingrin's labor, enabling him to anticipate the experience of future readers encountering his book for the first time.[2] When readers encounter a physical copy of *De historia stirpium*, Fuchs's insistence that Isingrin is "the most painstaking printer of Basel" can be readily verified in the very weight and materials of this folio. Held in the hands, Fuchs and Isingrin's volume is appreciably, monumentally, *voluminous*.

De historia stirpium's magnitude makes it obvious that Isingrin took a considerable risk in supplying the immense capital needed to publish the volume. As the grateful Fuchs explains, Isingrin's industry has been protected by an "imperial decree," and Fuchs's phrasing makes explicit the way that Renaissance legal protections over books primarily concerned not the intellectual property of their authors but the financial interests of their publishers. As a professor at the University of Tübingen, Fuchs received an annual subsidy from his employer to supplement the costs of his publications, and his sympathies for Isingrin's costs are impossible to separate from this shared investment in the publisher's role.[3] Nonetheless, though Fuchs claims authority over "these our commentaries" as both an author and a publisher, his phrasing makes it clear he understands that the ultimate rationale for the imperial decree is to guard Isingrin's outlay of the capital needed to produce the printed volumes rather than his own investment of scholarly and creative labor in the production of the verbal text and the illustrations it contains.

Much to Fuchs's indignation, however, the imperial decree protecting *De historia stirpium* was insufficient to keep unauthorized agents from mimicking elements of the book. Nearly immediately after it appeared, *De historia*'s carefully produced illustrations were copied and adapted to accompany a new edition of Dioscorides' *De materia medica* edited by

[2] On the practical advantages of printing preliminary material last, see Peter W. M. Blayney, *The Texts of King Lear and Their Origins* (Cambridge: Cambridge University Press, 1982), 95–96.

[3] Fuchs's salary in 1535 was 160 florins, with an additional 15 florins each for housing and for "publishing his own books" (Meyer et al., *Great Herbal*, 1:283). Assuming a Rhenish florin and an exchange rate of 41 pence sterling per florin, Fuchs's annual salary as a professor was roughly equivalent to £27, and his publishing subvention added another £2.5. See John H. Munro, "The Coinages of Renaissance Europe, ca. 1500," in Thomas A. Brady (ed.), *Handbook of European History, 1400–1600: Late Middle Ages, Renaissance, and Reformation*, Vol. 1 (Leiden: Brill, 1994), 671–678.

Walther Ryff and published in Frankfurt by the printer and block-cutter Christian Egenolff (1543, *USTC* 683351). Egenolff's encroachment on Fuchs's work was neither surprising nor unprovoked: even as Fuchs praised the quality of Isingrin's printing in his 1542 epistle, he also expressly condemned Egenolff's skill as a printer and implied that the university-educated Egenolff lacked the knowledge needed to publish works of botany. In condemning Egenolff's ignorance, Fuchs elevates his own professional status as a physician by implying that the study of botany is too sophisticated to be understood by lay figures without appropriate scholarly instruction. Later in his epistle, Fuchs notes that he has simplified some of his botanical descriptions specifically to suit the needs of such unprofessional readers: "since in relating the history of plants we had to use terms somewhat abstruse and remote from the knowledge and understanding of the lay reader, we have judged it worthwhile to add some short explanation of these terms so that the less knowledgeable reader would not be handicapped."[4] While it is possible to read Fuchs's readerly concerns as genuine, his condemnation of "drug sellers, a largely ignorant class of men" and "stupid and frightfully superstitious old wives" elsewhere in the epistle suggests that his remark about lay readership is part of a larger performance of self-promotion, making his concerns about the lay reader a form of intellectual *noblesse oblige*.[5] When it is seen within this broader intellectual context, Fuchs's attempt to position Egenolff outside of professional and authentic studies in German natural history can be recognized as it was intended: as a deliberate and pointed affront.

Fuchs's insult was also motivated by Egenolff's history of unauthorized herbal publication. A decade earlier, in 1533, Egenolff had published the first edition of Eucharius Roesslin's *Kreuterbuch* and copied the woodcuts of physician Otto Brunfels's *Vivae eicones herbarum* (Strasbourg, 1530–1536), which had been published by Johannes Schott under the protection of imperial privilege. Schott sued Egenolff for violation of his privilege, and Egenolff defended himself by claiming that images of the natural world such as plants could not be protected as works of art by virtue of their innate similarities: a daffodil could only ever look like itself, and the ultimate artist responsible for its image is God.[6] As I explain in Chapter 3, Fuchs had devoted considerable effort in hiring artists to render *De historia*'s botanical illustrations to his precise specifications, and his

---

[4] Meyer et al., *Great Herbal*, 1:214.   [5] Meyer et al., *Great Herbal*, 1:204.
[6] Sachiko Kusukawa offers an account of the dispute between the two men in *Picturing the Book of Nature*, 87–89, as does Meyer et al., *Great Herbal*, 1:801–804.

attack on Egenolff suggests that Fuchs thought the printer's illicit replication of Brunfels's woodcuts would make Fuchs's own botanical scholarship
vulnerable to the replication of errors caused by unauthorized reprinting.
"Among all the herbals extant today," Fuchs claims, "none are so full of
stupid errors as those the printer Egenolff published again and again."[7] He
points out that Egenolff's herbals reused woodcuts to illustrate two distinct
species of plants, and these errors stemmed as much from the printer's
avarice as from Egenolff's botanical ignorance: "he does not regard the
rewards of scholarship as of much account and is more intent on making
money, it is no wonder that books of this sort come from his workshop."[8]
Fuchs's easy dismissal of a publisher's livelihood as merely "intent on
making money" finds an analogue in some modern accounts of herbals,
where historians find it inexplicable that sixteenth-century craftsmen were
"out to make quick money" rather than to produce their wares primarily
for the benefit of authorities attempting to lay claims to a new discipline.[9]

Fuchs's preface makes it clear that he separates publishers into two
distinct categories. There are those publishers who, like Isingrin, put
their livelihoods into the service of herbal authors like himself, and there
are nefarious privateers like Egenolff who resist such authorial deference
and seek to publish herbals for their own financial gain. In setting himself
up as Isingrin's champion, however, Fuchs once again bolsters his own
intellectual and authoritative pretentions. He conveniently elides his reliance on a publisher for the propagation of his authoritative herbal knowledge, masking the way that his authorship depends entirely on the
dissemination of printed books. While unillustrated and anonymous
botanical works like *Agnus castus* might have flourished in manuscript,
Fuchs's *De historia stirpium* relied entirely on the precise correspondence of
image and text that could be maintained only through a medium as
relatively stable – and as technically difficult to produce – as print. It is
through such rhetorical sleight of hand that Fuchs attempts to prevent his
readers from understanding that, without the likes of Isingrin or Egenolff,
there would be no illustrated printed herbals for sale at all.[10]

Egenolff's issuance of Dioscorides' text alongside copies of the *De
historia* woodcuts thus did not just violate privilege; it threatened the

[7] Meyer et al., *Great Herbal*, 1:210.   [8] Meyer et al., *Great Herbal*, 1:210.
[9] Morton, *History of Botanical Science*, 123.
[10] Similar sentiments also appear in England. J. W. Binns's work on the printing of Latin texts suggests
    that by the 1570s such accounts of the "mercenary unimaginativeness of English printers" were
    commonplace. See *Intellectual Culture in Elizabethan and Jacobean England: The Latin Writings of
    the Age* (Leeds: Francis Cairns Press, 1990), 402–403.

terms of Fuchs's status as an expert, and Fuchs publicly condemned Egenolff's thievery in a work that was both published and printed by Isingrin. In *Apologia . . . qua refellit malitiosas Gualtheri Ryffi veteratoris pessimi reprehensiones* (*Apologia, by which he refutes the malicious criticism of the sly fox, Walther Ryff*; Basel, 1544, *USTC* 602518), Fuchs cites both the financial loss to Isingrin and the damage by copying done to the reputation of the cutter of the *De historia*'s original woodblocks, Veit Rudolf Speckle. Having had this fight over botanical images before, Egenolff was well equipped to answer Fuchs's charges, and he quickly countered with his own pamphlet: *Adversum illiberales Leonhardi Fuchsij, medici Tubingensis . . . calumnias, responsio* (*A refutation of the unjust, false accusations of Leonhart Fuchs, doctor of Tübingen*; Frankfurt, 1544, *USTC* 609318). In *Responsio*, Egenolff repeated his earlier defenses and even extended his argument to attack the originality of Fuchs's botanical commentary. In defending his use of Fuchs's woodcuts, Egenolff claimed that, because much of the text of *De historia* had been lifted not from Fuchs's own experience but from the works of other botanists, it was hypocrisy for Fuchs to identify himself as the text's author with a full-length title portrait. By clothing himself in the scholarship of his botanical betters, Egenolff argued, Fuchs's expert status was vulnerable, as once these scholars come to reclaim their authority, "very soon we shall see him completely skinned, this mangy, quite hairless little fox."[11] Not only, Egenolff claimed, were Fuchs's images of plants mere copies of the book of nature but Fuchs's own expertise was merely the stuff of so many other books. The implicit fraud that Egenolff leveled against Fuchs's skill as a botanist is an insult that would later resonate with herbalists like Turner and Gerard, who used their paratexts to try to foreclose the possibility that readers might level the same accusation at them.

Egenolff's acerbic quarto prompted Fuchs to respond in kind: *Adversus mendaces et Christiano homine indignas Christiani Egenolphi typographi Francofortani suique architecti calumnias responsio* (*A reply to the mendacious calumnies, unworthy of a Christian, of Christian Egenolff, the Frankfurt publisher, and his architect*; March 1545). Fuchs had intended for his second tract against Egenolff to circulate through the continental republic of letters via the 1545 Frankfurt Book Fair, but agents working for Egenolff managed to purchase all of the copies that its Basel publisher, Ulric Morhart, offered for sale and then presumably destroyed the pamphlets. None is now extant. In a print battle between an author and

---

[11] Quoted and trans. in Meyer et al., *Great Herbal*, 1:846n9.

a publisher, the publisher clearly has an advantage. Defeated, Fuchs was forced to seek out another publisher for the work's second edition (Basel: Erasmus Zimmermann August 1545; *USTC* 602515), where he offered his account of what had happened to the first.[12]

Fuchs had many such disputes in print over the course of his long career as a herbalist and as a physician, and they were eagerly followed by contemporaries throughout Europe. His dispute with Egenolff, Fuchs suspected, was really with Janus Cornarius (1500–1558), a humanist physician who felt not only that Fuchs's writings on Greek medicine had effectively plagiarized his own but also that Fuchs was dishonest in allowing successive editions of his own books to be printed under different titles, presumably to confuse potential buyers who had already purchased a previous edition. Thus, in condemning not only Egenolff but also "his architect" throughout this second tract, Fuchs responded to the accusation that he plagiarized the work of his predecessors by once again calling the publisher's intellect into question and by condemning Egenolff's mendacity. Egenolff's criticisms must have been spurred at the behest of some other agent, Fuchs maintained, someone with a greater intellectual investment in botanical authority, rather than a mere publisher who is interested only in the commercial bottom line. Regardless of that bottom line, however, the artisanal fraternity that bookselling engendered in its practitioners enabled Egenolff to snuff out all evidence of Fuchs's authorship of a particular pamphlet. Fuchs's status as a botanical authority was assured for the remainder of his lifetime, but to his continued dismay, publishers held a great deal of power over those who wished to benefit from the broadcast potential of print. To succeed in print, therefore, even widely esteemed herbalists needed to know their place.

To examine how Renaissance authorship was a mode of self-fashioning, this chapter highlights that authors' claiming of an expert knowledge domain depends upon readers' willingness to recognize that authority. I suggest that to better understand the circumstances in which Renaissance herbals were commissioned, authored, and sold within a trade of ideas, scholars need to make a "bibliographic turn," to see herbals not just as verbal texts but also as printed commodities. I argue that by conceiving of a "stationer-function," a discourse of textual authority that is able to operate even in the absence of an author, we have a better way of accounting for the popularity of both named and anonymous books with

---

[12] On Fuchs's dispute with Egenolff, see Meyer et al., *Great Herbal*, 1:801–804 and Kusukawa, *Picturing the Book of Nature*, 125–126.

Renaissance readers. Further, by attending to the circumstances in which printing took place, scholars attuned to a stationer-function can provide a more complete picture of the conditions in which natural history and medical knowledge circulated in sixteenth- and seventeenth-century England. Instead of valorizing authors as if they alone were responsible for making their works publicly available to readers, this approach can help us recognize that botanical works like herbals circulated because of the concerted efforts of booksellers and printers.

Self-Fashioning and the Sociology of Truth

The above-discussed account of Fuchs's *De historia stirpium* demonstrates how Renaissance publishers were attentive to, and sometimes directly implicated in, disputes about the authorship of herbal texts. It is also evidence of the way that clashes over the accurate representation of details of natural history and medicine could rapidly descend into accusations of piracy (the unauthorized reproduction of material documents owned by another publisher) and the related but separate offense of plagiarism (the unauthorized reproduction of verbal works written by another author). When scholars account for these conflicts, however, they can sometimes conflate these two activities in ways that confuse the distinct concerns of the affected parties and mistake the text of verbal work for the material document that contains it.[13] So too, it seems, did early modern authors, though when they conflated plagiarism and piracy they did so for deliberate and self-aggrandizing purposes. As they dedicated their works to esteemed would-be patrons, ambitious authors of herbals like Fuchs had a vested interest in downplaying their dependence upon the financial means of publishers and the technical skill of printers, and it served their attempts at self-fashioning to use their paratexts to depict these agents simply as arms-length financial backers or unlearned mechanicals rather than as powerful figures and artisans responsible for instigating the creation of an author's books. Fuchs's complimenting of Isingrin's "diligence" and "elegant type" thus betrays his anxieties over this dependency just as much as his condemnation of the "inept copying" of "drone bees" like Egenolff. As Fuchs insists that only the integrity of the individual agent involved separates a good printer-publisher from a bad one, he reveals his uneasy

---

[13] Sometimes both offences can – and did – occur simultaneously. The crucial point, however, is that plagiarism is a crime against authors and piracy is a crime against the legal owner of a text. In the Renaissance, the owner of a text was most often its publisher, not its author.

awareness that his botanical labors can be broadly recognized as "authorial" only through the publication efforts of another party, one with their own vested interest in the production of printed herbals. As Adrian Johns has succinctly remarked, "[t]here could be no substitute for publication if one wished to establish knowledge, and ways of securing knowledge, in a wider world."[14]

The denigration of other agents' motivations, particularly others' *economic* motivations, is a crucial part of establishing the veracity of "scientific" truth claims. Steven Shapin's research has demonstrated that, despite seventeenth-century scientists' attempts to characterize factual knowledge about the world as grounded in their own direct experience, what scientists put forward as "truth" was in fact socially constructed via the testimony, and the authority, of other scientists and invested onlookers. Readers' knowledge of early modern natural history was thus based in scientists' relationships with those figures who were trusted to accurately represent and verify their accounts of their world.[15] "What we call 'social knowledge' and 'natural knowledge' are hybrid entities," Shapin writes. "[W]hat we know of comets, icebergs, and neutrinos irreducibly contains what we know of those people who speak for and about these things, just as what we know about the virtues of people is informed by their speech about things that exist in the world."[16] Shapin asserts that the paradigm of seventeenth-century veracity was the English gentleman, a figure like Robert Boyle whose breeding, discretion, and financial acumen enabled him to be sufficiently indifferent to possible outcomes and therefore unbiased in his accounting of reality: "[a] selfless self was a free actor in a world of knowledge; all others counted as constrained."[17] In Fuchs's articulation of his authority over herbal knowledge, he follows a similar strategy by celebrating the efforts of a publisher such as Isingrin, who, like Fuchs himself (and unlike the seemingly acquisitive Egenolff), is motivated not by money but by civil and scientific truth. Fuchs notes that Isingrin's labor and expense were designed not for profit but to serve the higher purpose of attending to the needs of scholars of botany, "in order to serve

---

[14] Adrian Johns, *The Nature of the Book: Print and Knowledge in the Making* (Chicago: University of Chicago Press, 1998), 489. On natural historians' anxieties about print publication in seventeenth-century England, particularly those of John Aubrey, see Elizabeth Yale, *Sociable Knowledge: Natural History and the Nation in Early Modern Britain* (Philadelphia: University of Pennsylvania Press, 2016), 128–129. On the naturalist community of letters more broadly, see Ogilvie, *Science of Describing*, esp. 74–86.

[15] Steven Shapin, *A Social History of Truth: Civility and Science in Seventeenth-Century England* (Chicago: University of Chicago Press, 1994).

[16] Shapin, *Social History of Truth*, xxvi.   [17] Shapin, *Social History of Truth*, 182.

their convenience and aid their pursuits."[18] So, even as Fuchs speaks of the value that Isingrin brings to Fuchs's own botanical project, he makes the publisher's material and economic needs secondary to Fuchs's own intellectual ambitions. Thus, while the quality of the material form of the book is being celebrated, the product of the printer is demoted, and the importance of the verbal text created by the author is made superior to the material text produced by the printer.

The authority that Fuchs claims for himself derives from his creation of a verbal and illustrative work that represents a host of knowledge about plants, but his feuds with Egenolff and others make it clear that he realizes his authority does not fully extend to the representation of that work in book form. In other words, the way that readers received Fuchs's knowledge was mediated by the efforts of other figures who had the power to reinforce or to undermine Fuchs's expertise. Fuchs understood that his authority was dependent upon stationers, and he resented it. While authorial fears about loss of control are perennial, the technology of print led to an intensification of these concerns.[19] This observation suggests that Shapin's claims need to be modified to account for the material means by which knowledge was transmitted. In the case of authority derived from individual reading acts, historians of ideas need to account for the reality – and the sociology – of printed books.

In my Introduction, I argued that scholars of early English printed herbals have focused their efforts so intently on the content of botanical works that they have often overlooked the material means by which these works were disseminated. As upcoming chapters will show, the popularity with lay readers of small anonymous works like the little *Herball* spurred London publishers to invest in newer, larger, and more comprehensive botanical works, many of which they specifically commissioned from authors, artists, and translators. Authorized English herbals were thus not fully autonomous textual creations that affirmed the reality of plants with varying degrees of accuracy but speculative books that publishers sometimes asked authors to produce in order to appeal to particular clienteles. In turning herbal scholarship towards an appreciation of the work of printers and booksellers, I want to suggest that these other agents need to be considered authoritative in the process of making botanical works available to early modern readers. The histories of these other agents have largely

---

[18] Meyer et al., *Great Herbal*, 1:215.
[19] See Elizabeth Eisenstein, *Divine Art, Infernal Machine: The Reception of Printing in the West from First Impressions to the Sense of an Ending* (Philadelphia: University of Pennsylvania Press, 2011), esp. 21–22.

been hidden from view as authors' social and intellectual pretentions required them to downplay the important role of those who literally constructed the material means through which their botanical works reached audiences.

"Print Culture," "Piracy," and "Plagiarism"

In this extension of authority to include the artisans who financed and manufactured the verbal works of authors, I am engaging with arguments similar to those made by Adrian Johns in *The Nature of the Book: Print and Knowledge in the Making*. By drawing what he calls "the first real attempt to portray print culture in the making," Johns explains the means by which printed books "became trustworthy."[20] Johns refers to "print culture" in his 1998 monograph, a phrase that has declined in use in recent years. He acknowledges that the phrase was popularized by Marshall McLuhan in his 1962 book *The Gutenberg Galaxy: The Making of Typographic Man*, but Johns draws his concept of "print culture" directly from Elizabeth Eisenstein, who situates the term as a catchall phrase designed "to refer to post-Gutenberg developments in the West when setting aside its possible relevance to pre-Gutenberg developments in Asia."[21] As the subtitle of her own volume suggests, Eisenstein's goal in her monumental *The Printing Press As an Agent of Change* is to explore the role that the products resulting from Gutenberg's new technology played in "cultural transformations in early-modern Europe." Google Books Ngram Viewer, which displays a graph showing how a word or phrase has occurred in a corpus of digitized English books over a selection of years, records increased frequency in the phrase "print culture" from the early 1960s, corresponding with McLuhan's work, while a steep spike in the use of the phrase can be seen from 1980 onwards, corresponding with the reception of Eisenstein's book. As debates have raged over the agency and ontology of inanimate print, "print culture" has been in sharp decline since 2006, possibly as a result of its replacement by the related phrase "book history," which has been in increasing use. (In 2013, Peter W. M. Blayney surveyed the discipline in his history of the Stationers' Company of London and dryly remarked, "[t]he only sentence in this book in which the words *print* and *culture* both appear is this one.")[22] Johns repeatedly insists that Eisenstein

---

[20] Johns, *Nature of the Book*, 19, 3.
[21] Johns, *Nature of the Book*, 2n1; Eisenstein, *Printing Press As an Agent of Change*, xiv.
[22] Blayney, *Printers of London*, xvii.

characterizes print culture chiefly through print's capacity to endow "fixity" upon knowledge domains; however, her two-volume work of historical synthesis also explores myriad other features of cultural change that she sees resulting from the mass production of textual products, including dissemination, reorganization, data collection, preservation, amplification, and reinforcement, all of which, I argue, have particular relevance to the development of English botanical science throughout the sixteenth century.

In *Nature of the Book*, Johns recasts Eisenstein's arguments about "fixity" to note that it is a "transitive" quality of printed texts that is "recognized and acted upon by people." Johns's new formulation of fixity is instructive for the arguments of the present volume, as Johns's approach to print culture turns towards both the agents responsible for producing books and the varied readers who used them. Johns's understanding of what he calls print's "credit" builds directly on Shapin's concept of trust but moves the focus from trusted individuals to the ways trusted individuals can be understood through printed artifacts. He maintains that a Renaissance reader first approached a printed book cautiously and sought to make "a critical appraisal of its identity and credit" chiefly by assessing "the people involved in the making, distribution, and reception of books."[23] While earlier historians had viewed early modern readers as unthinkingly credulous, Johns finds readers to be highly apprehensive and even suspicious, attuned to the ubiquitous possibility that the texts of printed books may be something other than what they seem. To Johns, "[p]iracy and plagiarism occupied readers' minds just as prominently as fixity and enlightenment. Unauthorized translations, epitomes, imitations, and other varieties of 'impropriety' were, they believed, routine hazards."[24] To reassure themselves of the authority of a particular publication, Johns asserts, readers would first have to evaluate the credibility of printers and booksellers who produced and marketed it for sale, using the artifact as a surrogate for the agents who manufactured it. "The ways in which such agents thought of and represented themselves," he writes, "were therefore of central importance to the received credit of printed knowledge."[25] Through what Johns calls the "character" of printers and booksellers, an author's credibility over a knowledge domain might then safely be established.

Johns expands upon this point by exploring the particular means in which England's Royal Society in the later seventeenth century came to be

---

[23] Johns, *Nature of the Book*, 31–32.   [24] Johns, *Nature of the Book*, 30.
[25] Johns, *Nature of the Book*, 34.

viewed as an authoritative locus for natural philosophy by highlighting the ways that its members harnessed all elements of the medium of print, from maintaining its own printing houses and periodical journal, *Philosophical Transactions* (1665 –), to overseeing a series of public-facing correspondences between its membership. Johns demonstrates that the scientific authority claimed by the Royal Society was due in no small part to the social status accorded its members, whose status as witnesses to the experiments it conducted "would be apportioned credit according to their place in the social hierarchy, and in particular according to their received status as gentry."[26] Johns asserts that the establishment of epistemological credit in printed works of natural philosophy was the result of a concerted effort among not only authors and authorized witnesses to experiments but also book producers and sellers – namely stationers. Yet as book producers, stationers mediated the relationship between authors and readers, and their reputation could influence the reception of a particular book:

> In managing publications, Stationers, and often booksellers in particular, controlled events. The practices and representations of their domains affected every character and every leaf of their products. Isolating a consistent, identifiable, and immutable element attributable to the individual author would be virtually impossible in these circumstances. Attributing authorship was thus intensely problematic for both contemporary and future readers. A priori, virtually any element in a work might or might not be the Stationers' responsibility, in virtually any field of writing ... [t]he reading of a book could in consequence be substantially affected by the perceived conduct, and above all the perceived character, of the Stationer or Stationers who had produced it.[27]

Johns's evidence is derived primarily from the later Stuart period, which influences how he reads earlier events that adhered to different customs and systems of textual ownership.[28] As he is particularly invested in the machinations and social pretentions of figures associated with the dissemination in print of works of natural history created by gentry and members of the Royal Society, it is unsurprising that Johns's research primarily concerns evidence not only from the later seventeenth century but that foregrounds the identity of texts' purported authors – as well as the identity of the stationers who supported or undermined these scientific endeavors. This focus, however, has the consequence of misrepresenting the nature of bookselling in the first century of English printing and leaves Johns

---

[26] Johns, *Nature of the Book*, 470.   [27] Johns, *Nature of the Book*, 137–138.
[28] Peter W. M. Blayney shares my concerns; see *Printers of London*, 181nB.

without the ability to explain how the book trade operated before the Stationers' Company of London gained a monopoly over printing in 1557 or how anonymous popular texts like the little *Herball* and *The Grete Herball* found eager purchase at the hands of thousands of early modern readers. This deficit becomes particularly acute in Johns's articulation of piracy, or illicit printing, which he claims to be inextricably bound up in accusations of textual transgression from the period.

Johns uses the term "piracy" to denote:

> the unauthorized reprinting of a title recognized to belong to someone else by the formal conventions of the printing and bookselling community. But it soon came to stand for a wide range of perceived transgressions of civility emanating from print's practitioners. As such, almost any book could, in principle, find itself accounted a piracy, whatever its actual circumstances of production and distribution.[29]

In his opening "Note on Conventions," Johns acknowledges the anachronism concomitant with his extended definition of the term, which scholars such as John Feather, among others, caution should be limited to serving its contemporary legal sense of "printing without his or her permission of a text that was clearly and legally owned by another agent."[30] Johns, however, demurs:

> while such precision is probably necessary in matters of technical bibliography, the stipulation seems rather too restrictive for a work such as this, which deals with social, cultural, and intellectual history. Such a book is entitled to recover the broader meanings recognized by contemporaries – indeed, it is its duty to do so. Contemporary usage provides warrant. Someone might call an unauthorized printing of personal letters a piracy, for example, even though their ownership had not been registered beforehand; similarly, an unauthorized reprint produced in another country for sale on the Continent might be accounted a piracy, although it was outside English legal jurisdiction. There are no legal terms for such cases, although individuals certainly felt them to be transgressions of some sort. It would be awkward to have to resort every time to "unauthorized reprint" or some such formula. For the sake of conciseness and dramatic value, then – and not least to capture something of the sheer sense of outrage displayed by the aggrieved – I have chosen to follow what I take to be the emerging usage of the time, and call these activities by the generic label of piracy.[31]

---

[29] Johns, *Nature of the Book*, 32.
[30] Johns, *Nature of the Book*, xx; John Feather, "English Book Trade and the Law," *Publishing History* 12 (1982): 51–76.
[31] Johns, *Nature of the Book*, xx.

Johns labors throughout *The Nature of the Book* to provide "the first extensive taxonomy of practices labeled piratical – from piracy itself, through abridgment, epitomizing, and translation, to plagiarism and libel ... In short, it addresses precisely the epistemic significance of piracy."[32] As Eisenstein later noted, Johns's definition unhelpfully serves to "stretch[] the term 'piracy' to cover nearly every kind of printed output that was not specifically authorized."[33] While there may be cause to expand textual impropriety in this way in very specific contexts, such as the reception of works by members of the Royal Society, it is all but useless in understanding the publication of books in the sixteenth century. A book such as John Skot's reprint of Bankes's edition of the little *Herball* (*STC* 13175.4), being anonymously authored as well as printed prior to the incorporation of the Stationers' Company in 1557 (thus lacking both author and Company authority), would be implicated by Johns's concept of piracy, irrespective of any logical applicability to this particular publication or to its other pre-1557 reprints.[34]

Another concern with Johns's use of the term "piracy" lies in the way that his preference for "dramatic value" allows him not only to ignore the scholarly "precision" presumably favored only by "technical bibliographers" but also to misrepresent the agents who were responsible for coining and popularizing the term, in order to accord with his book's thesis that the strictures of fixity and veracity associated with printed books of natural philosophy were constructs hard-won by books' various producers. Early in his first chapter, Johns claims (without a source) that "the term [piracy] seems to have been coined by John Fell, Bishop of Oxford, to describe the rapacious practices of London printers and booksellers"; nearly 300 pages later, a footnote reveals that "It was in the early 1670s, as part of the closely related struggle between Oxford University and the Stationers' Company, that Bishop John Fell seems to have coined the term 'pirates' to refer to printers and booksellers who invaded others' literary propriety: see below"; thirty-one pages later, persistent readers eventually learn that "when John Fell, bishop of Oxford and the leading proponent of Oxford printing,

---

[32] Johns, *Nature of the Book*, 33.

[33] Elizabeth Eisenstein, "An Unacknowledged Revolution Revisited," *American Historical Review* 107 (2002): 87–105; 96.

[34] Johns modifies this position slightly in *Piracy: The Intellectual Property Wars from Gutenberg to Gates* (Chicago: University of Chicago Press, 2009), where he asserts that "piracy was an invention of the seventeenth century" (19). His account of the regulatory function of the Stationers' Company of London in this book, however, is extremely short (24–27) and does not cite any of the numerous and detailed studies of the Company or the Stationers' Registers by bibliographers and historians of the book.

wanted to describe to Sir Joseph Williamson his frustration at the invulnerable community of London Stationers who violated the university's 'propertie in Printing,' Fell called them 'land-pirats.' It was an evocative phrase, and one that would last."[35]

Johns's footnote on "land-pirats" cites a manuscript letter dated August 6, 1674, held in the Public Record Office, and Johns notes that "[t]his is the earliest reference given in the *OED*; similar phrases occur in several writers of the time, however, and those who concern themselves about such things may question Fell's absolute priority."[36] As of the *OED*'s updated third edition of June 2006, the first recorded usage of "pirate" to denote "[a] person or company who reproduces or uses the work of another (as a book, recording, computer program, etc.) without authority and esp. in contravention of patent or copyright; a plagiarist. Also: a thing reproduced or used in this way" (*n*.3.a) was Thomas Dekker in his exhortation to "[b]anish these Word-pirates (you sacred mistresses of learning) into the gulfe of Barbarisme," found on sig. A4r of his 1603 plague pamphlet *The Wonderful Yeare*. The earlier *OED* entry for "pirate" and the one cited by Johns in his 1998 text derives from the second edition of the *OED* published in 1989, which then offered as its first entry an exemplar reading "[s]ome dishonest Booksellers, called Land-Pirats, who make it their practise to steal Impressions of other mens Copies." This entry, however, is not ascribed to John Fell, Bishop of Oxford in "the early 1670s," but rather is credited to the authorship of the London bookseller John Hancock in 1668. As an "invulnerable" London stationer, Hancock was presumably the sort of "land-pirat" that so incensed Bishop Fell that Fell was moved to write the English Secretary of State Joseph Williamson to request the issuance of some kind of appropriate sanction. Johns's appreciation of the "dramatic value" of the term "piracy" has limited the usefulness of his analysis, causing him to mistake the concerns of the agent who coined an evocative phrase. As a London stationer, Hancock was frustrated with "pirates" not merely out of a concern for propriety but because such behaviors put his (and others') livelihoods at risk by undermining their exclusive rights to sell particular titles they'd registered with the Stationers' Company. By ascribing Hancock's words to Bishop Fell, Johns has confused the stakes of the dispute by turning a coinage derived from an internal commercial matter into one of civic decorum.

---

[35] Johns, *Nature of the Book*, 33, 313n126, 344.
[36] SP 29/361, nos. 188–188(i). The PRO merged with the Historical Manuscripts Commission to become The National Archives in 2003.

Considering the earlier usage of 1603 now credited in the updated *OED* only adds to the problem. Thomas Dekker's use of "Word-pirates" needs to be appreciated in light of Dekker's career as a prolific and opportunistic playwright and pamphleteer whose vested interests in self-promotion were so well known to his contemporaries that he was lampooned in Ben Jonson's *Poetaster* and *Cynthia's Revels*. Dekker is mentioned dozens of times in Philip Henslowe's diary between 1598 and 1602, often for revising or "script-doctoring" other authors' plays – collaborative activities that have complicated scholarly attempts at authorship attribution.[37] Dekker's repeated imprisonment for debt and his continued dependence on his pen for his livelihood require careful contextualization to unpack the motivations behind his portmanteau coinage of a term like "Word-pirates."[38]

Too easily accepting at face value the many accusations of textual impropriety that pervade texts of natural history throughout the sixteenth and seventeenth centuries would mean claiming, unreasonably, that all the herbals of the period were "pirated" in one form or another. Though modern discourses of scholarly authorship regularly seek to credit specific figures with idiosyncratic discovery or inventive composition, sixteenth- and seventeenth-century authors of herbals produced their works not *sui generis* but largely by incorporating and building upon the printed works of botanical scholarship that already existed.[39] As Egenolff noted of Fuchs, Renaissance herbalists composed their texts primarily by "gathering," synthesizing, and commenting upon the materials of their predecessors and using this information as a scaffold upon which they could then record their own differing or dissenting experience. Frances E. Dolan links this kind of "compost/composition" with flourishing Renaissance cultures of recycling, while Jeffrey Todd Knight locates a "culture of compiling" that appreciated books' material status as "thing[s] to actively shape, expand, and resituate as one desired."[40] Brian W. Ogilvie characterizes this period of natural history as necessarily bibliographic, pointing out

---

[37] See R. A. Foakes, ed., *Henslowe's Diary*, 2nd ed. (Cambridge: Cambridge University Press, 2002). As a representative example of Dekker's role in attribution scholarship, see D. J. Lake, "Three Seventeenth-Century Revisions: *Thomas of Woodstock*, *The Jew of Malta*, and *Faustus B*," *Notes and Queries* 30 (1983): 133–143.

[38] See John Twyning, "Dekker, Thomas (c. 1572–1632), playwright and pamphleteer." *ODNB*, accessed June 10, 2019.

[39] This problem is receiving increasing attention. In 2004, a trio of essays appeared in the journal *Isis* to surmise what the history of reading can offer to the history of science. See Blair, "Early Modernist's Perspective"; Jonathan R. Topham, "A View from the Industrial Age," *Isis* 95: 431–442; and Daston, "Taking Note(s)."

[40] Frances E. Dolan, "Compost/Composition," in Hillary Eklund (ed.), *Ground-Work: English Renaissance Literature and Soil Science* (Pittsburgh: Duquesne University Press, 2015), 21–39.

that published texts were not the end product of the process of natural history research; rather, they were themselves employed as tools by naturalists seeking to make sense of their particular experience . . . Their technology of observation shaped habits of observation, and was in turn shaped by those habits, in a continuing dialectic that focused attention above all on defining and describing new species or varieties of plant.[41]

Historians of botany who valorize invention and discovery have frequently struggled to account for this imitative and materialist method of composition and have often identified an author or publisher's replication of a previous herbal text as suspect, repeating and endorsing the claims that herbal authors themselves made to distinguish their works in a competitive print marketplace. These misgivings have even led historians to label some herbals as mere "piracies" of earlier volumes or some authors meager "plagiarists" of another's work. Scholarly narratives about reprints of the early *Herball* first published in 1525 thus characterize figures like Robert Wyer as a pirate of other stationers' books, while John Gerard is reviled for being a plagiarist owing to his use of a now-lost manuscript by one "Dr. Priest."

Attention to the context of the Tudor trade in vernacular books demonstrates that many of the seemingly illegitimate textual behaviors that have been ascribed to herbal publishers are instead normal stationer practice, while claims of "plagiarism" were often rhetorical ploys that served the interests of subsequent herbal authors leveling charges against their predecessors' scholarly credibility. The rest of this chapter attends to what is at stake in modern scholars' ratification of past claims of textual impropriety by explaining why it is crucial to distinguish between the agents who are responsible for the texts of verbal works (authors) and those who are responsible for producing copies of printed documents for sale (publishers and printers). While the financial and intellectual benefits to all of these figures frequently overlap, especially when an edition sells well, the particular motivations that lie behind authors' and publishers' investments in a text frequently differ, and it is instructive to separate the two roles. For example, while a herbalist's reputation as a man of letters might suffer after attacks from a competitor in print, a publisher will benefit from an intellectual controversy so long as their books continue to sell. Conversely, because the print publication of a book will establish the

---

Jeffrey Todd Knight, *Bound to Read: Compilations, Collections, and the Making of Renaissance Literature* (Philadelphia: University of Pennsylvania Press, 2013), 4. See also Leah Knight, *Of Books and Botany.*
[41] Ogilvie, *Science of Describing,* 207.

priority of a discovery or idea, a natural historian can benefit socially regardless of an edition's success in the marketplace. Printed books enabled naturalists to gain a larger public, making their private labors known to a wide audience. As Ogilvie remarks, "while manuscripts preserved experience for their authors, published [i.e. printed] natural histories reproduced it for others."[42]

Furthermore, the standards of intellectual propriety and legal ownership changed drastically over the course of the sixteenth century, shifting the norms of behavior for both authors and publishers. Chapter 2 therefore offers a history of the important changes in the way the Stationers' Company of London, the civic organization governing English printers and publishers, sought to regulate the production of books. When the Stationers' Company received a royal grant of incorporation in 1557, the Company's new means of authorizing printed texts began to place a latent value on unpublished works, which could theoretically underpin any number of future editions. While earlier systems of English patents such as the one held by Richard Bankes in 1525 allowed a patent-holding publisher to declare a particular text off-limits for a fixed period of time (usually seven years), the emergence of the Stationers' Company Registers permitted this kind of protected future speculation to become available to every London stationer who chose to register a title and to declare their ownership of those rights in perpetuity. Through the Stationers' new system of textual authorization, it therefore becomes possible to recognize precisely when piracy occurred, because a stationer could sue another for damages. Further, a textual work came to be recognized as a commodity in its own right – something that could be owned and something that therefore could be transferred – regardless of whether the would-be publisher ever actually had the work printed. By more thoroughly understanding the implementation and effects of the Stationers' system of title ownership, historians of herbals are in a better position to determine how both English booksellers and authors evaluated the dynamic market for printed books of natural history throughout the sixteenth and early seventeenth centuries.

---

[42] Ogilvie, *Science of Describing*, 181. Deborah Harkness argues that a "failure to publish proved fatal" to a sixteenth-century London community she titles the "Lime Street naturalists" who suffered anonymity as a result of the publication of John Gerard's *Herball or General Historie of Plants* of 1597 (*Jewel House*, 55).

A Bibliographic Turn of the "Author-Function"

As they were able to circulate through the channels of the early modern book trade both in England and on the continent, herbals were locations for plant investigators to publish theories that could later be confirmed or refuted by their fellows in their own publications. For example, in his *A New Herball* (London, 1551), Englishman William Turner refuted the Italian Pietro Andrea Mattioli's description of *Orobanche* or broomrape that the latter offered in his printed commentaries on Dioscorides' *Materia medica*. Mattioli had rebuked Dioscorides' milder account of the plant and asserted that broomrape was so chemically destructive that it could kill other plants living nearby without any physical contact. In *A New Herball*, Turner corrects Mattioli, suggesting that the Italian had not properly investigated his subject – if he had, Mattioli would have seen that in fact broomrape's roots strangle those of other plants. Agnes Arber sees Turner's clarification of his fellow herbalist as indicative of both his delight in "pouring scorn upon any superstitious notions which he detected in the writings of his contemporaries" and his respect in asserting the authority of ancient authors such as Theophrastus, whose commentary on broomrape Mattioli had summarily dismissed.[43] To Brian Ogilvie, this kind of exchange is typical of "the dialectic between producing and consuming knowledge" that may be seen throughout Renaissance Europe as authors struggled to make and to communicate accurate observations of the natural world through the medium of the printed book.[44]

This dialectic reveals that the herbalists' dispute occurred neither in isolation nor in a restricted republic of letters between a handful of interested parties but publicly, in a marketplace filled with printed volumes of plant knowledge. The texts of Mattioli and Turner testify to the long-contested fight for scholarly authority over Europe's botanical landscape, with broomrape and other plants serving as individual battles in an enduring transcontinental war. Printed books were the field in which this battle for botanical description was fought, and the capital to produce these books was fronted not by herbalists but by booksellers eager to see their investments pay off. While the herbalists' attentions were, understandably, primarily focused on the content of their own authored works and the particulars of a plant, tree, or herb, the material fact of their works' sale as books in a public marketplace also concerned a group of figures who

---

[43] Arber, *Herbals*, 124.   [44] Ogilvie, *Science of Describing*, 43.

were attentive to the ways that such texts (and their authors) could be marketed to as many readers as possible.

Historians who focus on herbals primarily as transcriptions of botanical or medical data make an implicit distinction between books and the words that books contain in order to justify their focus on the intellectual and social history of a genre. By separating forensic history of material documents as the proper concern of bibliographers, such historians have good company – the distinction between words and books is one that is also frequently employed by literary and textual scholars as they edit and interpret written documents. Because verbal works are immaterial, originating from the mind of an author and ultimately recognized in the mind of a reader, because they can be translated between languages, and because they can be copied innumerable times and still be identified in terms of their linguistic similarities, works are often seen as divorceable from the medium in which they appear. There is, between the copies of the first quarto and first folio editions of Shakespeare's *King Lear* in 1608 and 1623, enough similarity between the words of the two works to suggest that they are versions of the same thing, some idea of the play that has been rendered into a readable form with various degrees of perfection.[45] In the same vein, the variations between Bankes's first edition of the little *Herball* in 1525 and Robert Wyer's first edition in or around 1540 are negligible enough to view the texts of both books as versions of a single work, something that can then lead to a charge of "piracy" against Wyer for copying Bankes's printed text.

The question of what constitutes the essential components of a given work has been central to the occupation of textual scholars and editors for centuries, most of whom have been interested in uncovering an original, "intended" work of an author as it existed before it was rendered physically into the text of a manuscript or book.[46] While recently textual theorists such as Jerome McGann have used sociological methodologies to defend critical editions of particular printed texts on the grounds that such enterprises better reveal the historical and social circumstances relating to the production and reception of copies of these particular documents,

---

[45] On the two texts of *King Lear*, see Gary Taylor and Michael Warren (eds.), *The Division of the Kingdoms: Shakespeare's Two Versions of King Lear* (Oxford: Clarendon Press, 1986).

[46] Two of the most prominent proponents of authorial intention as an editorial goal are Fredson Bowers and G. Thomas Tanselle, whose writings outline methodologies for its application and respond to criticism of its use. See Fredson Bowers, "Authorial Intention and Editorial Problems," *Text* 5 (1991): 49–62 and G. Thomas Tanselle, "Textual Instability and Editorial Idealism," *Studies in Bibliography* 49 (1996): 1–60.

scholarly interest in *works*, which are the products of authors, has not substantially waned.[47] Along with the division of the text from its material form, central to many such literary studies of authorial intention is a curious, and often undisclosed, notion of property that insists that a text of a work belongs to its creator, an intellectual right that is distinct from the conventions of physical property governed by common law.[48] Such a view holds that a book might be owned by anyone who purchases it, but regardless of how many copies of that book have been sold, the *text* of the book, or that material which represents the author's verbal *work*, is the intellectual property of the person who labored to compose it.[49] Those who duplicate such texts without offering credit to the originating author are guilty of "plagiarism," the usurping of an author's authority over their own labor and a form of theft.[50] In such interpretations, even as a text is unyoked from one documentary form to produce another document, the verbal work that underlies both documents is nonetheless bound firmly to its author. The copying of the texts of works to form the texts of new documents can lead to confusion, though, and a slippage that enables the words "work" and "text" to become synonyms sometimes occurs as a result of the two terms' similar relationship to their originating author. Scholarly focus on authorial works rather than physical documents elides the ways that the meaning of a text is shaped by a given medium.

Once it was examined in detail by poststructuralist critics such as Michel Foucault, whose 1969 essay "What Is an Author?" attempted to delineate the purpose of this "solid and fundamental unit of the author and the

[47] See Jerome McGann, *A Critique of Modern Textual Criticism* (Charlottesville: University Press of Virginia, 1983). As Tanselle points out, a sociohistorical critical viewpoint and an editorial methodology that supports intentionality are not mutually exclusive: "an edition focusing on authorial intention, does not necessarily signify that the editor has failed to take the whole book, or the whole historical context, into account" ("Historicism and Critical Editing," *Studies in Bibliography* 39 (1986): 1–46; 17). This essay also features a critique of McGann's *Critique*. See also Neville, '*Nihil biblicum.*'

[48] On issues in copyright, see Mark Rose, *Authors and Owners: The Invention of Copyright* (Cambridge, MA: Harvard University Press, 1993).

[49] "Labour gives a man a natural right of property in that which he produces: literary compositions are the effect of labour; authors have therefore a natural right of property in their works," William Enfield, *Observations on Literary Property* (London: 1774), quoted in Mark Rose, "The Author As Proprietor: *Donaldson v. Becket* and the Genealogy of Modern Authorship," *Representations* 23 (1988): 51–85. Also quoted in Roger Chartier, *The Order of Books: Readers, Authors and Libraries in Europe between the Fourteenth and Eighteenth Centuries*, trans. Lydia G. Cochrane (Cambridge: Polity Press, 1994), 100n14.

[50] "Plagiarism," *OED*: "The action or practice of plagiarizing; the wrongful appropriation or purloining, and publication as one's own, of the ideas, or the expression of the ideas (literary, artistic, musical, mechanical, etc.) of another" (1621). On historical constructions of an author's work, see Chartier, *Order of Books*, chap. 2: "Figures of the Author."

work,"[51] this covalent stance on authorship became, in Roger Chartier's terms, an "obligatory reference" for all scholars of the history of books.[52] Foucault's demarcation of what he called the "author-function" served to establish that the idea of an authorial subject's production of an intended verbal work was, rather than an historical fact, merely a "discourse" constructed by later readers in order to unify and limit the boundaries of that work within a document. In Foucault's reading, an author's name became synonymous with cultural authority over a given subject matter or narrative by virtue of this author-function, which provides

> more than an indication, a gesture, a finger pointed at someone . . . it is the equivalent of a description . . . an author's name is not simply an element in a discourse (capable of being either subject or object, of being replaced by a pronoun, and the like); it performs a certain role with regard to narrative discourse, assuring a classificatory function. Such a name permits one to group together a certain number of texts, define them, differentiate them from and contrast them to others . . . it is a speech that must be received in a certain mode and that, in a given culture, must receive a certain status.[53]

Foucault continues his examination of the author-function to surmise that it does not affect all discourses or texts in a similar fashion, drawing a distinction between "literary" texts (which he explains includes "narratives, stories, epics, tragedies, comedies") and those texts "that we would now call scientific – those dealing with cosmology and the heavens, medicine and illnesses, natural sciences and geography."[54] While the authors of literary works were long permitted their anonymity owing to "their ancientness, whether real or imagined, [which] was regarded as a sufficient guarantee to their status," "scientific" works were

> accepted in the Middle Ages, and accepted as "true," only when marked with the name of their author. "Hippocrates said," "Pliny recounts," were not really formulas of an argument based on authority; they were the markers inserted in discourses that were supposed to be received as statements of demonstrated truth.[55]

---

[51] "What Is an Author?" was first delivered to the *Société française de Philosophie* in February 1969 and published as "Qu'est-ce qu'un auteur?" in *Bulletin de la Société française de Philosophie* later that same year. Josué V. Harari's translation quoted here in *Early Modern Herbals and the Book Trade* is of a revised version of the paper delivered at SUNY–Buffalo, and Harari discusses the variants between the two versions in Jousé V. Harari, *Textual Strategies: Perspectives in Post-Structuralist Criticism* (Ithaca, NY: Cornell University Press, 1979), 43.

[52] Chartier, *Order of Books*, 29.   [53] Foucault, "What Is an Author?," 105–107.

[54] Foucault, "What Is an Author?," 109.   [55] Foucault, "What Is an Author?," 109.

According to Foucault, the essential characteristics of these "literary" and "scientific" discourses reversed positions "in the seventeenth or eighteenth century," when "scientific" discourse no longer needed the influence of an author's proper name in order to be considered authoritative, bolstered instead by

> the anonymity of an established or always redemonstrable truth; their membership in a systematic ensemble, and not the reference to the individual who produced them, stood as their guarantee. The author function faded away, and the inventor's name served only to christen a theorem, proposition, particular effect, property, body, group of elements, or pathological syndrome.

While "scientific" texts gradually gained authority through the methods of experiential and experimental science, which in turn anonymized their author-functions, Foucault argues, "literary" discourses began to depend upon the identification of the author as a pretext for the establishment of their authority.

Scholars of the Middle Ages have since challenged the accuracy of Foucault's historical account of literary and scientific authorship.[56] However, I am less interested in the accuracy or generic particulars of Foucault's chronology of historical change than I am in the useful distinction he makes between an authorial subject and the role that an author's presumed *assumption* of status, or "authority," takes in a particular text or body of literature. Without this separation between authorship and authority, both textual scholars and historians may unwittingly collapse distinct forms of textual agency and fail to recognize the contingencies and constraints of the material artifacts that mediate our understanding of the past. It is the discourse of the author-function that textual scholars who support the constraints of authorial intention implicitly endorse in their methodologies, while it is likewise the discourse of the author-function that many historians of sixteenth- and seventeenth-century herbals employ in their analyses as they investigate the history of an "authoritative print herbal tradition."[57] All too often in both kinds of scholarship, however, the role of the author as a discourse that can be constructed *ex post facto* by later readers as a method of limiting and differentiating interpretations is overlooked. Foucault's assertion that the author-function is constrained

---

[56] Guillemette Bolens and Lukas Erne (eds.), *Medieval and Early Modern Authorship* (Tübingen: Narr Verlag, 2011); Alexandra Gillespie, *Print Culture and the Medieval Author: Chaucer, Lydgate, and their Books 1473–1557* (Oxford: Oxford University Press, 2006).

[57] Laroche, *Medical Authority*, 5.

by its context demands the establishment of that context for the unique circumstances of every would-be author: "it is a speech that must be received *in a certain mode* and that, *in a given culture*, must receive *a certain status*."[58] The *function* in Foucault's author-function thus offers historians two crucial practical benefits in their discussions of the texts of written documents. First, the author-function presumes the existence of readers who will encounter the deployment of an authorial subjectivity and interpret such authorship in contingent and diverse ways. Secondly, by highlighting readers' role in the construction of meaning, the author-function implicitly calls attention to the materials and technologies of text that enable readers to construct their interpretations.

In their primary focus on the intellectual content, or *works* of herbals, scholars have sought to identify the provenance of specific ideas and concepts central to the development of modern botanical science, and in so doing, they have risked elevating the status of particular authors beyond the import garnered by authorship in given historical moments. This traditional logic proceeds as follows: the provenance of herbal works requires unraveling because as the texts of herbals were translated, copied, and distributed through the media of script and print, they were altered by figures other than their authors and potentially infused with meanings different from the ones originally intended. As herbal texts were transmitted through the physical vehicle of books, they could be separated from this accepted form of authority, rendering authored works anonymous or ascribed to authors who had nothing whatsoever to do with them. To remedy such confusion, many accounts of herbals have been preoccupied with locating the first author of a given classification scheme or method of plant description, considering it absolutely crucial to give authorial credit to the correct person in order to reassert the stability of the author-function. In such accounts it is the role of the historian to set acknowledgments to rights, to redeem the underappreciated author and condemn those "copyists" who shamefully and deliberately usurped the work of others. For example, Anna Pavord's popular history of plant taxonomy *The Naming of Names* is as much a history of plant classification schemes as it is a clarion call highlighting the decisive roles played by such early botanists as the Greek Theophrastus (371 to ca. 287 BCE), whose work was "shamelessly plagiarized and regurgitated" by Pliny the Elder in his *Historia naturalis*.[59] "Remember him," urges Pavord, who titles chapter 4 of her work "Pliny the Plagiarist." The same sentiments are also found in the works of mid-twentieth-century botanical historians, whose

---

[58] Emphasis mine.   [59] Pavord, *Naming of Names*, 24.

attitudes still seem to influence more recent accounts.[60] In a 1963 published lecture on "Herbals, their history and significance," George H. M. Lawrence repeats a similar refrain as Pavord. As he closes his speech with "the late British herbals of the seventeenth century," Lawrence maintains that "three are deserving of mention: one because it is so bad, the others for their excellence."[61] The one that is "so bad" is

> John Gerard's *The herbal; or general historie of plantes*, published in London in 1597. The iniquities associated with it, ably reviewed by Arber and others, are too many to be recited here. Suffice it to say that Gerard (1545–1612), an unscrupulous barber surgeon of London, purloined an unfinished English translation of the last edition of Dodoens' *Pemptades* of 1583, bungled his part in the completion of the translation, laced it throughout with anecdotes, legends and fables – usually presented as facts – and published the whole as his own! Today's amateur herb lover may cherish the volume for its massiveness and antiquity and because its quaint English is readable. But the student of the history of science knows that almost every statement is suspect and that it is the production of a rogue.[62]

The botanical biographer Charles Raven is even more insistent on the issue: "Gerard was a rogue: of that there can be no doubt ... Gerard was a rogue. Moreover, botanically speaking he was, as has been indicated, a comparatively ignorant rogue."[63]

As scientists writing from the context of twentieth- and twenty-first-century post-Enlightenment science, the botanists uncovering the history of botany are keen on distinguishing between fact and fiction and often work backwards from their own knowledge of plants derived from modern empiricism to evaluate the accuracy of the texts printed in early botanical books. Yet Renaissance naturalists weren't always governed by the same prescriptions for empiricist fact-finding as their modern counterparts, and such assumptions often misunderstand their earlier intentions.[64]

---

[60] Brian W. Ogilvie, for example, twice refers to Gerard as a plagiarist. See *Science of Describing*, 37, 188.

[61] George H. M. Lawrence, *History of Botany: Two Papers Presented at a Symposium held at the William Andrews Clark Memorial Library December 7, 1963* (Los Angeles and Pittsburgh: The Clark Memorial Library and The Hunt Botanical Library, 1965).

[62] Lawrence, *History of Botany*, 17. A similar attitude towards medieval and early modern authors' "plagiarism" when they fail to properly cite sources can be found in the writings of botanical historian Jerry Stannard.

[63] Charles E. Raven, *English Naturalists from Neckham to Ray: A Study of the Making of the Modern World* (Cambridge: Cambridge University Press, 1947), 207–208.

[64] See Lorraine Daston and Katharine Park, *Wonders and the Order of Nature, 1150–1750* (New York: Zone Books, 2001). For the epistemological debates underpinning this topic, see Mary Poovey, *A History of the Modern Fact: Problems of Knowledge in the Sciences of Wealth and Society* (Chicago: University of Chicago Press, 1998).

Nonetheless, scholars of the history of herbals consistently value the writings of those authors who claim that their works are written upon the basis of firsthand evidence, while those herbalists whose publications were derived not from their own experience but from book-learning are barely acknowledged as natural historians at all. Charles Raven's claim that Gerard, "botanically speaking . . . was . . . a comparatively ignorant rogue" is bolstered by the fact that Gerard's investigation into plants "seems to have been almost exclusively in the home counties," of which he then admits that Gerard "spoke with accuracy."[65] Though he offers a paragraph celebrating Gerard's charm ("Rogue their author may have been: but when we have ceased to respect him as a botanist or esteem him as a man of honour we cannot fail to enjoy him"), Raven nonetheless refuses to consider the value that the *publication* of Gerard's *Herball* may have presented to the discipline beyond the narrow prescriptivism of the scientific method: "[b]ut we are concerned not with the charm of his writings but with their value as natural history; and beyond the defects already noted there are others."[66] To scholars who privilege a form of authority derived from firsthand experience, the work of early herbal authors is degenerate unless it records and promulgates evidence of hands-on activity or originality. Thus, while Theophrastus' study of prior works, coupled with his own investigations, offered "a synthesis of the information about plants that was available at the time," and was "great and original," for Anna Pavord, Pliny's listing of more than 100 sources for his *Historia naturalis* "added little new to the existing debate" and demonstrated only the names of those whose "work he plundered for his own."[67] The possibility that, however unoriginal, Pliny's synthesis could provide a useful contemporary service in an age before print, where the survival of manuscripts was uncertain and rapid distribution of them impossible, is left unacknowledged. Because of his lack of originality in the content of his writing, Pliny's practical service to the field of botany is not only dismissed but condemned. For his use of the books of others, Pliny, the compiler of 37 books of *Natural History*, is a "plagiarist," while Gerard's 1,400-page *Herball or General History of Plants* is the work of an "unscrupulous rogue" even as Gerard acknowledges his debts to Dodoens and L'Obel in his pages. Yet, as anthological gatherers, both Pliny and Gerard were well

---

[65] Raven, *English Naturalists*, 208, 201.   [66] Raven, *English Naturalists*, 214, 215.
[67] Pavord, *Naming of Names*, 25, 104, 64.

within the norms of the different modes of textual transmission in which they labored to produce their work.

Such condemnations serve little purpose but to express either the contemporary moral outrage of historians on behalf of their various authorial subjects or their appreciation of what Adrian Johns calls "dramatic value." Without the recognition that the texts of works were created and distributed not as nebulous, free-floating ideas but as physical objects, books that were manufactured, sold, and circulated, scholars' righteous indignation does not fully appreciate the wider context in which botanical knowledge was made public in the early modern period. Before modern systems of copyright (or literary theory) yoked author and text together, such historical accounts of herbals accord with Adrian Johns in viewing all but the most modern forms of textual transmission to be illicit and immoral.[68] The motivations for such illegality are naturally assumed to be economic, and as we saw with Fuchs's attacks on Egenolff, the economic motivations of a stationer are often understood to be at odds with the civic-minded nature of scientific truth. Further, cause and effect are often uncertain. It is unclear, for example, whether the popularity of the work with readers led to its frequent reprinting or if the reverse is true and the wider availability of a work in multiple editions led to its popularity with readers. Anna Pavord may argue that the publisher Peter Schoeffer's edition of a vernacular German herbal, *Der Gart der Gesundheit* (*The Garden of Good Health*, Mainz, 1485), was popular because "a pirated edition" was immediately published by Johann Schoensperger in the same year, along with the "seven plagiarized editions in the next four years," but without investigating the book as a commodifiable object unto itself we are left with only a limited understanding of the role played by *Der Gart der Gesundheit* in its various "popular" forms.[69] Because scholars have been preoccupied with herbals' authors, they have erroneously assumed that the correct ascription of authorship will solve the questions of authority that preoccupy many of these texts. In the early modern period, however, botanical authority is vested as much in the printed book form as it is in the verbal texts that authors composed.

---

[68] John Feather, "The Book Trade in Politics: The Making of the Copyright Act of 1710," *Publishing History* 8 (1980): 19–44.

[69] Pavord, *Naming of Names*, 160.

Considering the "Stationer-Function"

Though Roger Chartier generally endorses Foucault's "What Is an Author?" as an invitation "to a retrospective investigation that gives the history of the conditions of the production, dissemination, and appropriation of texts particular pertinence," he nonetheless finds fault with Foucault's simplistic characterization of the "radical reversal" in the role of the author-function "between the seventeenth or eighteenth centuries."[70] Citing Steven Shapin, Chartier finds Foucault's depiction of scientific discourse without an identifiable author-function as authoritative to be inaccurate in the face of historical record. Chartier notes that, particularly in the case of experimental science,

> the validation of an experience or the accreditation of a proposition presupposed the guarantee provided by a proper name – the proper names of those who, by their position in society, had the power to proclaim the truth. The fact that scholars and practitioners disappeared behind aristocratic authority in no way resulted in the anonymity of a discourse whose authenticity was not exclusively dependent on its compatibility with an already constituted body of knowledge. During the seventeenth and the eighteenth centuries a number of scientific texts displayed a characteristic that Foucault (perhaps wrongly) reserved to medieval works alone: later scientific texts were also "accepted . . . and accepted as 'true,' only when marked with the name of their author" – an "author", however, who was long understood as someone whose social position could lend "authority" to intellectual discourse.[71]

This is the point that Adrian Johns expands upon in his examination of how England's Royal Society came to be viewed as an authoritative locus for natural philosophy through its attention to publication. Chartier's and Johns's research suggests that the responsibility for a given discourse or text often rests in more than one person, indicating that the cognates "authorship" and "authority" are not always equivalent.

Often the locus of a work's creation is as much a publisher as it is a writer, calling into question which responsibilities should be allowed to define the author-function and demonstrating a need to keep the terms "work" and "document" distinct. Roger Chartier makes a similar point in his *Order of Books*, examining definitions of the word *auteur* in seventeenth-century French-language dictionaries to reveal that the word was not originally invested with the writerly connotation that modern

---

[70] Chartier, *Order of Books*, 32. Chartier's translator uses the term "radical reversal" in reference to Foucault's depiction of the shift in literary-scientific authorial discourses on pages 31 and 58.
[71] Chartier, *Order of Books*, 58–59.

scholarship often takes for granted but has something closer to the English meaning of "agent." César-Pierre Richelet's *Dictionnaire françois* (1680) defines *auteur* as "the first who has invented something, who has said something, who is cause of something that has been done"; while Antoine Furetière's *Dictionnaire universel* (1690) likewise validates a number of practical and technical meanings, including "said also of those who are the cause of something" and "said in particular of those who are the first Inventors of something."[72] Within such vagaries of import, the two definitions that Chartier views as precursors to *auteur*'s later literary meaning, "he who has composed some printed book" (Furetière) and "those who have brought some book into the light" (Richelet), may be viewed as denotations of what we now understand as the printer or publisher of the book.

Though Chartier's intent with this chapter in *Order of Books* is not to link the terms *bookseller* and *writer* under the rubric of author- or *auteur*-ship but rather to contextualize Foucault's author-function within the pre-print eras, Chartier's efforts nonetheless manage to highlight the authoritative status accorded to *all* those producers of the book who can be said to be responsible for "bringing it into the light." Examining the systems of order employed by sixteenth-century French book catalogues, Chartier finds that "the author-function had no trouble harmonizing with the dependency instituted by patronage" and that "the patronage connection and the affirmation of the author together define the regime of assignation of texts."[73] He cites La Croix du Maine's *Grande bibliothèque françoise* as a case in point, a catalogue of "the works or writings of every author," which listed for all works "by whom they were printed, in what format or size, in what years, how many sheets they contain, *and especially the names of the men or women to whom they were dedicated, without omitting all their entire qualities.*"[74] The above emphasis is Chartier's, whose main interest in this passage is addressing the subject of patronage, but the part of La Croix du Maine's quotation that Chartier does not emphasize is as relevant in locating historical conceptions of authority or responsibility, which apply not only to the agent who serves as a text's prime origin but also to those agents facilitating its distribution to a reading public, that is, publishers.

Such a broadening of the author-function to include multiple agents also opens up the venue for censorship and punishment that Foucault supplies in "What Is an Author?" In explaining the potential advantage of

---

[72] Chartier, *Order of Books*, 40.   [73] Chartier, *Order of Books*, 43
[74] Chartier, *Order of Books*, 43.

such a discourse, Foucault suggests that the author-function became necessary to provide a hierarchy that could adjudicate the responsibilities for textual production: "[t]exts, books and discourses really began to have authors . . . to the extent that authors became subject to punishment, that is, to the extent that discourses could be transgressive."[75] In his support of Foucault on this point, Chartier underplays the role of book producers and distributors in his efforts to locate the historical importance of "the" singular author, but his evidence nonetheless demonstrates just how transgressive and subversive the producers and distributors of books were understood to be in sixteenth-century France. The edict of Châteaubriant of June 27, 1551, affirms that "the author-function was thus constituted as an essential weapon in the diffusion of texts suspected of heterodoxy," but what Chartier's emphasis again demonstrates is a curious exclusion of other evidence that heralds the multiplicity of the author-function's subjectivity, for the edict also restrains *printers*:

> It is forbidden to all printers to perform the exercise and status of impression except in good cities and orderly establishments accustomed to do this, not in secret places. And it must be under a master printer whose name, domicile and mark are put in the books thus printed by them [with] the time of the said impression and *the name of the author*. The which master printer will answer to faults and errors that either by him or under his name and by his order will have been made and committed.[76]

In the hierarchy of multiple responsibility, the Châteaubriant edict holds the master printer as primarily liable for the profusion of unorthodox texts, a fact that Chartier's later anecdotal evidence of convictions under the edict supports enough to lead him to assert that "it was printing that extended, hence that made more dangerous, the circulation of texts that defied authority."[77]

The Châteaubriant edict of 1551 finds a contemporary analogue in England, where a proclamation of Edward VI dated July 8, 1546, includes a similar decree:

> that from henceforth no printer do print any manner of English book, ballad, or play, but he put in his name to the same, with the name of the author and the day of the print, and shall present the first copy to the mayor

---

[75] Foucault, "What Is an Author?", 108. On the effects of censorship on writers, and the possibilities for overcoming it by means of "purposeful ambiguity," see Annabel Patterson, *Censorship and Interpretation: The Conditions of Writing and Reading in Early Modern England* (Madison: University of Wisconsin Press, 1984).
[76] Chartier, *Order of Books*, 50, emphasis in the text.   [77] Chartier, *Order of Books*, 51.

of the town where he dwelleth, and not to suffer any of the copies to go out of his hands within two days next following.[78]

Later proclamations and statutes of both Edward VI and Mary I emphasize that the "penal appropriation" Foucault sees at play in the author-function was also located within the producers of books (here defined not just as printers but also as booksellers) and "players of interludes" – in other words, all those with the power to broadcast seditious material:

> Be it enacted . . . That if any p[er]son or p[er]sons after the xxth day of February next ensuing . . . maliciouslie devise write printe or set forthe any maner of Booke Rime Ballade Letter or Writing, conteining any false Matter Clause or Sentence of Sclander Reproche and Dishonor of the King and Quenes Majesties or either of them . . . or whosoever shall maliciouslie procure any suche Booke Rime Ballade Letter or Writing to bee written printed or set forthe . . . that then and in every such cace the Offender and Offenders therein . . . shall for his or their first Offence . . . have his and their right hande stricken of. (January 1555)[79]

The English state's need to control the distribution of unorthodox and treasonable viewpoints ultimately led to the crown's seeking assistance from the civic body best able to monitor the movements of one particularly effective broadcasting medium: print. Though in his biography of the Company Cyprian Blagden downplays the importance of Mary Tudor's granting of the privy seal to the Stationers' Company's charter of incorporation on May 4, 1557, the act clearly marked the state's official recognition that the technology of the handpress posed a threat considerably more significant in scale than that proposed by the circulation of manuscripts or the singing of ballads.[80] Unlike a synchronous sermon, printed pamphlets and treatises could be manufactured in the hundreds and thousands and, once produced, were available to be read, reread, and passed on.[81]

---

[78] Paul L. Hughes and James F. Larkin, eds., *Tudor Royal Proclamations*, 3 vols. (New Haven, CT: Yale University Press, 1964–1969), 272.

[79] Thomas E. Tomlins and John Raithby, eds., *The Statutes at Large, of England and of Great Britain: From Magna Carta to the Union of the Kingdoms of Great Britain and Ireland*, 20 vols (London: G. Eyre and A. Strahan, 1811), 4:240–241. This statute was used by Elizabeth I in 1579 to punish both John Stubbes, author of the anti-Anjou pamphlet *The Discovery of a Gaping Gulf* (*STC* 23400), and the work's publisher, William Page. Printer Hugh Singleton was also convicted, but his sentence was rescinded out of compassion for his advanced age. Both Stubbes and Page had their right hands severed and were imprisoned. Despite the risks, however, many printed editions failed to adhere to this edict.

[80] Cyprian Blagden, *The Stationers' Company: A History 1403–1959* (London: George Allen & Unwin, 1960), 19–20.

[81] Blagden, *Stationers' Company*, 29.

Foucault's identification of the "penal appropriation" of the author-function is confirmed through historical research – indeed, this discourse did allow legal systems such as the English crown to control dialogue by the means of discipline – but it also serves a secondary function relevant in contemporary scholarship of the development of natural history. While it offers a vehicle for state censorship over the original *production* of discourses, the author-function simultaneously allows scholarly systems of accreditation and historical account to offer a form of censorship over the *reception* of discourse, as they license certain types of writing acts (such as accounts of personal experience) and condemn others (such as copying). A preoccupation with the writer in the author-function has led scholars of early printed books to disregard the multiplicity of the authorial subject (which includes booksellers and producers along with writers and government censors) in favor of a narrative that supposes, first, that texts are produced in a vacuum outside of the material realities of the printed book and, secondly, that the material book's productive agents are necessarily in competition with authors for the benefits resulting from the commodification of the text in question. Implicit in such a narrative is the belief that printers, publishers, booksellers, distributors, and anyone else involved in the book trade are parasites feeding on their writerly hosts. It is understandable that authors like Leonhart Fuchs traded in such narratives, but there is much less justification for scholars taking authors' biased accounts at face value.

The case of early modern herbals suggests that texts lacking an author are not necessarily without the advantages that Foucault ascribes to the author-function, which indicates that the relationship between authorship and authority is less causal than correlative and may be replaced by the characteristics of a particular artifact. Eleanor F. Shevlin finds that a paratextual element common to medieval texts, the incipit, serves a classificatory purpose in much the same way as Foucault's author-function, but it manages to do so while respecting the multiple agencies of both the artifact's form and its content. Shevlin suggests that the *incipit* was seen as an "informal" address, behaving "like conversational markers that featured authors introducing readers to their subject matter," highlighting the dialogic relationship between not only reader and author but also reader and publisher, the *auteur* responsible for "bringing the book into the light."[82] Through Shevlin's model of titles as contracts, texts are

---

[82] Eleanor F. Shevlin, "To Reconcile Book and Title, and Make 'Em Kin to One Another: The Evolution of the Title's Contractual Functions," *Book History* 2 (1999): 42–77; 46, 47.

united not with their authors but with their material vehicles and therefore may be seen as the product of the multiple agencies responsible for a document's physical creation. Given this helpful intervention, the term "text" may be defined as any artifact that expresses a meaning, one that is subject to interpretation by various human agents.[83]

Shevlin's influence might be seen in this volume's Introduction, which opened with an analysis of the word "herbal" and suggested that a book's title signified a publisher's approach to their production. Shevlin writes that a title

> participates in the world outside the text. Situated on the border of the text, the title commands a far larger audience than the actual work that it labels – a location that presents vast opportunities for its participation in cultural arenas. By casting such a wide contractual net, titles embody the potential to illuminate not just individual works, but reading processes, authorial composition, publishing practices, marketing trends, and generic transformations as well.[84]

Agnes Arber's 1912 work *Herbals, Their Origin and Evolution: A Chapter in the History of Botany 1470–1670* is still considered one of the most influential texts on the subject and can be found cited in nearly every article and book on herbals that has since followed. Yet despite her focus not on the bibliographic elements of herbals but on their botanical content, Arber is unable to ignore the materiality of the book. Just as the publisher Robert Redman's renaming of Richard Bankes's 1525 *Here begynneth a newe mater* as a "boke of the properties of herbes" serves to illustrate the concerns of a book producer, so Arber's title demonstrates that herbals are objects operating in physical space through the notion of the book as a metaphor for understanding the botanical discipline. Herbals, those books "containing the names and descriptions of herbs, or of plants in general, with their properties and virtues," are to be understood as being but a "chapter" in a larger "history."

The appearance of such a metaphor is not altogether surprising. In the same manner that "herbal" is at once both a signifying noun for a specific type of book and an adjective describing that book's content, so is the word "history" heavily linked to its physical manifestation as written text. The second and third definitions of "history" in the *OED* emphasize the primacy of its *written* form, both citing as primary examples prefaces by

---

[83] My thinking here is indebted to D. F. McKenzie, "The Sociology of a Text: Oral Culture, Literacy, and Print in Early New Zealand", in *Bibliography and the Sociology of Texts*, 79–130.

[84] Shevlin, "To Reconcile Book and Title," 43–44.

England's first printer, William Caxton.[85] In his 1485 translation of *Paris and Vienne*, Caxton tells his readers that he has "undertaken to draw the history for you," an outlay spanning an intellectual effort not only in his translation from French to English but also in his literal construction of the printed pages that readers hold in their hands. Like Fuchs in his dedicatory epistle calling attention to the physical features of the printed book that materialize his status as an author, Caxton, as a printer, recognizes that intellectual and material responsibilities intersect in the artifact of a printed book. In "histories" as well as in "herbals," the physical book is never absent, a fact that herbalists themselves recognized as they composed the texts of their herbals by integrating information from the printed herbals that had been published earlier. While such activities have sometimes been understood as "plagiarism," such a description misses the point of the exercise: the work of herbalists was deliberately meant to be accretive and anthological rather than being entirely new and entirely original. In doing so, herbalists worked with the printers and booksellers who stood to profit from their sale and who pushed herbal authors to present their work in recognizable – and saleable – ways. In serving their "stationer-function," these agents of the book trade had the most to gain – and the most to lose – from the printing of a herbal. The history of printed English herbals necessarily requires recognizing them as commercial artifacts, and such an inquiry might start with the Stationers' Company of London, the dominant organization that structured the ways in which English books were produced, distributed, and sold.

---

[85] From the *OED*: "2. *Spec.* A written narrative constituting a continuous methodical record, in order of time, of important or public events. Those connected with a particular country, people, individual, etc."; "3. (Without *a.* or *pl.*) That branch of knowledge which deals with past events, as recorded in writings or otherwise ascertained; the formal record of the past, esp. of human affairs or actions; the study of the promotion and growth of communities and nations."

CHAPTER 2

The Stationers' Company and Constraints on English Printing

To better acquaint readers with the way that early modern publishers thought about textual ownership, which directly impacts the way that herbals were produced, this chapter takes a deep look at the early history of English printing. Though such a history may appear to take us far afield from the specifics of the trade in botanical books, it provides an important context for the arguments I make in later chapters about specific herbals and demonstrates how the regulatory constraints upon the manufacture of all type of books in sixteenth- and seventeenth-century London affected the production of herbals. These regulatory constraints involve both the crown's early directed efforts to control the spread of seditious and heretical material and the customs of the City of London, which citizens and denizens were required to follow. Because the restrictions upon print publication changed dramatically in 1557 when a London civic organization identifying itself as the Stationers' Company became a corporation, scholars of herbals need to consider how these shifting circumstances both effected and affected how herbals could be produced and sold. In order to appreciate how herbals moved from the relatively small books of Bankes and his fellow stationers to the massive tomes of Joyce Norton or Richard Cotes, historians need to better understand the legal and political restraints that guided booksellers' decision-making processes. This chapter explains how the provenance of particular editions was largely determined by the shifting regulatory and economic contexts in which booksellers and printers operated.

The 1557 incorporation of the London Stationers' Company had its roots in the Company's efforts fifteen years earlier, when its members first approached Edward VI at the Convocation of Canterbury in March 1542 with a document petitioning for their right to govern the conduct of their trade.[1] The specific details of that petition, which was unsuccessful, remain

---

[1] Blayney, *Printers of London*, 514–515.

unknown, but the Stationers' efforts seemed to encourage the crown's increasing attention to the potential dangers in the medium of print, which already had prompted a series of royal proclamations designed to censor the publication of seditious material. Evidence of extant historical records suggests a growing desperation on the part of the English government to control the spread of undesirable information. The reforming reign of Edward VI had encouraged the spread of printed materials like vernacular bibles, homilies, and prayer books, which proved a major problem for the Catholic Queen Mary I. Casting about for solutions to the ever-increasing profusion of now-heretical texts, the Marian government may in 1557 have recognized in the Stationers' Company's petition of 1542 an opportunity for offloading an otherwise impossible undertaking: complete authority over printing, the most effective broadcast medium the world had ever seen. In exchange for keeping tabs on subversive material, incorporation allowed the Stationers' Company collectively to hold property in its own name, to conduct lawsuits on its own behalf, and to make ordinances to which their members were legally bound, without "molestation or disturbance" from other London companies or governing bodies.[2] London citizens had been practicing the trades of bookmaking and bookselling for centuries, but incorporation was the means through which the Stationers' Company of London officially took regulatory control over the craft and the technology of printing. After 1557, the procedures put in place to manage Stationers' licensing and insurance systems, including the optional policy of entering titles into the Stationers' Company Registers, radically changed booksellers' understanding of market forces. It is crucial, then, for scholars investigating the products of the early printed English book trade, particularly in the shifting mores of the sixteenth century, to consider the ways that the incorporation of the Stationers' Company altered the motivations of the printers and booksellers who produced books.

The Stationers' Company before 1557

While the first recorded use of the term "stationer" referred to a bookseller in Bologna in the thirteenth century, the earliest use of the word in England suggests that "stationer" referred to almost anyone engaged in the business of making, finishing, or selling books.[3] Graham Pollard's

---

[2] Blayney, *Printers of London*, 927–935.
[3] Graham Pollard, "The Company of Stationers Before 1557," *The Library*, 4th Series, 18 (1937): 1–38; 2.

investigations into the manuscript documents of the City of London testify that, by the fourteenth century, "stationer" readily signified "parchemeners" or parchment merchants, illuminators, and bookbinders.[4] The term is a curious choice, as the medieval Latin *stationarius* was used to describe any person in a fixed situation and did not signify any particular activity or craft associated with bookmaking or bookselling. Instead, what "stationer" suggested was the retail or commercial fixity of the agent concerned. Pollard surmises the term "emphasizes ... the individual's importance as a dealer rather than a craftsman, as an intermediary between the producer and the public rather than an actual maker of the goods he sells."[5] Pollard's point is reinforced by George Unwin's exploration of the way the London economy came to differentiate its productive and distributive functions over the course of the sixteenth and seventeenth centuries.[6] In Peter W. M. Blayney's estimation, the term as it was used in 1417 and after probably meant something closely synonymous with the modern term "bookseller."[7]

In the fourteenth century and earlier, freemen of the City of London who employed the crafts of illumination and scriptwriting were members of a single *mistery* that included the "Writers of Court Hand and Text," legal clerks who wrote deeds and contracts.[8] In 1373, this latter group split to form their own company, the Scriveners, and, on July 12, 1403, the Textwriters' and Lymners' Company gained the Mayor and Aldermen's approval to superintend over all elements pertaining to their trade in the making, binding, and selling of manuscript books.[9] Over the next fifty years, however, the term denoting this Company in the Guildhall records varied considerably, from "Limners and Scriveners" in 1416, to "Scriveners, Limners and Stacioners" in 1417, to "Lymners and Textwriters" in 1423, and to "Lymnours and Stacioners" in 1433.[10] Regardless of nomenclature,

---

[4] Pollard, "Company of Stationers," 3.

[5] Pollard, "Company of Stationers," 5, but see Blayney's rejoinder in *Printers of London*, 8–10.

[6] George Unwin, *Industrial Organization in the Sixteenth and Seventeenth Centuries* (Oxford: Clarendon Press, 1904).

[7] Blayney, *Before the Charter*, 17.

[8] Blayney is careful to note that the medieval term "guild," while synonymous with "craft" in many of England's cities, did not apply in London, where "mistery," "craft," or "company" were the contemporary terms used to describe civic organizations that could train apprentices (*Printers of London*, 16–19).

[9] See Edward Arber, *A Transcript of the Registers of the Company of Stationers of London, 1554–1640 A.D.*, 5 vols. (London: Privately Printed, 1875–1894), 557. See also Pollard, "Company," 13–14. For a translation of the foundation document, see Blayney, *Printers of London*, 5.

[10] As Blayney explains, though the terms "scrivener" and "stationer" were sometimes confused, the Scriveners were a separate company and craft altogether, whose members engaged in activities similar to those of a modern solicitor (*Printers of London*, 1, 461–462).

however, the mistery that later became known as the "Stationers' Company" had been in existence in London since 1403 and was consequently subject to the guiding customs of the City.[11]

Members of the Stationers' Company could specialize in any one or more of the specific trades associated with bookmaking (text writing, illuminating, or bookbinding), the efforts of which were usually coordinated through the enterprises of a broker with a fixed, stationary retail shop. While most of the products of a fifteenth-century bookshop were labor-intensive and bespoke, stationers also imported bound works from abroad and carried secondhand books for ready purchase.[12] As the mistery that controlled the manufacture and retail selling of books in London, members of the Stationers' Company were thus quickly able to appropriate the rapid influx of products that followed Gutenberg's development of movable type and consequently the rapid spread of printed material in Western Europe. While the craft of text writing may have been threatened by the new technology, the efforts of limners and especially bookbinders remained in demand; as Pollard points out, "[bookbinding] remained for some time the last bottle-neck of handicraft through which the finished book had to pass."[13]

There were two ways that English manufacturers and importers offered their commercial products for sale. The first was by retailing their goods directly to customers. This right to sell goods by retail was governed by civic custom, and towns and cities could restrict retailing as a carefully protected privilege held exclusively by their citizens, freemen with membership in a town craft guild or city company. While within the boundaries of a municipality retailing wares was a privilege held only by citizens or authorized denizens, events that occurred outside of city walls such as country marts and fairs were free from such restrictions. The second way

---

[11] For an account of the organization of City companies and their civic responsibilities, see George Unwin, *The Gilds and Companies of London*, 3rd ed. (London: Allen & Unwin, 1938), and "Introduction," in A. H. Thomas, ed., *Calendar of Plea and Memoranda Rolls Preserved among the Archives of the Corporation of the City of London at the Guildhall*, 6 vols. (London, 1929–1961), 1:vii–lxiv.

[12] Henry R. Plomer, "The Importation of Books into England in the Fifteenth and Sixteenth Centuries: An Examination of Some Customs Rolls," *The Library*, 4th Series, 2 (1923): 146–150. See also Blayney, *Printers of London*.

[13] Pollard, "Company," 20. For the first eighty years of English printing, however, Stationers were not the only company engaged in the craft. Prior to the incorporation of the Stationers' Company in May 1557 (which gave them jurisdiction over printing), freemen of the Haberdashers, Salters, Grocers, Barber-Surgeons, and Drapers had been printers as well as holders of royal monopolies to print profitable works like grammars and psalters. This intercompany rivalry likely resulted in the failure of the Stationers' first attempt at incorporation in 1542 (Blayney, *Printers of London*).

that manufacturers and importers of goods might sell their products was wholesale, offering their products for sale to the civic merchants who were eligible to retail them inside a municipality's confines. Then, as now, wholesale transactions usually involved the transference of a quantity of items, and retail merchants would sell individual articles to customers at a sizable mark-up. The publishers named on colophons and title pages largely made their money not by selling individual copies of their editions to customers (although publishers who owned bookshops also did exactly this) but by wholesaling multiple copies of their books to other booksellers for sale in their shops. As well as enabling Foucault's strictures of penal accountability that I outlined in the previous chapter, the name of a publisher in the imprint of a book thus primarily served a wholesaling rather than a retail function and served to inform other merchants where they could buy multiple copies of the book in question. Therefore, while the title page of the first edition of John Gerard's *Herball* (1597) claimed that it was "Imprinted at London by Iohn Norton," the book could theoretically have been available for sale in any of London's bookshops.[14] From Caxton onwards, the economics of the English printed book trade depended upon publishers wholesaling their editions as widely as possible, making their wares available in bookshops not only across London but throughout the British Isles and, on occasion, even upon the continent.

Though to modern eyes the emergence of printing in England in the latter decades of the fifteenth century may seem like a technological sea change for the English trade in manuscript books, at the time a much greater contemporary economic threat to London's stationers (and indeed to all citizens of the City) was widely believed to come from the influx of foreign merchants and craftsmen who set up shops in the suburbs outside of the City's jurisdiction. Though only citizens or freemen of the City of London could retail products, many of these "aliens" were better equipped to import continental goods that could be sold wholesale or to retail their English-made works outside of civic regulations.[15] Thus, while in the

---

[14] In this case, "imprinted" means not that John Norton literally printed the *Herball* but that, as its publisher, he *caused it to be printed* (see Blayney, *Printers of London*, 30). Confusion over the relationship of printers to publishers has occasionally led historians astray, as in Deborah E. Harkness's *The Jewel House*, where she imagines recently inked pages of Gerard's *Herball* hanging in John Norton's shop in 1597. The fantasy is inaccurate because John Norton hired Edmund Bollifant, one of the members of the Eliot's Court Press syndicate, to print the *Herball* from Bollifant's house without Newgate. Norton, like most Elizabethan booksellers, had his retail shop in St. Paul's Churchyard.

[15] "Alien" or "stranger" were the standard terms used to describe foreigners on English soil. A "denizen" was an alien who had been granted a form of permanent residency via letters of

fifteenth century the craft of printing was not yet formally regulated by any
London company (allowing foreign printers such as John Lettou and
William de Machlinia to set up printing houses within the walls of
London and make books), early printers would have been prevented by
the customs of the City from binding and selling their product to customers directly. Within the City limits, aliens' printed books might only be
sold wholesale to London citizens, whose freedom of the City meant that
they were the only ones legally eligible to retail books to a paying public.[16]
As members of the established mistery that governed retail bookselling,
limning, and binding, stationers were therefore best positioned to take
advantage of the increased number of books supplied by the new technology of print.[17]

Printers, however, were operating under a different paradigm. William
Caxton aside, the majority of England's earliest printers were not native
stationers but foreign-born aliens, and the English book trade depended
upon these foreigners both for their printed products and for their importation of high-demand printed books from abroad. These circumstances
explain why, when a 1484 Act of Parliament sought to limit the deleterious
effects of foreign merchants and craftsmen on the English economy
(including their ability to retail goods at country fairs), King Richard III
explicitly exempted those strangers working in the book trade:

> Soit fait come il est desire [let it be done as desired] Prouided alwey that this
> acte or any part therof, or any other acte made or to be made in this p[re]sent
> p[ar]liament in nowise extende or be p[re]iudiciall any lette hurte or impedi-
> ment to any Artificer or m[er]chaunt straungier of what nacion or Contrey he
> be or shalbe of for bryngyng in to this Realme or sellyng by retaill or otherwise
> of any man[er] bokes written or imprynted, or for the inhabitynge within the
> said Realme for the same intent, or to any writer lympner bynder or imprinter
> of suche bokes as he hath or shall haue to sell by way of m[er]chaundise or for
> their abode in the same Reame for the exc[er]cisyng of the said occupac[i]ons
> this acte or any parte therof notwithstondyng.[18]

naturalization, the usual precondition to an alien being given freedom of the city via membership in
a company. In London, "foren" was the term used to describe Englishmen who were not free of the
City.

[16] With only a few exceptions for foodstuffs and other products requiring heavy regulation, freemen of
the city of London could retail anything of their choosing regardless of their company affiliation.
Thus, booksellers were by no means limited to the selling of books, nor were other citizens prevented
from selling books among their own preferred goods.

[17] On the ways that established trade routes enabled the rapid spread of printed materials, see
Andrew Pettegree, *The Book in the Renaissance* (New Haven, CT: Yale University Press, 2010).

[18] As quoted in Peter W. M. Blayney, *Printers of London*, 40–41, where a facsimile of the King's proviso
appears (42). Contractions in the facsimile have been expanded. A modernized and re-pointed

The act of 1484 (1 Richard III, c. 9) was designed to restrict the economic activities of aliens residing in England, but the king's proviso sought to prevent these restrictions from affecting the nascent trade in printed books. The importance of the importation of books printed on the continent to the fifteenth-century English book trade can be seen in the priority that the king's proviso grants to the activity of "bringing into this realme or selling by retail or otherwise of any manner [of] books," whether those texts be "written" (in manuscript) or "imprinted," because regardless of their media, such imported items would contribute to the English economy by being illustrated, bound, and retailed by native-born Englishmen or denizens.[19] With a few exceptions, the king's proviso did not override the existing rules governing trade within cities, so London's restriction that prevented noncitizens from retailing wares directly to customers was still in effect, and foreign printers and booksellers in London were still limited to selling their works wholesale unless they were able to obtain their freedom of the City.[20]

By the turn of the fifteenth century, native-born English stationers had begun to develop a mutually beneficial relationship with their book-dealing foreign neighbors. In exchange for admittance into the freedom of the City through membership in the Stationers' Company, foreign-born printers not only provided the skill and capacity to train native apprentices in the new craft but also offered trade connections to the much-needed supplies of paper and type that were then available primarily from the continent. While the traditional way of being made free of the City of London was via an apprenticeship in a City company (or by patrimonial affiliation if one's father had been a member of that company), citizens could also be made via "redemption," by paying a fee and/or signing a bond to a company in exchange for membership.[21] Richard Pynson,

---

version of the proviso is available in *Statutes of the Realm*, 2:493 (1 Richard III, c. 9); for a list of the errors in quotations of this statute, see Blayney, *Printers of London*, 41nA.

[19] For an examination of bookbinders' dependence on booksellers, see Stuart Bennett, *Trade Bookbinding in the British Isles, 1660–1800* (New Castle, DE: Oak Knoll Press, 2004), esp. chap. 1.

[20] Ian Archer, "Responses to Alien Immigrants in London, c. 1400–1650," in Simonetta Cavaciocchi (ed.), *Le migrazioni in Europa secc. XIII–XVIII: Atti della "venticinquesima settimana di studi"* (Istituto Internazionale di Storia Economica 'F. Datini' Prato, Serie II – Atti delle 'Settimane di Studi' (Florence: Le Monnier, 1994), 755–774, esp. 768–769. On the way liberties and royal peculiars within the City were a source of confusion (and opportunity) for foreign artisans and merchants, see Shannon McSheffrey, "Stranger Artisans and the London Sanctuary of St. Martin le Grand in the Reign of Henry VIII," *Journal of Medieval and Early Modern Studies* 43 (2013): 545–571.

[21] See Steve Rappaport, *Worlds within Worlds: Structures of Life in Sixteenth-Century London* (Cambridge: Cambridge University Press, 1989), 24. On paper and type respectively, see John Bidwell, "French Paper in English Books," in Barnard and McKenzie, 583–601, and Nicolas Barker, "The Old English Letter Foundries" in Barnard and McKenzie, 602–619. On importation, see Paul

a Norman-born printer, had gained his freedom of the City sometime before 1520, while Wynkyn de Worde, a Dutchman and William Caxton's onetime foreman, was a "citizen and staciouner of london" at the time of his writing of his will in 1534.[22] As both men had trained London apprentices and retailed books throughout the early decades of the sixteenth century, Blayney surmises that they were both able to purchase freedom of the Stationers' Company sometime around 1500.[23] Pynson may have been motivated to join the Stationers out of fear for his life and livelihood; in 1500, he brought an action under the Star Chamber charging a Henry Squire and others for an assault in Middlesex, a crime that Pynson believed stemmed from their hatred of Frenchmen. In his testimony, Pynson reported that he feared he would be unable to keep his employees because they had been so terrorized.[24]

For the fifty years following the exemption act of 1484, England's foreign-born printers were able to import, manufacture, and wholesale books alongside locals; and, for a few decades, this arrangement suited members of the Stationers' Company well. Once enough native-born stationers had mastered the new craft of printing, however, the activities of these foreign printers posed a threat to the London book industry. Aliens importing books printed and bound on the continent were threatening the economic interests of freemen, and the Stationers joined a larger City-wide cry for London's authorities to place further limitations on foreigners' trade activities, including their employing of journeymen and binding of apprentices. As their authority was restricted to the City limits, London's mayor and aldermen were forced to petition the crown to pass an act that would require all London area aliens, including those living in the suburbs and liberties, to submit to the jurisdiction of the City's relevant craft

Needham, "The Customs Rolls As Documents for the Printed-Book Trade in England," in Lotte Hellinga and J. B. Trapp (eds.), *The Cambridge History of the Book in Britain, Vol. 3: 1400–1557* (Cambridge: Cambridge University Press), 148–163, and Blayney, *Printers of London.*

[22] Pynson was born in Normandy and, as until 1450 Normandy was under the obeisance of Henry VI, he would have been considered a native-born Englishmen had he been born earlier than 1451 (see Blayney, *Printers of London*, 49). Regardless of his status as a native-born Englishman, however, Pynson was technically not free of the City of London until he gained membership into a City company willing to have him. On de Worde, see Mary C. Erler, "Wynkyn de Worde's Will: Legatees and Bequests," *The Library*, 6th Series 10 (1988): 107–121; 118.

[23] Blayney, *The Stationers' Company before the Charter*, 24. Blayney reports a legal document of June 28, 1502, identifying Pynson as a London "Ciuem & Stacionarium" (*Printers of London*, 69).

[24] E. Gordon Duff, *A Century of the English Book Trade* (London: Bibliographical Society, 1905), 126. Blayney offers a fuller account that suggests that the attack on Pynson was less xenophobic and more personally motivated than has been traditionally reported (*Printers of London*, 56–60).

wardens. Such an act was passed in 1523, though it was designed to benefit *all* of London's citizens, not just its Stationers.[25]

Yet the 1484 exemption for foreign craftsmen and dealers in books, which explicitly benefited those importing bound books from abroad, remained. This exception directly harmed English bookbinders, who were a sizable percentage of the members of the Stationers' Company. After petitioning the crown for a number of years to repeal it, the Stationers finally succeeded in 1534. Henry VIII's "Acte for printers & bynders of boks" recognized that the act of Richard III had once been necessary,

> for that there were but fewe bokes and fewe prynters within this Realme at that tyme which cold well exercise and occupie the seid science and craft of pryntyng; Never the lesse sithen the makyng of the seid p[ro]vysion many of this Realme being the Kynges naturall subjectes have geven theyme soo dylygently to lerne and exercyse the seid craft of pryntyng that at this day there be within this Realme a greatt nombre co[n]nyng and expert in the seid science or craft of pryntyng as abyll to exercyse the seid craft in all point[s] as any Stranger in any other Realme or Countre; And furthermore where there be a great nombre of the Kynges subject[es] within this Realme which [leve] by the crafte and myst[er]ie of byndyng of bok[es] and that there be a greate multytude well expert in the same ... Be it therefore enacted by the Kyng our Soveraigne Lorde the Lordes spirituall and temporall and the Comons in this present parliament assembled and by auctoritie of the same, that the seid provyso made the furst yere of the seid Kyng Richard the thride frome the feast of the natyvytie of our Lorde [God] next co[m]myng shalbe voyde and of none effect.[26]

As a result of the 1534 repeal, all English citizens, denizens, and aliens were now forbidden to purchase imported books that had been bound abroad. Such a restriction prevented an industrious bookseller from importing copies of continental herbals to sell in London, Cambridge, or Oxford. By removing the proviso that exempted foreign booksellers from the act of 1484, the crown ensured that foreigners operating in the book trade were now just as subject to the act's decrees as other aliens, and thus were now unable to retail their printed wares anywhere in England – they could only sell their works wholesale to local citizens. The combination of the 1484 and 1534 statutes had the effect of ensuring that, as the mistery that held within its membership the largest group of bookbinders and booksellers,

[25] *Statutes of the Realm*, Vol. 3 (14 and 15 Henry VIII); see also Blayney, *Before the Charter*, 230–231.

[26] *Statutes of the Realm*, 3:456 (25 Henry VIII, c. 15). Blayney offers a compelling rationale for believing that the "gratuitous history lesson" accounting for Richard III's proviso was written by John Rastell, printer, member of Parliament, and brother-in-law of Sir Thomas More (*Printers of London*, 335–336).

the Stationers' Company remained an integral part of the making and selling of books within the City of London. It also created a space in which herbals produced by English booksellers could thrive without competition from foreign publishers. Until the incorporation of the Stationers' charter in 1557, however, the specific craft of printing was still able to be practiced by anyone, foreign or otherwise.

Regulatory Procedures and Religious Controversy

As print became an increasingly popular medium for books and the demand for books of all kinds grew, some publishers were progressively more able to divest themselves of the technical details of manufacturing to focus instead on estimating which books would fare most profitably in the marketplace. By contracting out the actual setting of movable type to produce copies by impression, a number of stationers (as well as a handful of freemen from other companies) were able to invest in retail speculation, moving beyond the economic limitations of bespoke products that had followed books from their manuscript foundations. In separating the agency of the provider of capital from the agency of the manufacturer, publishing booksellers of this stripe could make considerable profit without needing the technical skill and materials to become master printers themselves. Though printers regularly published works for themselves, by the end of the sixteenth century more than half the books printed in England were manufactured for a publisher other than the printer.[27] Thus, when discussing the provenance of a particular early modern English book, the printer who literally manufactured the book should be understood as being of less import than its publisher, who, by "causing the book to be printed," functioned as its actual architect or producer.

Particularly in the first half of the sixteenth century, the production of early modern books was impacted by a number of papal and crown regulations designed to limit and control the spread of anti-Roman Catholic sentiment. This, too, had an effect on herbals. Herbalist William Turner was a Protestant divine as well as a Tudor physician and naturalist who authored numerous anti-Catholic polemics throughout his lifetime. A 1546 prohibition against "any maner of booke printed or written in the english tongue, which be or shall be sette forth" that listed Turner by name may have inadvertently been responsible for the destruction of copies of Turner's first botanical publication, *Libellus de re Herbaria novus*

[27] Blayney, *Before the Charter*, 36.

(London, 1538; *STC* 24358), of which only a handful of copies now survive. To better track the publication of seditious material, Tudor responses to Lollardy and Lutheranism regularly mandated policies that required identifying those responsible for causing a book to be printed as well as those responsible for printing and selling it. Further, throughout fifteenth-century Europe, ecclesiastical authorities issued edicts requiring all books and sermons to receive official approval prior to "publication," a noun that was generally understood to encompass both printed material intended for private reading and that which was broadcast live to audiences. While the transitive forms of the verb *to publish* necessarily imply that it is a book object that is "prepared and issued in copies for sale to the public" (*OED* 3.a), chiefly "in print" (*OED* 3.c), the intransitive verb is less stringent: "To bring a matter to public notice" (*OED* 5.a). That in early modern English both meanings could be in use simultaneously even in the noun may be evinced in Francis Beaumont's commendatory verse to John Fletcher's first quarto of *The Faithful Shepherdesse* (*STC* 11068), printed after that play's unfavorable debut at Blackfriars, the play's *first* publication:

> Since it was thy happe to throw away,
> Much wit, for which the people did not pay,
> Because they saw it not, I not dislike
> This second publication, which may strike
> Their consciences, to see the thing they scornd,
> To be with so much will and art adorned.   (sig. ¶3v)

This meaning of "publish" as "broadcast" can be seen as early as 1407, when Thomas Arundel, Archbishop of Canterbury, sought to quash Wycliffean sympathies by ordering that all books read in the universities should be preapproved by a group of twelve ecclesiastically preferred censors. Even prior to the widespread use of movable type, then, English authorities were concerned about how books could quickly disperse undesirable and heretical information in ways that were difficult to contain. *De haeretico comburendo*, passed in 1401, went so far as to suggest that preaching and writing are both threats to doctrine:

> none from henceforth any Thing preach, hold, teach or instruct openly or privily, or make or write any Book contrary to the Catholic Faith and Determination of the Holy Church ... and also that none from henceforth in any wise favour such Preacher, or Maker of any such and like Conventicles, or holding or exercising Schools, or making or writing such Books ... and that all and singular having such Books or any Writings of such wicked Doctrine and Opinions, shall really with Effect deliver or cause

to be delivered allsuch Books and Writings to the Diocesan of the same Place within xl. Days from the Time of the Proclamation.[28]

Prepublication licensing was designed to forestall the problems caused by heretical publications and broadcasts. These attempts were prevalent on the continent as well; a bull of Leo X dated May 1515 required that

No one shall presume to print or cause to be printed, in Rome or in any other city or diocese, any book or other writing whatsoever unless it has first been carefully examined and its publication approved by our vicar and master of the Sacred Palace, in other cities and dioceses by the bishops or by competent persons appointed by them and by the inquisitor of the city or diocese in which the books are to be printed.[29]

By July of 1520, the circulation of heretical sentiments in print would result in Leo X's decree to round up and burn such books, and that anyone inclined to "read, hold, print, publish or defend" them would be subject to excommunication. Cardinal Wolsey dutifully sought Luther's imported works throughout the realm, and on May 12, 1521, the apprehended books were burned in Paul's Cross Churchyard, the center of England's book trade as well as London's civic pride. Four and a half years later, the spectacle was repeated on a rainy Sunday in February 1526, shortly before imports of William Tyndale's translation of the New Testament began to circulate in England. After twice watching their products go up in smoke at the behest of doctrinal command, the Tudor booksellers who in the 1530s and 1540s reprinted the little *Herball* first printed by Bankes in 1525 had considerable reason to be concerned about the crown's regulations governing the printing and selling of books.

Bishop of London Cuthbert Tunstall was soon issuing more edicts in an attempt to stop the spread of Lutheran books. On October 12, 1524, a select group of London booksellers was summoned to Tunstall's palace and ordered not to sell imported books printed abroad without first showing them to himself, Archbishop William Warham, Cardinal Wolsey, or Bishop of Rochester John Fisher.[30] Shortly thereafter, the printer

---

[28] *Statutes of the Realm*, 2:127 (2 Henry IV, c. 15). Also quoted in a slightly different translation in A. W. Reed, "The Regulation of the Book Trade before the Proclamation of 1538," *Transactions of the Bibliographical Society* 15 (1917–1919): 157–184; 158–159.

[29] H. J. Schroder, ed., *Disciplinary Decrees of the General Councils* (London: B. Herder Book Company, 1937), 504–505.

[30] Though the record of Tunstall's warning to the booksellers did not explicitly mention the act of *printing*, it is clear from the subsequent summons and questioning of publishers that the bishop implicitly required locally printed books to be subject to the same process of censorship as imports (Peter Blayney, private communication, September 30, 2008).

Thomas Berthelet was summoned to account for his publishing of four works without having sought ecclesiastical approval, and when Berthelet admitted his guilt, he was forbidden to sell them. Even in such a politically charged era, financial penalties were more successful motivators of religious compliance than theological ones. For instance, in a letter dated January 5, 1526, John Longland, Bishop of Lincoln, described a conversation with the king about burning Lutheran books and binding the Stationers with recognizances against importing more: "The King approved the plan, especially as to the recognizances, which many would fear more than excommunication."[31]

As the four texts published by Berthelet were unlikely to meet with the bishops' disapproval (one of them was a copy of an anti-Lutheran sermon preached by Bishop Fisher at Paul's Cross before the second book burning), A. W. Reed surmises that this case illustrates "a tightening of the hold which the Bishop's officials had put upon the Printers."[32] Having not actually printed seditious material, Berthelet's fault was a technical one, and his prosecution was perhaps designed to demonstrate to other booksellers the seriousness with which the censors intended to pursue their authority.[33] Tunstall had a second meeting with London's booksellers in October 1526, in which he made that authority explicit and forbade them not only from importing Latin or vulgar books from abroad but also from producing any works native to England without first exhibiting them to a group of censors. The effect of this proclamation on the London book trade may have been more profound than is currently recognized, as such an order immediately established that books in print currently accredited with the king's privilege were assumed to have already met with the approval of ecclesiastical authorities and could thus be reprinted without falling afoul of the church or crown. Contemporary booksellers could reasonably surmise that, as no company yet had authority over the craft of printing, and as disputes over printing privileges were still resolved by a king and his council who were becoming increasingly concerned with the profusion of heretical material, reprinting other booksellers' privileged works was considerably less risky than attempting to get ecclesiastical approval for new texts.

Over the next decade or so, it would become increasingly easier for booksellers to follow such a pragmatic policy; by 1538, up to 40 percent of

---

[31] Reed, "Regulation," 165.   [32] Reed, "Regulation," 167.

[33] As the books in question were soon issued by Berthelet *Cum privilegio a rege indulto*, Reed suggests that "ample amends were done to the Printer and the innocent authors" for being made such an example of ("Regulation," 169). See also Blayney, *Printers of London*, 244–246.

the books printed in England claimed to be printed under the protection of the king's privilege.[34] Yet the expansive use of the king's privilege soon created other problems, one of which mirrors the difficulties of distinguishing between works and documents that I have been discussing more broadly. When the king's privilege began to be appended to radical books, Henry was forced to clarify what, exactly, his privilege entailed. In November of 1538, the king issued a proclamation designed to refute

> sondry printed books, in the englyshe tonge, that be brought from outwarde parties, and by such lyke bokes as haue bene printed within this his realme, *set forth with priuilege*, conteynynge annotations and additions in the margines, prologes, and calenders, imagined and inuented aswell by the makers, deuysers, and priynters of the same bokes.[35]

The 1538 proclamation reiterates Henry's enthusiasm for preprint licensing, expanding this requirement to include *all* books printed in England or in English and extending the prerogative to be that of a secular body (the king's Privy Council) rather than a religious one. The second matter restricts the language of his printing privilege:

> ITEM that no persone or persons in the realme, shall from hensforth print any boke in the englyshe tonge, onles vpon examination made by some of his gracis priuie counsayle, or other suche as his highnes shall appoynte, they shall haue lycense so to do, and yet so hauynge, not to put these words *Cum priuilegio regali*, without addyng *ad imprimendum solum*, and that the hole copie, or els at the least theffect of his license and priuilege be therwith printed, and playnely declared and expressed in the Englyshe tonge vnderneth them.[36]

Unfortunately, scholarly confusion over the squinting modifier *solum* has since led to misunderstandings about the nature of the printing privilege. While the king's addition sought to clarify that the royal privilege supported only the commerce surrounding the printed book object, as held distinct from royal support of the nature of the printed object's *text*, some publishers and bibliographers have held that *ad imprimendum solum* signifies the exclusivity of the patent owner's claim.[37] That certain booksellers and readers had viewed *cum privilegio* as royal endorsement rather than simply as a time-limited grant of monopoly issued by the crown is clear

---

[34] Blayney, *Printers of London*, 484.   [35] *STC* 7790, my emphasis.

[36] *STC* 7790, emphasis in original.

[37] As Peter W. M. Blayney points out, this interpretation "simply adds a redundant definition of what a privilege is" (private communication, September 30, 2008). For a more detailed account of the confusion, see Blayney, *Printers of London*, 480–487.

from its use as a legal defense in Essex in 1534.[38] There, a group of Lutherans, having been arraigned by a local vicar and his questman for reading books deemed inappropriate, claimed that, because the books were issued with the imprimatur of royal privilege, they were not only protected by the crown but *recommended*. By the time of his writing the 1538 proclamation it had become necessary to clarify that booksellers' use of his privilege was in no way related to this prepublication licensing. In other words, the king's privilege is the protection of the printed book as an economic commodity, not an endorsement of a text therein contained. To make the distinction between texts (which require ecclesiastical licensing) and documents (which, like other commodities, can be protected by privileges), the 1538 act also required that booksellers print both their license and their privilege in their books, and such accounts soon began to appear in colophons and in addresses to the reader.

I have elaborated the early history of the Stationers' Company at such length because a comprehensive understanding of the systems and practices of textual ownership in Renaissance England better equips us to evaluate the surviving evidence of herbals and other printed books of natural history. In Chapter 4 of this volume, I will show how the effect of Henry VIII's 1538 proclamation provides evidence that helps to explain the choices made by printers and publishers, providing an answer to the question of the enormous popularity of the text of the little *Herball* after Richard Bankes's exclusive privilege to print the title had expired. Yet before accounting for the ways that changing civic and company regulations influenced that book's many editions, I need to address the ways that changing attitudes towards botanical illustration likewise grew to become a material and promotional concern for English publishers. By accounting for the regulatory and economic concerns of publishers alongside the appearance of naturalized botanical illustrations, I can explain not only the little *Herball*'s enormous popularity but also the reason why that enormous popularity eventually started to wane.

---

[38] This case is discussed in Reed, "Regulation." For a vicar's similar mistrust of privilege, see Blayney, *Printers of London*, 481.

CHAPTER 3

Salubrious Illustration and the Economics of English Herbals

Over the course of the sixteenth century, herbals grew from small, unillustrated octavos to giant, illustrated folios and shifted from reprints of anonymous medieval works to commissioned authorial tomes. I argue throughout this book that, by making a bibliographic turn, scholars of English herbals can better understand the context in which English botanical science developed. Thinking bibliographically about herbals requires a consideration of herbal texts from the perspective of the publishers who invested capital in their manufacture. To reveal the sophisticated and nuanced calculus of English stationers, this chapter explores the recursive relationship between readers' responses to printed herbals and the activities of the publishers who catered to them, as well as the shifting regulatory mechanisms that enabled stationers to navigate the amount of financial risk that herbal publication increasingly asked of them.

The Emergence of Illustration in English Botany

Renaissance herbals frequently contain explanations of how plants can serve as remedies for ailments, but in his 1621 endorsement of study as a defense against melancholy, Robert Burton argued that even material books themselves could ease the disordered mind. Along with his recommendation that melancholics improve their moods by studying wholesome volumes of cartography, geography, and mathematics, Burton suggested that readers examine the figures of plants in large botanical books:

> To see a well cut herball, all Hearbs, Trees, Flowers, Plants expressed in their proper colours to the life, as that of *Mathiolus* upon *Dioscorides*, *Delacampius*, *Leobel*, *Bauhinus*, and that last voluminous and mighty herball of [Besler of] *Noremberge*, wherein almost every Plant is to his owne bignesse ... such is the excellency of those studies, that al those

ornaments and bubbles [baubles] of wealth are not worthy to be compared to them.[1]

In advocating for the benefits of herbals that are "well cut" – that is,
illustrated with woodcuts – Burton is by no means dismissing the medical
remedies contained within these texts (he regularly cites the expertise of
"herbalists" throughout his *Anatomy*) but is demonstrating what Heidi
Brayman calls "the extent to which the very materiality of the book
matters" in establishing readers' attachment to the printed medium.[2] As
Sachiko Kusukawa's work has detailed, herbals were among the printed
genres that most benefited from new technological developments in book
illustration, so it is unsurprising that Burton finds that herbals' salubrious
effects can be gained not just by reading but by *gazing* upon their engraved
or woodcut pictures of plants.[3] To that end, the large-format herbals that
Burton explains are of particularly healthful use are those widely known for
their distinctive illustrations, like the Czech edition of Pietro Andrea
Mattioli's 1544 commentary on Dioscorides with new, full-page woodcut
illustrations (Prague, 1562; *USTC* 568706); Pierre Pena and Matthias de
L'Obel's *Stirpium aduersaria noua* (London, 1570–1; *STC* 19595); Jacques
Dalechamps's *Historia generalis plantarum* (Lyon, 1586–1587; *USTC*
83985); and the *Prodromos theatri botanici* of Swiss physician Caspar
Bauhin (Frankfurt am Main, 1620; *USTC* 2135791), an illustrated preamble
to what would later be his magnum opus, *Pinax theatri botanici* (Basel,
1623; *USTC* 2045504). Since Burton was writing his *Anatomy* with the
resources of Oxford's Bodleian Library close to hand, his awareness of
large, illustrated continental herbals is unsurprising, and it explains his
ability to access a copy of Basilius Besler's notoriously expensive florilegium
Hortus Eystettensis (Eichstädt, 1613), which featured copperplate engravings
of plants intended to show, in extravagant detail, the riches of that
particular garden.[4]

   Burton's investment in the affordances of printed botanical illustrations
is of a piece with the health effects of "reading green" that Leah Knight

---

[1] Robert Burton, *The Anatomy of Melancholy* (Oxford: John Lichfield and James Short for Henry
Cripps, 1621), sig. Z1r.
[2] Heidi Brayman Hackel, *Reading Material in Early Modern England: Print, Gender, and Literacy*
(Cambridge: Cambridge University Press, 2005), 1.
[3] Kusukawa, *Picturing the Book of Nature*.
[4] William Ostler notes that "so laden with quotations is the *Anatomy* that it has been called 'The
Sweepings of the Bodleian'" ("The Library of Robert Burton," *Proceedings and Papers of the Oxford
Bibliographical Society* [Oxford: Oxford University Press, 1922–1926], 182–190; 184). On the printing
and publication of *Hortus Eystettensis*, see Nicholas Barker, *Hortus Eystettensis: The Bishop's Garden
and Bessler's Magnificent Book* (London: British Library, 1994).

finds is a recurrent feature of seventeenth-century English literary culture, including the phenomenon's association with the elite readers who could afford such large and lavishly illustrated books.[5] As Knight shows, the recursive effects of "green reading" could be seen not only in approaches to wellness but also in architecture and interior design, as Renaissance readers manipulated the leaves of herbal texts into new forms as imagined and literal decor. Leonhart Fuchs, who was particularly invested in illustration, puts the benefits of such books this way:

> there is the wondrous pleasure that will permeate your soul on contemplating so many kinds of plants and will invite you not only to the love, but to the defense, of herbal medicine. For what could be more pleasurable, more enjoyable, than to gaze upon plants, which Almighty God has painted with so many varied colors, has decked with the most elegant flowers, whose colors no painter ever could completely express, and then has adorned with fruits and seeds of the greatest use as condiments and medicine?[6]

As I discussed in Chapter 1, Fuchs's account of the beauty of his herbal conveniently elides the mechanical reproductive processes of printing and publishing that make such "wondrous pleasures" available to readers. More ironically, Fuchs's celebration of gazing upon books also inadvertently endorses the position of his rival, printer Christian Egenolff, as Egenolff copied the illustrative woodcuts of Fuchs's and Brunfels's herbals on the grounds that the natural world could be copywritten only by God himself. For Fuchs, the material forms of printed herbals are not a surrogate but a supplement to real-world botanical experience, useful primarily because their pictures can spur others to the godly and wholesome study of plants. The book is an inspiration, in other words, one that can force people out of their studies and into the fields to marvel in God's creation.

Given that Renaissance readers had such widespread appreciation for botanical illustrations, it is not surprising, then, that printed images of plants also found their way into the needlecraft of gentlewomen by providing them with patterns. The herbalist John Parkinson recognized this potential in his *Paradisi in sole paradisus terrestris* (London, 1629):

> Although Borage and Buglosse might as fitly haue been placed, I confesse, in the Kitchen Garden, in regard they are wholly in a manner spent for Physicall properties, or for the Pot, yet because anciently they haue been entertained into Gardens of pleasure, their flowers hauing been in some respect, in that they haue alwaies been interposed among the flowers of

[5] Leah Knight, *Reading Green in Early Modern England* (Burlington, VT: Ashgate, 2014).
[6] Meyer et al., *Great Herbal*, 1:218.

womens needle-worke, I am more willing to giue them place here then thrust them into obscurity.[7]

Parkinson's woodcut illustrations in *Paradisi* are roughly four times larger than those in other herbals, taking up the entirety of the folio's page, and it is small wonder that women would find them useful as patterns for needlecraft (Figure 3.1). As Rebecca Laroche suggests, Elizabeth Isham made use of the woodcuts of printed botanical books like Parkinson's in just this way to quiet her agitated mind.[8] Isham's autobiographical diary, dated 1638/9, reveals that through embroidery she "delight[ed] much in [flowers'] seuerall shaps & collers ... it kept me from those thoughts w[hich] was hurtfull to me," seemingly echoing the way that her contemporary Robert Burton also made use of printed herbals to distract from his own melancholy.[9] Other readers found these books so attractive that they were dangerously distracting: the diary of Puritan Samuel Ward lists looking at herbals among sinful behaviors: "May 17, 1595. Thy wandring mynd on herbals att prayer tyme, and at common place. Also thy gluttony the night before."[10]

By the time that Robert Burton and Elizabeth Isham were writing in the 1630s, herbals had been so long associated with botanical illustrations that they had become a requisite part of the genre. Samuel Ward's remarks suggest that botanical illustrations in printed books may have been appealing – and potentially damnable – even forty decades earlier. Yet, though the benefits of pictures now seem obvious to readers, particularly those inclined to marvel at herbals for their beauty, Renaissance authors' appreciation of printed book illustration emerged more slowly. Not all authors of works of natural history or medicine were initially convinced that illustrations were useful substitutes for traditional verbal description.

---

[7] John Parkinson, *Paradisi in sole paradisus terrestris* (London, 1629), sig. X5r. On the relationship between herbals and women's embroidery, see Jennifer Monroe, *Gender and the Garden in Early Modern English Literature* (Burlington, VT: Ashgate, 2008) and Linda Levy Peck, *Costuming Splendor: Society and Culture in Seventeenth-Century England* (Cambridge: Cambridge University Press, 2005).

[8] Laroche reports that a copy of Parkinson's *Theatrum botanicum*, now housed at the Library of Congress, features "eighteenth-century embroidery patterns ... pressed between the pages" (*Medical Authority*, 128).

[9] On the relationship between needlecraft and textuality, see Jones and Stallybrass, *Renaissance Clothing*, esp. chap. 6. On the manner in which Isham's textual process is figured through her embroidery, see Laroche, *Medical Authority*, esp. chap. 3, and Margaret J. M. Ezell, "Elizabeth Isham's Books of Remembrance and Forgetting," *Modern Philology* 109 (2011): 71–84. See also Susan Frye, *Pens and Needles: Women's Textualities in Early Modern England* (Philadelphia: University of Pennsylvania Press, 2010).

[10] M. M. Knappen, ed., *Two Elizabethan Puritan Diaries* (Chicago: American Society of Church History, 1933), 103–104.

The Vertues.

We know no vse they haue in Physick, but are cherished in Gardens for their beautifull flowers sake.

CHAP. LXIX.

Caryophyllus hortensis. d Gilloflowers.

TO avoide confusion, I will diuide Gilloflowers from Pinkes, and intreate of them in seuerall Chapters. Of those that are called Carnations or Gilloflowers, as of the greater kinde, in this Chapter, and of Pinkes, as well doubles as single, in the next. But the manner to treate so large a pointe, hauing great diuersitie in them often all verie endlesse, as the least should: for I will therefore set downe onely the descriptions of three or foure sorts of euery kinde referred all the other sorts, for their fashion and manner of growing, either to the seuerall varieties or to the vsually called with varieties in it, with other varietie and manner of colours in the flowers, wherein consisteth all their difference. I will not diuide them called Carnations to be the greatest, both for leafe and flower, and Gilloflowers for the smaller part to be kept in booth, and there fore will, as you read the greatest part, and the Orenge tawny or yellow Gilloflower liken it by it selfe, as differing very notably from all the rest.

1. *Caryophylus maximus Harwichensis siue Anglicus.*
The great Harwich or old English Carnation.

I take this goodly great old English Carnation, as a president for the description of all the rest of the great sorts, which for his beauty and statelinesse is worthy of a prime place, hauing becne alwayes very hardly preserued in the Winter, and therefore not so frequent as the other Carnations or Gilloflowers. It riseth vp with a great thicke round stalke, diuided into seuerall branches, some whereof lye flat with ioynts, and at euery ioynt two long greene leaues rather long, whitish leaues, broader then the Gilloflowers leaues, turning or winding in two or three circles round; in some other sorts of Carnations they are plaine, but bending the points downewards, and in front of a darker reddish greene colour, and in others not so darke, but rather of a whitish greene colour; the flowers stand at the toppes of the stalkes in huge, great, and round greene huskes, which are diuided into fiue points, out of which rise many long and round bottome leaues, deeply iagged at the ends, set in order round and comely, making a gallant great double flower, of a deepe Carnation colour, almost red, spotted with many blush spots and strakes, some great and some lesse, of an excellent sweete sent, neither too quicke as many others of these kinds are, nor yet too dull, and with two whitish crooked threads like hornes in the middle: this kinde neuer beareth many flowers, but as it is slow in growing, so in bearing, not to be often handled, which flowereth a kinde of statelinesse, fit to preserue the opinion of magnificence: the roote is branched into diuerse great, long, woody rootes, with many small fibres annexed vnto them.

2. *Caryophyllus hortensis flore pleno ruber.* The red or Cloue Gilloflower.

The red Cloue Gilloflower, which I take as a president for the second sort, which are Gilloflowers, grow like vnto the Carnation, but not so thicke set with ioynts and Leaues: the stalkes are more, the leaues are narrower and whiter for the most part, and in some doe as well a little turne: the flowers are smaller, yet very thicke and double in most, and the greene huskes wherein they stand are smaller, like vnto the ordinary maner: the ends of the leaues in this flower, as in all the rest, are denied or iagged, yet in some more, them in others, some also hauing two small white threds, crooked at the ends like hornes, in the middle of the flower, when as diuers other haue none. Their kindes,

Figure 3.1 John Parkinson, *Paradisi in sole paradisus terrestris* (1629), sigs. 2C3v–2C4r. The Huntington Library, San Marino, California (RB 14065).

Like Thomas Johnson in his account of bananas discussed in the Prologue, some authors were concerned that portraits drawn from living examples represented only a particular specimen and thus were inadequate to describe a species' fuller, more varied appearance.[11] Copious and detailed verbal descriptions that required readers to apply their own judgment as they evaluated their particular specimens could be seen as far more useful. Nonetheless, a combination of the advancement in printers' technical expertise and an increased authorial investment in illustration eventually enabled herbals to be used as identification tools for the description and classification of plant species that early modern English readers found at home and abroad.[12] These improvements in both the form and the content of herbals were valued both by needleworkers and by melancholics.

While the typically large folio size of these publications limited their utility as field guides, the comprehensive nature of their verbal texts in outlining plants' agricultural and medicinal virtues made them of pragmatic interest to medical practitioners, scholars, and literate laypeople alike. In some cases, a demand for large books could lead directly to the production of smaller ones. After experiencing the indignity of seeing his carefully designed woodcut images for *De historia stirpium* copied for a translation of Dioscorides's *De materia medica* by the Frankfurt publisher Christian Egenolff, Leonard Fuchs had smaller copies of the images recut for *Primi de historia stirpium* (Basel, 1545), an octavo edition of a much-reduced text of *De historia stirpium* designed to be used in the field. Likewise, William Ram created an unillustrated abridgment of Henry Lyte's English translation of Rembert Dodoens's *Cruydeboeck* (Antwerp, 1554) that he titled *Ram's Little Dodeon* [sic] (London, 1606; *STC* 6988). Ram wrote that he hoped to make the most salient features of Dodoens and Lyte's work available to readers unable to afford the large volume by "draw[ing] that into a handful, which before was in the compass of a great garden: or else to bring that into a little Garde[n] which before was (as to be looked for in many fields and disperced places) not to be found but by great labour and industry)."[13] Ram suggested that he needed

---

[11] On natural historians' ambivalence to illustrations, see Kusukwa, *Picturing the Book of Nature* and Ogilvie, *Science of Describing*.

[12] For further examination of the role played by illustration in the publishing history of herbals, see Sachiko Kusukawa, "Illustrating Nature," in Marina Frasca Spada and Nick Jardine, eds., *Books and the Sciences in History* (Cambridge: Cambridge University Press, 2000), 90–113; on Renaissance usage of naturalism, see James S. Ackerman, "Scientific Illustration," in Allan Ellenius, ed., *The Natural Sciences and the Arts* (Uppsala: Almqvist & Wiksell International, 1985), 1–17.

[13] William Ram, *Ram's Little Dodeon* (London: Simon Stafford, 1606), sig. A2v.

to create the epitome to serve the underprivileged, but deserving, herbal reader:

> So as where the geat [sic] booke at large is not to be had, but at a great price, which ca[n]not be procured by the pooer sort, my endeuor herein hath bin chiefly, to make the benefit of so good, necessary, and profitable a worke, to be brought within the reach and compasse aswell of you my poore Countrymen & women, whose liues, healths, ease and welfare is to be regarded with the rest, at a smaller price, than the greater Volume is.[14]

The publisher Simon Stafford, however, took his time bringing the book into print: though he entered the volume into the Stationers' Registers on June 9, 1600, Stafford didn't actually print Ram's epitome until 1606, and he never reprinted it.[15] For Stafford, then, the little book didn't seem especially "profitable" after all.

What herbal authors' hesitancy about illustration means is that, for a time, the images accompanying printed works were not drawn from authors' descriptions but supplied from publishers' existing stocks of woodcuts, many of which were copied from manuscripts. Wynkyn de Worde's 1495 English translation of Bartholomaeus Anglicus's illustrated encyclopedia *De proprietatibus rerum* (*The Properties of Things*, STC 1536) features a chapter on botany headed by a large woodcut of an orchard foregrounded by a field of plants. Even by the standards of incunabula, de Worde's early woodcuts are primitive, likely copied from his manuscript original, and the single illustration accompanying the chapter on trees offers little to make *De proprietatibus rerum* useful to fifteenth-century readers as a tool to identify distinct specimens of plants and herbs.[16] Though the leaves on the trees in de Worde's woodcut differ slightly from each other, they largely share the same trunk morphology, while the herbs in the foreground are similarly patterned rather than distinctive. Over the next century, however, two publishers saw enough in Bartholomaeus Anglicus's text to risk publishing it again. Thomas Berthelet's edition appeared in an unillustrated version in 1535 (*STC* 1537), and Thomas East published an updated and revised version in 1582 (*STC* 1538) after he entered the work into the Stationers' Company Registers.

---

[14] Ram, *Rams Little Dodeon*, sig. A2r. Lyte's revised edition in 1586 (STC 6986) required 125.5 edition-sheets per copy; Ram's epitome was a quarter of the size (32 sheets).

[15] Arber, *Transcript*, 3:162.

[16] Edward Hodnett, *English Woodcuts 1480–1535* (London: Bibliographical Society, 1973), 10.

Figure 3.2 *De proprietatibus rerum* (1495), sig. M5v. By courtesy of the Department
of Special Collections, Memorial Library, University of Wisconsin–Madison
(Thordarson 230).

Between Berthelet's edition of 1535 and East's publication of *De proprietatibus* in 1582 occurred a turning point for botanical book illustration.
Brunfels's and Fuchs's illustrated herbals were extremely popular on the

continent, going through dozens of editions in multiple vernacular languages. Despite being printed abroad, their books often appear in English
library catalogues and booklists, suggesting that they were regularly
imported.[17] In England, William Turner's three-volume *A New Herball*
(1551–1568) and Pierre Pena and Matthias de L'Obel's *Stirpium aduersaria
noua* (1570–1571) were likewise authoritative volumes that offered clarifying
illustrations to accompany individual plant descriptions wherever possible.
East's *De proprietatibus* bears evidence of the publisher's awareness of this
shift in readers' expectations for botanical book illustration, as does the
new woodcut that East commissioned for his edited text; the image clearly
exhibits the artist's awareness both of distinct species of plants, like the
plantain (bottom left) and violet (bottom right), and of the changing trunk
shapes that might result from the different locales where trees might grow.
The tree overlooking the river slopes down towards the water, while its
roots mound to keep it fixed firmly on the bank. East's decision to change
the botanical illustration accompanying his text (he could simply have
commissioned copies of the 1495 woodcut instead of designing a new one)
demonstrates the ways that Elizabethan publishers considered the norms
established by other printed books in the marketplace as they added
features and affordances to distinguish new volumes.[18] As Chapters 4 and
5 will show, this attentiveness to generic norms was observed even fifty
years earlier, as Henrician, Edwardian, and Marian publishers likewise
considered the competing books offered for sale by their contemporaries
as they brought their own books to market, innovating wherever they
perceived an opportunity to distinguish their product.

The first illustrated book printed in England exclusively devoted to the
study of plants appeared in 1526, the year after Bankes's edition of the
little *Herball* offered the first appearance of the word "herbal" in print.
However, the illustrations in Peter Treveris's *The Grete Herball* (*STC*
13176) suffered from some of the same problems as those in de Worde's
edition of *De proprietatibus*. Treveris's *Grete Herball* contains 481

[17] Leedham-Green, *Books in Cambridge Inventories*.
[18] The fact that each of East's woodcut images was printed on one side of a single folio leaf for insertion,
as an individual leaf, into the appropriate gathering is curious. In this regard, his woodcuts resemble
illustrations made from engraved and/or etched copperplates. Because the latter had to be printed on
a specialized rolling press, they often appear on inserted leaves of the kind we see in East's book.
Woodcuts, however, can be positioned alongside movable type and, because of this, were usually
printed as part of regular gatherings. The fact that East's woodcuts were printed in an atypical
manner, separately from the sheets of printed text, might suggest that their inclusion was an
afterthought or that the illustrations were designed to allow sale separately from the rest of the
volume.

Figure 3.3 *De proprietatibus rerum* (1582), a page inserted between sigs. Zz5v and Zz6r. The Huntington Library, San Marino, California (RB 97017).

woodcut illustrations of plants and animals, which, as Edward Hodnett notes, was "the record for an English press" at the time.[19] As with de Worde's text, however, precision in the rendering of illustrations suffered at the level of accuracy; Blanche Henrey calls *The Grete Herball*'s pictures "completely out of touch with nature."[20] Though attractive, many of the figures are deliberately stylized to fit into the woodblocks, and the occasionally preternatural and Galenic doctrine of the late medieval text is aptly represented in the accompanying illustrations, where mandrakes look like men and plants both flower and produce fruit at the same time.[21] In addition, some of the same figures are repeated as representing different species of plants, complicating attempts an early modern reader might make to use *The Grete Herball* as a guide to identification. I will explore the publication history of Treveris's *Grete Herbal* more fully in Chapter 5. My interest here is to use illustrated herbals to demonstrate more broadly some of the ways that early modern English stationers evaluated the existing market of books when they considered the viability of their own speculative publications.

While the "slavish copying" of medieval botanical manuscripts followed herbals in their initial foray into print,[22] some authors and compilers of Renaissance herbals began to include their own experiential accounts of plants, and such interest soon led to herbals' inclusion of botanical images drawn from life. The *German Herbarius* (Mainz, 1484; *USTC* 740862), an illustrated work printed by Johannes Gutenberg's sometime foreman Peter Schoeffer, appears to be the first example of a printed herbal text in any language that was primarily written from firsthand knowledge.[23] The preface to the *German Herbarius* claims that it was the joint work of a wealthy traveler to the east and a Frankfurt physician.[24] The *Herbarum vivae icones* (Strasburg, 1530–1536; *USTC* 662094) of Otto Brunfels promised its readers "living portraits of plants," while, as I've noted, Leonard Fuchs's *De historia stirpium commentarii insignes* (Basel, 1542) sought precision in every detail, including in the rendering of the text's printed images. Along with a woodcut portrait of the author, the opening pages of *De historia stirpium* featured portraits of *De historia*'s various craftsmen at

[19] Hodnett, *English Woodcuts*, 63.   [20] Henrey, *British Botanical*, 1:21.

[21] On contemporary debate over the usefulness of botanical illustration in the identification of plants for medical purposes, see Kusukawa, "Illustrating Nature."

[22] The term is quoted from John Gilmor, *British Botanists* (London: William Collins, 1944), 8.

[23] Henrey, *British Botanical*, 1:5–6; Arber, *Herbals*, 18.

[24] For a translation of the preface to the second edition of the German *Herbarius*, see Arber, *Herbals*, 23–26.

Figure 3.4 Portraits of the illustrators and block-cutter of *De historia stirpium* (1542). By courtesy of the Department of Special Collections, Memorial Library, University of Wisconsin–Madison (Thordarson T 1651).

work illustrating directly from the plants themselves and transferring the images to the woodblocks before the woodblocks were cut by Viet Rudolf Speckle (Figure 3.4).[25]

Fuchs was expressly invested in the utility of illustrations to reinforce the extent of his own botanical investigations, and he instructed his artists to use a diachronic strategy to display the various stages of a plant through the seasons to illuminate bud, flower, and fruit. Fuchs's illustrations display the entire plant right down to the root and both sides of a leaf, and varietals among a particular species might also be displayed as if they were growing on a single plant to show diversity while also minimizing the number of separate woodcuts needed in the volume. His accompanying text suggests that Fuchs assumed considerable botanical foreknowledge among his readership, and Kusukawa demonstrates that Fuchs uses his book's illustrations to provoke his readers' recall of sensible features of known plants (like taste and smell) to enable them to "adjudicate[] between competing opinions among ancient and contemporary authorities."[26] In this way, the technology of printed images constituted Fuchs's contribution to a raging humanist debate between the proper relations of theory and practice, particularly in the practice of medicine. Rather than the practice of reading standing in as a surrogate for firsthand expertise, the publication of an illustrated printed book could serve as an authoritative supplement designed to arbitrate readers' own experience of handling plants. As Kusukawa persuasively argues, "[t]exts worked in tandem with pictures to produce a powerful form of argument – a visual argument, encompassing both demonstration and persuasion," and authors like Fuchs exploited the new affordances available to them in the medium of the printed book to promote their professional agendas.[27]

Thinking Materially

Though it is easy to represent these developments in botanical illustration as a simple linear progression (herbal images were crude and then they became more sophisticated), the history of English herbals in print reveals that the process was recursive. After all, authors create *texts*, not books, and the concerns of those who make and market the codicological vehicles in which verbal texts find their readers do not always align with the

---

[25] See Sachiko Kusukawa, "Leonard Fuchs on the Importance of Pictures," *Journal of the History of Ideas* 58 (1997): 403–427.
[26] Kusukawa, *Picturing the Book of Nature*, 122.
[27] Kusukawa, *Picturing the Book of Nature*, 250–251.

preoccupations of authors. The progression in Renaissance naturalism was not linear either, as later publishers and compilers often copied classificatory images that had initially been drawn from an author's personal experience and placed them in "un-authorized" new contexts. The woodcuts of plants and herbs that illustrated the *German Herbarius* were for decades copied by other continental publishers in their own botanical books. Similarly, despite their author's efforts to defend a visual and verbal ethos in plant description and the efforts of the publisher to name the artists within the volume, the woodcuts in *De historia stirpium* were quickly divorced from Fuchs's text to join the works of other authors, much to his dismay. Fuchs's woodcuts were so popular that they were copied by herbals in Germany and the Low Countries, and reproductions of the images eventually found their way into William Turner's *A New Herball*, which was so celebrated for being the first of the great English herbals that Turner is widely heralded as the "Father of British Botany." (That the illustrations to Turner's magnum opus were copied from Fuchs often goes unmentioned in such celebratory accounts.)

As the genre of illustrated herbals became more familiar to English readers over the course of the sixteenth century, these botanical works gradually grew in both size and scope, cumulating in such extensive books as Turner's three-volume *A New Herbal* (1551–1568) but also in the 1,400-plus-page folio of John Gerard's *Herball or General Historie of Plantes* of 1597 and in the equally massive *Theatrum botanicum* of John Parkinson published in 1640. The names of these large, illustrated folio herbals frequently turn up in the libraries of physicians and apothecaries, a reasonable inclusion given the attention that herbals typically pay to the use of plants in treating ailments and disease. Mention of these folio herbals also crops up in the diaries and account books of aristocratic women who worked as lay healers: Grace Mildmay specifically mentions Turner's *A New Herball* in her diary; Margaret Hoby has "the Herball" read to her three times in 1599; while Anne Clifford is featured in her great triptych portrait at Appleby Castle standing in front of a wall of books that includes a manuscript epitome of Gerard's.[28] Given his declared interest in

---

[28] On Mildmay, see Linda Pollock, *With Faith and Physic: The Life of a Tudor Gentlewoman Lady Grace Mildmay, 1552–1620* (New York: St. Martin's Press, 1993). On Hoby, see Margaret Hoby, *The Private Life of an Elizabethan Lady: The Diary of Lady Margaret Hoby, 1599–1605*, ed. Joanna Moody (Stroud: Sutton Publishing, 1998) and Laroche, *Medical Authority*. On Clifford, see Mary Ellen Lamb, "The Agency of the Split Subject: Lady Anne Clifford and the Uses of Reading," *English Literary Renaissance* 22 (1992): 347–368; 365. Critics have misidentified the work as a printed copy of Gerard's *Herball*, but Rebecca Laroche points out that, as an epitome, the volume in the

illustrated herbals, it is perhaps not surprising that Robert Burton singled out his copy of Gerard's *Herball* in his will to bequeath it to one "Mrs Iles."[29] Such an itemized note testifies that Burton saw Gerard's *Herball* as an especially valued book to pass along, and Blanche Henrey provides evidence that Gerard remained in use as a standard botanical textbook through to the nineteenth century.[30] Indeed, scholars still regularly invoke Gerard's, Turner's, and Parkinson's illustrated herbals as authorities: editors of early modern texts view them as valuable resources that explain early modern authors' medical and botanical knowledge.[31]

And well they should – the large English folio herbals, whose authors are widely heralded as the fathers of British botany, are thick, informative compendia. Their contents contain "the names and descriptions of herbs, or of plants in general, with their properties and virtues," and they bear evidence of their authors' study of other printed and manuscript herbals as well as their own informed experience as gardeners. The images in these books served as a vital means for disseminating visual information about exotic "New World" varietals that few old world botanists ever got to see firsthand. Gerard's herbal of 1597 offered readers the first printed illustration of the potato, while, as we've seen, Thomas Johnson's 1633 revision of Gerard offered what was then cutting-edge: a cross-sectioned banana.[32] Over the course of the sixteenth and seventeenth centuries, herbals grew through such botanical one-upmanship until their ever-more comprehensive contents reached the upper limits of binding a single-volume codex. Such accumulated bulk accounts for Richard Cotes's choice of words when he entered Parkinson's *Theatrum botanicum* in the Stationers' Registers as "*an herball of a* Large *extent.*"[33]

---

painting better displays Clifford's deliberate effort at self-fashioning in echoing her mother's alchemical practice (see *Medical Authority*, 17–18).

[29] Osler, "Library," 184.   [30] Henrey, *British Botanical*, 1:53

[31] A few representative examples taken from the Arden Shakespeare series: James C. Bulman cites Gerard to explain "mandrake," the nickname whores gave Justice Shallow in *King Henry IV, Part II* (London: Bloomsbury, 2016), 315; A. S. Cairncross cites Parkinson's *Paradisus terrestris* in his note on "balm" in his edition of *The Third Part of King Henry VI* (London: Bloomsbury, 1964), 116; R. A. Foakes cites both Turner and Gerard in a note on "century" in his edition of *King Lear* (London: Bloomsbury, 1997), 322.

[32] As Redcliffe N. Salaman notes in *The History and Social Influence of the Potato* (Cambridge: Cambridge University Press, 1949), the potato's absence from Nicholas Monardes's *Joyful News out of the New World* (first English translation, 1577) and William Turner's works of 1551–1568 offers a "a datum line before which we may be reasonably certain that the potato was unknown in Europe" (77). The first printed mention of the potato was in Gerard's Latin catalogue of the plants in his Holborn garden in 1596 (*Papus orbiculatus*), Englished in its translated edition of 1599 to "Bastard potatoes."

[33] Emphasis mine. See Arber, *Transcript*, 4:307.

Yet, as the impressive popularity of the unillustrated *Herball* first published by Richard Bankes in 1525 suggests, such heavily illustrated folio herbals did not emerge from print shops *sui generis*, invested in by their publishers simply on the grounds that a market for such vernacular works likely existed in England as readily as it did on the continent. Publishing a work such as Gerard's *Herball* in 1597 required a substantial outlay of capital to purchase or rent not only the book's 2,200 woodcuts but also sufficient paper for the entire print run, the printer's expenses for composition and presswork, and the copy of the manuscript produced by Gerard. To better compare the costs involved in publishing books of various sizes, bibliographers invoke a unit of measurement known as an "edition-sheet." Because a four-page (two-leaf) folio, an eight-page (four-leaf) quarto, and a sixteen-page (eight-leaf) octavo gathering are all created from one sheet of paper, considering the total number of sheets of paper required to print a copy of a book allows for a comparison of relative cost among formats.[34] Each copy of Gerard's 1597 folio *Herball*, for example, contained 371 edition-sheets, so a print run of 500 copies of the volume would have required the Nortons to purchase 185,500 sheets of large-size paper, more than 386 reams.[35] (Printing a single copy of Bankes's 1525 quarto *Herball*, by contrast, needed only nine edition-sheets.) The cost and quality of white paper suitable for printing varied, but the paper used in a volume of comparable format, the 1596 edition of John Foxe's *Book of Martyrs*, cost seven shillings a ream; at such a rate, the paper alone for the 1597 *Herball* would have cost its publishers more than £135 before a single word or image had been printed upon it.[36] Once the paper and Gerard's manuscript copy had been acquired, the booksellers Bonham and John Norton needed to provide the printer, Edmund Bollifant, with these supplies, as well as with sufficient funds to employ Bollifant's workers in manufacturing the massive volume. In order for a herbal to be printed, publishers' significant material and financial concerns needed to be accommodated. Illustrations required woodblocks to be manufactured, rented, or purchased, and large illustrated texts could be financed only by the wealthiest stationers.

[34] Blayney, *Printers of London*, 938–939.
[35] I am calculating a ream of twenty quires at twenty-four sheets per quire. Blayney, *Printers of London*, 100–101; see also "Publication of Playbooks," 408–410.
[36] This amount assumes a print run of 500 copies. The figure for the paper cost of *Book of Martyrs* comes from W. W. Greg and Eleanore Boswell, eds., *Records of the Court of the Stationers' Company 1576–1602 from Register B* (London: The Bibliographical Society, 1930), 51.

Managing Risk

Early modern publishers could not begin selling copies of books and recouping their costs until every page of every copy of a volume had been printed, and they still would not break even until they had sold about two-thirds of the books wholesale to other booksellers.[37] Such risks to financial outlay in the creation of an edition motivated stationers to pay the fee to license their right to copy and record their intention to print a particular work within their civic organization, the Stationers' Company. While some earlier Tudor publishers held individual time-limited, crown-issued patents that protected their editions from piracy (I will detail these patents more in Chapter 4), the Stationers' incorporation in 1557 granted the Company the legal means to assert control over the technology of print. Only members of the Company were now permitted to do so, and all stationers were required to license their titles in advance. The earliest records post-incorporation record payments of the Company's licensing fee.[38]

As the edition-sheet totals for herbals like Gerard's suggests, printed book manufacturing was expensive and financially risky. What protected stationers' investments was the Company's internal regulations: once the right to copy a title had been claimed, another stationer could not also print an edition of the text without risking Company sanction. Licensing was therefore largely designed to protect members' economic investments: "it was problems of infringement, rather than of censorship, that the Company's license was intended to regulate."[39] An extant record of a stationer having paid for a license to publish a work was typically recorded in an entry in the Stationers' Registers, and thus has since come to be known as a "register entry." Such licenses could be exchanged, bequeathed, or transferred among stationers.[40] Register entries were primarily designed to record the fee that the Company charged for a license to print a work, but they eventually also came to indicate, within the Stationers' Company, a stationer's ownership of a particular textual property and their right to profit from the income that property could generate through print publication. Under the rights granted to the Stationers by virtue of their charter, precautions such as licensing enabled the Company to charge anyone who usurped a stationer's right to copy with a breach of

---

[37] For an overview of the economics of book publication in the period, see Blayney, "Publication of Playbooks."

[38] Peter W. M. Blayney, "If It Looks like a Register . . .," *The Library* (2019): 230–242; 239.

[39] Blayney, "Publication of Playbooks," 399.   [40] Blayney, "Publication of Playbooks," 400.

contract, subjecting the thief to fine and seizure of the surreptitious copies.[41] Without the insurance of Register entries, even wealthy stationers such as the Nortons could not afford to hazard their finances on such large-scale products as bibles, lawbooks, and herbals, as avaricious colleagues could, in theory, have easily appropriated others' finished texts and reprinted them to sell at a reduced price.

There were additional costs to putting a book into press for the first time. The editorial labor involved in compiling, organizing, and (especially in the case of large books like Gerard's *Herball*) indexing a text only affected the profits of its first edition; a page-for-page reprint of a text required little new editorial work. Yet, while sizable folios with complicated editorial constraints such as bibles and statutes of law were always in popular and professional demand, the market for more specialized treatments of scientific and literary subjects usually needed to be readily established by smaller projects along similar themes before a publisher would reasonably invest in a larger book. Only after a clear market for Francis Beaumont and John Fletcher's play quartos was demonstrated, for example, did it make sense for the publishers Humphrey Moseley and Humphrey Robinson to risk their capital publishing a folio of their collected dramatic works.[42] Similarly, before examining the Nortons' or other publishers' investments in the illustrated herbal phenomena of the latter half of the sixteenth century and first decades of the seventeenth, it will be helpful to investigate the period when the market for such works was first established.

This discussion brings us back, at last, to the first and most popular printed herbal in early modern England: the unillustrated little *Herball* of 1525 that was first printed by Richard Bankes. With eighteen editions in less

---

[41] Some publishers also sought ad hoc patents, which gave them a monopoly on a title, genre, or given class of books, enabling them to seek redress of illicit copyists with the backing authority of the crown. (Books and sheets printed with the protection of such patents did not need to be entered into the Registers.) Such patents for genres like playbills were derived from the "generic" or all-purpose privileges that a number of individual printers and booksellers had held prior to 1557, which entitled them to remove their new titles from the public domain for a fixed period of time.

[42] In his introduction to the readers of the Beaumont and Fletcher folio of 1647 (Wing B1581), Moseley explains that the widespread availability of printed quartos of many of Beaumont and Fletcher's plays necessitated his avoidance of including them in his collection, to avoid his being accused of codicological double-dipping: "I would have none Say, they pay twice for the Same book" (sig. A4r). Along with his dismissal of the seemingly ubiquitous quartos, contrasting the nascent Beaumont and Fletcher folio with other books is an important part of Moseley's marketing strategy; the convenience of the current printing of the authors' "entirely New" plays together in a single tome is offered in a direct contrast to other collections that are "commonly but a *new Impression*, the Scattered pieces which were printed Single, being then onely Republished together: 'Tis otherwise here" (sig. A4r).

than fifty years, this small book was a runaway bestseller, and the *Herball*'s demonstrated profitability for many publishers later made it possible for the larger, illustrated herbals of William Turner and John Gerard to be produced. The little *Herball* does more than simply pave the way for later, larger editions, though: as different publishers experimented with different ways of presenting the *Herball* in print, they tested new affordances and marketing strategies that would influence how English readers would respond to the herbal genre. The decisions made by innovative publishers like Robert Wyer and William Copland as they repackaged the little *Herball* demonstrate that authority – and authors – gradually became a useful mechanism for distinguishing one's wares in the competitive print marketplace of early modern London.

PART II

Anonymity in the Printed English Herbal

CHAPTER 4

Reframing Competition
The Curious Case of the Little Herball

The previous chapter showed how seventeenth-century figures like Robert Burton and Elizabeth Isham believed that viewing ornate woodcuts of plants was a form of healthy recreation. The robust contemporary trade in botanical images cut from the pages of antique books indicates that these printed illustrations of plants continue to attract and fascinate our gaze. Yet one of the most regularly reprinted books in sixteenth-century England was a short, anonymous herbal that contained no illustrations at all. As I have outlined in the Introduction, in 1525 the London printer Richard Bankes issued from his shop a quarto "whiche sheweth and treateth of [the] vertues & proprytes of herbes" (*STC* 13175.1), and he saw fit to republish the book in the following year. By 1567, the text and variations upon it had been reprinted at least eighteen times by at least fifteen other publishers, testifying to the value that both booksellers and readers saw in this profitable little book.[1] Despite an influx of recent scholarship on the influence of printed botanical texts on early modern authors and readers, scholars have largely dismissed these early books as being of little interest to those concerned with issues of textual or intellectual authority. If the little *Herball* publications are mentioned at all, they are generally noted only to display the comparatively "authoritative" status of William Turner and then quickly dismissed. Leah Knight, for instance, finds that "[Turner's] work is implicitly contrasted with that of his medieval predecessors, and even with slightly earlier sixteenth-century works like Banckes' herbal, a book conventionally named for its printer instead of its author and one which is more of a translation and compilation than a recognizably 'authored' work."[2] In a similar vein, Rebecca Laroche notes that "[t]hose herbals printed before [William Turner's] in England, namely *Bancke's*

---

[1] After Bankes's reprint of his edition of 1526 (*STC* 13175.2), all other reprintings of the text were in octavo (*STC* 13175.4–13175.19c).
[2] Knight, *Of Books and Botany*, 46.

Herbal (1525) and the *Grete Herball* (1526), though interesting in their own right, are not infused with issues of textual authority that we find in Turner and post-Turner publications."[3]

While the little *Herball* does not fit with modern expectations of the genre, the surviving evidence of the text in print testifies that sixteenth-century readers found much to like in the book. This chapter will demonstrate how and why the little *Herball* became such an amazing commercial success, and it will raise the possibility that the audience for English herbals did not rise and fall with the expensive texts preferred by elite scholarly readers or gentry. The publishing history of the little *Herball* reveals that the purchasing preferences of Tudor London's middling readers, as well as the regulatory constraints upon bookmaking and bookselling, created the economic conditions that later enabled the large, illustrated folio herbals of Turner, Gerard, and Parkinson to come into being. In other words, these large books with named authors on their title pages were a secondary development in the tradition of the printed English herbal, suggesting that the "author-function" that governed a text's authoritative value was initially irrelevant to English readers. The association between herbals and particular botanical authorities did not result from readers' perceptions of their accuracy but can be traced to commercial concerns: their publishers' desire to sell an old and profitable text in innovative new ways.

The curious case of the little *Herball* demonstrates that, to uncover the origin and evolution of the printed English herbal, historians need to be attentive to the economic and material circumstances governing the production and circulation of books. My Introduction explained how, in printing the first edition of the little *Herball* in 1525, the publisher Richard Bankes sought to exploit the popularity of a late medieval manuscript work that had circulated widely, capitalizing on its existing familiarity with readers to sell many more copies of the text in a new medium. The evidence of Bankes's immediate reprinting of his herbal the following year reveals his accurate reading of the marketplace for print in the mid-1520s, while the investment of other publishers in their own editions during the latter half of the 1530s confirms that the little *Herball* continued to be a vendible and valuable commodity – and was widely recognized as one. The evidence shows that, throughout the 1540s and 1550s, publishers continued to print new editions of this book. Even as the regulations and

[3] Laroche, *Medical Authority*, 29. For slightly more thorough accounts of the texts of the *Herball*, see Eleanour Sinclair Rohde, *The Old English Herbals* (London: Longmans, Green and Co., 1922), 55–65, and Henrey, *British Botanical*, 1:12–15.

the market forces governing the English book trade shifted with the incorporation of the Stationers' Company in 1557, the little *Herball* continued to be seen as worth publishing and protecting: John King sought a license for *"the little herball"* and thereby entered it into the Stationers' Company Registers between November 30, 1560 and March 8, 1561, effectively removing the work from the public domain.[4] The license was an insurance policy in more ways than one. By entering the title, King both secured his right to profit indefinitely from any number of his future editions of the book free from the threat of piracy and eliminated the possibility that the little *Herball* could return to compete with any *other* botanical books he wished to publish in the future. (That King entered the rights to copy *The Grete Herball* at the same time suggests that he was thinking in exactly these terms.)

Taken as a whole, the efforts of the little *Herball*'s many publishers confirm that, once in print, this little book was in unusually high demand among Tudor book purchasers. The use of quantitative analytics helps to determine the relative popularity of books in the London book trade and prove, categorically, that the little *Herball* was a runaway bestseller. Only 1.8 percent of speculative books first printed between 1473 and 1580 reached eighteen editions by 1640; less than 1 percent of speculative books first printed between 1473 and 1580 reached eighteen editions within forty years.[5]

The little *Herball* thus raises the same issues as those examined by Andy Kesson and Emma Smith in their study of print popularity in early modern England.[6] As it is an unqualified "best-seller" by any measure, interest in the little *Herball* in its many editions surpassed that of the three-volume *New Herbal* of William Turner, which was published in its entirety only once (1568), and the three editions of John Gerard's commodious *Herball or Generall Historie of Plants* (1597; rev. 1633, 1636). As I noted in Chapter 3, Gerard's *Herball* regularly appears in the notes of editions of Shakespeare, and Turner's *New Herbal* is used by A. C. Hamilton to explain Edmund Spenser's account of "the Poplar never dry" in book 1 of *The Faerie*

---

[4] See note for *STC* 13175.19. A recording of the entry is transcribed in Arber, *Transcripts*, 1:153, but also see Blayney, "If it looks like a register . . .," 240–242. King perhaps had recognized the value of the text earlier when he had been hired to print a shared edition of the little *Herball* for John Walley and Abraham Veale in 1555 (*STC* 13175.16 and *STC* 13175.17).

[5] Alan B. Farmer, private communication. See also Alan B. Farmer and Zachary Lesser, "What Is Print Popularity? A Map of the Elizabethan Book Trade," in Andy Kesson and Emma Smith (eds.), *The Elizabethan Top Ten: Defining Print Popularity in Early Modern England* (Burlington, VT: Ashgate, 2013), 19–54.

[6] Kesson and Smith, *Elizabethan Top Ten*.

Queene.[7] Yet while both Turner's and Gerard's herbals are often used as resources by scholars seeking to uncover Shakespeare's or Spenser's botanical understanding, the little *Herball* is virtually ignored as a viable botanical resource to explain an author's use of plants like rosemary, borage, catmint, or wormwood. Unlike its much longer descendants, the little *Herball* lacks a clear author to demarcate its botanical authority, and scholars writing commentaries for literary texts evidently prefer to rely on, or default to, impressive-looking illustrated works with these more legible pedigrees. Gerard's *Herball or Historie of Plants* has been found in the libraries of John Milton, Anne Clifford, and John Donne,[8] but it is hard to argue that it was anywhere near as popular as its smaller forebear. It is quite possible that more copies of the little *Herball* were circulating in sixteenth-century London than of all the other "authoritative" herbals combined, yet this little volume remains relatively unknown. The most popular early modern texts, in other words, were not always the largest and most imposing ones that have had a better chance of survival in famous libraries or notable collections.

Such obscurity in the face of quantity is characteristic of the paradoxical notion of print popularity. As Kesson and Smith note, the phrase "best-selling" can thus be at odds with "other, less quantifiable indices of value, or, to put it another way, the hyphenated term 'best-selling' is under some strain, as 'best' starts to serve less as an adjectival modifier to 'selling' and more its ideological opposite."[9] In some respects, then, the popularity of the little *Herball* with Tudor readers seemingly justifies scholars' lack of attention to it. Kesson and Smith remark that the very notion of popularity, particularly in its focus on the preferences of "non-elite" readers, "has odd and unexpected implications for the canon." This too can be seen in the little *Herball*'s publication history. Richard Bankes's decision to draw an old manuscript text forward into the new medium of print calls into question the typical "protocols of periodisation" that separate examinations of natural history in the medieval and Renaissance periods. An examination of the evidence of public demand can show that traditional literary and historical categories are much more complicated than they may initially seem.[10]

[7] A. C. Hamilton (ed.), *Spenser: The Faerie Queene*, 2nd ed. (Toronto: Pearson, 2007).

[8] Donne's autographed copy of Gerard's *Herball* of 1597 is held by the Missouri Botanical Garden's Peter H. Raven Library (shelfmark MBG Pre-Linnean QK41. G3 1597 [#670]). See Hugh Adlington, "Seven More Books from the Library of John Donne," *The Book Collector* 67 (2018): 528–533.

[9] Kesson and Smith, *Elizabethan Top Ten*, 1.

[10] Kesson and Smith, *Elizabethan Top Ten*, 6, quoting John Simons, "Open and Closed Books: A Semiotic Approach to the History of Elizabethan and Jacobean Popular Romance." See also Gillespie, *Print Culture*.

This chapter attends to the publication history of the little *Herball* as a series of calculated investments by London booksellers as they navigated the dynamic English economy in printed books between 1525 and 1567. I first explain how the regulatory practice of generic privilege influenced Richard Bankes's choice to print and then reprint the little *Herball*, as well as the influence that Bankes's privilege had on the behavior of the other Tudor publishers who were the first to reprint the book. As part of that discussion, I explain how Bankes's publication of the little *Herball* was one of several texts that he was issuing concurrently that readers could bind and sell together in a single, composite volume. I then explore how the editions of printer-publisher Robert Wyer changed the functionality of the little *Herball*, which has subjected Wyer to accusations of piracy. My analysis will show that these accusations are both anachronistic and unfounded. Finally, I examine another marketing innovation that booksellers hoped would attract new customers to the little *Herball*: the addition of a named author on its title page.

Richard Bankes and Generic Print Privileges

The colophon of *Here begynnyth a newe mater / the whiche sheweth and treateth of [the] vertues & proprytes of herbes / the whiche is called an Herball*, the first printed herbal in English, is dated March 25, 1525. The quarto's title page also features the words "Cum gratia & priuilegio a rege induito," a Latin phrase of such importance to its publisher, stationer Richard Bankes, that he also repeated it on the final page of the volume: "Cum priuilegio. Imprynted by me Rycharde Banckes / dwellynge in Lo[n]do[n] / a lytel fro [the] Stockes in [the] Pultry / [the].xxv.day of Marche. The yere of our lorde. M.LLLLL.&.xxv."[11] Bankes reprinted the text the following year with an updated colophon but shortened his title page declaration: both the first and the last page of the 1526 text simply read "Cum priuilegio."[12]

In previous chapters, I outlined the forms of ecclesiastical, royal, and civic authority that adjudicated English publishers' rights to make, distribute, and sell copies of printed works in the first half of the sixteenth century. In particular, I explained the system of ad hoc privileges that temporarily removed texts from the public domain for a specified number of years, a system that was in use prior to the incorporation of the

---

[11] Anon., *Here begynnyth a new mater* (London, 1525), sig. I4v.
[12] Anon., *Here begynnyth a new marer* (London, 1526), sig. I4v. The second edition of Bankes's *Herbal* is dated June 25, 1526.

Stationers' Company in 1557, along with the subsequent economic protections that were created by the new company's regulatory systems. As an earlier form of pre-incorporation economic insurance, the *cum privilegio* patent was a crown dispensation that granted a publisher a chance to earn back their return on an investment by preventing another publisher from printing their privileged texts for a set period. On occasion, these patents secured a privilege over specific titles, but more common were what Peter W. M. Blayney calls "generic" privileges that granted the recipient "temporary protection for *any* book (legally) printed at his costs and charges."[13] In the case of some patents, such as those held by the King's Printer, the term of the privilege was usually for the king's life, but the patents granted to most booksellers were for a shorter and limited period of time up to seven years. In 1525, this is the sort of privilege that Bankes appears to have held and to have indicated with "Cum priuilegio" on the title page and colophon of his 1525 and 1526 herbals.

Bankes's time as a printer is split between two periods, 1523–1526 and 1539–1545, but he published books throughout his career. The exact terms of Bankes's privilege in 1525 are difficult to ascertain because no record of it from his earlier printing period survives outside of the claims he makes on his title pages and colophons; however, in accordance with King Henry's 1538 proclamation that books published with the protection of the king's privilege must also print "the effect" of that privilege in the text of the protected book, Bankes dutifully printed his privilege in full in a number of his works after 1538, and these instances provide a guide to what his earlier privilege may have looked like.[14] The text printed in his 1540 edition of the summer gospels (*STC* 2968) indicates that Bankes had been granted a seven-year monopoly on any work he chose to print at his own expense:

> Henry the eight by the grace of god kynge
> of Englande and of Frau[n]ce, defensour [*sic*] of the

[13] The quotation is Blayney's, from a private communication to the author. It is important to reiterate my earlier point that Blayney's use of the word "generic" to describe the privileges held by Tudor booksellers does *not* mean an adjectival form of "a particular style or category of works of art; esp. a type of literary work characterized by a particular form, style, or purpose" (*OED* "genre," *n.* 1.b.) but instead "applicable to a large group or class, or any member of it" (*OED* "generic," *adj.* 1.a.), here specifically meaning those texts that are published by the particular individual holding the patent. For a more detailed investigation of the privilege system, see Blayney, *Printers of London*.

[14] The text of the king's 1538 proclamation ordering that "the hole copie, or else at the least theffect of his license and priuilege be therewith printed" whenever the phrase "*Cum priuilegio regali ad imprimendum solum*" is used is found in *STC* 7790. Copies of the text of Bankes's privilege also appear in *STC* 2967, 2969, 2967.3, 2968.3, 2969.3, 2967.5, and 2969.5. For a similarly worded patent granted to Thomas Berthelet in 1538, see sig. A1v of *The dictionary of syr Thomas Eliot knight* (*STC* 7659).

fayth, Lorde of Ireland, and in earth Supreme head
immediatly vnder Christe of the church of Engla[n]d
to all prynters of bokes wythin thys oure Realme
and to all other our officers, ministers and Subiec-
tes, these our letters hearyng or Seynge: Gretynge.
We let you wit, that of our grace especial we haue
gyuen priuilege vnto our welbeloued Subiecte Ri-
charde Bankes, that no maner person wythin thys
our Realme, Shal prynte any maner of bokes, what
So euer our Sayd Subiecte Shall prynte fyrste wythin the Space of Seuen yeares next ensuyng the prin-
tynge of euery Suche boke So by hym prynted, vpon payne of forfetynge the Same. Wherefore we
woll and co[m]maunde you, that ye nor none of you
do presume to prynte any of the Sayde bokes du-
rynge the tyme aforesayd, as ye tender oure plea-
Sure, and woll auoyde the contrarye.

While it is prudent to note that it is possible that the 1540 privilege outlined
here may be a different or shorter privilege than the one that is actually
referenced by the *cum privilegio* of Bankes's prior publications, assuming
that he had a similarly termed, seven-year patent as early as 1525 may
explain why more than a decade passed between Bankes's second edition
of the little *Herball* in 1526 and its first reprinting by another publisher
sometime around 1537.[15] It is not clear how Bankes managed to acquire
a crown privilege to protect his works, but unlike his contemporary
privilege holder and fellow printer-publisher John Rastell (who was the
brother-in-law of Sir Thomas More), there is no clear indication that
Bankes was connected to the court. Bankes's motivation for publishing
the little *Herball* in 1525 must therefore be found through an examination
of the other books he printed and published during his twenty-four-year
bookselling career, as well as by putting Bankes in the wider context of the
early English book trade in the 1520s and 1530s. Blayney identifies Bankes as
one of the first English publishers to give up printing to concentrate their
efforts on the more lucrative activity of publishing, and this shift suggests
that he was a particularly astute reader of the marketplace for printed books
in Tudor London.[16]

At the time of Bishop Tunstall's October 1526 meeting with London's
booksellers to forbid them from printing the works of English authors

---

[15] The first reprint of the little *Herball* by someone other than Bankes appears to have been John Skot's
undated edition (*STC* 13175.4), which Blayney and the *STC* provide with a tentative date of 1537.

[16] Blayney, *Printers of London*, 182–183.

without first showing the books to a group of civic and ecclesiastical censors (a permission to publish later known as *allowance*), Bankes was operating his printing house at the Long Shop in the Poultry beside St. Mildred's Church, just a few doors away from the bustling Stocks Market. Bankes's first printed book, a short anonymous tract translated from Dutch, was issued from the Long Shop on October 5, 1523: *Here begynneth a lytyll new treatse or mater intytuled & called The.ix.Drunkardes* (*STC* 7260).[17] Playing on the established tradition of the Nine Worthies, Bankes's quarto retells a selection of biblical stories and apocrypha illustrated with seventeen unique woodcuts.[18] Featured stories include Noah and the Ark, Cham espying his father's drunken nakedness, Lot and his daughters, Judith beheading Holofernes, the banquet of Absalom, the foolish refusal of Nabal, and Belshazzar's feast with the writing on the wall. Despite its novel illustrations, *The. ix. Drunkardes* likely did not sell particularly well, as Bankes himself never found cause to reprint it, nor did any of his fellow stationers see fit to copy the book. Would-be competitors considering reprinting Bankes's text may have been deterred more by the work's copious illustrations than by the *cum gracia et privilegio* appended to the colophon, since reprinting the illustrations would have required another publisher either to borrow the figures from Bankes or to copy and recut the wood blocks at a considerable expense. By contrast, the "cum priuilegio" declaration on Bankes's twice-printed and unillustrated little *Herball* ably served its purpose, warning off other publishers to wait to reprint the book until after Bankes's seven-year privilege expired. Nonetheless, the simultaneous and quick emergence of new editions after its expiration testifies to the vendibility that early printers saw in this particular work. Once the little *Herball* returned to the public domain, editions soon issued undated from the presses of John Skot, Robert Redman, and Robert Wyer towards the end of the 1530s, and another appeared from the press of Thomas Petyt in 1541. Though bibliographers have sometimes accounted these editions "piracies" (particularly those published by Wyer), these Tudor booksellers were making rational and perfectly legal choices in response to the regulatory and material circumstances in which they produced books. The latest terms of the patent held by the little *Herball*'s first printer would have expired in 1532 or (counting seven years from Bankes's second edition) in 1533, when the text would

---

[17] On Bankes's shop, see E. Gordon Duff, *The Printers, Stationers and Bookbinders of Westminster and London* (1906; New York: Arno Press, 1977), 154.

[18] These woodcuts comprise most of the cuts in Bankes's collection. For a complete list of the cuts with descriptions, see Hodnett, *English Woodcuts*, 395–397.

have returned to the public domain. Skot, Redman, and Wyer were well within their rights to print the text.

The popularity of the little *Herball* may also have had something to do with characteristics of the verbal text itself. Later described by its twentieth-century editors Sanford Larkey and Thomas Pyles as being in manner "quaint, old-fashioned, yet racy and vigorous," the texts offer brief descriptions of plants listed under their Latin names, coupled with details of their virtues or medical import.[19] For the most part, the medical information contained in the pages of the little *Herball* is slight, but the "racy and vigorous" charm that Larkey and Pyles find remarkable can be found in the specific wording of remedies, as in this cure for gout:

> Take the rote of wylde Neppe & the rote of of [*sic*] wylde docke sothen by it selfe & cutte them in thynne pyces & pare a waye the utter rynde and cut them in quarters / than boyle them in clene water ii. or iii houres / than stampe them in a morter as small as thou can / than put therto a quantyte of sote of a chymnaye / than tempre the[m] vp with the mylke of a cowe that the heere is of one coloure / than take the vryne of a man that is fastynge & put thereo & make a playster therof & boyle it and laye it to the sore as hote as the seke maye suffre it / & let it ly styll a day and a nyght / & do so.ix. tymes & thou shall be hole on warantyse, by [the] grace of god.[20]

Some of the little *Herball*'s plant therapies are mystical as well as practical. If *Herba Joannis*, or Saint John's Wort (still prescribed by naturopaths to treat mild depression), is "putte in a mannes howse / there shall come no wycked sprite therin."[21] Other remedies demonstrate evidence more of folk belief than of medicine, such as the recommendation that supplicants carry "veruayne," or verbena, because "they that bere Veruayne vpon the[m] / they shall haue loue and grace of great maysters / & they shall graunte hym his asking / if his askynge be good and ryghtfull."[22] By bearing mother-worte, or mugwort, a man will avoid being grieved by venomous beasts, while he who "frots" his hands with Dragantia "without doubte he may take Adders they shall not venyme hym," but only in the month of May.[23]

---

[19] Larkey and Pyles, *An Herbal*, vii.

[20] *Herball* (1525), sig. I3r. "Take the root of wild nep [catnip] and the root of wild dock seethed [in water] by itself and cut them in thin pieces and pare away the outer rind and cut them in quarters, then boil them in clean water 2 or 3 hours, then stamp them in a mortar as small as thou can, then put thereto a quantity of soot of a chimney, then temper them up with the milk of a cow that the hair is of one color, then take the urine of a man that is fasting and put thereto and make a plaster thereof and boil it and lay it to the sore as hot as the sick [person] may suffer it, and let it lie still a day and a night, and do so 9 times and thou shall be whole on warrantee, by the grace of God." Except where noted, all quotations from the *Herball* are taken from the first edition of 1525.

[21] *Herball* (1525), sig. D2r.   [22] *Herball* (1525), sig. I2v.   [23] *Herball* (1525), sigs. E4r, C2v.

Editions of the Little *Herball* Post Bankes

Because many of the editions of the little *Herball* printed by other publishers did not include dates in their imprints, providing a precise sequence
of editions that allows a scholar to determine with certainty who copied
whom is difficult. Though Blanche Henrey speculates that Robert Wyer
was the first printer to copy the little *Herball* the year after Bankes's seven-
year royal privilege would have expired, in the revised *Short-Title Catalogue*
(*STC*) Katharine Pantzer gives Wyer's edition a queried date of 1543,
positioning printer John Skot as the little *Herball*'s first copyist sometime
around 1537.[24]

   Little is known about Skot, whose career, based on colophon evidence,
spanned the period 1521 to 1537. He rarely dated his works and often failed
even to append his name to his books. In his early career, he lived in
St. Sepulchre without Newgate parish before moving, sometime before
1528, to St. Paul's Churchyard. Present at Tunstall's second meeting with
the booksellers in October 1526, Skot was a hesitant printer-publisher,
choosing to supplement the profits he made printing his own publications
by also printing works for others. Early in his career, Skot sometimes
printed for Wynkyn de Worde, presumably when the house of Caxton's
former assistant was too busy with other publications and wanted to rush
into print an edition of a work like the second edition of *Here begynneth
a treatyse of this galaunt with the maryage of the bosse of Byllyngesgate. vnto
London stone* (1521?; *STC* 24242).[25] Skot printed his edition of *A boke of the
propertyes of herbes the which is called an Herball* for himself, issued undated
from his last recorded address, Foster Lane in St. Leonard's parish. Having
already been twice-printed by Bankes, it was reasonable for Skot to have
assumed that the little *Herball* posed no ecclesiastical hazard and, once
Bankes's privilege expired, could easily be copied and sold throughout
London without fear of ecclesiastical or chancery reprisal. Such concern
with penal appropriation may have been rather important to Skot's
decision-making, as he, like many of his contemporaries, had recently
run afoul of Thomas Cromwell. Skot had been one of the publishers of
a work about Elizabeth Barton, the Maid of Kent, who was notorious for

---

[24] The date of 1535 that Henrey provided for *STC* 13175.8C is far too early (*British Botanical*, 1:249);
both Pantzer and Wyer bibliographer Prudence Tracy confirm that Wyer's book was printed circa
1543, with *STC* 13175.6 printed first, likely around 1540. In his reevaluation of Tracy's work, Peter
W. M. Blayney pushes this date back slightly, to 1544 (Blayney, *Printers of London*, 1046).

[25] Peter W. M. Blayney has privately suggested to me that de Worde may have "farmed out" these early
works to Skot to help him get started, as he had done with his former apprentices Robert Copland
and John Byddell.

having opposed Henry VIII's divorce from Catherine of Aragon and was convicted of treason.[26] After 1537, Skot disappears from the records of early English printing.

Scholars have been preoccupied with accounts of piratical activity in the publication history of the little *Herball* in part because of Bankes's fellow stationer Robert Redman, whose aggressive and often illegal behaviors towards Richard Pynson and other booksellers left behind a number of records. Listed as being another attendant at Tunstall's October 1526 meeting, Redman printed his own edition of the little *Herball* from his shop at the sign of "The George" (St. George) in Fleet Street in or around 1539. Like Bankes, Redman had begun his career in 1523, when he set up his first shop in St. Clement's parish just outside of Temple Bar and began to produce copies of works printed by Richard Pynson, then both the King's Printer and the Printer for the City of London. Pynson, a native of Normandy, had paid a fee to join the Stationers sometime before 1500. After that, Pynson was technically a citizen of the City of London and was able to practice his trade within the City limits, so in 1500 he moved his shop at the sign of the George from St. Clement Danes parish in Middlesex to just inside Temple Bar in St. Dunstan's parish. By copying Pynson's sign and address from his very beginnings, Redman seems to have deliberately targeted Pynson's career as a model for his own, and his copying of Pynson's books was so overt that Pynson began to issue attacks on this "Rude-man" in his addresses to the reader.[27] When Pynson died in 1530,

---

[26] Duff, *Printers, Stationers and Bookbinders*, 151. Elizabeth Barton (*c.*1506–1534), also known as the Maid or Nun of Kent, was a Benedictine nun and visionary who gained her ability to prophesy after a protracted illness. Her miraculous recovery, which reportedly occurred during Lent 1526, was itemized in a no-longer extant work possibly entitled "A marveilous woorke of late done at Courte of Streete in Kent" that had been produced at Skot's press. Though her Catholicism was originally praised and supported by the crown, Barton publicly opposed Henry's divorce from Catherine of Aragon and she was convicted of high treason and executed on April 24, 1534. According to Diane Watt's entry on Barton in the *ODNB*, "[t]he act of attainder called upon the public to surrender any books, scrolls or other writings about [Barton's] revelations and miracles attributed to Barton and her adherents, on pain of imprisonment and the imposition of a fine." As Skot was resident in St. Sepulchre's parish of London in 1526, the same time that Barton was a nun in the Canterbury St. Sepulchre's priory, it is possible that some affiliation or loyalty to her cause motivated his surreptitious printing of an account of Barton's good works shortly after her execution. See Diane Watt, "Barton, Elizabeth (*c.*1506–1534)," *ODNB*.

[27] The attack appears in Latin in *STC* 15726, Pynson's edition of *Lytylton tenures newly and moost truly correctyd & amendyd* of 1525. Presumably Redman had copied *Leteltun tenuris new correct* issued by Pynson in 1522, but the earliest Redman edition still extant dates from 1528. None of the *Early English Books Online* copies display the preliminaries, and I am unable to verify the location of Pynson's attack, which is translated and paraphrased at length (but with no citation) by Duff in *Printers, Stationers and Bookbinders*, 178.

Redman moved shops, taking over Pynson's inside Temple Bar in St. Dunstan's, where he remained until his own death in 1540.

Redman's piratical activities were not limited to his attacks on the lawful material of Richard Pynson. Shortly after Pynson's death, Redman was ordered in 1533 not to sell copies of his edition of Christopher St. Germain's *The Division of the Spirituality and Temporalty*, the rights of which had been granted to Thomas Berthelet, who had succeeded Pynson as King's Printer. Berthelet had issued his edition of *The Division of the Spirituality and Temporalty (STC* 21587) *cum privilegio* in 1532, and an illegal edition pirated by Redman had appeared around the same time. The Star Chamber forbade Redman to sell his copies of the work and barred him from reissuing it or any other book that had been printed with the king's privilege, binding him with the threat of a 500-mark penalty.[28]

Bankes's own dealings with Redman seem not to have differed greatly from those of Pynson and Berthelet. In 1540, when he was brought before the Privy Council to account for printing a series of broadsides alternately condemning and defending Thomas Cromwell, Bankes blamed the late Redman, along with Richard Grafton (who later confessed his part in the publications), with deliberately falsifying Bankes's imprint.[29] The Council found both the authors of the broadsides, Thomas Smyth and William Gray, and the publisher Grafton guilty of sedition and sentenced all three to a prison term in the Fleet.[30] Here again, as early as the reign of Henry VIII in England, the "penal appropriation" that Foucault asserts is crucial to the "author-function" was linked as much to stationers as to authors, to the practical distribution of textual materials as well as their imaginative origins. By virtue of their ability to make information public, the bookselling publishers, those agents who initiated the production and oversaw the distribution of printed books, were seen by civic and royal authorities as being just as responsible as authors. Conversely, such punitive measures made previously circulated and uncontroversial works in print or manuscript more attractive for would-be publishers because they had already been publicly tested and had not found controversy.

---

[28] Duff, *Printers, Stationers and Bookbinders*, 132. See also Blayney, *Printers of London*, 257–258.

[29] Duff, *Printers, Stationers and Bookbinders*, 154–155; see also Duff, *Century*, 8.

[30] Such a confession and imprisonment may have ultimately proved fortuitous for Grafton, who had received Cromwell's patronage throughout his career. When Henry VIII began to feel regret for Cromwell's execution, the king granted Grafton a letters patent for the publication of service books. By 1545, Grafton was printer for the house of Prince Edward, and he was appointed King's Printer upon Edward's ascension in 1547, ousting Thomas Berthelet from what had previously been a privilege held for life. On Grafton, see Meraud Grant Ferguson, "Grafton, Richard (*c.*1511–1573)," *ODNB*.

Redman's explicit acts of violation of others' privileged texts do not necessarily mean that all of his activities should be seen as suspicious or that his behaviors were always objectionable. Like that of his contemporary Richard Bankes, Redman's extant output demonstrates that he had an especially keen eye for books that were likely to sell well, and he exploited the market to his advantage. All bibliographers have agreed that Redman's undated edition of the little *Herball* appeared after Bankes's privilege for the book had expired, when the work was once again a part of the public domain. Early reprints of the little *Herball* by other stationers thus are testimony not to criminality but to the marketability that savvy sixteenth-century publishers saw in this particular text. Redman's edition was later copied and reprinted by his widow Elizabeth and by her successors in the shop at the George, William Middleton and William Powell.[31]

One of Redman's final projects before he died was printing Thomas Berthelet's 1540 edition of the Great Bible (*STC* 2069) with Thomas Petyt.[32] Petyt had been hired by Berthelet to print editions of the New Testament twice in the previous year, and Redman's shop may have been contracted for the 1540 edition because Petyt's shop in St. Paul's Churchyard at the sign of the Maiden's Head was already working at maximum capacity. Petyt issued his own *A boke of the propertyes of herbes the whiche is called an Harbal* in an edition dated 1541, using Elizabeth Redman's edition as his copy-text. A group of other stationers thereafter took turns reprinting their own editions of the work until a new means of establishing a text's value emerged in 1557: the title was finally licensed and entered into the Stationers' Registers by John King in late 1560 or early 1561.

By 1541, then, the work that most scholars know as "Bankes's Herball" existed in seven distinct editions: two printed by Richard Bankes dated 1525 and 1526 and one each from the presses of John Skot (1537?), Robert Redman (1539?), Robert Wyer (1539?), Elizabeth Redman (1540?), and Thomas Petyt (1541). Such intensive publication of a single, popular title raises numerous questions: Why did the late 1530s and early 1540s create such a run on this particular book? If the little *Herball* was such a lucrative text with Tudor readers that four other publishers would seek to capitalize

---

[31] Although those who entered the Stationers' Company via patrimony and through apprenticeship were men, Stationer widows regularly printed and published after the death of their husbands. See Sarah Neville, "Female Stationers and Their 'Second-Plus' Husbands," in Valerie Wayne (ed.), *Women's Labour and the History of the Book in Early Modern England* (London: Bloomsbury, 2020), 75–93.

[32] Redman's will was dated October 21, 1540, and it was proved November 4 of the same year.

on its popularity, why did Bankes only reprint the work once before his privilege expired? The circumstances surrounding early attempts to control the book trade may provide some explanation.

With the exception of Elizabeth Pickering Redman (whose printing house was represented by the attendance of her husband Robert), all five printers had been present at Tunstall's meeting of October 25, 1526. Shortly thereafter, the same group began to print a selection of octavos on popular topics, seemingly "copying" each other's works; in addition to the *Herball*, Bankes's *The Seeing of Urines* (1525–6; *STC* 22153) and *Here beginneth a good boke of medicines intytulyed or callyd the treasure of pore men* (1526; *STC* 24199)[33] appeared from the Redman and Wyer presses, while Wyer's edition of Thomas Moulton's *This is the myrour or glass of helthe, necessary and nedefull*, printed earlier than 1531 (*STC* 18214), was variously reprinted both by the Redmans and by their successors at the George, as well as by Thomas Petyt and Robert Copland.[34]

As these octavo publications occur shortly after Tunstall's meeting that highlighted the dangers of unapproved texts, the concurrence of a small group of limited privilege-holding printer-publishers issuing the same short works en masse raises a variety of questions. Did these publishers, seeking to attract English readers to the variety of information available in the new medium, issue these works as part of a larger series? Was such copying between publishers the result of a fear of ecclesiastical reprisal in a turbulent age? Many miscellaneous bound collections were broken up by nineteenth-century book collectors, but Crynes 873, a composite octavo volume held at the Bodleian Library, Oxford, provides an indication of the ways that book buyers approached these texts as a group. The bound volume features the single surviving copy of Thomas Petyt's edition of the little *Herball* alongside Petyt's 1540 edition of *Medicines* (*STC* 24202) and his 1545 *Glass of Health* (*STC* 18225.4). It also includes editions of John Gough's *Regiment or Dietary of Health* (*STC* 3378.5, printed by Wyer) and Elizabeth Pickering Redman's 1541 edition of *Seeing of Urines* (*STC* 22155). While the Crynes 873 volume might suggest that such often-reprinted works all had a health-related theme, the stationers' recursive reprinting of

---

[33] The assumed interrelationship between these books is also directly evident in the works themselves, as the text of *The Synge of Uryns* ends with "All they that desyre to haue knowlege of Medycynes for all suche Uryns as be before in this boke go ye to the Herball in Englysshe / or to the boke of medycynes /and there you shall fynde all suche Medycynes that be most profytable for man" (Bankes 1525, sig. H3v).

[34] The *STC* records Wyer as publishing four editions of the text prior to Robert Redman's edition of 1540.

legal works – such as Anthony Fitzherbert's *The newe boke of iustices of the peas* (1538; *STC* 10969), translated from the French and originally printed by Robert Redman, or his *Offices of sheryffes, bailliffes [and]coroners* (1538; *STC* 10984) – suggests that the driving similarity may have been more broadly practical: small reference books with a high use value rather than books around a particular subject. Unfortunately, the rebinding habits of nineteenth-century book collectors make it difficult to do more than speculate. What such convergences in publication history do offer, however, is a cogent caveat to the inclination of print historians to see each new issue of a printed work as necessarily in competition with its precursors. Especially in an era preceding the Stationers' Company's control over the English book trade, booksellers occasionally worked together to increase consumer demand for their products, and Crynes 873 demonstrates that that form of collaboration could be recognized by readers and book purchasers.[35]

There is also a material feature of the first edition of the little *Herball* that is worth further attention. Bankes appears for the first time in any extant records in the lay subsidy rolls of 1523, where he is described as a bookbinder, a detail that informed his approach to both printing and marketing his editions of the book.[36] Like many of the English books printed in the early decades of the sixteenth century, Bankes's edition of the little *Herball* lacks both pagination and catchwords, leaving only the signatures that appear beneath the text in the right-hand corner of the first three recto pages of each quire to instruct a binder in the correct way to assemble the little *Herball*'s pages. In both the 1525 and the 1526 herbals, however, Bankes has set the abbreviated word "Her." in the gutter opposite the signature, signifying that the quarto pages marked with each signature refer to his book's title. If the little *Herball* was printed to be bound alone, Bankes's use of this abbreviated title in the signature line would serve no purpose; however, if Bankes conceived of his little *Herball* as part of a series of quartos designed to be sold and bound together, a bookbinder would need to be able to distinguish the individual quires of the little *Herball* from those of another book in order to avoid mis-sewing. Two other contemporaneous Bankes publications share this signature-line title feature: *Here begynneth the seynge of uryns*, dated May 28, 1525, (*STC* 22153,

---

[35] In her examination of the logistics of various publishers independently printing quarto works of Seneca under the same ordinal rubric, Tara L. Lyons sees evidence of a similar overarching codependence at work in London in the 1550s and 1560s (private communication).

[36] E. Gordon Duff, "Notes on Stationers from the Lay Subsidy Rolls of 1523–4," *The Library* Series 2, 35 (1908): 257–266; 258.

with a signature-line title of "Seyng of wa.") and *Here begynneth a new boke of medecynes intytulyd or callyd the treasure of pore men* (*STC* 24199, with a signature-line title of "Me."), printed in or around 1526. Both books were printed for Bankes by John Rastell. Later in the 1530s, editions of *The Seynge of Uryns* came from the presses of Robert Wyer, as well as Robert and Elizabeth Redman and their successors at the George. Many of the same stationers also reprinted *A New Boke of Medecynes*. It was not just Bankes, then, but his fellow Tudor booksellers who conceived of the little *Herball* as one in a series of short informative volumes that could be bound with others. The material form of the little *Herball* first printed by Richard Bankes, along with its capacity to be linked with other, related texts, was thus a fundamental part of its popularity with Tudor readers.

Robert Wyer and His Readers

Like his contemporary Robert Redman, Robert Wyer is often credited as being a notorious pirate of other printers' copy, but in the context of the English book trade prior to 1557, his three editions of Bankes's *Herball* were perfectly legitimate. Though by the time Wyer started printing in 1529 London had had several foreign-born printers, he was the only citizen printer active at the time who was not a member of the Stationers' Company. Wyer was free of the Salters' Company (which ranked ninth in London's "Great Twelve" livery companies from which the mayor was selected), a position that gave him considerable protection. As a bookseller, City custom decreed that Wyer had to obey the policies and standards of the Stationers' Company; however, until 1557 the Stationers' Company did not have authority over printing. What this meant was that, as a printer, Wyer had no specific governing customs and could do almost anything he wanted. What Wyer clearly wanted to do was print and wholesale as many books as possible; over the course of his career between 1529 and 1556, he published at least 140 items, many of which were reprints of works that had already established themselves in the marketplace. Yet Wyer was also willing to risk his capital on new works: of the 140 works he printed for himself, 74 titles were first editions. His biographer notes that he preferred to publish "small octavos dealing with subjects of a popular nature, and therefore readily saleable."[37] Such a prolific output, which included works that had been first printed by others, has sometimes led scholars to view Wyer as a pirate of other stationers' copy. In moralizing the legality of their subjects' activities,

---

[37] Henry R. Plomer, *Robert Wyer, Printer and Bookseller* (London: Bibliographical Society, 1897), 11.

narratives of the book trade sometimes miss the fact that stationers who copied others' books were simply well-attuned to the best means of making money, and not all of these means of copying were necessarily illegal.

Wyer's enthusiasm for popular books, coupled with his rather sloppy output (as bibliographer P. B. Tracy notes of Wyer's copies, "founts are used to death, re-castings are of poor quality, presswork is uneven"), has led to accounts of his career as a printer and publisher that echo the derisive attitudes scholars have expressed about "rogue" herbalist John Gerard.[38] In an article titled "Some Rogueries of Robert Wyer," H. B. Lathrop accuses him of publishing "dingy octavos" for the "uneducated" multitudes,[39] while Francis L. Johnson subjects Wyer to a more direct attack:

> Robert Wyer's methods of obtaining the copy for his handbooks stands revealed to the full measure of its unapologetic knavery. Neither the hiring of competent authors and translators nor respect for the rights of his fellow printers had any place in his system.[40]

Johnson supposes that Wyer's reprinting Bankes's *Herball* in a trio of modified editions is sufficient evidence to label him a "knave," but, given the willingness of other printers to enter into business relationships with Wyer, the animosity modern scholars surmise that early printers felt for his supposedly illicit trade practices is overstated. Everything Wyer was doing was completely legal within the terms of early Tudor printing and bookselling. That Bankes himself believed his privilege for the little *Herball* expired in the mid-1530s is confirmed by Bankes having hired Wyer to print for him after Bankes abandoned his own press at the Long Shop.[41] Neither Wyer's inferior press nor his supposed knavery was enough to prevent his colleagues in the book trade from entrusting him to manufacture their products.

As I suggested in the Introduction, the editions of the little *Herball* published by John Skot, Robert Redman, Elizabeth Pickering Redman, and Thomas Petyt have few variations between them. Wyer's reprints of the little *Herball* followed an entirely different approach,[42] one that has not

---

[38] P. B. Tracy, "Robert Wyer: A Brief Analysis of His Types and a Suggested Chronology for the Output of his Press," *The Library* 6th series, 2 (1980), 293–303; 293.

[39] H. B. Lathrop, "Some Rogueries of Robert Wyer," *The Library* 3rd series, 5 (1914), 349–364; 349.

[40] Francis R. Johnson, "*A New Herball of Macer* and Bankes's *Herball*: Notes on Robert Wyer and the Printing of Cheap Handbooks of Science in the Sixteenth Century," *Bulletin of the History of Medicine* 15 (1944): 246–260; 249.

[41] Bankes's last publication at the Long Shop address is dated 1528. He hired Wyer to print for him once in 1540 (STC 18052), four times in 1542 (STC 9343.7; 12047; 12468; and 24601), and twice in 1545 (STC 439.5; and 9343.8, though STC suggests this last title may be a false imprint).

[42] Skot and the Redmans were members of the Stationers; though the custom of the City mandated that Petyt be governed by the Stationers' trade practices, he was actually a Draper.

endeared him to history. In a detailed analysis of the differences between Wyer's three editions of the little *Herball* and Bankes's two, Johnson suggests that Wyer's changes were part of a fundamentally dishonest approach to bookmaking and bookselling. Johnson maintains that Wyer edited and reorganized the text of the little *Herball* in order to deliberately "gloss over his theft," which was supposedly intended to thwart any attempt by Bankes to "obtain redress" for Wyer's usurpation of his royal privilege.[43] Yet Johnson's argument is muted by his misunderstanding both the nature and the terms of Bankes's privilege. Once that knowledge is returned to the equation, Wyer's status as a rogue pirate dissolves. Wyer had no offense to mask because there was no offense committed.

When Wyer reprinted the little *Herball*, he chose to identify the work not with the title favored by most of its earlier printers, *Boke of the propertyes of herbes the which is called an Herball*,[44] but as *Hereafter foloweth the knowledge, properties, and the virtues of herbes (STC 13175.6)*.[45] Because he was working from the assumption that "enterprising" printers like Wyer engaged in outright piracy, Johnson makes several unqualified assertions about book production in an era preceding the regulatory effects of the Stationers' Company Registers and licensing system:

> by changing the title of the work and making a few minor alterations in the arrangement and wording of the text, the injured party, notwithstanding his royal privilege, would find it very difficult to obtain redress. The pirate need only maintain that his was a new book; then the Renaissance approval of free literary borrowing would force the complainant to rest his case on the debatable distinction between outright plagiarism and an unskillful, but not reprehensible, imitation.[46]

[43] Johnson, "*New Herball of Macer*," 248.

[44] *Boke of the propertyes of herbes the which is called an Herball* was used for the work not only by the Redmans, Petyt, and Skot but also by William Middleton (1546; *STC* 13175.10), Robert Copland (1547; *STC* 13175.11), and John Walley (1548; *STC* 13175.12).

[45] The record for *STC* 13175.6 gives the text a date of 1540, supported by Tracy's typographic analysis of Wyer's books, which dates this work between 1539 and 1542 ("Robert Wyer," 299). Blayney further refines this date to a speculative 1541 (*Printers of London*, 1046). In 1975, Henrey suggested that Wyer's first edition of the little *Herball* was *STC* 13175.8c, which she had dated 1535; during the revision of the *STC*, Henrey's date for 13175.8c was corrected to a queried circa date of 1543, confirmed by Tracy (see Henrey, *British Botanical*, 1:13; Tracy "Robert Wyer," 299–300). In *Herbal*, the editors Larkey and Pyles suggest that Wyer's undated works appeared in the reverse order than the one presented here, illogically suggesting that Wyer *removed* the Linacre and Macer information from his title pages as he put the work through three editions.

[46] Johnson, "*A New Herball of Macer*," 247–248. Johnson's critical arguments about piracy in 1944 appear to reflect the influence of A. W. Pollard's account of Shakespeare's "bad quartos" in *Shakespeare's Fight with the Pirates and the Problems of the Transmission of his Texts* (London: Alexander Moring, 1917). Though Peter W. M. Blayney's measured responses to Pollard ("The Publication of Playbooks" and an unpublished paper, "Shakespeare's Fight with *What* Pirates?"

Johnson's account of Wyer's production of the *Herball* is curiously inconsistent with his scholarly treatment of its other editions after Bankes. Though he notes that the largest group of these herbals (which includes the Redmans, Skot, and Copland editions) are essentially "page for page reprint[s]" of each other, Johnson nonetheless singles out Wyer's editions as emblematic of printing villainy.[47] Yet none of these three post-Bankes editions of the *Herball* had any more or less legal right to the title than Wyer himself did in 1539. The first change in Bankes's title came from Skot, not from Wyer. Johnson's illogical claim that Wyer's alteration of Bankes's text was the "easiest and least expensive way of obtaining the text for a new herbal" is an argument that strains against both the systems of privilege at work in the period and the work's extant publication history. For a sixteenth-century publisher like Wyer (as for the Redmans, Skot, Copland, and everyone else who followed Bankes, up to and including John King), by far the easiest way to obtain the text of an English herbal was simply to reprint something that had already been printed and that was no longer protected by an earlier privilege.[48] In 1539, Wyer could have legally printed Bankes's *Herball* verbatim, but he chose not to do so. By changing the title of the work and by reorganizing the text of the *Herball* to improve its functionality for readers (which served no regulatory or nefarious purpose), Wyer's alterations demonstrated not his roguery but his capacity for textual innovation.

Johnson supports his view of Wyer's "unapologetic knavery" by itemizing other examples of where the printer "extracted," "altered," "corrected," "augmented," "abridged," "compiled," or "paraphrased" – all activities that Johnson believes should be undertaken only by "competent authors and translators."[49] Though a selective collation, Johnson demonstrates that Wyer's edition of the *Herball* introduced substantive changes in Bankes's text by subtracting 27 of Bankes's 207 chapters and adding 3 others, as well as by altering the wording of those chapters that he did include. Johnson surmises that, in order to create his edition, Wyer

---

delivered at the Folger Shakespeare Library on May 11, 1987) have done much to mitigate the playbook piracy debate, critical exaggerations of the prevalence of illicit book-dealing in sixteenth-century England are still widespread, as evinced in Johns's *The Nature of the Book*.

47 Johnson, "*New Herball of Macer*," 246.

48 Johnson, "*New Herball of Macer*," 248. Though he has not seen them, Johnson acknowledges the existence of the Redmans, Skot, and Copland editions, but he seems to be under the impression that, because they are all copied from Robert Redman's edition, they are somehow less problematic than Wyer's eclectic text ("*A New Herball of Macer*," 258).

49 Johnson, "*New Herball of Macer*," 249.

himself, or some hack writer in his employ, goes through Bankes's *Herball*, revising it, with the object of bringing it out under Wyer's imprint. He adds supplementary material now and then from other sources ... he omits sections that prove too difficult or seem of minor importance. When the text seems to him faulty or obscure, he makes a crude attempt to correct it ... when a casual reference to these works fails to solve a problem, he makes a clumsy guess, and since he has no knowledge of botany to aid him in his task, his corrections, though they often replace an obsolete term with a seemingly familiar one, usually leave the meaning of the passage as obscure as it was before.[50]

To make a case, a prosecution must establish motive, and Johnson incorrectly surmises that Wyer made alterations to the *Herball* primarily to "make a crude attempt at covering up his tracks" while violating Bankes's privilege.[51] Yet in his desire to vilify Wyer, Johnson also makes an egregious claim about Wyer's (or his compiler's) lack of botanical knowledge. In doing so, he judges its botany by later standards, anachronistically turning to the evidence of later printed works such as William Turner's herbal of 1568, Henry Lyte's translation of Dodoens (1578), John Gerard's *Herball, or Historie of Plants* (1597), and John Parkinson's *Theatrum botanicum* (1640). Unsurprisingly, Wyer's short compilation is unable to demonstrate the detail of many of these celebrated folio texts. Wyer should have, Johnson argues, been more careful in his consultation of contemporary English works like *De proprietatibus rerum* (de Worde, 1495; Berthelet, 1535) or *The Grete Herbal* (Treveris, 1526, 1529), because "these books and manuscripts would in most cases have sufficed for his task had he been a conscientious and intelligent workman. As it was, they only abetted his ignorance, so that his text as a rule merely introduced new errors in place of old confusion."[52]

Johnson characterizes Wyer's use of compilation, his cross-referencing between various source texts, and his smoothing of elements that may prove confusing to his customers as "typical of Wyer's notorious system of compiling popular handbooks by appropriating as much as he found useful of other men's works and disguising them as his own."[53] That such behavior seems to be perfectly in keeping with the "Renaissance approval of free literary borrowing" that Johnson elsewhere asserts exists does not

---

[50] Johnson, "*New Herball of Macer*," 252.   [51] Johnson, "*New Herball of Macer*," 254.

[52] Johnson, "*New Herball of Macer*," 255. Because botanical and medical historians differ in the value they place upon the various types of information that herbals rightly contain, they also disagree about what constitutes a "better" text. Agnes Arber, for example, finds the little *Herball* to be superior to *The Grete Herball* specifically because the latter spends too much time on remedies (*Herbals*, 41) – which is exactly the opposite of Johnson's complaint about it.

[53] Johnson, "*New Herball of Macer*," 257.

dissuade him from calling Wyer's herbal "a clumsy revision and augmentation of Bankes's text, made with the intent of misleading the prospective purchaser."[54] Johnson does not appear to know that the revising and augmenting that Wyer does to the *Herball* is a considerable effort, one that, given the expiration of Bankes's original privilege, was also completely unnecessary to justify his activities with the text. After Bankes's privilege expired, Wyer was in no more danger from Bankes's royally sanctioned claim to the title than was Skot, Petyt, or Redman. Further, as the holder of his own royal privilege for books he'd created, if Wyer could have demonstrated to the king's council that he had spent money in creating his new adaptation of the *Herball*, he could have claimed protection for it – but he didn't.[55]

Wyer was one of many early English printer-publishers who recognized that the increased availability of printed texts shifted contemporary debates about experimental knowledge making, and his changes to the text demonstrate Wyer's investment in making the *Herball* more appealing to contemporary readers. In retitling the herbal *Hereafter foloweth the knowledge, properties, and the virtues of herbes*, Wyer ignored the stress on its status as a "boke" that other publishers were eager to emphasize in favor of an account of the text's "knowledge" or use value. The *OED* offers a fifteenth-century use of "knowledge" specifically denoting "the fact or condition of being instructed, or of having information acquired by study or research" (n.11). Just such a usage of the word appears in a popular work first printed by Caxton in 1477 that was reprinted in 1528, one that seems to have accorded with Wyer's similar handling of the term in 1539: "Knowlege is better than ignoraunce."[56] Wyer's addition to Bankes's title thus served to illustrate the effort that the printer put into producing the text of his new volume by adding supplementary material available in other manuscript and printed works. As Martha Driver notes in an article on Wyer's printing of Christine de Pisan's *The. C. Hystoryes of Troye* (an edition that is sometimes accused of "suppressing" de Pisan's authorship because of Wyer's anti-feminist agenda), "in the first hundred years of printing, the printer, the new maker, superseded the author, in the transmission of texts, similar to the way Hollywood overwrites literary authors today."[57] Driver's

[54] Johnson, *"New Herball of Macer,"* 258.
[55] I'm grateful to Peter W. M. Blayney for making this suggestion.
[56] Found in Earl Anthony Wydeville Rivers, *The dictes or sayenges of the philosophres* (Caxton, 1477, 1480, 1489; de Worde, 1528).
[57] Martha Driver, "Christine de Pisan and Robert Wyer: *The C. Hystoryes of Troye, or L'Epistre d'Othea Englished,*" *Gutenberg-Jahrbuch* 72 (1997): 125–139; 139.

account of Wyer and his contemporaries' "active self-promotion" easily explains Wyer's motivations in changing the title of Bankes's text to emphasize the "fact or condition of having information acquired by study or research." The changes that Wyer makes to the *Herball* suggest that there may be something more than the usual custom in Wyer's deliberate emphasis on his role as the maker of this particular book, which had been "Imprynted *by me* Robert Wyer."[58] Wyer's colophon simultaneously highlights his work as a publisher and printer as well as his labor in reorganizing and supplementing the work through activities that we now chiefly associate with authors and editors.

Even if in 1541 Wyer's original intent was to "deceive" potential customers with the uniqueness of *Hereafter foloweth the knowledge, properties, and the virtues of herbes*, the similarities between it and the products of other publishers may still have been too obvious to early modern readers to convince them that it was in fact a different version of the work, and in 1544, Wyer determined to reprint his text under a completely different scheme. Wyer's second edition of the work was published as *A newe herball of Macer, translated out of Laten into Englysshe* (*STC* 13175.8c)[59] and sought to capitalize on booksellers' familiarity with a medieval manuscript poem on plants known as the "Macer Floridus," often erroneously attributed to the classical poet Aemilius Macer (Figure 4.1).[60] Wyer's addition of Macer's name was wholly spurious and designed as an advertising feature – there was nothing added of Aemilius Macer or Macer Floridus that could justify the new title page claim. The improvements to Wyer's new edition did not end with the title, however; he also supplied an important new textual affordance that shows Wyer's understanding of the way readers engaged with such little books. Wyer added marginal notations alongside the body of his text, highlighting key words for readers scanning to locate plants appropriate to various ailments (Figure 4.2).

In the period before indexes were regularly keyed to either pagination or foliation, such marginal notations meant that readers searching for remedies for "wormes" or a means by which to "delyuereth a woman of a dead childe" needed only to scrutinize the margins of a herbal's pages. Wyer's *New Herbal of Macer* of 1544 was the first English herbal to recognize that such an edifying compendium might better serve its readers if it were

---

[58] Emphasis added. See also Larkey and Pyles, *An Herbal*, xv–xviii.
[59] On the revised date, see Blayney, *Printers of London*, 1046.
[60] An edition of *De viribus herbarum* (which was actually authored by the medieval French physician Odo Magdunensis) was published in Naples in 1477 (Henrey, *British Botanical*, 1:13; Arber, *Herbals*, 40).

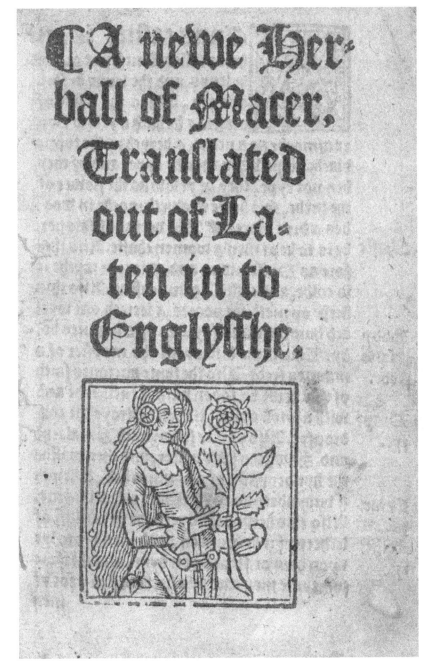

Figure 4.1 *A newe Herball of Macer* (Robert Wyer, 1544), sig. A1r. By courtesy of the Department of Special Collections, Memorial Library, University of Wisconsin–Madison (Thordarson T 2122).

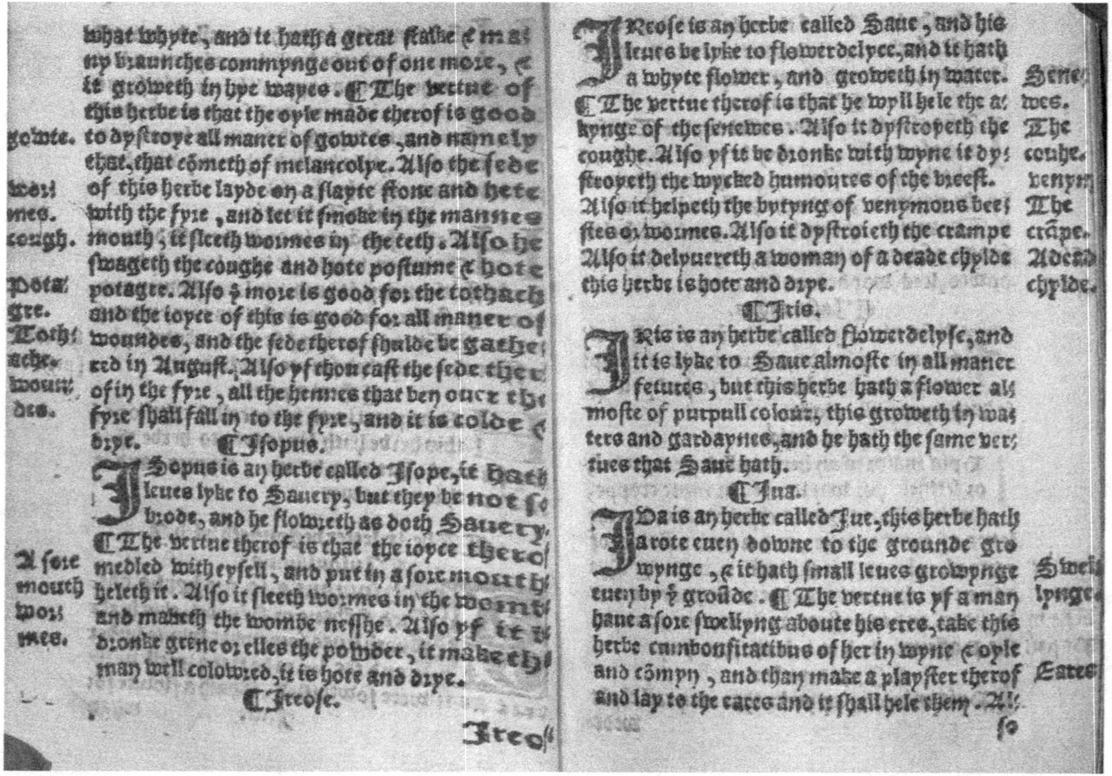
what whyte, and it hath a great stalke & ma-
ny braunches commynge out of one rote, &
it groweth in hye wayes. ¶ The vertue of
this herbe is that the oyle made therof is good
to dystroye all maner of gowtes, and namely gowte.
that, that cometh of melancolye. Also the sede
of this herbe layde on a slatte stone and hete Wor-
with the fyre, and let it smoke in the mannes mes.
mouth; it sleeth wormes in the teth. Also he cough.
swageth the coughe and hote postume & hote
potagre. Also ye rote is good for the tothache Pota-
and the iuyce of this is good for all maner of gre.
woundes, and the sede therof shulde be gathe- Toth-
red in August. Also yf thou cast the sede ther- ache.
of in the fyre, all the hennes that ben over the Woun-
fyre shall fall in to the fyre, and it is colde & des.
drye.

¶ Isopus.

Isopus is an herbe called Isope, it hath
leues lyke to Sauery, but they be not so
brode, and he floryssheth as doth Sauery.
¶ The vertue therof is that the iuyce therof
medled with eysell, and put in a sore mouth A sore mouth
heleth it. Also it sleeth wormes in the wombe Wor-
and maketh the wombe nesshe. Also yf it be mes.
dronke grene or elles the powder, it maketh
man well colowred, it is hote and drye.

¶ Ireos.

Ireos

Ireose is an herbe called Saue, and his
leues be lyke to flowerdelyce, and it hath
a whyte flower, and groweth in water. Sene-
¶ The vertue therof is that he wyll hele the a- wes.
kynge of the senewes. Also it dystroyeth the The
coughe. Also yf it be dronke with wyne it dys- coughe.
troyeth the wycked humoures of the brest. Venym.
Also it helpeth the bytyng of venymous bees- The
tes or wormes. Also it dystroieth the crampe crampe.
Also it delyuereth a woman of a deade chylde A dead
this herbe is hote and drye. chylde.

¶ Iris.

Iris is an herbe called flowerdelyse, and
it is lyke to Saue almoste in all maner
fetures, but this herbe hath a flower almoste of purpull colour, this groweth in waters and gardaynes, and he hath the same vertues that Saue hath.

¶ Iua.

Iua is an herbe called Iue, this herbe hath
a rote euen downe to the grounde growynge, & it hath small leues growynge Swel-
euen by ye grounde. ¶ The vertue is yf a man lynge.
haue a sore swellyng aboute his eres, take this
herbe cumbonsitatibus of her in wyne & oyle
and comyn, and than make a playster therof Eares.
and lay to the eares and it shall hele them. Also

Figure 4.2 *A newe Herball of Macer* (Robert Wyer, 1544), sigs. F3v–F4r. By courtesy of the Department of Special Collections, Memorial Library, University of Wisconsin–Madison (Thordarson T 2122).

accompanied by organizational markers in the margins that could quickly point readers towards the information they sought. Wyer's innovation has hitherto gone unnoticed by those seeking to vilify Wyer's contributions to the herbal genre.[61] Except for its new title and these marginal annotations, the 1544 work was otherwise a reprint of Wyer's 1539 edition.

Wyer may have gotten the idea for his Macer marketing ploy from the misprint in the title of Bankes's second edition of the text, which contained the error *marer* for *mater* in *Here bygynnyth a newe mater* (Figure 4.3). Such an error may have been the result either of poor composition (it was certainly an error in proof correction) or of an incorrectly distributed piece of type caused by a compositor's misreading. If the lay of Bankes's type case was anything similar to that illustrated in Joseph Moxon's *Mechanick Exercises on the Whole Art of Printing*, in which the *t* and *r* sorts are at sufficient distance from each other that a compositor's grabbing one for the other by mistake seems unlikely, the error likely resulted from a compositor's error of the type as he redistributed it.[62] However the error occurred, it provided a suggestive opportunity. In the black letter typeface used throughout Bankes's *Herball*, a lowercase *r* looks similar to a lowercase *c*. Wyer's initial misreading of a copy of the 1526 Bankes may have ultimately proved fortuitous.

Wyer's *New Herbal of Macer* was at least somewhat successful with customers, as he reprinted the text as *Macers Herbal* again in 1552 (*STC* 13175.13c), this time so confident in his marketing ploy that he splashed the title of his work across the running head of each page (Figure 4.4). In addition to Macer, Wyer seems to have wanted his book to advertise an endorsement from a more local authority; on his 1550 title page, he added that *Macers Herbal* is presented as "practysd by Dr Lynacro," or Thomas Linacre, founder of the Royal College of Physicians of London in 1518 (Figure 4.5). Linacre was instrumental in translating selections of Galen's work into Latin in a series of editions that were published by Richard Pynson in the 1520s, making Wyer's claimed endorsement particularly

---

[61] On the value of indexes for Renaissance readers, see Blair, *Too Much to Know*.

[62] Joseph Moxon, *Mechanick Exercises on the Whole Art of Printing*, ed. Herbert Davis and Harry Carter (Oxford University Press, 1958), 32. Moxon's description of the distribution process offers an easy explanation for how such an error can occur; a compositor grabs a finger-length's worth of cleaned type and then he "brings what he has taken off towards his Sight to read; then with a sleight thrusting the Ball of his Thumb outwards, and drawing inwards the Balls of his fore and middle Fingers, he spreads and *Squabbles* the shanks of the *Letters* between his Fingers askew; and remembering what *Letters* he read, he nimbly addresses his Hand with a continued motion to every respective *Box*, which his Fingers, as they pass by, lets a *Letter* drop into, till his *Taking off* be quite *Distributed*" (202).

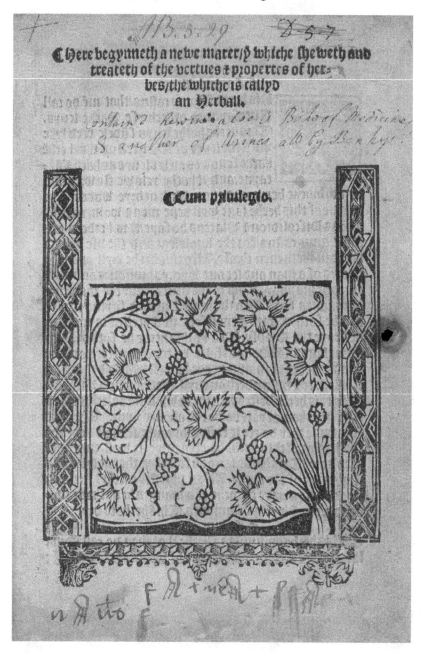

Figure 4.3 *Here begynneth a newe marer* [*sic*] (1526), sig. A1r. Reproduced by the kind permission of the Syndics of Cambridge University Library (Shelfmark Sel.5.175).

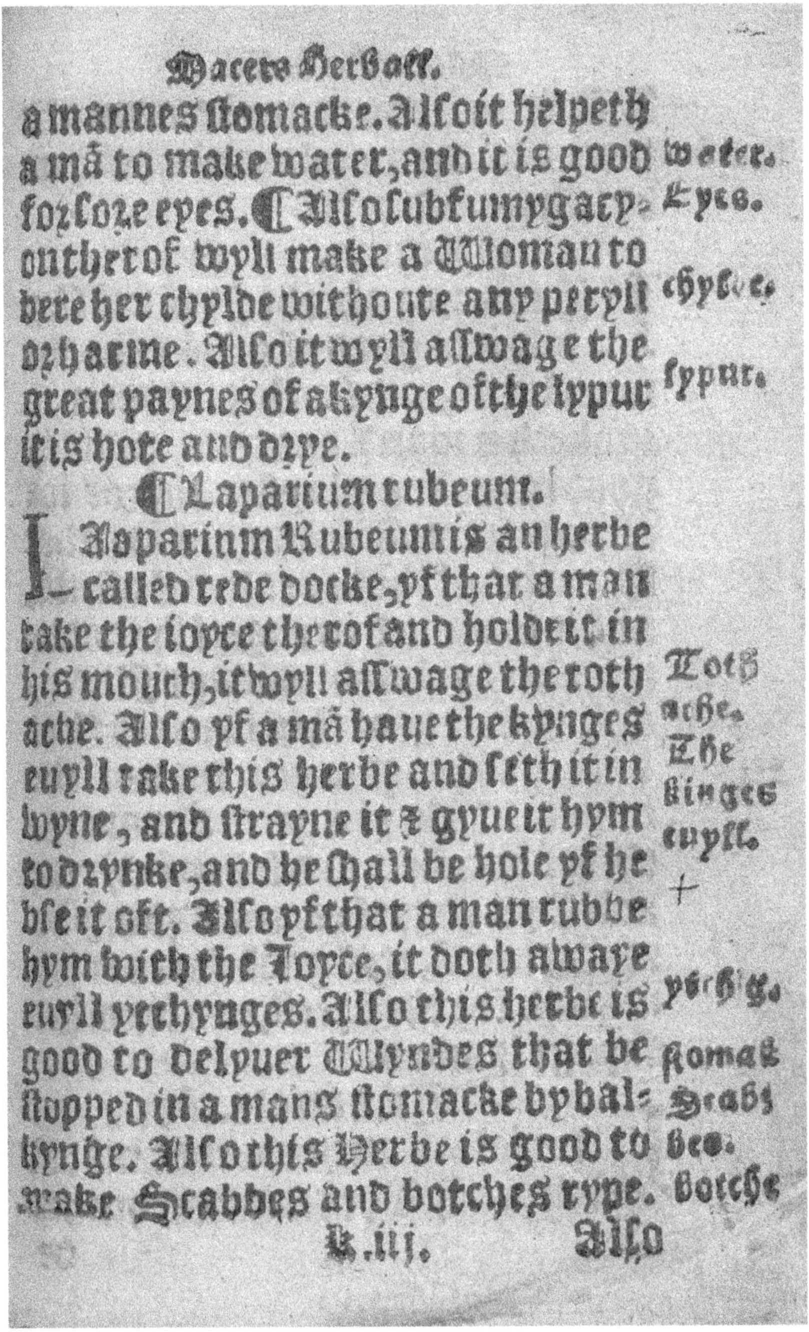

Macers Herball.

a mannes ſtomacke. Alſo it helpeth
a mā to make water, and it is good water.
for ſore eyes. ¶ Alſo ſumy gary- eyes.
on therof wyll make a Woman to
bere her chylde withoute any peryll chylde.
or payne. Alſo it wyll aſſwage the
great paynes of a kynge of the lyppur lyppur.
it is hote and drye.

¶ Laparium rubeum.

Laparinm Rubeum is an herbe
called rede docke, yf that a man
take the ioyce therof and holde it in
his mouth, it wyll aſſwage the toth Toth
ache. Alſo yf a mā haue the kynges ache.
euyll take this herbe and ſeth it in The
wyne, and ſtrayne it & gyue it hym kinges
to drynke, and he ſhall be hole yf he euyll.
vſe it oft. Alſo yf that a man rubbe +
hym with the Ioyce, it doth awaye
euyll yechynges. Alſo this herbe is yechings.
good to delyuer Wyndes that be Romac
ſtopped in a mans ſtomacke by bal- Scabs
kynge. Alſo this Herbe is good to &c.
make Scabbes and botches rype. Botche
K.iij.   Alſo

Figure 4.4 *Macers Herball* (Robert Wyer, 1552), sig. K3r. The Huntington Library, San Marino, California (RB 59462).

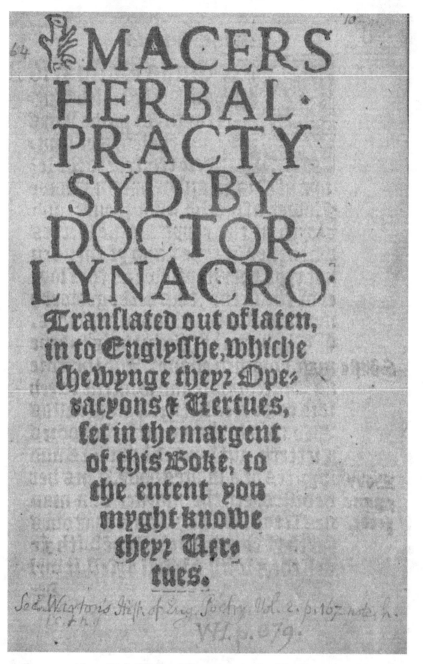

Figure 4.5 *Macers Herball* (Robert Wyer, 1552), sig. A1r. The Huntington Library, San Marino, California (RB 59462).

clever since none of Linacre's writings, including a Latin grammar, were yet available in English. Wyer's marginal annotations also return in his 1550 text, this time as an affordance he considered worthy enough to advertise on his book's title page.

Though Rebecca Laroche finds that early herbals "are not infused with issues of textual authority that we find in Turner and post-Turner publications," the artifacts produced by Wyer demonstrate that named authorities did find their way onto the title pages and running titles even of the small-format herbals available for sale prior to William Turner's *New Herbal* of 1551.[63]

The Little *Herball* Variations of William Powell and William Copland

Wyer's success between 1539 and 1550 with his versions of the little *Herball* later provided the publishers William Powell and William Copland with a model for their own "Askham's Herbal" (*STC* 13175.13) and "W.C. Herbal" (*STC* 13175. 18) versions of the text, which were printed between 1550 and 1567. Anthony Askham was a patronage-seeking Yorkshire physician known to would-be readers as the brother of humanist Roger Askham, Cambridge fellow and tutor to the young princess Elizabeth. Given that Powell was the publisher of a series of Askham's astrological octavos, his choice to supplement his 1550 edition of the little *Herball* with Askham's work to compete with Wyer's Macer variations was a reasonable one. Powell had little competition to fear from the remnants of the Redman or Middleton editions, if those were still circulating in London's retail book market; as the husband of Elizabeth Middleton, William Middleton's widow, Powell would have succeeded to all of Middleton's remaining stock at the time of his death, including all the unsold copies of various editions of the little *Herball* that Middleton may ultimately have acquired from his forerunner at the George, Elizabeth Pickering Redman.

Like the Macer herbals, Powell's motivation in creating his Askham herbal was to offer readers something apparently novel. His herbal's full title also promised additional astronomical information with the seeming imprimatur of an expert physician, and the title's length left some ambiguity about who was responsible for its botanical information: *A lytel herball of the properties of herbes newely amended and corrected, with certayne*

---

[63] Laroche, *Medical Authority*, 29.

addicions at the end of the boke [as] appointed in the almanacke, made in M.D.L. the xii. Day of February by A. Askham. The ambiguity of the squinting modifier "made and gathered" left dangling at the end of the title when this edition was reprinted by John King in 1561 (*STC* 13175.19) led to some confusion in the first edition of the *STC* (which is organized by author name) as well as the *Oxford Dictionary of National Biography* (*ODNB*) (which still insists that Askham wrote the 1550 herbal). However, a collation of Powell's edition with its most likely copy text, William Middleton's edition of 1546, reveals that there is so very little change offered by Powell in 1550 that even Powell's use of the phrase "newely amended and corrected" on the title page is suspect. The *STC* notes that "the additions mentioned were presumably to be a reissue of 857a.5," or *A lytel treatyse of astrouomy [sic], very necessary for physyke and surgerye,* which was also published by Powell; however, no extant editions of Powell's herbal survive that are bound with any Askham material, and it seems possible that the chief distinction of the text of the Askham herbal in the marketplace of Tudor London was located primarily on its title page. Powell's retail customers may have been encouraged to bind their copies of his herbal with *A lytel treatise;* however, if readers who bought their texts elsewhere wished to read "Askham's herbal" without the text of STC 857a.5, they were free to do so.

Such is not the case for the fourth variant in the Bankes's *Herball* canon, those texts known as the W. C. herbals, which came first from the press of William Copland printing on behalf of the Draper John Wight and the stationer Richard Kele in 1552.[64] The title of Wight's book in full is *A boke of the proprerties [sic] of Herbes called an herball, wherunto is added the time [the] herbes, floures and Sedes shold be gathered to be kept the whole yere, with the vertue of [the] Herbes when they are stilled. Also a generall rule of all manner of Herbes drawen out of an auncyent booke of Phisyck by W.C.* (*STC* 13175.15). As in the case of Powell's Askham herbal, a squinting modifier comes into play in the title to confuse scholars desperately seeking title page authorship in the absence of clearer textual authority. The first edition of the *STC* originally listed this book under the name of Walter Cary, creator of such medical works as *The Hammer for the Stone* (1580, *STC* 4733) and *A Briefe Treatise Called Cary's Farewell to Physic* (1583, *STC* 4730); however,

---

[64] The variant title page signifies that the costs of the edition were split between publishers Wight (named on *STC* 13175.15) and Kele (named on 13175.15A). Wight was made free of the Drapers' Company by his master, Thomas Petyt, on July 30, 1541, and was likely still bound to him as Petyt was preparing his own edition of the *Herball.* If so, Wight would have had firsthand experience of seeing the *Herball* through the press.

this Walter Cary was still a child in 1552. The W. C. who drew a general rule of all manner of herbs from some unidentified "Ancient Book of Physic," was likely someone else, possibly the work's printer, William Copland, doing exactly what Wyer had done with his reorganization of the little *Herball* the decade before. Such a division in responsibility for the book's manufacture likewise demonstrates the emergence of non-printing publishers like Wight and Kele, as well as the common occurrence of shared labor or expense in the printing of an edition.

The printer-translator Copland displayed his continued interest in the text by reprinting an edition for himself in 1559 (*STC* 13175.18), while in 1555, John Walley and Abraham Veale (another of Petyt's former apprentices) hired John King to print for them a shared edition of the W. C. herbal of their own (13175.16, Walley; 13175.17, Veale).[65] In deciding upon an edition of the little *Herball* to print for himself in 1561 (*STC* 13175.19), King chose the Askham version of William Powell. King was also the first stationer to seek a Company license for the text, as is recorded in the Registers along with the licensing of two other titles sometime between November 20, 1560, and March 8, 1561. (Notably, the entry does not mention Askham's name.) King's death in August of that year meant that his records in the Registers didn't prevent Antony Kytson from later printing another edition of the W. C. herbal circa 1567, which was at least the eighteenth and the last edition of the phenomenally popular work first printed by Richard Bankes in 1525.[66] The remedies the little *Herball* depicted, however, would resurface half a century later in another bestseller: Gervase Markham's *The English Housewife* (1615).[67]

Once we disaggregate the provenance of the work's many editions, the publication history of Bankes's *Herball* reveals that early English stationers were operating within a complex and dynamic marketplace that complicates a simple narrative of copyright ownership and competition. The

---

[65] Though these editions are clearly the same imprint, King provided distinct colophons for each publisher. As Vele was freed on April 16, 1543, there is little question that he was employed as an apprentice and would have seen Petyt's 1541 edition of the *Herball* in press.

[66] Blayney, *Printers of London*, 785.

[67] In his edition of *The English Housewife*, Michael Best suggests that "Markham, or whoever compiled the remedies, must have read systematically through [Bankes's] herbal, noting all the herbs which were described as beneficial for the frenzy, for dim or sore eyes, for the dropsy, and so on; he then devised a recipe for each sickness by including each herb which was recorded as effective in its treatment" (Gervase Markham, *The English Housewife*, ed. Michael Best [McGill-Queen's University Press, 1986], xix). See also Best, "Medical Use." For insight into the ways that the paratexts of Markham's work enabled new modalities for domestic reading, see Wendy Wall, "Reading the Home: *The Case of The English Housewife*," in Helen Smith and Louise Wilson, eds., *Renaissance Paratexts* (Cambridge: Cambridge University Press, 2011), 165–184.

combination of ecclesiastic control over seditious printing and the system of royal privilege during the pre-charter period actually did the opposite: it encouraged the spread of popular titles through the 1550s when the supply of printed books was outpaced by an increasing demand. Yet as England's officials struggled to keep tabs on religious controversies, the solutions they used to control printed books had a knock-on effect upon nonreligious titles. The incorporation of the Stationers' Company and their attendant regulations eventually pushed such early popular works out of the market: by the late sixteenth century, new editions of the little *Herball* were no longer available for sale to early modern readers. Despite its disappearance, however, the *Herball* in its multiple editions later served to convince cautious stationers that there was a sufficient English demand for printed botanical books in the vernacular to risk publishing much larger and more expensive editions. As a result, the London publisher Steven Mierdman could, in 1551, be assured that producing the illustrated folio of William Turner's *A New Herball* in English was a good economic risk – after all, lay English readers were still buying copies of a 25-year-old, unillustrated octavo on a similar subject. Before accounting for the publication of this "authoritative English herbal" authored by the "Father of British botany," however, I first need to discuss *The Grete Herbal*, another anonymous English herbal that helps us better understand how Tudor readers responded to printed works of natural history and medicine.

CHAPTER 5

The Grete Herball *and Evidence in the Margins*

Sometime in spring 1526, Peter Treveris squinted over a page, red pencil in hand. He was correcting pages of his latest publication, an English translation of a French herbal that had been in print on the continent since 1487.[1] With nearly 500 woodcuts, Treveris's illustrated folio herbal was an expensive and complicated undertaking, especially for a new printer who'd published only a handful of works before.[2] The new herbal was designed to supplement another illustrated folio that Treveris had published immediately upon settling in Southwark the prior year, Hieronymus Brunschwig's *Noble Experyence of the Vertuous Handy Warke of Surgeri (STC* 13434). This work, too, was a substantive investment for Treveris, and he had gone to some trouble in printing its strikingly illustrated title page in both red and black ink. Treveris intended to use a similarly eye-catching design for the title page of his herbal, and he even planned to reference the surgery book on the title page of this new volume to reinforce how the two books were designed to complement each other (Figure 5.1).[3] He further planned to add to the title

---

[1] *Arbolayre … Le grant herbier en francois (USTC* 59437), published by Petrus Metlinger in Besançon between 1486 and 1488. On this text see Henrey, *British Botanical*, 1:6, and Arber, *Herbals*, 26, 28.

[2] Treveris, an alien probably from Trier, Germany, settled in Southwark in 1525. Southwark was then outside of the formal boundaries of London, which enabled Treveris to escape the stringent controls of the City. See Blayney, *Printers of London*, 191–194. On *The Grete Herball*'s 481 woodcuts, see Hodnett, *English Woodcuts*, 63, and Arber, *Herbals*, 17.

[3] The full title of Treveris's text is: *The grete herball whiche geueth parfyt knowlege and vnderstandyng of all maner of herbes & there gracyous vertues whiche god hath ordeyned for our prosperous welfare and helth/ for they hele & cure all maner of dyseases and sekenesses that fall or mysfortune to all maner of creatours of god created/practysed by many expert and wyse maysters/as Auicenna & other.&c. Also it geueth full parfyte vnderstandynge of the booke lately prynted by me (Peter treueris) named the noble experiens of the vertuous handwarke of surgery.* The title page is xylographic, or block book, in which an illustration and accompanying text are cut from a single block of wood.

157

Figure 5.1 *The Grete Herball* (1526), sig. ✠ 1r. By courtesy of the Department of
Special Collections, Memorial Library, University of Wisconsin–Madison
(Thordarson T 1823).

that the remedies in his volume were "practysed by many expert and
wyse maysters/ as Auicenna & other. &c.," an endorsement that
suggested there was more to these titles than what was available for

sale elsewhere.[4] As the unillustrated quarto herbal that Richard Bankes had printed the previous year was only a fraction the size of his own, Treveris may have been especially pleased to title his new work *The* Grete *Herball* (*STC* 13176, emphasis added).[5]

Before Treveris could attend to the printing of his herbal's preliminaries, however, he had to print the remainder of the volume, and something was amiss in his chapter on juniper. As he checked the newly printed pages against his manuscript copy, Treveris noticed that a few clarifying words were missing from the instructions on how to make juniper oil, a remedy for quartan fevers caused by melancholy. With his red pencil, Treveris made a note in the margin. To accommodate the new words, he would need to reorient a few lines and respell some of the surrounding text. No matter: "the" could easily be shortened to "y^e" and "with" abbreviated to "w^t" to provide the necessary space. Treveris likewise marked for correction a misspelled and incoherent word, "pacyon," a dittography error likely caused by the compositor's inadvertently echoing the ending of a word in the chapter's subheader. In the margins, he noted that the ending needed to be revised so that the word read "pacient." Most of Treveris's corrections assured the accuracy of his translation of the verbal text from a manuscript into print, but as a craftsman he was also concerned with the technical errors that marred the aesthetics of his page with unsightly blotches, conspicuous errors that might preclude his being hired by another publisher as a trade printer sometime in the future. At one point, a space had risen to take ink; a few lines later, the kerning of one form of lowercase *r* in his textura type pushed against a long-*st* ligature in "first," creating another blemish. The *r* would need to be replaced with the other sort of the letter. Treveris marked these errors for correction, too.[6]

---

[4] Treveris lifted Islamic physician-astronomer Ibn Sina's name (Latinized throughout the Middle Ages as Avicenna) from the preface to the volume, where the work's pedigree is established: "This noble worke is compyled / composed and auctorysed by dyuers & many noble doctours and expert maysters in medycynes / as Auicenna. Pandecta. Constantinus. Wilhelmus. Platearius. Rabbi moyses. Iohannes mesue. Haly. Albertus. Bartholome{us}. & more other. &c," sig. ✠ 2r. Several of these names appear within the text of the volume itself, testifying to its provenance as a compiled text. As Eleanour Sinclair Rohde notes, "the preface ... bears a strong resemblance to that of the German Herbarius" (*Old English Herbals*, 67–69), though Treveris or his translator took considerable liberties. See also H. M. Barlowe, "Old English Herbals, 1525–1640," *Journal of the Royal Society of Medicine* 6 (1913): 108–149.

[5] A copy of the little *Herball* usually required nine edition-sheets to produce; a copy of Treveris's *Grete Herball* required eighty-seven.

[6] In keeping with Joseph Moxon's assertion that the master printer was "the Soul of Printing," I have speculated that the corrector working in Treveris's printing house in 1526 was the master printer himself and not a hired agent. See Moxon, *Mechanick Exercises*, 12, 246–251.

We know the specifics of Treveris's activities as a corrector of his text of *The Grete Herball* because his proof-sheet for leaves N2–N5 survived in the binding of a 1526 indenture held at Queen's College, Oxford.[7] Scrap papers and other forms of printers' waste were regularly recycled into the paste downs and board bindings in Renaissance books, and as Strickland Gibson observes in his account of the proof-sheets, these "tiny pearls" can provide insight into the mechanics of textual transmission.[8] In the case of the first edition of *The Grete Herball*, the proof corrector's notes testify to Treveris's careful attention both to his copy-text and to the aesthetics of his printed page, demonstrating his awareness that errors could easily creep into the documents he offered for sale. Both forms of correction were relevant to Treveris's livelihood: as a bookseller who may have commissioned the translations of the works he published, Treveris had a vested interest in ensuring that his texts were sufficiently accurate and free from nonsensical errors that readers (and fellow booksellers) would value their verbal content enough to purchase them; as a printer whose press and type might be hired by another publisher, he likewise had a vested interest in ensuring that his printed pages were clean and legible. More than four centuries later, Jerome McGann would need to remind scholars that "texts ... are embodied phenomena, and the body of the text is not exclusively linguistic," but for a Renaissance printer-publisher like Treveris, such concerns were perfectly obvious and wholly commonplace.[9]

Treveris's (and McGann's) attention to the embodiment of texts as material documents results from their awareness that the interaction between verbal and illustrative texts produces meaning. *The Grete Herball* lacks even the basic descriptions of plant morphology found in the editions of the little *Herball*, and in many cases, Treveris's woodcut illustrations, flawed and stylized as they were, provided the only evidence that could enable a user of the text to identify an unfamiliar plant. Along with the volume's preface, his woodcuts had been copied from those in a continental herbal, the *German Herbarius*, which purported to be the product of a wealthy traveler to the east who'd commissioned an artist to accompany him on his travels and illustrate plants firsthand.[10] Recognizing

---

[7] Strickland Gibson, "Fragments from Bindings at the Queen's College Oxford," *The Library* series 4, 12 (1932): 429–433.

[8] Gibson, "Fragments," 429.

[9] Jerome McGann, *The Textual Condition* (Princeton, NJ: Princeton University Press, 1991), 13.

[10] Agnes Arber offers E. G. Tucker's translation of the preface from an edition printed in Augsburg, 1485 (see *Herbals*, 25). A cursory check of the cartoonish "mandrake" woodcut, which depicts both its "male" and its "female" versions, attests that *The Grete Herball*'s illustrations are indeed copied from the *German Herbarius* but for one crucial distinction – the more prudish cutter of the English

that some of the utility of his product depended on this precise coordination of text and image, Treveris's press-correcting efforts therefore extended to making sure that his copious woodcuts matched up with the correct chapter. Here, too, there was a problem. Treveris noticed only as he was perfecting sheet D3–4 that the illustration accompanying chapter 58 on borage had been switched with the illustration for an earlier, unnumbered chapter on bombax, or cotton, which he had already printed on the outer side of the same sheet (Figure 5.2). Treveris made the only correction available to him short of scrapping the page entirely and starting over: he inserted a vertical note running alongside the inaccurate cotton illustration that was now heading the borage chapter, noting "Nota [the] pictour of bo[m]bax & borago [the] one is put for [the] other."[11] The illustrations were restored to their proper places in Treveris's second edition of *The Grete Herball* in 1529, which Treveris printed as a joint investment with his fellow London printer Lawrence Andrewe.[12] The remaining two sixteenth-century editions of *The Grete Herball*, by Thomas Gibson in 1539 (*STC* 13178) and John King in 1561 (*STC* 13179), were largely unillustrated.[13]

Marginalia

Treveris's careful attention in ensuring the quality of his printed books was justifiable because errors of textual transmission not only promulgate themselves in future editions; they also lead to readers taking matters of correction into their own hands.[14] The manuscript annotations early modern readers left in their books testify that they too were aware of the

woodcut neglected to give the naked male mandrake his genitals. Copies of the illustrations in the *German Herbarius* also found their way into the popular continental work, *Hortus sanitatis*, which simplified and stylized many of the images. Sachiko Kusukawa notes that many of the illustrations in the *Hortius sanitatis* were "mnemonic pictures" designed to enable users to recall particular details of a remedy's origin or usage (Kusukawa, *Picturing the Book of Nature*, 18).

[11] *The Grete Herball* (1526), sig. D3v.

[12] *STC* 13177/13177.5. Andrewe, a sometime resident of Calais, translated and printed Hieronymous Brunschwig's *Book of Distillation* (*STC* 13435–6), which he illustrated with the woodcuts that Treveris had used for *The Grete Herball*. It, too, had a xylographic title page. Given the shared interests and clear association between the two men, it has been suggested that Andrewe was responsible for translating *The Grete Herball* from French (Blayney, *Printers of London*, 1, 92).

[13] Gibson's edition is completely unillustrated save for a title page border; King's edition features an illustrated title page featuring a pair of foresters but the interior offers only two woodcuts of a Lord and Lady, incongruously used to illustrate the male and female mandrake (the Lord is later reused to head the chapter on urine). See Ruth Samson Luborsky and Elizabeth Morley Ingram, *A Guide to English Illustrated Books 1536–1603*, 2 vols. (Tempe, AZ: Medieval & Renaissance Texts & Studies, 1998), 1:435.

[14] Errors can also lead to fellow booksellers getting new marketing ideas: as I argued in the previous chapter, Richard Bankes's printing error of "Marer" for "Mater" (matter) on the blackletter title

stie and plydes / and sethe them in vynep=
gre / and wete a sponge in the sayde decoc=
cyon / and lay it to the pytte of the stomake
¶ Igaynst flur. ℔

¶ Agaynst flux of the bely caused of wey=
kenesse make a decoccyon of balaustie / ᵹ
plides with rayne water / and with this
decoccyon make fomentacyon / that is to
say lete the bely be longe chaufed therwᵗ
The powdre of balaustie reioyneth woū=
des / ᵹ in stede of bol armenyc is put pow=
dre of balaustie / but take for a generall
rule whan thou fyndest ony medcyne in
a recept put none other in p place of other
so that thou may gete ony of that whiche
is expressly named.

¶ De Boragine. Borage.   Ca. lviii.

Here is put the picture of borage   Borage

ᴮOrage is an herbe ᵱ hath rughe le
   ues and is named borrage. It is
   hote and moyst in the fyrst degre
the leues be good in medcyne whyle they
ben grene / but not dry / and next the leues
take the sede. It engendreth good blode
and therfore it is good for them that haue
be seke of late.

¶ Agaynst cordyake passyon. ᴬ

¶ For them that ben dysposed to fall in
swowne / or ben faynt at the herte / and ha
ue cordyake passyon / that is payne at the
herte / and for them that haue melancoly=
ke humours in theyr body / lete them ete
borage wᵗ theyr flesshe / or in theyr potage
¶ Agaynst swownynge ℔

¶ Agaynst swowninge make syrope with
iuce of borage and sugre.

¶ Agaynst passyon of ᵱ hert ℭ

¶ Agaynst passyon of ᵱ herte make syrope
with this iuce / and put therto powdre of
the bone in the herte of a harte.

¶ Agaynst melancolyke. ᴰ

¶ Agaynst melancolyke passyons / and
agaynst epylence or fallynge euyll / sethe
sewet in iuce of borage and make a syrope
therof / and yf ye haue no leues sethe the
sedes therof in water / and strayne them ᵹ
make a syrope. The sedes may be kept. ii.
yere in vertue. The rote is not vsed in me=
dycyns / yf the herbe be eaten rawe it bre=
deth good blood.

¶ Agaynst Iaundys. ℰ

¶ Agaynst Iaundys ete this herbe often
soden with flesshe / and lete the pacyent vse
the iuce therof with iuce of scaryol / that
is wylde letuse.

Figure 5.2 *The Grete Herball* (1526), sig. D3v. By courtesy of the Department of
Special Collections, Memorial Library, University of Wisconsin–Madison
(Thordarson T 1823).

possibility that errors could appear anywhere in their printed books. The popularization of "Faults Escaped" or errata lists in sixteenth-century European books helped readers normalize difficulties in textual transmission when they encountered them, and as William Sherman and Seth Lerer have demonstrated, readers regularly corrected by hand both those errors listed in printers' errata lists and those they found on their own.[15] A reader of Thomas Petyt's 1545 edition of Thomas Moulton's *Mirror, or Glass of Health* (*STC* 18225.4), for instance, confronted in the table of contents with the nonsense chapter heading "yf one womysshe to moche," correctly surmised that "womysshe" must mean "vomiteth."[16] John Locke's copy of the 1526 edition of *The Grete Herball*, now held in the Bodleian Library, features manuscript notes detailing an error in that particular copy's binding, while John Donne's copy of John Gerard's 1597 *Herball* contains a series of corrections to that edition's errors in page numbering. Other readers corrected a printer's technical omissions, such as a note furnishing a missing chapter number in Treveris and Andrewe's 1529 edition of *The Grete Herball*,[17] or a dutiful attempt to supply pagination throughout Robert Redman's 1539 reprint of Bankes's little *Herball*.[18] Yet sometimes readers' attempts at correction could make matters worse. A reader of Treveris and Andrewe's 1529 edition realized that two items on sig. O5r were not given chapter numbers and added them, also correcting the numbers in the register of chapters; however, the inattentive reader seems not to have realized that doing so would necessitate advancing all the other chapter numbers in the volume by two.[19] Nonetheless, readers' marks such as these testify to moments when readers found fault in their books, and as producers of the printed artifacts in question, booksellers had a vested interest in offering products for sale that were as correct as it was possible to make them.

As Treveris realized, though, just as readers recognizing the vicissitudes of textual transmission could correct printers' errors in the construction of

page of his 1526 edition of the little *Herball* may have inspired Robert Wyer to add Aemilius Macer's name to the title page of his edition of the text as a marketing ploy.

[15] Seth Leher, "Errata: Print, Politics, and Poetry in Early Modern England," in Kevin Sharpe and Steven N. Zwicker (eds.), *Reading, Society, and Politics in Early Modern England* (Cambridge: Cambridge University Press, 2003), 41–71; Sherman, *Used Books*, 79. See also Blair, "Errata Lists."

[16] Bodleian Library, Crynes 873. The note appears at the top of sig. A4r. Petyt's edition of this version of text follows a 1540 edition by Robert Wyer (*STC* 18225.2) that does not make the error. Petyt also shared in an edition of a slightly modified version of the text printed for him and four others by Nicholas Hill.

[17] Note appears on sig. A2v of British Library C 27 L 3.   [18] British Library 546.b.31.

[19] Bodleian Library, Vet. A1 f.8.

the book artifact, so too could they correct the content of the verbal and illustrative texts that such books contained. The evidence of contemporary marginalia left in Renaissance books likewise indicates that early modern readers, much like modern scholars, were capable of using books as authorities over knowledge domains only inasmuch as it suited them to do so. Readers who took their pens to printed works could express their disagreement with the verbal text at hand, as did one reader of *The Secrets of Alexis* (London, 1580) who, upon altering several recipes, wrote "All theas receipts ar verye falsly written, but being corrected heer they ar trew."[20] Manuscript evidence contained in several extant printed herbals likewise reveals that, when sixteenth-century readers sought medical advice from their pages, they did so with an evaluative and utilitarian eye, changing the physical artifact of the book to better suit their individual needs as book users and consumers. Wyer's Macer editions, discussed in the previous chapter, offered readers printed marginal annotations that quickly highlighted key terms to facilitate the scanning of its pages, but the clear margins of the Bankes and Copland editions (and their successors) allowed readers to do such annotating for themselves.[21] The single surviving copy of Thomas Petyt's 1541 edition (*STC* 13175.8) contains manuscript notations from a sixteenth-century reader who found some plant names too Latinate to be helpful, and after reading their vernacular monikers in the text that follows the Latinate heading, they added the English names in the margin. Sig. A3ᵛ's "Absinthium" is thus annotated with "Wormewoode," and on the following leaf, "Arthemesia" is renamed "mugworte." A British Library copy of the "W.C. herbal" (published by John Wight in 1552) was read by someone particularly vested in the remedies for flatulence contained in the text, as this document is annotated to highlight those simples that alleviate "wycked wynd."[22] A Folger Library copy of *Ram's Litle Dodeon* (1606; *STC* 6988) features heavy annotation in both red and black inks; as Katarzyna Lecky has noted, several of the receipts "are distinguished with sketches of

---

[20] Quoted in Sherman, *Used Books*, 18.

[21] Ann M. Blair has noted that such marginal notation also serves readers who will later use their marginalia to facilitate the creation of a commonplace book. See *Too Much to Know*, esp. chap. 2, "Note-Taking as Information Management."

[22] *STC* 13175.15. Shelfmark 449a.9. The reader has written "Good for wynde" beside "let passe wyked wyndes" on sig. A5r, highlighted that Alium can be used "To Vnbind wynde" on sig. B1r and noted on sig. B1v that Ansium is similarly useful for those who suffer from bound "wycked wynds." The same reader is also preoccupied with recipes for "to brek stone" on sig. B5r, sig. B8r, and sig. C8v, and the making "oyle of roses" on sig. H3v and sig. H4v. Clearly, at some point in the sixteenth or seventeenth century, this reader made careful use of this text, looking for specific material.

the body part that they treat; others reveal a reader's reactions to the sugarcoated language referring to women's health issues."[23]

Attuned to his customers' use of books to catalogue and note their own reading experiences, Treveris supplied *The Grete Herball* with sophisticated finding aids to provide readers with opportunities for using – and marking up – the book in a variety of different ways. Both the 1526 and 1529 editions feature a "registre of the chapytres in latyn and in Englysshe," which provide each entry in the volume with its own chapter heading and number.[24] The chapters are alphabetized by the first letter of the entry's Latinate name, usually immediately followed by the corresponding name for the plant or substance in the English vernacular.[25] In addition to the initial "registre," Treveris's editions of *The Grete Herball* conclude with "a table very necessary and prouffytable for them that desyre to fynde quyckely a remedy agaynst all maner of dyseases."[26] Organized into ailments affecting body parts from the head to the feet, remedies in the table are "marked by [the] letters of the.A.B.C. in euery chaptyre." Those readers interested in, for example, remedies "Agaynst a balde heed" are instructed to seek out section A in chapter cccclxxxi (481) where they learn that Abrotanum powder muddled with "oyle of Rafanus" and anointed on the head will cause hairs to grow.[27] Freed from the tyranny of consecutive reading, consumers of *The Grete Herball* could either use the work as a pharmacological guide, by seeking out individual remedies in the initial register and learning what ailments each could treat, or use the herbal's concluding table to read the work as a book of cures, organized by complaint.[28] Later publishers of *The Grete Herball* like Thomas Gibson would clarify the organization still further by splitting the register to provide separate lists of Latin and English names.[29] These

---

[23] Katarzyna Lecky, "The Strange and Practical Beauty of Small-Format Herbals," *The Collation*, Folger Shakespeare Library, March 15, 2018 (collation.folger.edu/2018/03/small-format-herbals/).

[24] Except where noted, quotations from Treveris's two editions of *The Grete Herball* are taken from the corrected second edition of 1529.

[25] Treveris had previously used the same system of an introductory "registre" in the edition of *Vertuous Handy Warke of Surgeri* he published the year before. See Jean A. Givens, "Reading and Writing the Illustrated *Tractatus de herbis*, 1280–1526," in Jean Ann Givens, Karen Reeds, and Alain Touwaide, eds., *Visualizing Medieval Medicine and Natural History, 1200–1550* (Burlington, VT: Ashgate, 2006), 136–145.

[26] *The Grete Herball* (1526), sig. 2D3v.   [27] *The Grete Herball* (1526), sig. 2B3v.

[28] On the way the format of the codex encourages discontinuous reading practices and facilitates annotation, see Peter Stallybrass, "Books and Scrolls: Navigating the Bible," in Jennifer Andersen and Elizabeth Sauer, eds., *Books and Readers in Early Modern England* (Philadelphia: University of Pennsylvania Press, 2002), 42–79.

[29] It is worth noting that a reader of Gibson's 1539 edition now held by the British Library was unimpressed with that book's ailment index, oriented from head to foot – they chose instead to

pharmacologically inflected affordances pioneered by Treveris and Gibson would eventually be adopted and modified by publishers of later "authoritative" herbals like John Gerard's of 1597, whose considerable size made discontinuous reading preferable. Reading such a massive tome straight through would be nearly impossible.[30]

Most of the British Library copies of *The Grete Herball* contain annotations that suggest readers engaged with the book for specific purposes. A reader of John King's 1561 edition was particularly concerned with women's health, noting that chamomile is useful "for to provoke the flowers," and inserting a manicule (☞) alongside the same effect of calendula.[31] On sig. N2r, under "to lose the wombe," this same tactful reader has noted "to cause the flowers to flowe," while later they opine that a recipe to "cause you to be laxe and go too the Stole" is "a good purgation."[32] A reader of a British Library copy of William Copland's 1559 little *Herball* (*STC* 13175.11) has numbered its pages from one to seventy-eight but there gave up the enterprise. They did not correspond to the numbered pages to the work's ending table (which offers nothing more than an alphabetical listing of the plants contained), but it is clear that the reader was attempting to organize and annotate their reading. On sig. A5r, the word "wormes" is inserted into the margin at "destroyeth wormes," while on the facing page they repeat "morphew" and offer three hasty manicules. Worms continue to preoccupy the reader on the following page, while "palsey" and "dropsy" appear to annotate lavender and wormwood respectively.

Because readers of herbals turned to these books as tools that helped them solve problems, these volumes also provided readers with an occasion for recording their own receipts or modifications of verbal details. The same abovementioned British Library copy of Copland's little *Herball* is bound with handwritten lists of recipes "For purgation," written on three pieces of smaller format paper that had presumably been tucked into the

---

reindex the book alphabetically, keying their data to the printed index's numbered columns (a digitized copy of the edition is available on *Early English Books Online*).

[30] Size was a particular concern for the publishers of large folios, especially those wanting to ensure their products' appeal to women readers. In his 1647 edition of the collected plays of Francis Beaumont and John Fletcher (Wing B1581), Humphrey Moseley noted that he deliberately did not include certain plays in the large folio volume because they "would have rendred the Booke so Voluminous, that Ladies and Gentlewomen would have found it scarce manageable, who in Workes of this nature must first be remembered" (sig. A4r).

[31] Sig. G3r. On these "severed hands, frozen in gestures that cannot fail to catch the eye," see Sherman, *Used Books*, chap. 2: "☞:Toward a History of the Manicule," 25–52. The King volume is British Library shelfmark 448g.3.

[32] *The Greate Herball* (1561), sig. Q6v.

volume for safekeeping.[33] That they are recipes is not in question: "For purgation" is clearly legible, as are the words "take," "boyle," "oz," and "draught." A handwritten recipe for a distillation contains marigolds and roses and advises that the concoction should only be used in May and June. Such use of herbals as locations for early modern readers to store their own or acquired remedies was widespread, as was the tendency of readers to modify the recipes to suit their own particular religious or geographic affiliations. R. T. Gunther found a copy of Gerard's 1597 *Herbal* with notes that indicate the work's contemporary usage, while a Protestant reader of Treveris and Andrewe's 1529 edition of *The Grete Herball* removed the work's Catholic sentiments.[34] In a remedy "for the byting of a madde dog," where the text reads "go to the chyrche and make thy offrynge to our lady and pray her to helpe and hele thee," the reader has crossed out "our lady" and inserted the word "God."[35]

This kind of readerly alteration was made possible by a verbal text's incarnation in a book, whose physical manipulability enabled readers to highlight certain details and ignore others. As Lorraine Daston has observed, "[t]aking notes entails taking note – that is, riveting the attention on this or that particular." Note-taking, whether it occurs as a result of reading or of observation, "imparts a distinctive economy of attention to practitioners, sharpening their senses and whetting their curiosity for certain domains of phenomena at the expense of others."[36] The surviving annotations of Renaissance readers thus indicate that they were not passive agents of the advice that they received from books but rather active mediators who evaluated the diverse claims of written advisors against the body of their own knowledge and experience.[37] Though some scholars of early printed books conclude that the shift from script to print

---

[33] Shelfmark 546.b.30.

[34] R. T. Gunther, *Early Botanists and Their Gardens: Based on the Unpublished Writings of Goodyer, Tradescant, and Others* (Oxford: Oxford University Press, 1922), 238.

[35] *The Grete Herball* (1529), sig. S3v.   [36] Daston, "Taking Note(s)," 445.

[37] Barbara Howard Traister sees a similar integration of personal and practical authorities at work in the manuscripts and annotations of notorious seventeenth-century physician Simon Forman: "Forman wrote constantly. He used his books to hold information, to convey information, to shape and present himself, and to make orderly and comprehensible a world that might otherwise have seemed merely chaotic and diseased. Books offered him a way to manage the past, present and future from within the confines of his study." See *The Notorious Astrological Physician of London: Works and Days of Simon Forman* (Chicago: University of Chicago Press, 2001), 144. See also Hannah Murphy, "Common Places and Private Spaces: Libraries, Record-Keeping and Orders of Information in Sixteenth-Century Medicine," *Past and Present* Supplement 11 (2016): 253–268. The phenomenon does not seem to be exclusive to the Renaissance; for a similar claim about Roman women, see A. Richlin, "Pliny's Brassiere," in Laura K. McClure (ed.), *Sexuality and Gender in the Classical World* (Oxford: Blackwell, 2002), 225–255.

ultimately resulted in the creation of a passive reader who largely agreed with a text, William Sherman finds that "Renaissance marginalia usually offer clues not just about the context in which books were circulated and read, but about how they were used; indications of the kinds of training that readers brought to bear on their encounters with texts, and the kinds of needs they could be made to serve."[38]

The Use Value of Herbals

This evidence of reading and note-taking habits contained within extant books is crucial to challenge accounts of herbals that assume contemporary readers simply treated these books as authoritative sources of medical and botanical information in the absence of professional authorities. In so doing, these scholarly accounts support not objective facts about early moderns' credulity or epistemology but the subjective advertising strategies deployed by publishers as they sought to differentiate their books in the marketplace. For example, H. S. Bennett's influential work *English Books & Readers, 1475 to 1557* identifies herbals as "invaluable first-aid books of reference, and to those far from medical care, often served as the only means whereby a patient's ailments might be treated. Of course, they were far from scientific in many particulars; but, expressed in simple language, and at times adorned with crude woodcuts of the plants, they met an obvious need."[39]

Bennett's interpretation takes *The Grete Herball*'s own preface as a model in describing the book's utility for readers. In his preface to the work in 1526 and 1529, Treveris claimed that the herbal provided readers with

> fortune as well in vilages where as nother surgeons nor phisicians be dwell-yng nygh by many a myle/as it dooth in good townes where they be redy at hande. Wherfore brotherly loue compelleth me to wryte thrugh [the] gyftes of the holy gost shewynge and enformynge how man may be holpen w[ith]

---

[38] William H. Sherman, "What Did Renaissance Readers Write in Their Books?," in Andersen and Sauer, *Books and Readers*, 119–137; 126. Paul Saenger and Michael Heinlen argue that the advent of printed marginalia was a form of oppression that preempted a reader's critical engagement with a text, ultimately resulting in a passive acceptance of the printed page: "throughout the Middle Ages readers, even long after a book had been confected, felt free to clarify its meaning through the addition of . . . marginalia. Under the influence of printing, reading became increasingly an activity of the passive reception of a text that was inherently clear and unambiguous." See "Incunable Description and Its Implication for the Analysis of Fifteenth-Century Reading Habits," in Sandra Hindman (ed.), *Printing the Written Word: The Social History of Books circa 1450–1520* (Ithaca, NY: Cornell University Press, 1991), 225–258; 254.

[39] Bennett, *English Books and Readers*, 98.

grene herbes of the gardyn and wedys of [the] feldys as well as by costly receptes of [the] potycarys prepayred.[40]

Putting his book to press within a year of Bankes's little *Herball* being offered for sale (and its being popular enough to quickly merit a second edition), Treveris sought to differentiate his more expensive work from the unillustrated little quarto. To do so, he explicitly presented his herbal as a surrogate for medical care in the absence of knowing professionals, and he likewise positioned himself not merely as a broker in printed commodities but as a thoughtful would-be Englishman engaging in dedicated Catholic service.[41]

In *English Books & Readers*, Bennett takes Treveris at his word. Yet, as Paul Slack notes, such introductory or title page appeals to "brotherly love" or the good of the "common weale" were routine in the vernacular medical literature of Tudor England.[42] Though they are compelling evidence for a publisher's motivations in putting a particular text to print at a particular time, these remarks function more as

> pious hopes or calculated advertisements rather than statements of fact. Such works can scarcely have reached the illiterate poor, and the extent of their diffusion even among the literate may well be questioned . . . they were one small and specialized part of a medical world in which there were several alternative sources of knowledge and advice, from the educated practitioners to the more numerous "cunning" men and women who represented a well-worn and well-known tradition of magical and folk medicine.[43]

Slack concludes that, while works such as *The Grete Herball* may have offered ancillary help to literate lay readers, they were not primarily viewed as replacements for the myriad forms of professional and "cunning" medicine available for purchase. Yet books such as herbals did serve as a supplement to medicine, a means for readers to learn about some common tricks of the medical trades and how to avoid being taken in. In addition to the remedies for common ailments contained in its entries on aloe, garlic, honey, and other plants and minerals, *The Grete Herball* details the methods by which unscrupulous medical practitioners could forge expensive medicaments: "And

---

[40] *The Grete Herball* (1526), sig. ✠ 2r.

[41] The preface to the *German Herbarius* shares a similar spirit of commonweal, making it difficult to determine the source. See Arber, *Herbals*, 23–26. If he translated the text of *The Grete Herball*, this phrasing may be Lawrence Andrewe's; despite his residency in Calais, Andrewe identifies England as "my natyfe Countrey" in *STC* 13437 on sig. ¶1r. See also Blayney, *Printers of London*, 188–190.

[42] Paul Slack, "Mirrors of Health and Treasures of Poor Men: The Uses of the Vernacular Medical Literature of Tudor England," in Hilary Marland and Margaret Pelling (eds.), *The Task of Healing: Medicine, Religion and Gender in England and the Netherlands* (Rotterdam: Erasmus Publishing, 1996), 239–273.

[43] Slack, "Mirrors of Health," 237.

though in this boke we put the craftynesse or deceyt of medycynes / It is not bycause we wolde not that it shoulde be made / but to eschew [the] frawde of them that selleth it / and thus it is made decytful."[44]

The title pages of herbals indicate that their publishers recognized how these books offered opportunities for readers to exercise their own independent critical judgments, yet, in scholarship, the notion of deferential English readers is nonetheless pervasive. The implicit but usually unacknowledged assumption rests on the notion that the credulous early modern herbal reader accepted anything written down or printed at face value, unquestioningly following the directions depicted in an authoritative book. Readers are often assumed to have attempted anything they encountered in a book's pages in their desperation to cure. Sometimes scholarly sympathy for the ignorant reader is cited to amplify the misconduct associated with a non-authorial textual agent. For instance, in his extended condemnation of Robert Wyer's alterations to the little *Herball*, Francis Johnson bemoans the way that

> Wyer makes purely mechanical changes in the wording of sentences that originally were perfectly clear, and thus creates sentences that are either vague or have a different meaning. Note, for example, the condensation of the last part of the section "Anetum." Bankes's text was clear, but Wyer, perhaps because his changed order of words led to a mental association of roasting the seed and hotness, directs that the plaster be applied hot to the hemorrhoids. One winces at the agony that many patients must have endured because of this ignorant compiler's mistake.[45]

Medical doctors and historians evaluating the value of these herbal remedies of printed medical books likewise assume readers' naïveté when they make a point of emphasizing that seldom did such remedies actually work. In their facsimile edition of the little *Herball* of 1525, editors Sanford V. Larkey and Thomas Pyles assert that "undoubtedly a number of the prescriptions may have had some efficacy, but in many cases it is difficult to see where they could have been of any value whatsoever. The diseases treated cover a very wide range, and there is little evidence of any rationale."[46] Agnes Arber's approach is similar: in her examination of *The Grete Herball*, Arber remarks that the work gives "a definite idea of the utilitarian point of view of the herbalist of the period" and that "from

---

[44] Sig. A1r. Later, in chap. 319, "Of the bone in the heart of a hart," a remedy for both melancholy and hemorrhoids, the text warns that apothecaries sometimes sell the bones of goats' hearts in lieu of the bones of the genuine article. "But the dyfference is knowen by that the gotes bone hath no flesshe styckynge on it / & is not browne of coloure / but is whyte & softer" (sig. S2r).

[45] Johnson, "A New Herball of Macer," 254.   [46] Larkey and Pyles, *An Herbal*, xxii.

the twentieth-century point of view, [it] contains much that is curious, especially in regard to medical matters . . . the remedies for various ailments strike the modern reader as being violent in a terrifying degree, and adapted to a more robust age than the present."[47] Ludmilla Jordanova has identified such presentist accounts as following a "use/abuse model" that "does not challenge historians to unravel the mediating processes involved in the creation of knowledge, leaving the 'best' science and medicine as unhistoricized, because true and acceptable, and capable of being used for worthy purposes."[48] She advocates instead for the deployment of a social constructivist approach to the history of medicine that can better integrate multiple perspectives and ideologies of healing.

An attention to the materiality of books further aids in the recognition of multiple perspectives. As Jonathan R. Topham observes, the very act of manipulating artifacts enables readers to contest the meaning of verbal texts, which requires rethinking default assumptions about readers' credulity or innate trust in written objects. "[T]he new history of reading highlights the recalcitrant materiality of the printed works through which readers encounter texts and the hermeneutical significance of that material form," he writes. "The fact that readers encounter texts in particular material objects – whether books, newspapers, or computer monitors – makes a difference to the meaning they derive from them, because they read more than merely the works."[49] Adrian Johns's work has likewise demonstrated that it took considerable effort for seventeenth-century scientists to make their printed books appear trustworthy, and as we have seen, Renaissance authors themselves were well aware of this phenomenon, using various rhetorical strategies to assert hermeneutic control over their texts.[50] In Chapter 1, I pointed out how Leonard Fuchs's praise of Michael Isingrin, the Basel printer and publisher of Fuchs's *De historia stirpium*, served to elide Fuchs's dependency upon Isingrin's dissemination of printed books as a means of establishing and maintaining Fuchs's own scholarly authority. Chapter 6 of this study offers an investigation into the way the authority of printed books was broadly understood by early modern Londoners by considering how books were deployed on the popular English stage, while later chapters on William Turner and John Gerard further reveal how these authors' anxieties over their credibility with readers caused them to attempt to "authorize" themselves through

---

[47] Arber, *Herbals*, 45; 47–48.
[48] Ludmilla Jordanova, "The Social Construction of Medical Knowledge," *Social History of Medicine* 8 (1995): 361–381; 367.
[49] Topham, "A View," 431–432.   [50] Johns, *Nature of the Book*.

various strategies. The remainder of the present chapter demonstrates that this authorial "authorization" in English herbals, paradoxically, derives from the reprinting of an anonymous work. As *The Grete Herball* found its way into the hands of Protestant physicians looking to instrumentalize print to suit their professionalizing and evangelical ends, they recognized that books like herbals could reach an audience of self-healers that may have otherwise been resistant to authorized forms of medical care. The books then served as advertisements, not for the services of particular authors or physicians but for the integrity of the emerging practice of professional physic more generally.

Thomas Gibson and the Authoritative Move

I began this chapter with an account of the first illustrated herbal in English, *The Grete Herball* published by Peter Treveris in 1526, which offered its users innovative affordances like indexes and tables of contents to enable discontinuous reading. Like his contemporary Richard Bankes, Treveris thought of his herbal as part of a sequence of related books about healing, relating it both to his recent handbook on surgery (1525) and later to Lawrence Andrewe's publication of a book of distillation (1527), which made use of *The Grete Herball*'s woodcuts. Treveris reprinted *The Grete Herball* in a joint publication with Andrewe in 1529. My analysis continued by suggesting that the printer Treveris's concern for the appearance of error in his books indicated his latent anxiety about readers' expectations for the printed artifacts they purchased and his awareness that readers could do whatever they liked with his books once they took them home from his bookshop. The evidence of annotative reading found in contemporary marginalia indicates that Treveris's concerns were justified: Renaissance readers *were* skeptical of the information presented in books, capable of recognizing the limitations of both textual transmission and a verbal text's authoritative claims. An attentiveness to the materiality of books as repositories for authorized and regularized attitudes towards knowledge establishes a crucial context for what comes next: the third edition of *The Grete Herbal* published by grocer-printer Thomas Gibson in 1539. This edition included the first appearance in English printed herbals of an authorizing figure who attempts to delimit or mark the interpretive boundaries of his verbal text.

Thomas Gibson, a Morpeth native, made his way to London to apprentice as a grocer in or around 1518. He was made free of his apprenticeship and was a citizen of the City by August 30, 1524, and immediately set up shop as a grocer, successful enough in his trade to bind apprentices in 1526 and 1528.[51] By 1535, however, Gibson had also begun printing, joining the ranks of several other non-stationers who were engaging in the craft before the Stationers' Company's incorporation in 1557 enabled Stationers to have full control over the technology. Gibson's religious sympathies can be gleaned from his publications: his first known printed book was an edition of Coverdale's concordance to the Tyndale Bible (*STC* 3046), and he printed Tyndale's New Testament (*STC* 2841) a few years later. Within the next four years, Gibson had printed a total of twelve works, eleven for himself as well as an English primer (*STC* 15998) that he printed for William Marshall.[52] In 1537, the bishop of Worcester, Hugh Latimer, wrote to Thomas Cromwell asking that Gibson (who was the messenger of the letter) be entrusted with the printing of *The Institution of a Christian Man* (*STC* 5163–7), a privilege that would normally be granted to the King's Printer Thomas Berthelet (which it ultimately was). Latimer notes in the letter that he himself is only passingly acquainted with Gibson; he remarks that he is vouching for the printer at the behest of one "Doctor Crome," probably Edward Crome, a clergyman and fellow of Gonville Hall.[53] Gibson seems to have done his best to ingratiate himself to the king; Blayney records finding among Cromwell's papers an eleven-page letter of pro–Henry VIII prophecies that Gibson had collected in the hopes of being useful, as well as a proposed bill to "regulate the use of confiscated monastic property."[54]

Gibson's petitions for advancement were not particularly successful, and he appears to have left England around 1543 to acquire a medical degree.[55] John Bale would later record in a notebook kept between 1548 and 1552 (which had once belonged to Gibson) that Gibson was "olim calcographus, nunc medicus" ("formerly a printer, now a physician").[56] Such medical

---

[51] Because there are a number of Thomas Gibsons in and around London during the decades under discussion, the printer Gibson's biography has proved difficult for historians. Blayney offers a cogent summary of the confusions in *Printers of London*, 390–398. See also, *pace* Blayney, Ian Gadd, "Gibson, Thomas (d. 1562)," *ODNB*.

[52] Gibson would also publish two books that he had printed by others. He hired Richard Lant in 1539–1540 to print *The Sum of the Acts and Decrees made by Divers Bishops of Rome* (*STC* 21307 a.7), the second edition of a work Gibson had first printed in 1538, and in 1552 he hired William Copland to print it again (*STC* 21308). See Blayney, *Printers of London*, 398.

[53] Susan Wabuda, "Crome, Edward (d. 1562), Church of England clergyman and religious controversialist," *ODNB*.

[54] Blayney, *Printers of London*, 397.

[55] Blayney, *Printers of London*, 393. On trends in Englishmen seeking continental MDs, see Margaret Pelling and Charles Webster, "Medical Practitioners," in Charles Webster (ed.), *Health, Medicine and Morality in the Sixteenth Century* (Cambridge: Cambridge University Press, 1979), 165–235.

[56] Blayney, *Printers of London*, 391.

sojourns by Englishmen were themselves not unusual; the physician Thomas Linacre took his MD at the University of Padua in 1496 before forming the College of Physicians of London in 1518.[57] Linacre's fellow Oxford graduate Edward Wotton and Cambridge's William Harvey also took their MDs at Padua, later having their credentials incorporated by their home universities. Archivists have found Gibson practicing medicine in Strasbourg in 1555–1558, and upon his return to England he was granted a license to practice medicine by Cambridge University in 1559.

One of the last books that Gibson printed before he left England testifies to his medical interests: a new and unillustrated 1539 edition of *The Grete Herball* (now spelled *The Great Herball*). Given *The Grete Herball*'s investment in enabling patients to forgo the "costly receipts of the pothecaries prepared" in favor of their own knowledge of "green herbs of the garden and weeds of the fields," Gibson's choice to republish Treveris's text is a curious one. Why would a grocer-apothecary undermine his craft by publishing a book that seeks to expose trade secrets? What seems to have happened is that, by 1539, Gibson had already decided to ally himself with a more professionalized medical calling than that of the apothecary-grocers. Hints of Gibson's philosophy may be seen in the changes that he made to the text of *The Grete Herball*, which he chose to advertise as "*The great herball newly corrected.*" In place of Treveris's xylographic red and black title page with its illustrated gardens, florals, and a pair of coy mandrakes, Gibson's title page made use of an architectural window-frame border that had previously belonged to printer William Rastell, who had used it to print Fabyan's *Chronicle* and Thomas More's rebuttals to Tyndale (Figure 5.3).[58] Unable or unwilling to locate botanical woodcuts to illustrate his text, Gibson may have thought it appropriate to suggest instead that his text of *The Great Herball* could stand alongside such commanding books. He did not use the border in his other publications.[59]

More telling, however, are Gibson's editorial changes to the contents of the work that justify his editorial pledge of "newly corrected." As he reprinted Treveris's text, the Protestant Gibson stripped *The Grete Herball* of its inherent Catholicism, removing the advice to pray to "our

---

[57] Vivian Nutton, "Linacre, Thomas (c.1460–1524), humanist scholar and physician," *ODNB*, 2004.

[58] R. B. McKerrow and F. S. Ferguson, *Title-Page Borders Used in England and Scotland 1485–1640* (London: Bibliographical Society, 1932), 18–19.

[59] Rastell had last used the border in 1534 to print John Heywood's *A Play of Loue* (*STC* 13303) and stopped printing shortly thereafter, and it is unclear when or how Gibson acquired it; by 1542, the border was in the hands of William Bonham, who used it for his own editions of Fabyan's *Chronicle* and Chaucer's *Workes*.

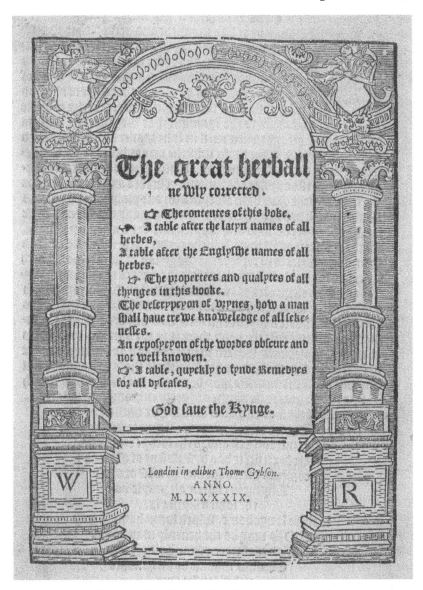

Figure 5.3 *The Great Herball* (1539). The Huntington Library, San Marino, California (RB 61431).

Lady" from the account of what to do for a bite from a "wood" or mad dog.[60] In addition to changing the work's religious bent, though, Gibson's text also used his printer's address to the reader to endorse the professionalization of healing as it was practiced by English physicians, shifting the nature of *The Grete Herball*'s medical authority from the individual self-healer to the dutiful patient who seeks out the resources of informed practitioners. While Treveris's preface emphasized the potential of the "gyftes of the holy gost" to enable a man to heal all manner of diseases himself, without the recourse of the "costly receipts of the apothecaries,"[61] apothecary Gibson's preface, now headed "The Prenter to the Reder," is careful to note that the authority of the text's remedies stems primarily from the professional status of its compilers. Though the 1539 *Great Herball*'s simples are still those "which God hath ordeyned for our prosperous welfare, & helthe," their virtues are reframed. Gibson's readers should take note of the remedies in his volume because they "ware practysed by many experte and wyse masters of physyke who also co[m]pyled this most necessary volume, for the comforte of all those, whiche tender theyr owne helth."[62] The volume's "*exposycyon of the wordes obscure and not well knowen*" appeared at the end of Treveris's editions of the book, but Gibson finds the glossary (which defined words like "appoplexie," "conglutinative," and "sirop") worth advertising on his title page. Gibson's highlighting of the list as a selling feature likewise serves to suggest the professional expertise of those who use such a vocabulary. Gibson's volume teaches, but it also implicitly sends the message that those who would heal themselves must rely on professionals for instruction. Without the intervening expertise of editorially employed masters of physic, "studies" like *The Great Herball* would be unable to "te[m]per prosperytye . . . mytygate aduersytye . . . kepe vnder the hastye and rashe mocions of yeuth, and make yonge persons semblable and equalle to me[n] of great age."[63] Education and scholarship are great equalizers, but as Gibson carefully reframes the work, *The Great Herball*'s contents are particularly valuable *because* they originate in professional masters who were motivated by a higher power to share their knowledge with the ignorant. Those compilers who "set forth first this herball, which geueth perfyte knowledge and vnderstandynge of all maner of herbes and theyr gracious vertues," were inspired by God, "as God is the causer of all good studyes . . . euen in lyke maner as it hath

---

[60] *The Great Herball* (1539), sig. R3v.   [61] *The Grete Herball* (1526), sig. ✠ 2r.
[62] *The Great Herball* (1539), sig. πIv.   [63] *The Great Herball* (1539), sig. πIv.

pleased God to styrre and moue those (whyche no doubte of it ware his elect) to set forth first this herbal."[64]

Gibson claims that printed books of medical remedies authored by learned, Galenic physicians serve the interest of the public, because

> sekenesses may be cured & healed by those which knowe the gracyous natures of herbes through the influe[n]ce course of the four eleme[n]tes which God hath set in theyr order, whiche order bryngeth all men to knowledge of all infyrmitees, and to the spedye remedyes therof.[65]

Medical authorities' education of readers through the distribution of printed books of remedies may be a benefit to the public at large, but as Gibson reframes his argument, it is also one that reaffirms the intellectual superiority of the English medical establishment and its construction of authorized forms of healing. Crucially, there is one exception to the diseases that the listed herbal remedies can cure: "excepte it be a dysease sent of God, as comenly men haue one dysease or other whyche bryngeth all people as the comen saying is, to theyr longe home."[66] Gibson's reworking of *The Grete Herball* therefore serves to provide his version of the text with a particularly authoritative medical standpoint, repeating the early modern physician's ultimate excuse that his inability to heal a sick patient results not from his lack of expertise but from the will of God.

Gibson likewise removed from his edition a closing address to readers that had previously appeared in Treveris's and Andrewe's editions and that would reappear in John King's 1561 edition. The address suggests that the volume would benefit both readers and "practicyens," a Middle French word that originally meant a practicer of a particular, usually medical, art, one who operates on the basis of practical rather than theoretical experience.[67] In equating readers with practicians, *The Grete Herball* of 1526 offers equal benefit and opportunity to all, regardless of intellectual or authoritative status:

> OYe worthy reders or practicyens to whome this noble volume is prese[n]t I beseche yow take intellygence and beholde ye workes & operacyo[n]s of almyghty god which hath endewed his symple creature mankynde with the graces of ye holy goost to haue parfyte knowlege and vn|derstandynge of the vertue of all maner of herbes and trees in this booke comprehendyd / and eueryche of them chaptred by hymselfe / & in euery chaptre dyuers clauses wherin is shewed dyuers maner of medycynes in one herbe comprehended

---

64 *The Great Herball* (1539), sig. πιν.   65 *The Great Herball* (1539), sig. πιν.
66 *The Great Herball* (1539), sig. πιν.   67 OED, "practicisian," *n.*

whiche ought to be notyfyed and marked for the helth of man in whome is
repended ye heuenly gyftes by the eternall kynge / to whom be laude and
prayse euerlastynge. AMEN[68]

Gibson's edition of 1539 eliminates this closing note. The herbal for
Gibson thus confirms a Tudor Reformer's moral value of the medical
arts, one whose practitioners heal the body just as the minister of the
Gospel heals the soul. A decade later, in his *Summarium* of 1548, John
Bale would credit Gibson with authorship of a now-lost treatise on
unskilled alchemists, suggesting that Gibson was invested in authorizing discourses even beyond what we see in this small printer's
preface.[69] Though he was trained as an apothecary and a member of
the Grocers' Company, Gibson had his eye on more professional
advancement, and he sought preferment both in direct appeals to
the crown and in the books that he offered for sale.

As discussed, Peter Treveris's reading of the print marketplace led
him to experiment with marketing his texts in new ways, like offering
his innovative "register" to enable different types of reading acts and by
declaring his work of particular use to his English readership in the
absence of readily accessible medical professionals. Gibson's edition is
largely structured like Treveris's, but Gibson improves upon the earlier
herbal's multiple articulation systems to offer distinct alphabetized
tables for both Latin and English chapter headings, and he expressly
uses the space of his new title page to advertise them. Within the
border's corniced columns, *The Great Herball*'s title page in 1539 offers
a careful list of "The contentes of this boke," which includes "A table
after the latyn names of all herbes, / A table after the Englysshe names of
all herbes." Along with the closing index of diseases he provides,
Gibson's opening tables allow his readers to search for individual medicaments in both languages, expanding upon Treveris's single table that
had been organized solely by simples' Latin names. These, too, are
carefully advertised on *The Great Herball*'s new title page. As we will
see in Chapter 7, Gibson's approving attitudes towards the professionalization of medicine, as well as the utility of the form of the printed
book to further these professionalizing ends, will resurface in
the writings of William Turner and color the way that scholars have
since read English herbals.

---

[68] *The Grete Herball* (1526), sig. 2D3v. The passage appears on the same page in Treveris's reprint of
1529 and on sig. Y8r in John King's version of 1561.
[69] Blayney, *Printers of London*, 390nC.

John King Plays the Odds

More than two decades after Gibson's revised *The Great Herball* appeared, John King suggested his familiarity with Gibson's "newly corrected" 1539 edition by advertising on the title page of his 1561 publication of *The Grete Herball* (as *The Greate Herball*) that the work was not only "newly corrected" but also "diligently ouersene." King's highlighting of correction as a feature of his text demonstrated his familiarity with the advertising language of his competitors in the English book trade: William Powell's 1550 edition of the "Askham" herbal, discussed in Chapter 4, advertised its text as being "newly amended and corrected," and it was this text that King saw fit to print for himself at the same time that he printed his edition of *The Grete Herball*. King's text, however, was not a reprint of Gibson's but a copy of Treveris's text that King saw fit to reprint unillustrated, perhaps because he was unable to locate suitable woodcuts or because he was unwilling to pay to have new ones cut at his own expense. Given the increasing demand for botanical accuracy that stemmed from popular continental publications like Otto Brunfels's *Herbarum vivae eicones* (Strasbourg, 1530–1536) and Leonard Fuchs's *De historia stirpium* (Basel, 1542), King may have surmised that the old illustrations simply would not serve the turn. There was also a new illustrated herbal complicating matters: the first part of William Turner's illustrated *A New Herball* had first been issued from John Gybkyn's shop in Paul's Churchyard in 1551, and King may have seen this authoritative book's impressive and detailed woodcuts in the copies that continued to circulate in London's bookshops. There was therefore good cause for eliminating illustrations entirely, despite their potential utility for readers.

King had started printing in 1554 and was one of the stationers listed in the Company's charter of incorporation.[70] Sometime between November 20, 1560, and March 8, 1561, King sought Stationers' Company licenses for three books: "the one Called *the little herball* the ij^{de} *the grete herball* the iij^{de} *the medicine for horses*."[71] King had been fined 2 shillings 6 pence by the Company in 1558–1559 "that he Ded prynte *the nutbrowne mayde* without lycense," so perhaps he, once burned, was

---

[70] Blayney helpfully provides both a transcript of the Stationers' charter of incorporation and an English translation in appendix J of *Printers of London*.

[71] Arber, *Transcript*, 1:61. Prior to 1582, the standard price of a book license was determined by the number of sheets of paper used in the composition of the book: 3 sheets for a penny; minimum 4d per item. See William A. Jackson, "Variant Entry Fees of the Stationers' Company," *Papers of the Bibliographical Society of America* 51 (1957): 103–110. King began by publishing his book on horses, which came out in 1560 (*STC* 24237.5).

particularly shy of being subjected to another Company sanction.[72] It is also possible that King was, like Peter W. M. Blayney's hypothetical stationer in "The Publication of Playbooks," either an "optimist (hoping that his [books] would do well enough to attract thoughts of piracy) or a pessimist (anticipating unspecified problems of infringement)."[73]

The calculated nature of John King's business strategy is confirmed by his choice in 1561 to pay to acquire the rights to two vernacular English herbals. By doing so, King eliminated both books from the public domain so long as he kept them in print, and he dutifully printed the little ten edition-sheet octavo (*STC* 13175.19) and the much larger, seventy-five edition-sheet double-column folio (*STC* 13179) immediately.[74] King's decision to market simultaneously two different English herbals testifies to the economic diversity he saw in the marketplace for printed books in the first decades of Elizabeth's reign. The longer, more expensive herbal could provide for users who were able to afford a more comprehensive text, while the smaller octavo could be bound with other related octavo works that King was issuing around the same time, like his new English translation of the book of secrets of Albertus Magnus (*STC* 258.5), which had been printed by William de Machlinia nearly eight decades before.[75] It was a clever scheme: by controlling both forms of herbals, King could ensure that the pair of texts were positioned to compete not with each other but within different markets and with different classes of users in mind.

Throughout this chapter, I have argued that, though historians of herbals have often ascribed credulity to early modern English readers, such accounts strain against the evidence of authors' paratextual explanations for their texts, the evidence of publishers' paratextual explanations for their books, and finally, the evidence of the marginalia left behind by contemporary readers. A publisher's decision to print an anonymous herbal text allowed readers to use their copies of books as locations to record their own local knowledge and experience free from authorial anxieties about intellectual influence. Yet, as Thomas Gibson's edition of the *Great Herball* shows, publishers' use

---

[72] Arber, *Transcript*, 1:93.   [73] Blayney, "Publication of Playbooks," 404.

[74] King's edition of what he calls *A litle herbal* collates A-I8 K8 (-K8), for a rounded total of ten edition-sheets. King's edition of *The Grete Herball* collates ✠ 6 A-X⁶ Y⁸ 2A⁶ 2B², for a total of 296 pages of 74 edition sheets.

[75] King secured his license to print this book, too, on August 30, 1560 (Arber, *Transcript*, 1:150). The text went through a number of editions by William Copland and William Seres before again being entered into the Registers by William Jaggard in 1595.

of anonymous texts could also provide an opportunity for would-be medical authorities to step into the breach. When William Turner turned his attentions to the genre at the end of the 1530s, the market was primed to christen a new – and named – figure upon the title pages of printed herbals.

CHAPTER 6

"Unpublished Virtues of the Earth"
Books of Healing on the English Renaissance Stage

As the previous chapter showed, marginalia offer a means for qualifying debates in the history of ideas to show that early modern readers did not automatically trust the information they found in printed books. This chapter uses evidence from the English stage to demonstrate that, for early moderns, the book form was often as important as its content. The material aspect of book knowledge was most pronounced in matters of medicine, where books were especially well-suited as stage properties that could serve characters' authoritative pretentions. What's more, an appreciation of books as properties reveals how early modern readers engaged in medical care not exclusively through deference to professional medical authorities but as individualized and idiosyncratic acts of self-healing.

Renaissance Credulity

In considering Renaissance English approaches to the marvelous, Madeline Doran sets out "to recapture the spirit of the cultured and adult Elizabethan, who saw his world through his own eyes, not ours" in order "to understand what to them is normal and what strange, in other words, what their standard of reasonable judgment is."[1] While post-Enlightenment standards of classification and independent verification of facts were obviously not yet in use in the period, Elizabethans nonetheless "had certain positive principles of reference by which they could judge of the probability of things firsthand," such as the use of analogies and the doctrine of signatures.[2] Doran proposes that scholars acknowledge the distinct degrees of "responses to the marvelous" that contemporary individuals might hold about various subjects, degrees that range from complete acceptance, through "entertainment of the possibility," to "complete

---

[1] Doran, "On Elizabethan 'Credulity,'" 151, 156.
[2] Doran, "On Elizabethan 'Credulity,'" 163. See also Poovey, *History of the Modern Fact*.

rejection ... with a willingness for reasons of convention or of symbolism to entertain the fiction imaginatively."[3] As she notes, such a range of credulity accounts for the message of John Donne's popular poem "Go and catch a falling star," where "it does matter in what state of belief we are in with regard to mandrakes or mermaids, for if we believe in them too thoroughly we shall miss the point of the poem, that a constant woman is as strange as they."[4]

Even by the standards of modern knowledge, humanists may have made their assertions about early modern credulity and the efficacy of medieval and Renaissance herbal remedies too easily. An article in the *Journal of Ethnopharmacology* by scientists examining sixteenth-, seventeenth-, and eighteenth-century herbals for evidence of plants that were supposed to effectively treat rheumatoid illness found that more than half so identified by the herbals do work.[5] The authors have since followed up this study with others on Renaissance herbalists' remedies for epilepsy and malaria.[6] While Francis Johnson may have disagreed with Wyer's assertion of a hot plaster to cure hemorrhoids in 1944, the same remedy was advocated by master barber-surgeon John Gerard in his herbal of 1597 and may have been a common treatment.[7] The appearance of such remedies suggests that early modern writers who addressed a wide public audience assumed that their readers had a considerable body of personal and common knowledge upon which they could draw to evaluate a book's claims. Such critiques likewise made their way into popular entertainment. In his mockery of

---

[3] Doran, "On Elizabethan 'Credulity,'" 170–171.
[4] Doran, "On Elizabethan 'Credulity,'" 173. For a more extended treatment, see Daston and Park, *Wonders and the Order of Nature*. Donne's poem appears in dozens of surviving seventeenth-century manuscripts (Peter Beal (ed.), *Catalogue of English Literary Manuscripts 1450–1700*, accessible at www .celm-ms.org.uk).
[5] See Michael Adams, Caroline Berset, Michael Kessler, and Matthias Hamburger, "Medicinal Herbs for the Treatment of Rheumatic Disorders: A Survey of European Herbals from the 16th and 17th Century," *Journal of Ethnopharmacology* 121 (2009): 343–359.
[6] Michael Adams, Sarah-Vanessa Schneider, Martin Kluge, Michael Kessler, and Matthias Hamburger, "Epilepsy in the Renaissance: A Survey of Remedies from 16th and 17th Century German Herbals," *Journal of Ethnopharmacology* 143 (2012): 1–13; Michael Adams, Wandana Alther, Michael Kessler, Martin Kluge, and Matthias Hamburger, "Malaria in the Renaissance: Remedies from European Herbals from the 16th and 17th Century," *Journal of Ethnopharmacology* 133 (2011): 278–288.
[7] "The leaues of Elder boiled in water vntill they be very soft, and when they are almost boyled inough, a little oile of sweet Almonds added thereto, or a little Lineseed oile; then taken forth and laide vpon a red cloth, or a peece of scarlet, and applied vnto the Hemorrhoides or Piles, as hot as can be suffered, and so remaine vpon the part affected, vntill it be somewhat colde, hauing the like in a readines, applying one after another vpon the diseased part, by the space of an hower or more, and in the end some bounde to the place, and the patient warme a bed: it hath not as yet failed at the first dressing, to cure the said disease; but if the patient be dressed twice, it must needes do good, if the first faile" (Gerard, *Herball* (1597), sig. 4K8r).

grocers, *The Knight of the Burning Pestle* (1607), Francis Beaumont could assume that enough early moderns recognized the value of licorice to "maketh a mannes brest / his throte / & his lo[n]ges, moyst and in good tempre" (Bankes 1525, sig. E1v) to squeeze even more of a laugh out of a pushy character's unnecessary interruptions of the action of a play-within-a-play:

WIFE   I pray, my pretty youth, is Rafe ready?
BOY   He will be presently.
WIFE   Now, I pray you, make my commendations unto him, and withal carry him this stick of licorice. Tell him his mistress sent it to him, and bid him bite a piece; 'twill open his pipes the better, say. (1.1.69–76)[8]

Just as apprentice Rafe echoes nothing but popular speeches by the likes of Hotspur, Mucedorus, and Hieronimo, his master and his mistress offer their customers nothing but widely known popular remedies. Wife Nell's disturbance is made the more aggravating (and more humorous) because she assumes her knowledge is specialized whereas it is widely held in common, a usurpation of medical authority that mimics the way she and her grocer-apothecary husband George have usurped the public stage of the fictional play *The London Merchant.*[9] In a similar way to Nell and George, the booksellers operating during the first century of print endeavored to commodify much common herbal and medical knowledge for their own profits. Although the resulting books supplemented the information circulating in folklore and public discourse, they did not necessarily supplant it.[10]

Authorizing Stage Medicine

Francis Beaumont's assumption of his audience's familiarity with simple remedies in *The Knight of the Burning Pestle* is a reminder that Renaissance dramatists regularly drew both on common knowledge and on contemporary

[8] Francis Beaumont, *The Knight of the Burning Pestle*, in Arthur F. Kinney (ed.), *Renaissance Drama* (Oxford: Blackwell, 1999).

[9] Margaret Pelling calls such homey recipes "kitchen physic." See Margaret Pelling, "Compromised by Gender: The Role of the Male Medical Practitioner in Early Modern England" in Hilary Marland and Margaret Pelling (eds.), *The Task of Healing: Medicine, Religion and Gender in England and the Netherlands 1450–1800* (Rotterdam: Erasmus Publishing, 1996), 101–133; 104. On the epistemological ramifications of kitchen physic practiced by women in domestic spaces, see Wall, *Recipes for Thought*, 219–226.

[10] More specialized studies of readership reinforce this readerly resistance. For example, J. Wogan-Browne's work on hagiography and virginity literature reinforces the ways in which female readers in particular deployed complex strategies of interpretation to challenge dominant narratives about women's bodily autonomy. See *Saints' Lives and Women's Literary Culture: Virginity and Its Authorizations* (Oxford: Oxford University Press, 2001).

cultural debates to furnish the worlds of their plays. Here, too, can we find evidence that the material forms of books caused readers to take matters of influence into their own hands. Renaissance dramatists widely recognized that, as props, books could figure synecdochally on stage to endorse and to under-mine characters' authority.[11] In a number of plays by Shakespeare and his contemporaries, lay healers (that is to say, medical practitioners other than physicians and surgeons) are explicit in their use of written materials to validate their own successful healing acts. Other characters defend their right to self-medicate, which provides a larger context for understanding how herbal authors attempted to assert their dominance over the administration of herbal remedies. Such an interruption in my analysis of the printing history of Renaissance herbals may seem to mistake the symptom for the cause, but this chapter is designed to illuminate the setting in which sixteenth-century pub-lishers, herbalists, and medical authors competed for readers. As Jean E. Howard has remarked in her study of the Elizabethan public theatre's role in cultural transformations, "the scripts themselves embody social struggle . . . they enact a contest between and a negotiation among competing ideological positions."[12] Only in an environment where readers already assumed that they had a responsibility to heal themselves did it make sense for medical authors to take such pains to position themselves as gifted advisors and specialized counsellors. Such attention also offers a literary payoff: drawing out this lost history of self-medicating as it appeared not only on the Renaissance English stage but also on the extant pages of popular sixteenth-century herbals enables me to account for the curious disappearance of Cordelia's attendant "Doctor" – a character who exists in the 1608 quarto *History of King Lear* but whose role is replaced by an indistinct "Gentleman" in the 1623 folio *Tragedy of King Lear*. Given Shakespeare's attitudes towards physicians and lay healers elsewhere in his canon, I propose that this famous crux concerning the character's identity is inflected by debates over who has the right to authorize what should be *common* knowledge. To understand Beaumont's joke about George and Nell is thus to understand something of the King's Men's revision of *King Lear*: both cases highlight the ways that English healers tried to assert their scholarly and literary credentials upon resistant subjects.[13] Printed books played a major part in this jockeying for authority.

---

[11] On the role of properties on the Renaissance English stage, see Andrew Sofer, *The Stage Life of Props* (Ann Arbor: University of Michigan Press, 2003).

[12] Jean E. Howard, *The Stage and Social Struggle in Early Modern England* (London: Routledge, 1994), 83.

[13] I remain convinced by the argument that Shakespeare was the agent behind the revision of Quarto to Folio texts provided by John Kerrigan's essay "Revision, Adaptation, and the Fool in *King Lear*," in Taylor and Warren, *The Division of the Kingdoms: Shakespeare's Two Versions of King Lear* (Oxford:

In the 1520s, when both the little *Herball* and *The Grete Herball* were first published, members of the nascent College of Physicians of London were still struggling to situate themselves within a diverse medical marketplace.[14] London's Company of Barber-Surgeons, like the Stationers, had a long history within the City and would soon get a royal charter of their own in 1540. Apothecaries like George and Nell would remain part of the Grocers' Company until the Society of the Apothecaries would split apart from them (with the physicians' help) in 1617, but the Grocers' status as one of London's great twelve livery companies ensured that such medicament-dispensing grocers were both plentiful and powerful.[15] When, in 1518, the College of Physicians of London was granted their charter, its members were profoundly outnumbered by London citizens well-equipped to manage the commercial and civic aspects of healing. The handful of physicians could not realistically compete for practical dominance, but members of the College had other, far more important, social goals in mind.

Margaret Pelling has written at length about the College's struggles during the seventeenth century to differentiate itself from other healers and empirics through a concerted program of professionalization and "aggressive intellectual activity" that sought to demonstrate the ways that physicians' considerable humanistic training raised them above the menial "body-service" performed mostly by women.[16] Pelling's work shows that, while early modern English physicians might have been able to obtain high social status on an individual level, their professional body remained insecure about their intellectual pretensions as a group. "[T]he College seem[ed] to be manifesting a form of self-consciousness unusually well developed for the period," Pelling writes, "composed of anxieties, insecurities, and a mode of self-righteousness, allied to an entirely anomalous institutional position and lack of effective connection with the political process."[17] Seeking to establish physicians not only as healers but more importantly as intellectual counselors

---

Clarendon Press, 1986), 195–245, which highlights the ways that a "tinkering" playwright would revise earlier work; other critics, however, reserve from passing judgment on just who, exactly, was responsible for making alterations to the Quarto to produce the Folio text.

[14] See Margaret Pelling, *Medical Conflicts in Early Modern London: Patronage, Physicians, and Irregular Practitioners 1550–1640* (Oxford: Oxford University Press, 2003). Pelling points out that the term "medical marketplace" is Harold Cook's, which she explains describes "the relative (and increasing) lack of regulation of medicine in an England heading towards laissez-faire economics and partisan politics" (2).

[15] C. R. B. Barrett, *The History of the Society of Apothecaries of London* (London: Elliot Stock, 1905).

[16] Margaret Pelling, "Compromised by Gender," 114. See also Pelling and Webster, "Medical Practitioners," and Pelling, *Medical Conflicts*, esp. chap. 6, "Gender Compromises: The Female Practitioner and Her Connections."

[17] Pelling, *Medical Conflicts*, 14.

with the ear of royal and civic authorities, the College even went so far as to implement a code of elevated dress for its members in 1597, stipulating "scarlet for feast-days and solemn meetings, purple for other occasions."[18] Such sumptuary dress signified a distinction between a College physician and any other practitioner of medicine such as a barber-surgeon or an empiric, whose services were not only cheaper but apparently preferred by laity at all levels of status. Francis Bacon was espousing popular opinion when he noted in his *Advancement of Learning* that "in all times, in the opinion of the multitude, witches and old women and imposters have had a competition with physicians." It is evident, however, that Bacon didn't really blame the public for their preferences, as his opinion of the College was not much better: "Medicine is a science which hath been (as we have said) more professed than laboured, and yet more laboured than advanced; the labour having been, in my judgement, rather in circle than in progression. For I find much iteration, but small addition."[19]

Since the granting of their charter of 1518, the College of Physicians had endeavored to "regulate" medical practice in London (and within a seven-mile radius of the city) by prosecuting unlicensed healers who fell outside the civic guilds of Barber-Surgeon and Grocers, such as empirics, mountebanks, and cunning women. This right was granted them by their charter's patent, which was designed "with a view to the improvement and more orderly exercise of the art of physic, and the repression of irregular, unlearned, and incompetent practitioners of that faculty."[20] Such "irregular practitioners" were viewed as a practical threat not only to the physicians' attempted monopolization of physic but also to the decorum and status of medicine itself, an anxiety that did not go unnoticed by Elizabethan dramatists alert to such moments of social struggle. Throughout Thomas Heywood's city comedy *The Wise Woman of Hoxton* (performed 1602–1603), for example, the disguised heroine Luce 2 critiques the eponymous character's "lawless, indirect and horrid means / For covetous gain!"[21] Sympathizing with the

---

[18] George Clark, *A History of the Royal College of Physicians of London* (Oxford: Clarendon Press, 1964), 137–138.

[19] Francis Bacon, *Advancement of Learning*, ed. William Aldis Wright (Oxford: Clarendon Press, 1869), 135, 137.

[20] William Munk, *The Roll of the Royal College of Physicians of London*, 3 vols. 2nd ed. (London: Royal College of Physicians, 1878), 1:1. For a copy of the original Letters Patent (in Latin), see Munk, *Roll*, 1:2–6. For a history of the College, see Harold Cook, *The Decline of the Old Medical Regime in Stuart London* (Ithaca, NY: Cornell University Press, 1986) and Clark, *History*.

[21] All quotations from *The Wise Woman of Hoxton* are taken from Sonia Massai's edition of the play for the Globe Quartos series. Thomas Heywood, *The Wise Woman of Hoxton*, ed. Sonia Massai, Globe Quartos (New York: Routledge, 2002).

status quo of professionalized medical authorities, Luce 2 dismisses the Wise Woman's pretensions, asking "How many unknown trades / Women and men are free of, which they never / Had charter for?" (3.1.43–45) and ultimately concluding that the Wise Woman's efforts are "no trade, but a mystery" (3.1.68). For her own part, the Wise Woman views herself as a veritable civic polymath:

> Let me see how many trades I have to live by: first, I am a wise woman and a fortune-teller, and under that I deal in physic and forespeaking, in palmistry, and recovering of things lost. Next, I undertake to cure mad folks. Then I keep gentlewomen lodgers to furnish such chambers as I let out by the night. Then I am provided for bringing young wenches to bed. And for a need, you see I can play the matchmaker.
> She that is but one and professeth so many,
> May well be termed a wise woman, if there be any. (3.1.164–82)

The Wise Woman's bravado, which celebrates not only her healing prowess but also her skills as prophet and bawd, later serves to suggest that the play's outcome derives less from any inherent cleverness that she might have than it does from the naïve foolishness of her victims.

Luce 2 ends Heywood's play as its unmistakable hero, making clear that the Wise Woman is simply a charlatan; but not all early modern dramatists were quite so sympathetic as Heywood to the cause of the professional medical authorities. William Kerwin points out the ways that the "medical theater" of John Webster's *The Duchess of Malfi* serves to display "how claims to ancient and disinterested tradition can cover up base interests," ultimately revealing the ways that "medical power legitimates itself."[22] At the root of Kerwin's argument is an association that Webster makes between Malfi's corrupted court and the tenuous medical authority of the play's physicians, best illustrated by the Doctor's overestimation of his ability to intimidate Ferdinand's madness right out of him:

> Let me have some forty urinals filled with rose water: he and I'll go pelt one another with them; now he begins to fear me. Can you fetch a frisk, sir? Let him go, let him go upon my peril. I find by his eye he stands in awe of me: I'll make him as tame as a dormouse. (5.2.68–73)[23]

---

[22] William Kerwin, "'Physicians Are Like Kings': Medical Politics and *The Duchess of Malfi*," *English Literary Renaissance* 28 (1998): 95–117; 96.

[23] All quotations from *The Duchess of Malfi* are taken from John Webster, *The Duchess of Malfi*, ed. Elizabeth M. Brennan, New Mermaids (London: Ernest Benn, 1964).

As Pescara and Bosola witness, the Doctor's bombast fails; instead of submitting to the Doctor's authority, Ferdinand beats him, adding:

> Can you fetch your frisks, sir? I will stamp him into a cullis; flay off his skin, to cover one of the anatomies, this rogue hath set i'th' cold yonder, in Barber-Chirurgeons' Hall. Hence, hence! you are all of you like beasts for sacrifice, there's nothing left of you, but tongue and belly, flattery and lechery. (5.2.73–80)

Adding insult to the injuries he showers upon the Doctor, Ferdinand's reference to the barber-surgeons' public anatomies serves to remind audiences that, of the major competitors for medical authority in Jacobean London, it is the surgeons' skills that were practically and empirically obtained.[24] Evidence of physicians' lax morality, as well as their middling success at healing, is presented throughout the play, from a remark about doctors' overreliance on urine analysis, "which some do call / The physician's whore, because she cozens him" (1.2.58–59), to their preoccupation with lucrative trivialities like cosmetics, or "scurvy face physic . . . the very patrimony of the physician" (2.1.25–44).[25] In her own mistrust of physicians' practice of raising the expense of medicine to little curative effect, Julia notes that unreactive gold "hath no smell, like cassia or civet, / Nor is it physical, though some fond doctors / Persuade us, seethe't in cullises" (2.4.64–66). Webster's play endeavors to remind its audience that physicians' labored proximity to royal and ecclesiastical authorities so readily corrupts them that, despite their Hippocratic Oath, they are as suspect as

---

[24] In order to be admitted to the freedom of the Barber-Surgeons' Company, a candidate had to have met the general requirements for admittance to a London mystery (by serving an apprenticeship for no less than seven years' time, by being the son of a member of the company, or by redemption) as well as pass an examination assuring that the candidate was "well exercised in the curing of infirmities belonging to surgery of the parts of a man's body commonly called the anatomy." See Sidney Young, *The Annals of the Barber-Surgeons of London* (New York: AMS Press, 1978), 316. In contrast, as Pelling and Webster note, "the profile of the academically educated physician which gradually emerged was that of a humanistically inclined scholar, familiar alike with classical tongues and the medical sciences. This physician had spent many years studying at English universities, and sometimes also a few years abroad at one or more of the continental medical schools. This course of education frequently involved seven years in preparation for an MA, and a further seven years or more accumulating medical qualifications" ("Medical Practitioners," 189). Though both the College and the Company required their members to participate in anatomical demonstrations, it was not the Physicians but the Barber-Surgeons who both enforced this regulation and opened their dissections for the interest of the curious public ("Medical Practitioners," 176; see also Young, *Annals*).

[25] On physicians' anxieties about their association with urine, see Margaret Pelling, "Recorde and *The Vrinal of Physick*: Context, Uroscopy and the Practice of Medicine," in Gareth Roberts and Fenny Smith (eds.), *Robert Recorde: The Life and Times of a Tudor Mathematician* (Cardiff: University of Wales Press, 2012), 39–56.

any other indentured menial. As Bosola muses, "all our fear, / Nay, all our terror, is lest our physician / Should put us in the ground" (2.1.61–63), an opinion the Duchess shares: "physicians thus, / With their hands full of money, use to give o'er / Their patients" (3.5.7–9).[26]

Such dramatic anxiety over devious physicians was also apparent in the works of Webster's predecessors and contemporaries. In *The Jew of Malta*, Marlowe's murderous Barabas (who famously "go[es] about and poison[s] wells") claims to have learned his trade when

> Being young, I studied physic, and began
> To practice first upon the Italian;
> There I enriched the priests with burials,
> And always kept the sexton's arms in ure
> With digging graves and ringing dead men's knells. (2.3.185–189)[27]

The city comedies of Thomas Dekker, Francis Beaumont, and John Fletcher likewise demonstrate an awareness of popular apprehensions surrounding medical authorities' access to poison;[28] and with good reason: the widely publicized trial of Dr. Roderigo Lopez in 1593 and the murder by poison of Sir Thomas Overbury in 1613 kept such medical dangers in the forefront of the public imagination. When Ben Jonson's Corbaccio (himself a would-be poisoner) insists that the sleeping draught he offers Volpone is safe, he admits to having overseen its preparation just to make sure that the untrustworthy physician didn't slip in anything lethal: "I myself / Stood by, while 't was made; saw all th' ingredients" (1.4.14–15).[29] Later in the play, as Volpone imitates a mountebank, such guile is extended beyond physicians to include anyone engaged in medicating others for profit, and the drama's humor rests in depicting the absurdity and futility of the commodified medical marketplace of Jacobean London (in its Venetian disguise). Mosca's repeated claim that "He hath no faith in physic" is sufficiently broad to make a jest of anyone fool enough to hand over coin in exchange for an assurance of health.

---

[26] Compare the "true physic" of Ben Jonson's *Volpone*: "'Tis *aurum palpabile*, if not *potabile*" (1.4.73).

[27] All quotations from Christopher Marlowe's *The Jew of Malta* are from David Bevington's edition in *English Renaissance Drama* (New York: W. W. Norton, 2002).

[28] For a reading of a similar perspective on the physicians of Ben Jonson's *Sejanus, his Fall* and *Volpone*, see Tanya Pollard, "'No Faith in Physic': Masquerades of Medicine Onstage and Off," in Stephanie Moss and Kaara L. Peterson (eds.), *Disease, Diagnosis and Cure on the Early Modern Stage* (Burlington, VT: Ashgate, 2004), 29–41, as well as Pollard's monograph *Drugs and Theater in Early Modern England* (Oxford: Oxford University Press, 2005).

[29] All quotations from Benjamin Jonson's *Volpone, or The Fox* are from David Bevington's edition in *English Renaissance Drama* (New York: W. W. Norton, 2002).

As far as the efficacy of medical authorities is concerned, Shakespeare seems to have been more of Webster's persuasion than either Heywood's or Jonson's, seeing medicine as something that *could* be successfully practiced – but by empirics, lay people, or cunning women, and *not* by physicians. Of the eight characters in Shakespeare's plays designated as "doctors" by their speech prefixes, all are men, unsurprising given the exclusively male makeup of the College.[30] Yet, while Shakespeare's *doctors* are universally male professionals, the same cannot be said of his *healers* both on and off stage. *Twelfth Night*'s Fabian urges that Malvolio's urine be carried "to th' wise woman" for analysis of the cause of his madness (3.4.88), while *The Comedy of Errors*' Adriana is dismayed that her wifely duties as caregiver have been usurped by the Abbess's sheltering of the seemingly mad Antipholus of Ephesus (5.1.99–102).[31] In explaining these and other medical moments in Shakespeare's plays, Barbara Howard Traister sees a general movement towards an acceptance of physicians' authoritative pretensions that they struggled so hard to maintain.[32] Traister suggests that Shakespeare's Jacobean doctors function less as healers than as authenticators of offstage action, valued for "their ability to observe and to pronounce judgment, rather than for their therapeutic skills."[33] She points out that, despite the prevalence of impotent or inactive medical professionals in the Shakespeare canon, two of his later plays offer lay medical practitioners who ultimately succeed where professional medicine has failed: in *All's Well That Ends Well*, Helena cures the French king's seemingly incurable fistula, while *Pericles*' Cerimon raises the entombed Thaisa from death. I will return to Cerimon's and Helena's activities in a moment.

Margaret Pelling's work has shown that one of the "aggressive intellectual activities" employed by the College was an attempt to mirror the religious and intellectual authority the clergy maintained through its elite

---

[30] Included in this count are the sometime-schoolmaster Dr. Pinch in *The Comedy of Errors*, the French Dr. Caius in *The Merry Wives of Windsor*, *Cymbeline*'s moral Cornelius, *Macbeth*'s Scottish–English physician pair, *Henry VIII*'s Dr. Butts, and the otherwise unnamed "Doctors" of *Two Noble Kinsmen* and the quarto of *King Lear*.

[31] Except where noted, quotations from Shakespeare are taken from the *New Oxford Shakespeare: The Complete Works, Modern Critical Edition*, ed. Gary Taylor, John Jowett, Terri Bourus, and Gabriel Egan (Oxford: Oxford University Press, 2016). For a comprehensive account of unofficial healers upon the stage, see M. A. Katritzky, *Women, Medicine and Theatre, 1500–1750: Literary Mountebanks and Performing Quacks* (Burlington, VT: Ashgate, 2007).

[32] Barbara Howard Traister, "'Note Her a Little Farther': Doctors and Healers in the Drama of Shakespeare," in Stephanie Moss and Kaara L. Peterson (eds.), *Disease, Diagnosis, and Cure on the Early Modern Stage* (Burlington, VT: Ashgate, 2004), 43–52.

[33] Traister, "Note Her a Little Farther," 45.

access to biblical texts. By representing the works of Galen as similarly sacred, choosing only to employ Galenic methodology in treatment and denying the feasibility of alternatives such as Paracelsianism, the College declared its respect for in-depth reading practices and aligned itself with the general humanistic linking of scholarship and gentle status.[34] Implicitly connected to physicians' authority over the public practice of physic was a connection to books and learning, an association most clearly emphasized in the distinction made between the elevated theory of medicine as described in books and the hands-on business of practical healing. With their extended university educations, physicians had a vested interest in the social elevation of book learning, while medical practitioners operating in the civic guild tradition such as Barber-Surgeons and Apothecaries, or "empirics" operating without a company affiliation such as Heywood's eponymous Wise Woman of Hoxton, emphasized the importance of successful practice. Pelling and Webster note that, over the course of the sixteenth century, members of both licensed groups became increasingly invested in authoring works of natural history, mathematics, and medicine as part of a larger effort to demonstrate both their authoritative knowledge and their hands-on experience.[35]

Such conflicting values may be seen in the title character's first scene, where the Wise Woman receives a suite of seven clients at once, all clambering for her attention. Presented with the urine of a Countryman's ill wife, the Wise Woman claims to diagnose from it the heartbreak and ill stomach from which the wife suffers, eventually crowing her success in a long speech that celebrates the practical expertise of empirics:

> I think I can see as far into a millstone as another. You have heard of Mother Nottingham, who, for her time, was prettily well skilled in the casting of waters. And after her, Mother Bomby. And then there is one Hatfield in

---

[34] "[I]n meetings with as well as outside the College, censorship was mainly exerted by means of the Censors' admonitions to aspirants and irregulars as to what works they should and should not read, quote from, or publicly applaud. It is fair to say that none of the moderns sufficed in the absence of Galen, and irregulars were never instructed to read a modern author. Indeed, the Galenic texts were represented to (male) irregulars as all-sufficing ... [a]s far as the officebearers were concerned, innovation was allowable only from within, not outside the College" (Pelling, *Medical Conflicts*, 70). See also 17, 57–83.

[35] Pelling and Webster, "Medical Practitioners," 172, 177. In the case of Barber-Surgeons, who, more than any other London medical organization, were invested in public health initiatives to treat illnesses such as the plague and pox, these publications were also designed to teach the literate to treat their illnesses themselves. See Margaret Pelling, "Appearance and Reality: Barber-Surgeons, the Body and Disease," in A. L. Beier and Roger Finlay (eds.), *London 1500–1700: The Making of the Metropolis* (London and New York: Longman, 1986), 82–112; 103.

Pepper Alley; he doth pretty well for a thing that's lost. There's another in
Coldharbour that's skilled in the planets. Mother Sturton in Golden Lane is
for forespeaking. Mother Philips of the Bankside for the weakness of the
back. And then there's a very reverend matron on Clerkenwell Green, good
at many things. Mistress Mary on the Bankside is for 'recting a figure. And
one – what do you call her – in Westminster, that practices the book and the
key, and the sieve and the shears. And all do well, according to their talent.
For myself, let the world speak. (2.1.21–37)

Yet, as the unimpressed Luce 2 notes in an aside, the Wise Woman can
actually only see "[j]ust so much as is told her" (2.1.14), and she bemoans
that the public's glorification of novelty overshadows the more important
problem of the Wise Woman's lack of a formal education:

> 'Tis strange the ignorant should be thus fool'd.
> What can this witch, this wizard, or old trot,
> Do by enchantment or by magic spell?
> Such as profess that art should be deep scholars.
> What *reading* can this simple woman have?

In Chapter 5, I explained how the materials of the printed book provided
a site for early modern readers to contest the intellectual authority of verbal
texts in their annotations by correcting, modifying, or otherwise changing
the book to suit their own particular ends. The materials of the printed
book likewise serve the idiosyncratic ends of a figure like the Wise Woman,
who recognizes that her customers settle questions of her authority over
medical and mystical matters by the mere appearance of learning: the Wise
Woman handles books, therefore she can handle whatever problems are
brought her way. "As is so often true in this period," Jean Howard writes of
Heywood's play, "power is shown to lie with the theatrically skillful, and in
this play the most theatrically skillful figures are women."[36] Because part of
the Wise Woman's theatrical skill depends on her careful deployment of
the materials of traditional medical authority, the physician's classically
steeped university education in Galen can easily be mimicked with the
assistance of appropriate properties. After Luce 2 has employed herself in
the Wise Woman's service, she continues to question her new mistress
directly:

LUCE 2 … But, mistress, are you so cunning as you make yourself? You can
neither write nor read; what do you with those books you so often turn over?

---

[36] Howard, *Stage and Social Struggle*, 89.

WISE WOMAN Why, tell the leaves. For to be ignorant, and seem Ignorant, what
     greater folly?
LUCE 2 [aside] Believe me, this is a cunning woman.

Andrew Sofer has observed that "props are not static symbols but precision
tools" that require interaction with an actor in order to achieve meaning.[37]
The acutely performative Wise Woman is well aware of this fact, and she
makes the most of the book props at her disposal. Even Luce 2 is sardonic-
ally impressed with her performance.

     While Heywood has an empiric's (and mountebank's) view of book
learning serve as a mere pretense to supplement her practical skills, both of
Shakespeare's successful lay healers actually *read* books alongside their
hands-on experience in order to construct their medical authority, mirroring
the scholarly humanistic shift that the physicians so self-consciously
attempted to employ. In scene 14 of *Pericles, Prince of Tyre*, the Lord
Cerimon restores Thaisa, the dead wife of the play's hero, back to life after
she died in childbirth during a Mediterranean voyage and was buried at sea.
The wooden box containing Thaisa's body eventually washes up on the
Ephesian shore and is promptly brought to Cerimon to open and investigate.
At the start of the scene, Cerimon enters attendant on the servants of two ill
masters who have sought out his medical advice. Nothing can be done for
the first, but he offers the second a prescription to be filled by an apothecary.
Such advice would not be remarkable coming from a real doctor, but as his
title suggests, Cerimon is not a trained physician but a lay healer, drawn to
medicine through its connection to what he calls "virtue and cunning"
(14.25). As a healer, Cerimon is apparently very successful, and the Second
Gentleman notes that "hundreds call themselves your creatures, who / By
you have been restored" (14.42–43). In order to account for his medical
knowledge, Cerimon offers the following explanation:

> 'Tis known I ever
> Have studied physic, through which secret art,
> By turning o'er authorities, I have
> Together with my practice, made familiar
> To me and to my aid the blest infusions
> That dwells in vegetives, in metals, stones,
> And so can speak of the disturbances
> That nature works, and of her cures . . . (14.29–36)

---

[37] Sofer, *Stage Life of Props*, 3, 12.

The "authorities" that Cerimon refers to here are learned writers, not only Galen but also those medical practitioners, like medieval Roger Bacon, whose texts outlining the manufacture of alchemical "blest infusions" were publicly denounced by the College of Physicians.[38] Cerimon's books reveal to him "secret arts," such as the method behind the mystic recoveries of bodies that have "nine hours lien dead" (14.82), or the principles espoused by Paracelsus of alchemical medicine found in metals and stones.

A similar emphasis on the authority of the written word can be seen in Helen's request to the Countess in *All's Well That Ends Well*. Helen's wish to go to Paris to cure the king by using her father's "prescriptions / Of rare and proved affects" (1.3.193–194) is well known both to the world of the play and to its critics (such as Lafeu's dictum to her in the play's first scene: "you must hold the credit of your father" [1.1.66]), but less critical attention has been paid to the *source* of her physician father's knowledge, which comes down to Helen through the reading habits that scholars have observed in the surviving records of actual Renaissance physicians.[39] As well as his "manifest experience" (1.3.195), Gerard de Narbonne's remedies, "notes whose faculties inclusive were / More than they were in note" (1.3.198–199), stem from his "reading" (1.3.194) and are conveyed to Helen only because Narbonne in turn "set down" (1.3.200) his knowledge in manuscript. Whether Narbonne's note-taking was a deliberate transfer of his own knowledge to his daughter (Helen remarks only that they are passively and ambiguously "left" her [1.3.193]) or whether he took notes for his own later benefit is unclear. However, what is crucial in my reading of this passage is the material means by which Helen receives this knowledge, means that are similar to the way her father would have first received his – by reading. Crucial, too, is that Narbonne was, as were the medical practitioners in attendance on the King of France, a physician with a humanist university education – he was neither a surgeon nor an apothecary who learned his trade by apprenticeship in accordance with civic custom. It is the Galenic theoretical underpinnings of physicians' educations learned by rote that the Countess surmises leaves them too "[e]mbowlled of their doctrine" to truly help their king (1.3.213).

Something more than skill, Helen claims, will allow her to try *her* receipt out on the King. Critics such as Susan Snyder see that "something more" in Helen's status as a virgin: in his address to the King, Lafeu "goes on to

[38] On Paracelsian remedies, see Charles Webster, "Alchemical and Paracelsian Medicine," in Charles Webster (ed.), *Health, Medicine and Morality in the Sixteenth Century* (Cambridge: Cambridge University Press, 1979), 301–334, esp. 313.

[39] See Traister, *Notorious*, and Murphy, "Common Places."

emphasize Helen herself as the curative application, rather than the pre-scription she carries."[40] Such a reading holds well in Lafeu's allusive emphasis that Helen will bawdily raise the King to "sprightly fire and motion" (2.1.70). Yet it is in these bawdy puns that we also see confirm-ation that the mode of authority that Helen carries with her is the *written* artifact – "to give great Charlemagne a pen in 's hand / And write to her a love-line" (2.1.72–73).[41]

Contextualizing Cordelia

In contrast with Shakespeare's other professional healers, *King Lear* offers an example of an *un*characteristic physician who is at once able to uphold both the intellectual authority espoused by his College and the practical success of the empiric or lay practitioner. In the Quarto of 1608, when Cordelia returns to the story in the fourth act, her attendants include a "Doctor" who counsels her how best to treat her ailing father's madness by using the Paracelsian method of "like cures like."[42] To counteract the mad King Lear's crown of weeds, the "rank fumitor and furrow-weeds, / With burdocks, hemlock, nettles, cuckoo-flowers, / Darnel, and all the idle weeds" (4.4.3–5), the doctor prescribes "many simples operative, whose power / Will close the eye of anguish" (4.4.14–15).[43] The phys-ician's exposition of the effects of simples, medicaments so-called for being made from the extracts of a single plant, here serves a dual

---

[40] William Shakespeare, *All's Well That Ends Well*, ed. Susan Snyder (Oxford: Oxford University Press, 1993), iiin70.

[41] Snyder here also makes much of Lafeu's claim of Helen's "profession" in 2.1.78, aggravating G. K. Hunter's 1959 gloss of "that in which she professes" to "amazing not in itself but in conjunction with *her sex, her years*." This, I think, takes Lafeu's perceived sexism too far, because many of the medical practitioners of the Elizabethan/Jacobean era were female and recognized as experts even within the patriarchal confines of membership in City companies (see Pelling, *Medical Conflicts*, 189–224). Women could not, of course, be university-educated physicians, and according to Aristotle, they were also notoriously stupid – but it does not necessarily follow that Shakespeare's audience believed that they were also inadequate to the practical task of healing. What is key for Lafeu is in Helena's intellectual status, not her gender, suggesting that what is most revealing about the phrase "Dr She" is the *Dr*, not the *She*.

[42] Galenic therapies insisted that illness was caused by an excess or lack in one of the four humors and sought to restore humeral balance by means of divesting surplus humors (usually bleeding or purging) or by supplying deficits. Paracelsian medicine saw illness and infection as occurring as a result of an outside agent entering the body, and its remedies often claimed to cure by offering a chemically modified version of the agent responsible for causing the illness. See entry on "Paracelsus," in Sujata Iyengar, *Shakespeare's Medical Language: A Dictionary* (London: Bloomsbury, 2011).

[43] Except where noted, all quotations from *King Lear* are taken from Foakes's edition. William Shakespeare, *King Lear*, Arden Shakespeare Third Series, ed. R. A. Foakes (London: Bloomsbury, 1997).

purpose.[44] The first offers a practical explanation for Lear's later difficulty waking in 4.7, a simple having presumably been given him as a sleeping aid in order that he might receive the "repose" denied him in his madness. Yet, in her questioning of the limits of "man's wisdom / In the restoring of [Lear's] bereavèd sense" (4.4.8–9), it is *Cordelia* who derives immediate solace from the physician's confident explanation of "simples operative," or the healing powers of plants.[45] She replies:

> All blest secrets,
> All you unpublished virtues of the earth,
> Spring with my tears. (4.4.15–17)

On stage, whether performed as an invocation of Nature's power or of Cordelia's own palpable relief that herbal medicine can restore her father, the affect of Cordelia's prayer, and the logic of its image, can mask her otherwise curious statement. By complementing the Doctor's knowledge as "blest *secrets*" of the "*unpublished* virtues of the earth," Cordelia's speech implies that flora's therapeutic properties are so impenetrable that only an expert can decode them.

Scene 4, Act 4 marks Cordelia's return to the stage after a three-act absence, and her concern with Lear's overthrow finds its expression in her preoccupation with the material circumstances of her father's madness. She describes in detail the disparate plants Lear wears in the place of his once unifying golden crown, descrying the "idle weeds" of her sisters that grow in England's "sustaining corn" (4.4.5–6). The analogy of a neglected garden for a state in turmoil is common to Shakespeare; Hamlet, too, complains of "an unweeded garden / That grows to seed" (1.2.135–136), while the Gardener in *Richard II* offers the metaphor an extended treatment, espousing a variety of horticultural activities that ensure the health of the estate by the means of preventing harm. The trope continues with an image of the King as a sickly plant fed upon by the weeds he shelters with his leaves, and little room is left for the possibility of Richard's redemption in gardener Bolingbroke's plucking up of everything "root and all" (3.4.53). In the case of *Lear*, however, the metaphor stops short of such drastic husbandry, and through their manipulation into medicaments, the plants

---

[44] As in *OED* "simple," sense 6: "A medicine or medicament composed or concocted of only one constituent, *esp.* of one herb or plant (*obs.*); hence, a plant or herb employed for medical purposes"; also "a single uncompounded or unmixed thing; a substance free from foreign elements, *esp.* one serving as an ingredient in a composition or mixture" (7.a).

[45] An editor's choice in modernizing punctuation can make Cordelia's question clearer, as in Kenneth Muir's Arden 2 edition: "What can man's wisdom / In the restoring his bereaved sense? / He that helps him take all my outward worth" (4.4.8–10).

in Lear's crown serve both as the symbol of the King's sickness and as the source of his cure.

Cordelia's admission of botanical ignorance is curious, because not only was a knowledge of plants and horticulture sufficiently understood by early moderns as to be a useful and common Shakespearean metaphor but by far the majority of medical care in the sixteenth and seventeenth centuries was self-administered. While physicians attempted to elevate the practice of physic by fighting unlicensed healers like Heywood's Wise Woman, their major impediment was the folk traditions that enabled people to take care of themselves. Simples, plant-based medicaments that could be gathered on one's own, were generally understood to be a part of an average early modern's personal medical repertoire, and as this study demonstrates, the books about herbs and simples that were a flourishing publishing niche throughout the sixteenth century and well into the seventeenth demonstrated that public interest in the topic was perennial.

In light of such material evidence that provides a broader sense of what some scholars call "history from below,"[46] Friar Laurence's knowledge of the "powerful grace that lies / In plants, herbs, stones and their true qualities" (2.2.15–16) is thus perhaps not as remarkable as our modern editorial tendency to separate spiritual and physical counsel might suggest:

> Within the infant rind of this weak flower
> Poison hath residence, and medicine power;
> For this, being smelt, with that part cheers each part;
> Being tasted, slays all sense with the heart. (2.2.23–26)

Though scholars frequently argue that Friar Laurence's botanical familiarity is highly specialized, the evidence found in extant botanical books suggests that the Friar's musing is rather a part of the common knowledge easily accessed by the nonmedical laity, a knowledge over which figures like Thomas Gibson were eager to claim authority.[47] In a similar vein, when Romeo seeks out a poison from the Apothecary, he demonstrates a familiarity with accessing medicine as an independent consumer, recognizing that the Apothecary's knowledge of the "[c]ulling of simples"

---

[46] Coined by the founder of the *Annales* school Lucien Febvre, "history from below" endeavors to produce historical narratives oriented around the perspectives of those ordinary or average people who have not previously been considered worthy of investigation.

[47] This perspective is offered in response to accounts such as Lynette Hunter's, who sees Friar Lawrence as "a serious physician and apothecary, not a fraudster" specifically designed to contrast with the play's devious, amoral apothecary (174). Lynette Hunter, "Cankers in *Romeo and Juliet*: Sixteenth-Century Medicine at a Figural/Literal Cusp," in Stephanie Moss and Kaara L. Peterson (eds.), *Disease, Diagnosis, and Cure on the Early Modern Stage* (Aldershot: Ashgate, 2004), 171–185.

(5.1.40) must necessarily include the familiarity with poisons that Friar Laurence had already demonstrated. A curious textual variant makes this interpretation explicit: in the text of the second quarto of the play, Romeo's entrance is early enough that he hears Friar Lawrence's talk about poison; in the Folio, he does not.[48]

It appears that, in Shakespeare's own medical ethos, so long as the medicament consumed is a simple, or a plant, such self-medicating is common and acceptable. The simplicity of simples, coupled with the reinforcement of such knowledge in print, enabled early moderns to treat their own illnesses. Buried in Iago and Cleopatra's references to "drowsy syrups" made from poppy or mandrake (*Othello* 3.3.324–325; *Antony and Cleopatra* 1.5.3–5), in King Richard's efforts to "prescribe, though no physician" (*Richard II* 1.1.154), and in John of Gaunt's accusation that the king is guilty of being "careless-patient" (*Richard II* 2.1.97) is the assumption of the early moderns' tendency and even their moral obligation to self-medicate. Moreover, though it may have been disputed by the self-appointed medical authorities of the College of Physicians, an individual's license to minister simple medicaments was entrenched in Tudor law, a boon to sellers of herbals and other books of remedies. A 1543 statute of Henry VIII now known as the "Quacks' Charter" permitted

> every person being the King's subject, having knowledge and experience of the nature of Herbs, Roots and Waters, or of the operation of the same, by speculation or practice within any part of the Realm of England, or within any other the King's Dominions, to practice, use and minister in and to any outward sore . . ., wound, apostemations, outward swelling or disease, any herb or herbs, ointments, baths, poultices and plasters, according to their cunning, experience and knowledge in any of the diseases, sores and maladies beforesaid, and all other like to the same, or drinks for the stone and strangury, or agues, without suit, berations, trouble, penalty or loss of their goods.[49]

---

[48] By 1652, in his *A Priest to the Temple* (London: T. Maxey for T. Garthwait, 1652), George Herbert could specify that the healing skills of a parson derive from reading books: "Now as the Parson is in Law, so is he in sicknesse also: if there be any of his flock sick, hee is their Physician, or at least his Wife, of whom in stead of the qualities of the world, he asks no other, but to have the skill of healing a wound, or helping the sick. But if neither himselfe, nor his wife have the skil, and his means serve, hee keepes some young practicioner in his house for the benefit of his Parish, whom yet he ever exhorts not to exceed his bounds, but in tickle cases to call in help. If all fail, then he keeps good correspondence with some neighbour Phisician, and entertaines him for the Cure of his Parish. Yet is it easie for any Scholer to attaine to such a measure of Phisick, as may be of much use to him both for himself, and others. This is done by seeing one Anatomy, reading one Book of Phisick, having one Herball by him" (96–97).

[49] See 34 and 35 Henry VIII c. 8, *Statutes of the Realm*, 3:906. On the relationship of the Quacks' Charter to an outbreak of the pox in London in the 1540s, see Pelling, "Appearance and Reality."

The ambiguous wording of the charter permits not only an individual's right to self-medicate but also the right of the individual to administer simples to any example of an "outward sore ... swelling or disease" of another person. The charter's intent was to protect the poor's right to receive medical care outside of the professional and costly options offered by the College of Physicians, whose major objection to lay medical practitioners centered on empirics' potential to cut into the physicians' sanctioned monopoly on practicing physic. The general knowledge of folk medicine that so concerned physicians was continually bolstered by an ever-increasing library of medical texts and pharmacopeias available in the English vernacular. Yet physicians also saw those texts as an opportunity to use print to bolster their own efforts at professionalization, a particularly effective means of publicly broadcasting their authority over medicine. This is the environment in which Robert Wyer thought it prudent to add the name of the founder of the College of Physicians, Thomas Linacre, to the title page of the third edition of his herbal in 1550.

Throughout the dramatic literature of the Elizabethan and Jacobean periods, there is evidence that the early modern public reserved the right to heal itself, despite increasing efforts made by licensed healers to control their behavior. It is worth noting that it was not just poor individuals but members of *all* classes who benefited from printed works of remedies; indeed, reducing dependency on potentially nefarious medical practitioners by medicating oneself could be particularly attractive to nobility concerned for their lives. To keep the Duchess of Malfi's pregnancy a secret from prying eyes, her steward claims that she was poisoned by one of her doctors, and he claims that she will neutralize such threats by taking care of herself: "She'll use some prepared'd antidote of her own, / Lest the physicians should repoison her" (2.2.175–176). That such an alibi works to deter doctors, if not the shrewd conniver Bosola, testifies that lay healing was both an established and acceptable early modern practice. The Duchess's knowledge of practical remedies is evident throughout the play; her last instruction to a servant is to "giv'st my little boy / Some syrup for his cold" (4.2.200–201), while a few lines later she welcomes death's improvement upon mandrake's soporific properties (4.2.231).

The Duchess of Malfi, like *Pericles* and *All's Well That Ends Well*, demonstrates that the medical knowledge of the play's characters is gleaned through study and the reading of books. The Duchess's brother Ferdinand cites Pliny's *Natural History*, and elsewhere Pescara admits to seeking out written authority to confirm medical conditions he'd never before heard about:

PESCARA Pray thee, what's his disease?
DOCTOR A very pestilent disease, my lord,
    They call it lycanthropia.
PESCARA What's that?
    I need a dictionary to't. (5.2.4–8)

Though the Doctor offers Pescara an explanation of the term he has used, Pescara's self-reliance upon easily accessed authorities diminishes a physician's traditional theoretical acumen, shrinking it down to the repetition of just so many books.[50]

Evidence from both early modern drama and the manuscript notations in printed books of remedies indicates that folk knowledge of basic medicaments was widespread in the period, and the publication history of herbals and other books of recipes testifies that more specialized treatments of plants' virtues were easily available in print. This raises the question: Why does Cordelia's prayer maintain that the therapeutic powers of plants are secretive and mysterious? How could they be the "unpublished," or secret, virtues of the earth? The answer may be found in the Folio revision to the *Lear* text, which, along with downplaying the French invasion, removes the character of "Doctor" and renames him "Gentleman," thereby changing the person who cares for Lear from a licensed authority to a lay practitioner like Helena or Cerimon.[51] The dramatic motivation for the change in the revised text may have been a simple desire for accuracy: by curing Lear though the Paracelsian therapy of like curing like, the healer's herbal remedy was inconsistent with the Galenic standards employed by Renaissance physicians.[52] It was, however, consistent with the procedures employed by apothecaries and surgeons as well as the unlicensed practitioners in the medical marketplace of Jacobean London.

For audiences, Cordelia's prayer is dramatically effective; but when I put aside the embedded affect of Cordelia's pathetic fallacy and read it through Shakespeare's usage elsewhere, I suspect that the key to understanding her claim of plants' secrecy lies in the French queen's use of the imperative

---

[50] Sarah Neville, "Referencing Pliny's *Naturalis Historia* in Early Modern England." *Notes & Queries* 64:2 (2017): 321–325.

[51] Gary Taylor, "The War in King Lear," *Shakespeare Survey* 33 (1980): 27–34.

[52] Pelling, "Compromised by Gender," 109.

mood. Cordelia prays, but she also commands, and it is her queenly assertion of authority over the virtues of the Earth that will ultimately heal her father:

> All blest secrets,
> All you unpublished virtues of the earth,
> *Spring* with *my* tears. (4.4.15–17, my emphasis)

In returning to her English homeland, Cordelia commands the Earth just as another of Shakespeare's returning English sovereigns had done so before her: in *Richard II*, the King, returning from Ireland, opens with a long speech of similar pathetic fallacy, ultimately concluding, "This earth shall have a feeling" (3.2.24); and, like Cordelia's, Richard's affective invocation to England's soil prompts the growths of plants: he urges that the earth might "Yield stinging nettles to mine enemies" (3.2.18), a passage that is soon ironically undercut by the Gardener's later allegorical transference of the King himself into a sick plant (3.4.49–50). Neither Cordelia nor Richard survives until the end of the play; both die in prison, ultimately defeated by events beyond their sovereign control. The botanical usage shared between King Richard and Cordelia is thus dramaturgically, narratively, and affectively similar, suggesting that, as he revised *King Lear*, Shakespeare may have had in mind the earlier play about another sovereign who was "careless-patient."

In transforming the Quarto's Doctor into the Folio's Gentleman, Shakespeare both eliminates the possibility that Cordelia may be understood to defer to the growing intellectual authority of physicians and sets up the character as a healer in her own right. While it is possible in the Quarto to read the Doctor's account of "simples operative" as a professional's answer to Cordelia's rhetorical question about the limits of "man's wisdom," in the Folio those details are provided by an unspecified member of the court. In other words, what had once been specialized knowledge becomes commonplace, able to be spoken by anyone. In the Folio, Lear's loyal daughter, now turned French queen, savior of England, and general of an invading army, does not submit to taking the council of a physician. Instead, Cordelia, whose name means "heart medicine," uses this common knowledge to take healing matters into her own hands. When speaking to a Doctor in the Quarto, Cordelia's "Be governed by your knowledge, and proceed / I' th' sway of your own will" (4.7.17–18) defers to a physician's authority to govern medical care, even when caring for the bodies of kings. Spoken to a Gentleman, however, the phrase serves to elevate the subjectivity that has guided Cordelia's actions throughout the play. Once Lear is brought onto the stage, Cordelia utters another assertion of a lay person's power to cure:

> O my dear father, restoration hang
> Thy medicine on my lips, and let this kiss
> Repair those violent harms that my two sisters
> Have in thy reverence made! (4.7.24–27)

For a brief moment, the mad king is lucid, cradled in his daughter's arms.[53]

An investigation of Cordelia's intention in this small speech indicates the increasing complexity of early modern attitudes towards the fields of botany and medicine and highlights the role that books could play in the performance of healing by both professionals and amateurs. By 1608, printed botanical works, along with the manuscript annotations contained within them, were widely available to serve as props that allowed Jacobean dramatists to consider the ways that medical and scholarly authority was constructed as part of the process of self-fashioning. Herbals could likewise serve as props off stage as these books appeared in portraits for figures like Anne Clifford and William Cunningham (see Figure 7.1), who used them to serve as evidence of their own medical, cosmographical, or botanical authority. It is unsurprising, then, that the English stationers who produced and profited from such books recognized their potential as status-conveying commodities. In the semiotic space of the early modern stage, herbals and other medical books held up a mirror to the tentative and conditional nature of scholarly and professional authority.

---

[53] Wayne Lewis, writing on doctors in literature in the back pages of a medical newsletter, calls *King Lear*'s physician "the original 'walk-on part' for the medic … He is there for plot and character development only." Nonetheless, Lewis finds meaning in the character's ability to signify the triviality of the physician's role: "Lear's doctor should remind us that we too have only 'walk on parts' in the great tragedies of our patients' lives." See Wayne Lewis, "Six Doctors in Literature: Number 5: The Doctor from *King Lear*, by William Shakespeare," *The British Journal of General Practice* 49 (May 1999): 416. On variant stage directions in the texts of *Lear*, see Sarah Neville, "The 'Dead Body Problem': The Dramaturgy of Coffins on the Renaissance Stage," in Annalisa Castaldo and Rhonda Knight, *Stage Matters: Props, Bodies, and Space in Shakespearean Performance* (Madison, NJ: Farleigh Dickinson University Press, 2018), 127–141, esp. 132–133.

PART III

Authors and the Printed English Herbal

CHAPTER 7

William Turner and the Medical Book Trade

In a November 28, 1550, letter to William Cecil, then secretary of state, Protestant divine William Turner demonstrated how intertwined his studies of natural philosophy were with his religious conviction and political maneuvering. After his reformist zeal led to his rejection from consideration for leadership positions at Oriel and Magdalen colleges, Turner feared that he might never find the preferment he sought in England, and he proposed to Cecil that a return to the continent would offer him some consolation. Turner had first left England in early 1541 after marrying in defiance of his diaconal vows, and this sojourn abroad had enabled him to obtain an Italian MD.[1] If Cecil obliged with funds, Turner wrote, a new tour would enable him to complete a number of writing projects on theology and natural history. Both of these interests, as well as Turner's careful study of textual transmission, are clearly on display in his request, as was his deep-seated conviction that the Roman Catholic church had corrupted doctrine:

> if that i myght haue my pore prebende cu[m]myng to me yearly i will for it correct ye hold [old] newe testament in englishe, and wryt a booke of ye causis of my correctio[n] & changing of the translatio[n]. I will also finishe my great herball & my bookes of fishes stones & metalles, if good sende me lyfe and helthe.[2]

Turner's play on "old" and "new" was characteristic; more than a decade earlier, he had translated works by Joachim von Watt and Urbanus Regius,

---

[1] Whitney R. D. Jones, "Turner, William (1509/10–1568), Naturalist and Religious Controversialist," *ODNB*.

[2] Quoted in Benjamin Daydon Jackson, *William Turner: Libellus de Re Herbaria 1538, The Names of Herbes 1548* (London: privately printed, 1877), iv. The letter is listed in R. Lemon (ed.), *Calendar of State Papers, Domestic Series, of the Reigns of Edward VI, Mary, Elizabeth 1547–[1603], Preserved in the State Paper Department of Her Majesty's Public Record Office*, vol. 1: *1547–1580* (London, 1856), 31; C. S. Knighton (ed.), *Calendar of State Papers, Domestic Series of the Reigns of Edward VI, 1547–1553; Mary I, 1553–1558*, 2 vols. (London, 1992, 1998).

and these works' English titles indicate Turner's preoccupation with textual corruption: *Of ye Olde God & the Newe* (1534; *STC* 25127) and *The Olde Learnyng & the Newe* (1537; *STC* 20840). Turner's exegetical interests in Protestant reform offered a valuable backdrop to his botanical investigations, encouraging him to couple textual analyses and corrections of classical and modern authorities with his own observations of plants. More often than not, on the title pages of his botanical works Turner's role is identified as a "gatherer," a figure who locates and assembles disparate information into a cohesive and useful whole. In his magnum opus, a three-part herbal of 1568 that was fully published only after his death, the unpublished third part of Turner's work is presented as "lately gathered."[3]

Turner's combination of observation, correction, and accretive book learning has appealed to modern critical sensibilities, and historians have hailed him as the "Father of British Botany" since the endorsement of that phrase by Benjamin Daydon Jackson in 1877. Turner's paternal moniker offers a useful framing for understanding how his specific form of rhetorical self-fashioning became naturalized within the history of "authorized" botanical books. The first named English herbalist carefully and explicitly signaled his use of his contemporaries, particularly continental herbalists, and Turner's paratexts demonstrate the way that herbals were conceived by their authors as an iterative and intertextual genre even as the medium of the printed book enabled authors to declare their authority as "herbalists" to the world. In both verbal and pictorial content and in codicological form, then, herbals as a genre were embedded within a textual ecosystem that calls singular authorship into question. Later texts build upon the findings of previous ones, and later authors stand to gain by arguing and correcting their predecessors. The herbal genre, in other words, is self-perpetuating, and it was this recursive propagation that made such books particularly attractive to the publishers who stood to profit from their sale.[4]

Turner and Cecil had become acquainted in the employ of Edward Seymour, Duke of Somerset, where Cecil had been Somerset's secretary

---

[3] The first part of Turner's *A New Herball* (*STC* 24365) was printed in 1551; it was a relatively slim forty-three edition-sheets. The second part was printed in 1562 (*STC* 24366), which also included a treatise on baths; this edition was much larger (100 edition-sheets). Finally, in 1568, the final version of Turner's herbal was published (*STC* 24367), comprising a reprint of the first part of 1551, a reissue of unsold sheets of the second part of 1562, a new third part, and a reissue of the unsold sheets of the treatise on baths; this edition was 184 edition-sheets.

[4] See Elizabeth Eisenstein, *The Printing Revolution in Early Modern Europe*, 2nd ed. (Cambridge: Cambridge University Press, 2005), esp. chap. 7, "The Book of Nature Transformed."

and Turner his physician. Through Cecil's intervention, shortly after the 1550 request, Turner succeeded to the deanery of Wells, but his religious successes were soon extinguished by the accession of the Catholic Queen Mary I in 1553. Turner, like many English reformers, fled to the continent. The hands-on studies of continental plants that Turner's exiles made possible, coupled with his understanding of English flora, enabled him to overcome the linguistic and biogeographical barriers that had stymied his fellow English natural historians who still subscribed to the works of Dioscorides and Pliny as if they were dogma. By demonstrating his respect for these classical authorities while simultaneously acknowledging that there were limits to the information that modern editions of their works could possess, Turner's lasting contributions to British botany have as much to do with his understanding of the ways that written texts can often lead the faithful astray as they do with his developing empiricist ethos, a codicological awareness Leah Knight describes as Turner's "botanical reformation."[5] I argue in this chapter that, throughout his careers as a naturalist and as a reformer, Turner strategically deployed print, using the medium to his advantage in both terrestrial and celestial fields to make his authoritative pretensions manifest. As a surrogate for his person, Turner's printed books could go places that he could not, and they could speak even when their author was in continental exile.

Turner's desire for authority is most on display in his medical works, where, after becoming a physician in the 1540s, he quickly adopted the domineering authorial posture characteristic of those who recognized that print could be instrumentalized to serve the medical establishment's larger professional goals. Yet there is also an ambivalence laced throughout Turner's writing. As he suggests that printed texts can usefully serve as surrogates for their authors, he also displays an increasing concern that the rapid and unauthorized transmission of books in print may lead to an author's original intentions becoming corrupted. Once made public, copies of a printed book take on a life of their own, and authors are unable to control how others read and receive their message. Authors therefore needed to manage early modern stationers, the makers and distributors of books, with careful rhetoric to try to prevent the stationers' agency over the printed artifact undermining the authority of authors over their subject matter. Like his continental contemporary Leonard Fuchs, Turner's

---

[5] See Knight, *Of Books and Botany*, chap. 3. Knight's chapter deftly uses Turner's reforming tendencies to account for his development of plant nomenclature, finding that "the subordination of the linguistic and elevation of the imaginative aspect of naming sets the botany of Turner's day in close relation to poetry" (66).

authorial self-fashioning responded to his dependency upon stationers by attempting to distinguish himself from those artisans whose skills were integral to his authoritative posturing.

Turner was not alone in his recognition that print could serve as a proxy for an author's expertise and professional standing. In Chapter 5, I argued that in his 1539 edition of *The Great Herball*, the grocer-apothecary and printer Thomas Gibson used his address to the reader to reframe that work's medical stance and support the professionalization of medicine. While the earlier and later editions of *The Grete Herball* of Peter Treveris and John King had suggested that books like herbals might serve as surrogates for medical practitioners like apothecaries, Gibson eliminated a closing address that recognized the way readers themselves could become practitioners of herbal medicine through study of the natural world. Instead, Gibson's paratextual materials foreground the Galenic expertise espoused by European physicians, which Gibson later became, and suggest that the most trustworthy medical books should be accompanied by medical doctors' endorsements or oversight. Thus did early modern physic and early modern bookselling become intertwined, as physicians quickly realized that printed books offered an opportunity for physicians to lay claim to public knowledge about the body. Over the course of his career in print, Turner, who may have known Gibson personally, eventually also came to assert that physicians' authority allowed them to control the discourses of healing provided by printed books like herbals.

Turner's authoritative posturing in his books of natural history complicates our understanding of his doctrinal positions because his professional status as a physician eventually required his endorsement of a hierarchy of knowledge that is seemingly at odds with the reformist position of *sola scriptura*. While, on the one hand, Turner's botanical writing simply grows to endorse physicians' traditional approaches to lay readership by assuming doctors' command over readers' understanding of their own bodies, reading Turner's herbals alongside his religious polemics reveals contradictions with his earlier insistence on Christians' informed but independent judgment in spiritual matters.[6] What gradually begins to emerge in his

---

[6] In *Avium praecipuarum* (*STC* 24350.5), his 1544 treatise on birds dedicated to Prince Edward, Turner suggests that it is vital that princely wisdom exceed that of his counselors, so that he is able to tell good advice from bad. Turner even goes so far as to insist that one should prefer the findings of one's own senses over those reported by others. See *Turner on Birds: A Short and Succinct History of the Principal Birds Noticed by Pliny and Aristotle*, ed. and trans. A. H. Evans (Cambridge: Cambridge University Press, 1903), 5. This linking of doctrinal and terrestrial matters comes to a head in Turner's *A New Book of Spiritual Physic* (1555).

botanical writing is evidence of an epistemological collision between Turner's dual roles as reformer and physician, as his affiliation with the latter group struggled to control an information medium that the former group had masterfully and strategically used to its advantage. Despite (and perhaps because of) this increasing ambivalence about authority, however, Turner's publications throughout his lifetime display his acute awareness of the ways that print can be deployed strategically to support authorial agendas, and his lasting status as "the father of British botany" shows that, at least in the field of natural history, his efforts were successful.

Others have found similar evidence of Turner's authorial ambivalence in the religious polemics he wrote attacking the Henrician bishop Stephen Gardiner, *The Huntyng & Fyndying out of the Romishe Fox* (1543; *STC* 24353) and *The Rescuynge of the Romishe Fox* (1545; *STC* 24355). Erin Katherine Kelly has shown that in these hunting tracts Turner instrumentalized the printed medium as a proxy for his devoted service in order to engage a "canny" posture that facilitated a simultaneous "assertion of status and an expression of utter servility."[7] In Turner's tracts, the publication of printed books are tools for making public the heretofore hidden efforts of Romish predators lurking in the king's dominion. The narrator's role as a reluctant hunter forced to seek out Gardiner, the Romish Foxe, aligns with his positioning the tracts as "hounds" dutifully deployed in service of Henry VIII. As Kelly notes, however, "the meanings attached to participants in the hunt, animal or human, change as Turner's argument requires," and Turner's chosen metaphor also enables him to "use[] the hunt to assert his own status, both as a commentator on religious affairs in England and as a potential loyal servant in a truly reformed England."[8] Yet the self-effacement is transient; when Turner returns to the hunt as a metaphor a decade later in his 1555 tract *The Huntyng of the Romyshe Vuolpe* (1555), Kelly says "the carefully calibrated humility that was evident in the earlier two tracts is discarded" in favor of a new declaration of expertise. However, Turner's appreciation of the role of the printed medium as a vehicle for his self-pretention is still in clear evidence:

> I haue for my parte found out these wolues, where as they were so dysgysed, that a man unexpert in thys kynde of hunting, which I do professe, would haue thought that they had been men, and not onely men, but honest men,

---

[7] Erin Katherine Kelly, "Chasing the Fox and the Wolf: Hunting in the Religious Polemic of William Turner," *Reformation* 20 (2015): 113–129; 116.
[8] Kelly, "Chasing the Fox and the Wolf," 118, 119.

and no Wolues. I haue in thys my boke shewed you where they be, & who they be.[9]

For Turner, in 1545, printed books are useful largely because they make hidden truths public, but, by 1555, the material form of print is the foundation of an author's authority to interpret. In both cases, however, the agents that Turner insists are responsible for "thys my boke" are not the stationers who made such works available to readers as publishers, printers, and distributors but the author who wrote its text.

Turner's attitude towards printed books, and the uses to which they can be put by clever authors, can be seen to shift over the course of his interrelated careers as a physician, divine, and naturalist. This chapter demonstrates how Turner's three herbals reflect a bibliographic self-consciousness in English botany that was emerging simultaneously with the efforts of English physicians to assert their influence over all elements of medicine. Anonymous bestselling English works like the little *Herball* as well as *The Grete Herball* were widely available during Turner's undergraduate studies at Cambridge, but despite their popularity with readers, Turner claimed that those works offered little of use to professional medical practitioners. It was to remedy what he called the "unlearned cacography" of these texts that Turner was prompted in 1538 to first offer up his own botanical studies in English for the good of the commonweal despite his fellow physicians' concerns that such an endeavor would make specialized professional knowledge widely available to laypeople.[10] Historians of botany have largely taken Turner at his word and consequently viewed him simply as a benevolent democratizer of medical information; however, the herbals that Turner wrote *after* he obtained a medical degree reveal that, like Thomas Gibson and Leonard Fuchs before him, Turner came to develop a mistrust of laypeople's judgment. The shift in the attitudes of his herbals likewise mirrors the way that Turner's approach to print changes through his hunting pamphlets: books that were first materially useful because of their wide distribution later become useful as a textual mechanism for asserting authoritative control. In either case, however, stationers profit so long as Turner's books sell to a willing public. In the wider context of the trade in Renaissance books, then, Turner's herbals result less from his personal

---

[9] William Turner, *The Huntyng of the Romyshe Vuolpe* (Emden: Egidius van der Erve, 1555), sig. A2v.

[10] William Turner, *The first and seconde partes of the herbal lately ouersene, corrected and enlarged with the thirde parte, lately gathered. Also a booke of the bath of Baeth* (Cologne: Heirs of Arnold Birckman, 1568), sig. *2v.

religious zeal or professional ambition than they do from Tudor printers willingly taking advantage of an anticipated market demand.

Turner Reads the Print Marketplace

At the time of writing his 1550 appeal to Cecil, Turner had only just returned to England after a decade of self-imposed exile on the continent that had been necessitated by Turner's marriage to Jane Alder.[11] Along with the ecclesiastical charges stemming from this marriage, Turner had also been wanted on charges of heresy for *The Hunting & Fyndyng of the Romishe Foxe* and *The Rescvynge of the Romish Fox*. The tracts had been printed in Germany and smuggled into England along with other reformer texts, and the crown, fearing that the pamphlets would fuel Protestant uprisings, had issued a prohibition on July 7, 1546, "[t]o auoide and abolish suche englishe bookes, as conteine pernicious and detestable erroures and heresies" (*STC* 7809). Along with Tyndale's and Coverdale's translations of the New Testament, no one in England

> shall receiue have take or kepe in his or their possession, any maner of booke printed or written in the english tongue, which be or shalbe sette forth, in the names of Frith, Tindall, Wicliff, Joy, Roy, Basile, Bale, Barnes, Couerdale, Tourner, Tracy, or by any of them, or any other boke or bokes conteining matter contrary to the kinges maiesties booke, called, A necessary doctrine and erudition for any christian man.[12]

Unaffected by this proclamation were Turner's Latin works that were less accessible to lay readers, including his botanical tract *Libellus de re Herbaria novus in quo Herbarum aliquot nomina greca, latina & anglica habes, vna cum nominibus officinarum* (*STC* 24358), a short quarto published by John Byddell and distributed from his shop at the sign of the Sun on London's Fleet street in 1538.[13] This "new booklet concerning herbal matters, in

---

[11] The marriage was solemnized on November 13, 1540; a statute effective July 12, 1539, had declared that those in religious orders who had sworn a vow of celibacy were forbidden to marry upon penalty of death. See Eric Josef Carlson, "The Marriage of William Turner," *Historical Research* 65 (1992): 336–339.

[12] Also available modernized in Hughes and Larkin, *Tudor Royal Proclamations*, 1:374. For an analysis of Turner's anti-Catholic tracts, see Rainer Pineas, "William Turner's Polemical Use of Ecclesiastical History and His Controversy with Stephen Gardiner," *Renaissance Quarterly* 33 (1980): 599–608, and Rainer Pineas, "William Turner and Reformation Politics," *Bibliothèque D'Humanisme et Renaissance* 37 (1975): 193–200.

[13] Byddell, who also went by the title of "John Salisbury," had been apprenticed to Wynkyn de Worde and served as his executor at the time of de Worde's death in 1534. Throughout the 1530s, Byddell was a frequent publisher of the works of Erasmus as well as many religious titles with an anti-papal bent, and the crown made particular use of Byddell to issue works sympathetic to Henry VIII's interests in

which you have some Greek, Latin and English names of herbs, together with names of medicaments,"[14] was effectively a simple glossary of 144 plants that included linguistic variants in plant names. Compared even to earlier botanical works like the multiple editions of the little *Herball* and *The Grete Herbal*, the practical or medical information contained in Turner's *Libellus* was slight. For every *Alsine* that offered "this is the herb which our women call Chykwede [chickweed] ... those who keep small birds shut up in cages refresh them with this when they are off their feed," there were a dozen *Athanasia* that stated merely "[this] is called *tagetes* in Greek, *tanacetum* in Latin, what the English have called *Tansy*."[15] The work is primarily a multilingual dictionary designed to enable readers to keep botanical signifiers in order as they read other texts. In other words, *Libellus* is a book that both relies upon and supports the existence of other books.

Turner's biographers have noted that his fellow exiles on the continent during Henry VIII's and Mary's reigns were significant contributors to both his medical and his botanical development. Because universities were major sites for both humanism and medical education, natural historians affiliated with universities on the continent were among the first to interrogate the philology of plant names and to connect these linguistic investigations to their own personal experience with plants.[16] The first botanical garden was established in Pisa in 1544; a second followed in Padua in 1545. The original purpose of such gardens was to provide an applied education in simples for students as part of their medical education, and after their humanistic instruction at Oxford or Cambridge, many would-be English physicians were granted permission to seek residencies at Italian, Swiss, French, or Dutch universities to further their studies.[17] During his first exile in the early 1540s, Turner took advantage of his

---

justifying the schism with Rome. See John Archer Gee, "John Byddell and the First Publication of Erasmus," *ELH* 4 (1937): 43–59. In 1534, Byddell had printed Turner's English translation of Watt's *Ye Olde God & the Newe* (*STC* 25127) for the publisher William Marshall as part of Marshall's Cromwell-approved anti-papal propaganda campaign, and perhaps Turner sought out Byddell as his *Libellus* publisher out of respect for the pair's shared religious sympathies. See Alec Ryrie, "Marshall, William (*d.* 1540?)," *ODNB*.

[14] Translation from William T. Stern, in *William Turner: Libellus de Re Herbaria 1538, The Names of Herbes 1548* (London: Ray Society, 1965), 4.

[15] Translation from Raven, *English Naturalists*, 68.

[16] On the relationship of English universities to those of the continent, see Faye Getz, "Medical Education in Later Medieval England," in Vivian Nutton and Roy Porter (eds.), *The History of Medical Education in Britain* (Amsterdam: Rodopi, 1995), 76–93.

[17] On the relative tolerance for Protestant students at Italian universities, see Paul F. Grendler, *The Universities of the Italian Renaissance* (Baltimore, MD: Johns Hopkins University Press, 2004), 191–193.

time on the continent to become a doctor of medicine at either Ferrara or Bologna, a degree that Cambridge incorporated upon his return to England in 1547. Such credentials enabled Turner to act as both physician and auxiliary chaplain to his patron, the Earl of Somerset, Lord Protector at Seymour's residence at Syon.[18]

Turner's interest in plants as medicaments becomes evident from the preface to *Libellus*, which displays a mild rebuke to those learned men who refuse to share their knowledge in print. In his 1538 address to the "Candid Reader," the thirty-year-old Turner explains why he, a "still beardless youth" (*imberbem adhuc iuuenem*), would attempt to write a herbal when he knows that there are, "in such studies, six hundred other Englishmen who precede me (as they say) on white horses."[19] Despite these numerous but nameless would-be English herbalists, however, there remains in 1538 no printed list of English and classical botanical equivalencies like the one Turner himself provides, and he admits that he "thought it best that [he] should try something difficult of this sort rather than let young students who hardly know the names of plants correctly go on in their blindness."[20] Such blindness, it seems, Turner himself had experienced as an undergraduate at Cambridge. He would later reminisce in the introduction to his 1568 *New Herball* that the *Libellus* was born from his frustration with inadequate instruction as an undergraduate, which could not be remedied by turning to the book market:

> euen beyng yet felow of Penbroke [*sic*] hall in Cambridge/ wher as I could learne neuer one Greke/ nether Latin/ nor English name/ euen amongest the Phisiciones of anye herbe or tre/ suche was the ignorance in simples at that tyme/ and *as yet there was no Englishe Herbal but one*/ al full of vnlearned cacographees and falselye naminge of herbes/ and as then had nether Fuchsius nether Matthiolus/ nether Tragus written of herbes in Latin.[21]

---

[18] Turner identified himself as the "servant" of Edward Seymour until Somerset's death in 1552 and dedicated his *Names of herbes* to him (Jackson, *William Turner*, 16). Jackson also notes that "whilst abroad [Turner] received a college benevolence of 26s. 8d in 1542" (17), indicating that Turner's first exile may have been at least partly legitimated as a necessary segment of his university studies.

[19] William Turner, *Libellus de Re Herbaria* (London: John Byddell, 1538), sig. A1v.

[20] Translation from Raven, *English Naturalists*, 69.

[21] Turner, *First and Seconde Partes*, sig. *2v, emphasis added. In *Abecedarium Anglico Latinum* (1552; *STC* 13940), Richard Huloet describes *cacographia* as "Ill wrytynge," a usage similarly employed by Thomas Blount a century later in his *Glossographia or a Dictionary* (1656; Wing B3334): "ill writing, or a writing of evill things." Raven maintains that the *Libellus* cannot be the Latin herbal that Turner speaks of in 1568 (*English Naturalists*, 68) and presumably assumes that what Turner meant was the *Historia de naturis herbarum scholiis & notis vallata* (1544) mentioned by Benjamin Daydon Jackson, but the existence of this text is disputed, even by Jackson. See Jackson, *William Turner*, 27.

At least as he reconstructs his motivations in 1538 thirty years later, Turner saw his *Libellus* as filling a void for scholarly English readers, who had no printed works fit to guide their botanical explorations that had been produced by a native natural historian of plants.[22] Anonymous works like the little *Herball* (1525) and *The Grete Herball* (1526) were increasingly available in new editions, but each offered so little in the way of descriptive information on plant nomenclature, morphology, or localities that they were virtually useless for bridging the gap between the various continental and English terminologies for plants that Turner had identified. Whichever work it was that Turner recognized in his condemnation of the only "vnlearned cacographee" that was available to early English readers, it is clear that he nonetheless saw the enterprise of herbalism (*cognoscendis herbis*) in England as a nascent scholarship open to those willing to investigate on their own. Throughout *Libellus*, Turner urges his candid reader to read critically and improve upon his work: "If I am caught blundering (and this is very easy) I will gladly be corrected by men of learning. For I am not too proud and pleased with myself to accept gladly the verdicts of the learned."[23]

Turner clearly saw the works of continental authors as a crucial aid to plant identification and classification, and their names appear throughout his many volumes of natural history to bolster his arguments or to offer inferior hypotheses that Turner then endeavors to correct. For example, in his later 1548 volume *The Names of Herbes*, Turner notes that

> Stachys semeth to Gesner to be the herbe that we cal in english Ambrose, & I deni not but that it may be a kynde of it. Howe be it I haue sene the true Italian staches, whiche hath narrower and whiter leaues then Ambrose hat. It maye be named in englishe little Horehounde or strayte Horehound.[24]

Because Turner's first herbal was a gloss or equivalency table of plant names, the text's nature mostly precluded his citation of other botanists; nonetheless, a few authoritative figures appear in the work's preliminaries. In 1538, those men esteemed by Turner as sufficiently "learned" included the Parisian physician Jean Ruel and German physician Otto Brunfels, whose works served as excellent exemplars of regionally inflected service to

---

[22] In 1568, Turner may simply have been following the example set for him by Fuchs, who had lamented in *De historia* (1542) that his contemporary physicians were not better versed in plant lore: "by Immortal God, is it to be wondered at that kings and princes do not at all regard the pursuit of the investigation of plants, when even the physicians of our time so shrink from it that it is scarcely possible to find one among a hundred who has an accurate knowledge of even so many as a few plants?" (translated in Arber, *Herbals*, 67).

[23] Translation from Raven, *English Naturalists*, 69.   [24] Turner, *The Names of Herbes*, sig. G5r.

a growing body of natural philosophy. In *Libellus*'s address to the reader, Turner mentions both men by name, and both also regularly appear in the references of his later botanical writings. The first volume of Otto Brunfels's three-volume *Herbarum vivae eicones* was printed by Johannes Schott in Strasburg in 1530, a work that, as its title ("Living Portraits of Plants") suggests, was chiefly notable for its illustrations by Hans Weiditz, a pupil of Albrecht Dürer. Later volumes followed the publication of this text in 1531–1532 and 1536. Ruel's translation of Dioscorides' *De materia medica* (first printed in Greek by the Aldine Press in 1499) had been published in Paris by Henri Estienne in 1516; by 1551, Turner seems to have owned or to have had access to a copy of one of Ruel's many editions. Both Ruel and Brunfels frequently appear in Turner's *A New Herball* among a group of continental authorities whose printed works "haue greatly promoted the knowledge of herbes by their studies, and haue eche deserued very muche thanke, not only of their owne countrees, but also of all the hole common welth of all Christendome."[25] Printed books of botany improved "the hole common welth" through their dissemination, which made what was once individual knowledge widely available, able to be shared in common.[26] Turner's investment in others' printed works was typical of the era, as Brian W. Ogilvie has noted: "published texts [of natural history] were not the end product of the process of natural history research; rather they were themselves employed as tools by naturalists seeking to make sense of their particular experience."[27] In other words, later herbals descended from earlier ones, and previously printed botanical books were a crucial location for herbalists' "gathering" behaviors.

A crucial and distinctive part of Turner's use of contemporary botanical authorities, however, is his recognition of their provenance. He is particularly attuned to the sources that individual authors used in their translations of classical authorities. For example, in his entry on *Nerium* in the second volume of his *Herball* (1562), Turner notes that the seed pod

> as it openeth/ sheweth a wollyshe nature lyke an thystel down/ as Ruellius tra[n]slation hath/ it semeth [that] hys greke text had ἀκάνθινοις παπποις. But my greke text hath ὑάκινθίνοις παπποις. And so semeth the old translator to have red/ for he he [*sic*] translatheth thus: *lanam deintus habens*

---

[25] Turner, *A New Herball*, sig. A2r. On the multiple editions of Ruel, see Stannard, "Dioscorides," 9.

[26] Eisenstein, *Printing Press*, 71–80. As books contributed to cross-cultural exchange, authors endorsed additional mechanisms for exclusion, such as "Christendome," that would later serve Orientalist discourses. See Angela Barreto Xavier and Ines G. Županov, *Catholic Orientalism: Portuguese Empire, Indian Knowledge (16th–18th Centuries)* (Oxford: Oxford University Press, 2014).

[27] Ogilvie, *Science of Describing*, 207.

similem hyacintho. Yet for all that I lyke Ruelliusses Greke text better then myne for the down is whyte and lyke thestel down/ & nothynge lyke hyacinthus . . .[28]

Printed Greek works were presumably available to Turner in the libraries of his friends and colleagues during his exiles on the continent between 1540 and 1558, but the availability of such texts in Cambridge in 1538 may have been limited, as only Ruel and Brunfels were mentioned in the text of the *Libellus.* Later, in the second part of the *New Herball,* Turner insists that the limited availability of good translations could be mitigated if publishers included the original work along with the vernacular conversion, "for so myght men the better examin theyr translationes."[29]

Turner notes that including both original and translated texts together would not only benefit plant knowledge by enabling correction but also encourage the spread of self-education, a secular form of the *sola scriptura* that was consistent with his devotion to religious reform. Turner's awareness of the limited availability of quality books motivated both his educational and his reform goals, and he insisted that authors themselves were responsible for helping to remedy this bibliographic problem. This pursuit accords well with modern standards of scholarly citation and, I argue, later helped to ensure Turner's botanical reputation.

Once he obtained his MD, Turner's reputation was also protected by his role as a physician. As Turner realized that printing made possible a widespread distribution of books, he also recognized an opportunity that could serve his pastoral and botanical interests: the diverging systems of professional and civic authority governing the three medical professions. While physicians were university-trained professionals who were required to complete a Master of Arts degree before even beginning their medical studies, surgeons and apothecaries were educated through a seven-year apprenticeship in accordance with the customs of the City of London. Surgeons were ostensibly required to be conversant in Latin in order to pass their church-mandated licensing examination, yet since this requirement was often waived or inconsistently applied, its lax enforcement provided physicians with a humanistic basis for asserting surgeons' inferior understanding: they did not know their Latin and were therefore wholly ignorant of the medical tradition. Apothecaries, originally included within the Grocers' Company, were unable to split off from it until 1617, when

---

[28] William Turner, *The Seconde Parte of William Turners Herball* (Cologne: Arnold Birckman, 1562), sig. L5r.

[29] Turner, *Seconde Parte,* sig. R4v.

their efforts were assisted by a College of Physicians that had a vested interest in the Apothecaries' pharmacological skills.[30] Though Turner was never admitted into the select and limited membership of the College of Physicians of London, his boasts of superiority over other medical practitioners were in keeping with the general attitude that the College took towards the subordinate practitioners it had, since 1518, been charged with overseeing.[31] By the end of the sixteenth century, all three groups of medical practitioners had attempted to use print to their advantage, but physicians' early strategic deployment of Tudor herbals gave them a head start in the quest for medical authority.

Turner's attitude towards printed books of English botany in 1538 might have been formed through a relationship to Thomas Gibson, whom I identified in Chapter 5 as the first figure in English botany to introduce an authoritative posture in order to limit the interpretive boundaries of his work. Gibson's unillustrated third edition of *The Great Herball* (1539) both removed that work's Catholic sentiments and added a preface that promoted physicians' authority over all elements of medical care. A reconsideration of Gibson's changes to the text sheds additional light on Turner's early dismissal of the English herbals available for study. While in 1538 he may well have shared with Gibson the latter conviction about the authority of medical doctors, Turner himself was not yet a medical doctor directly invested in the elevation of physicians at the expense of other kinds of authorized medical professionals.[32] Evidence of just such an attitude is apparent, however, in Turner's next botanical publication, published after he had become a physician.

The Names of Herbes (1548)

The Names of Herbes in Greke, Latin, Englishe, Duche & Frenche wyth the commune names that Herbaries and Apotecaries vse. Gathered by William Turner was published in 1548 by John Day and William Seres *cum gracia & priuilegio*

---

[30] See Pelling and Webster, "Medical Practitioners," 165–235.

[31] For an extended treatment of the regulatory activities of the College of Physicians throughout the sixteenth and seventeenth centuries, see Pelling, *Medical Conflicts*.

[32] Tudor analogies of the body politic that positioned certain agents as healing physicians were commonplace, but as Whitney R. D. Jones notes, "Turner's specialist knowledge enabled him to employ this device with particular and often picturesque effect, while his fervent advocacy of the need for religious reform encouraged him to extend its use into that field also." See *William Turner, Tudor Naturalist, Physician, and Divine* (London: Routledge, 1988), 3. Turner's *A New Booke of Spirituall Physik* (1555; *STC* 24361), ostensibly "Imprented at Rome by the vaticane churche," was Turner's most extended treatment of this device. See Rainer Pineas, "William Turner's *Spiritual Physik*," *The Sixteenth Century Journal* 14 (1983): 387–398.

and printed by Steven Mierdman. Eventually the holder of the patents for John Ponet's catechism, the works of Thomas Becon, the Sternhold and Hopkins metrical psalter, and *ABC with a Little Catechism*, as well as the publisher of John Foxe's *Acts and Monuments*, Day was arguably the most important stationer of his era and had an especially keen eye for saleable works, even early in his career. Day's willingness to invest in Turner's *The Names of Herbes* indicates that he believed there to be a viable market for a new English herbal, particularly one dedicated to the young King Edward VI. Day may have had a personal interest in herbals or simply wanted to flatter those who did, such as his patron William Cecil, who was especially fond of gardens. In his edition of physician William Cunningham's *The Cosmographical Glasse* (*STC* 6119), for which, with Cecil's aid, Day received a lifetime patent in 1559, Day commissioned a woodcut author portrait of Cunningham reading an illustrated herbal of Dioscorides beside a globe (Figure 7.1), signaling a relationship between cartography and botany that would increasingly figure in defenses of European colonial expansion.[33] Though Day printed most of his later books for himself, some of his earliest work was produced at the press of Steven Mierdman, an Antwerp printer resident in London between 1548 and 1553. In July 1550, Mierdman received a five-year generic grant of privilege from the king to print books at his own expense, but with the young king's death, the Protestant Mierdman was forced to flee to Emden, where he died in 1559.[34]

During the better part of a decade that he spent in Europe during his first exile, Turner had investigated continental vegetation, attempting to reconcile his studies of the works of Pliny and Dioscorides with the new plants he encountered and collating them with his working knowledge of English flora that John Byddell had published as the *Libellus* in 1538. *The Names of Herbes* builds on the linguistic equivalencies in the earlier work, adding plant locations where known, as in his entry for *Alnus*, or alder trees ("it growth by water sydes and in marrishe middowes").[35] Most of the work is devoted to reconciling his experience with classical description: "The best Gramen and moste agreying with Dioscoridis description, dyd I see in Germany with other maner of

---

[33] Christopher M. Parsons, *A Not-So-New World: Empire and Environment in French Colonial North America* (Philadelphia: University of Pennsylvania Press, 2018).

[34] On Day, see Elizabeth Evenden, *Patents, Pictures and Patronage: John Day and the Tudor Book Trade* (Burlington, VT: Ashgate, 2008), C. L. Oastler, *John Day, the Elizabethan Printer* (Oxford: Oxford Bibliographical Society, 1975); Peter W. M. Blayney "John Day and the Bookshop That Never Was," in Lena Cowen Orlin (ed.), *Material London, ca. 1600* (Philadelphia: University of Pennsylvania Press, 2000), 322–343; and Peter W. M. Blayney, "William Cecil and the Stationers," in Robin Myers and Michael Harris (eds.), *The Stationers' Company and the Book Trade 1550–1990* (New Castle, DE: Oak Knoll Press, 1997): 11–34, esp. 20–22. On Mierdman, see Duff, *Century*, 105.

[35] Turner, *The Names of Herbes*, sig. A7r.

Figure 7.1 Portrait of William Cunningham from *The Cosmographical Glasse* (1559), sig. A3v. The Huntington Library, San Marino, California (RB 60873).

rootes."[36] Occasionally, where he feels he has something to add or to correct in the works of authorities, Turner includes updated descriptions of plants that he mentions:

> Typha growth in fennes & water sydes amo[n]g the reedes, it hath a blacke thinge Almost at the head of the stalke lyke blacke Veluet. It is called in englishe cattes tayle, or a Reedmace, in Duche Narren Kolb, or Mosz Kolb.[37]

Throughout *The Names of Herbes*, Turner's research into nomenclature is diverse and nonjudgmental, much like a modern-day descriptive linguist would produce. He offers names for the herbs of the ancients in a variety of languages, as well as the names that his contemporary apothecaries and "herbarists" actually use: "Seseli massiliense is called in the Poticaies shoppes, siler montanum, it may be called in englishe, siler montayne"; "Pistacia are called of the poticaries Fistica, they may be called in english Fistikes or Festike nuttes"; "Oxycantha is called in englishe as it is named of the poticaries berberes."[38] By explaining how "poticaries" identify plants, Turner presumes a reader requesting simples at an apothecaries' shop, indicating that he expects an audience who engages with apothecaries in their role as public merchants, not necessarily with apothecaries in their role as private healers. Such a feature hearkens back to the "exposycyon of the wordes obscure" feature of *The Grete Herball*, and Turner's inclusion of "the Potecaries and Herbaries Latin" in his writings later becomes a central feature of the title page advertising for his larger, three-part herbal.

The distinction between apothecaries as vendors of prepared plants or as healers of patients is crucial to Turner's larger authoritative goals in *The Names of Herbes*. In the period between the publication of his first herbal in 1538 and his second herbal in 1548, William Turner became a physician, and Turner's investment in the medical authority of physicians over other members of the medical professions becomes clear. In the 1548 preface, Turner outlines the provenance of his latest botanical work, explaining that he had finished a Latin version of the text two years previously but had refrained from seeking to have it published after his fellow doctors urged

---

[36] Turner, *The Names of Herbes*, sig. D4r. In one entry, Turner limits his comments by virtue of the plant's familiarity with readers: "Fragraria is called in english a strawberry leafe, whose fruite is called in englishe a strawbery, in duche Erdeber, in frenche Fraysne. Euery man knoweth wel inough where strawberries growe" (sig. D2v).

[37] Turner, *The Names of Herbes*, sigs. G6v–G7r. See also the entry for *Astragalus*: "It growth in the mountaynes of Germany, and hath leaues and stalkes lyke a pease, blacke little rotes with knoppes lyke acorns, Fuchsius toke thys herbe to be apios, but the discription agreeth not" (sig. B4r).

[38] Turner, *The Names of Herbes*, sigs. G2v; F3v, E8v.

him to provide a more comprehensive guide to English plants. His colleagues suggested instead that he investigate more broadly and, in particular, that he replicate the features of Fuchs's successful *De historia*: "they moued me to set out an herbal in Englishe as Fuchsius dyd in latine with the discriptions, fisgures and properties of as many herbes, as I had sene and knewe."[39]

Yet an illustrated English work like Fuchs's *opus* was impossible for Turner, or indeed any author, to produce on his own. As we have seen, an illustrated herbal requires a considerable outlay of capital from a willing printer able to invest in woodcut illustrations that can support an author's text, as well as the support of craftsmen who can draw and carve them. Turner explains in his preface that he was unable to complete such a compilation at present, though he carefully suggests that he, as the author, is the limiting agent. He simply does not have the time, given his other responsibilities as physician and chaplain to the Lord Protector: "I could make no other answere but that I had no such leasure in this vocation and place that I am nowe in, as is necessary for a ma[n] that shoulde take in hande such an enterplise."[40] The codicological means by which his "vocation" could find its audience remains unmentioned – booksellers, blockcutters, and printers are nowhere to be seen. Turner's business was not an issue, however, in his acquiescence to his friends' other request, that he "at the least to set furth my iudgeme[n]t of the names of so many herbes as I knew whose request I have acco[m]plished, and haue made a little boke, which is no more but a table or regestre of suche bokes as I intende by the grace of God to set furth here after."[41] Here, again, Turner leaves unmentioned the role of the publishers whose finances would enable his books to be made and "set furth," as their agency and capital would undermine his careful maneuvering for political preferment. Characteristically, Turner follows up the account of his accomplishment with a direct request that the Lord Protector provide him with both leisure and a "co[n]venie[n]t place as shall be necessary for suche a purpose," a request that, as his above-quoted letter to Cecil reveals, Turner felt had still not been adequately satisfied by November 1550.[42]

Before concluding his 1548 preface with another appeal to the benevolence of Lord Seymour, Turner highlights his scholarly deference to the medical authority of classical authors, chiefly Galen, to signal his professional allegiance. In an assertion of his own empirical authority derived

---

[39] Turner, *The Names of Herbes*, sig. A2v.   [40] Turner, *The Names of Herbes*, sig. A2v.
[41] Turner, *The Names of Herbes*, sig. A3r.   [42] Turner, *The Names of Herbes*, sig. A3r.

from personal experience, Turner hints at a mistrust of apothecaries' judgment:

> And because men should not thynke that I write of it that I neuer sawe, and that Poticaries shoulde be excuselesse when as the ryghte herbes are required of the[m], I haue shewed in what places of Englande, Germany & Italy the herbes growe and maye be had for laboure and money, whereof I declare and teache the names in thys present treates [treatise].[43]

Turner's botanical knowledge, gained by firsthand experience, is newly strengthened by his professional standing as a physician, which extended his authority over the body. Just as, in 1539, Gibson's preface to *The Great Herbal* confirmed the righteousness of doctors' control over all elements of ministry to the sick, so Turner's 1548 preface concludes by declaring that the usefulness of his latest herbal will be confirmed by expert physicians: "howe profitable it shall be vnto al the sicke folke of thys Realme, I referre the matter vnto all them whiche are of a ryght iudgeme[n]t in phisicke."[44] While in his *Libellus* of 1538 the naturalist Turner would suffer to be corrected by any "man of learning," a decade later his work's success or failure might be properly estimated only by those members of the medical caste in which he is now a member: formally educated physicians.

There are some limits to Turner's new professional conceit as a doctor, but these are centered on the objects of his botanical observations. Though he is largely confident in his status as an authority, in *The Names of Herbes* Turner often indicates his unwillingness to pronounce a verdict on a given plant when the evidence is inconclusive: "Bacchar or Baccaris is the herbe (as I thynke) that we cal in english Sage of Hierusalem, but I wyll determine nothynge in thys matter tyl I haue sene further. Let lerned men examine and iudge"; "I heare saye that there is a better kynde of Buglosse founde of late in Spayne, but I haue not seene that kynde as yet"; "Chamaecyparissus is supposed of some men to be the herbe that we cal Lauander cotton, whose opinion as I do not vtterly reiect, yet . . ."[45] Such caution has suggested to botanical historians eager to cement Turner's status as "the Father of British Botany" that he employed the skeptical scientific rigor espoused by modern science more than a century before the founding of the Royal Society. This may be true, but as Turner's

---

[43] Turner, *The Names of Herbes*, sigs. A3r–A3v. Such an attitude is also evident in the body of the work itself, as in Turner's entry on Myrica: "The Poticaries of Colon before I gaue them warning vsed for thys, the bowes of vghe, & the Poticaries of London vse nowe for thys quik tree, the scholemaisters in Englande haue of longe tyme called myrica[m] heath, or lyng, but so longe haue they bene deceyued al together. It may be called in englishe, Tamarik" (sig. E5v).

[44] Turner, *The Names of Herbes*, A3v.   [45] Turner, *The Names of Herbes*, sigs. B4v, B6v, C1v.

estimations center on a recognition of his own elevated subjectivity as a physician, it also seems clear that he views some kinds of botanical judgments as better than others, depending on the professional status of those who pronounce them. By 1548, then, Turner had internalized what Steven Shapin identifies as a key element in intersubjective trust, using his social and professional status to present to his readers authorized truth claims within printed English works of botany.[46]

Authorizing the Medical Marketplace

Turner's allusions to the advice of other physicians suggest his increasing bias towards the superior role of the medical establishment in the construction of an updated body of English natural philosophy. While Turner's desire to discuss his botanical work with fellow physicians was perhaps not surprising, it is remarkable that he claims to have sought out their advice on the particulars of *publishing* it. As I have argued throughout this book, determining the reading market for a printed edition is the purview of a publisher who functions as a book's speculative investor. A number of concurrences in Turner's biography suggest that he was acquainted with at least one physician who was uniquely qualified to evaluate the saleability of his latest botanical work, someone who had recently edited, published, and printed an herbal himself: Thomas Gibson. Though no evidence survives suggesting a direct connection between the two men, biographers have charted several coincidences between Turner and Gibson: both were born in Morpeth and attended Cambridge, where they were noted for their commitment to Protestant reform.[47] Further, in 1548, both men had works published by the upstart publisher John Day shortly after Day had finally secured his right to retail books within the City. A short tract credited to Gibson, *A Breue Cronycle of the Bysshope of Romes blessynge* (*STC* 11842a), was published by Day and sold at his shop at the sign of the Resurrection "a little aboue Holbourne Conduite."[48] While such surmises are not demonstrable, the

---

[46] See Shapin, *Social History of Truth*, p. xxvi.

[47] Because neither man admits to knowing the other in extant records, any connection between Turner and Gibson remains conjectural. John Hodgson was among the first to note the parallels between Gibson's and Turner's careers: both were born in Morpeth and educated at Cambridge where they were influenced by growing Reformation sympathies. See John Hodgson, *Memoirs of the Lives of Thomas Gibson . . . Jonathan Harle . . . John Horsley . . . William Turner* (Newcastle upon Tyne: Charles Henry Cook, 1831), 9–11. See also Raven, *English Naturalists*, 52.

[48] Duff, *Century*, 55. Though John Bale credits Gibson with authorship of this pamphlet, Blayney notes that "we have only Bale's word that it was written by Gibson. See Blayney, *Printers of London*, 392.

coordination of two Morpeth-born physician-divines seeking publication from the same bookseller suggests that Day may have been particularly sympathetic to physicians' engagement with print.

Day's early biography provides additional hints that he was acquainted with printed medical texts, as well as those who used them. As a younger man, Day was apprenticed or otherwise in service to the physician Thomas Raynald, a printer of engraved pictures who was responsible for publishing the midwifery manual *The Byrth of Mankynd* (1540, *STC* 21153).[49] Raynald had been in London at least since 1540, when a deposition was made to the City on August 17 of that year by "Thomas Mannyng, John Borrell and John Day late servants to Thomas Reynoldes printer late dwelling at Hallywell nere unto London," which asserted that a series of goods were Raynald's own.[50] Among the jackets, gowns, and cloaks were a number of books, including works by Vincentius,[51] as well as two herbals, suggesting Raynald's interest in medical books.[52] His effects also include a series of engraving plates for printing male and female anatomical figures with paste-in illustrated flaps, demonstrating Raynald's awareness of how print could be used as a surrogate or supplement to a physician's medical training. The midwifery volumes that Raynald published likewise indicate his cognizance that much-needed books of physic were still missing from the marketplace. If John Day had been Raynald's apprentice or otherwise worked for him before he started printing and publishing on his own, Day would have directly observed Raynald's navigation of the London market for medical books.

---

[49] Eucharius Roesslin's *Rosengarten* was originally published in Worms in 1513. See Blayney, *Printers of London*, 439–443.

[50] Henry R. Plomer, "Notices of English Stationers in the Archives of the City of London," *Transactions of the Bibliographical Society* 6 (1901): 13–27, 20. See also Blayney, *Printers of London*, 440nA.

[51] Vincentius Bellovacensis, or Vincent of Beauvais, a French Dominican friar, was the author of the three-part *Speculum majus*, an encyclopedic work of natural history used as a medical resource by Chaucer and others. See Pauline Aiken, "Arcite's Illness and Vincent of Beauvais," *Publications of the Modern Language Association* 51 (1936): 361–369.

[52] Blayney identifies the item in the list as not two herbals, one of English and one of Latin, but a single bilingual herbal; however, if Blayney is correct, then what is referred to must be a manuscript book as no such printed text then existed. Herbals are often itemized together in book lists and more likely is Raynald having had a copy of either the little *Herball* or *The Grete Herball* as well as a copy of a text like Turner's *Libellus*. Along with John Wight and Abraham Veale, another Thomas Raynald ("Reynolds"), possibly the physician's son, was apprenticed to Draper Thomas Petyt in 1540 and was freed (as a Draper) on August 29, 1547. It is therefore probable that the Raynalde (his preferred spelling) the Draper saw Petyt's version of the little *Herball* through the press in 1541. After he was freed, Raynalde took over Petyt's shop, where he later printed the 1552 edition of *The Byrth of Mankynd*. See Blayney, *Printers of London*, 441–443.

Day is now best known as the publisher of John Foxe's *Book of Martyrs*, but his early skill at observation and his extraordinary ability to recognize opportunity were instrumental in his later success. As no London company yet had authority over the craft of printing, it could be practiced by anyone, but, as I explained in Chapter 2, goods could be retailed in London only by those who were free of the city. At the time he was working for Raynald, Day was a *foren*, an Englishman who had not been born in London, which restricted his employment and freedoms within the City limits until he could obtain the status of freeman. Raynald's standing in London was unclear, but as the deposition of 1540 does not identify him with any City company, it is likely that he primarily earned his living as a physician, a profession that did not take apprentices.[53]

Day began printing in 1546, the same year that the company of Stringers (bowstringers) were permitted by the City to admit twenty redemptioners to their company. These new members gained their admission by paying a fee and, once done, became freemen, eligible to buy and sell retail goods as well as practice their craft. Though the names of those who were made free by redemption by the Stringers in 1546 are unknown, it is almost certain that Day was one of them.[54] He was "translated" (transferred) to the Stationers' Company in 1550. By 1553, Day had received patents for a number of the most profitable books in England. These patents would eventually help Day become one of the wealthiest stationers of his era, but more than a decade before that he was in service to the physician Thomas Raynald at the same time that Raynald published the first (and possibly also the second) edition of *The Byrth of Mankynd*.[55] Raynald's publication was the first English book to feature engraved illustrations, and the expense and complexity of providing these high-quality images testify to Raynald's belief in their value.[56] The volume's preliminaries highlighted that most of the listed remedies for ailments were Greek or Latin terms that would be unfamiliar to most lay readers, highlighting the necessity of an English work of linguistic glosses for plants that Turner's *The Names of Herbs* later

---

[53] That Thomas Raynalde, his son or kinsman, bound himself to a Draper further hints that the elder Raynald did not have master status within a London company.

[54] Blayney, "John Day," 329.

[55] Day was also of sufficiently close acquaintance with Barber-Surgeon William Tylley that he witnessed Tylley's will. See Evenden, *Patents*, 4.

[56] On the masculine nature of the authoritative posturing of *The Byrth of Mankynd*, see Caroline Bicks, *Midwiving Subjects in Shakespeare's England* (Burlington, VT: Ashgate, 2003); on its reception, see Jennifer Richards, "Reading and Hearing *The Womans Booke* in Early Modern England," *Bulletin of the History of Medicine* 89 (2015): 434–462.

provided.[57] In bringing *The Names of Herbes* to Day to publish, then, Turner may have found himself a particularly sympathetic investor.

By the time that the first part of Turner's *A New Herball* appeared in print in 1551, he had become fully persuaded that physicians were expert witnesses over the medical domain. He also had become something of a botanical evangelical, claiming that the study of plants, being tied to medicine, was of the highest order of knowledge ordained for men by God. Turner writes that "[a]lthough ... there be many noble and excellent artes & sciences, ... yet is there none among them all, whych is so openy com[m]ended by the verdit of any holy writer in the Bible, as is [the] knowlege of plantes, herbes, and trees, and of Phisick."[58] Turner's musings throughout his preface use biblical and apocryphal exegesis to define the value of botanical study and demonstrate the elevated role of the physician, who learns of the fruits of the earth and uses that knowledge to heal, and to teach, others. The physician's status as an intellectual authority is central to these tasks, because "The knowledge of the Phisicio[n] setteth vp hys heade, and maketh [the] noble to wondre."[59] While apothecaries might temper medical mixtures together, their efforts are merely mechanical deployments of the wonders of God's creation: "his [the apothecary's] workes bringe nothinge to perfecyon, but from the lorde commeth furth helth into all the broade worlde."[60] By contrast, the physicians' appreciation of the causes of illness through their investment in the Galenic systems that underlay healing better recognize the complexity that underwrites creation. Turner thus ultimately urges his readers to place their trust in God – and in God's most hallowed professional servant: "My sonne in thy syckenes fayle not, but pray vnto God: for he shall heale [thee]: leue of synne, shewe straight handes, and clenge thy harte from all synne. And then afterwarde gyue place vnto the Phiscion, as to him: whom god hath ordened."[61]

This attitude of deference to physicians' theoretical knowledge is not unique to English books but is typical of the larger herbal genre; the *German Herbarius* features a large woodcut on its title page depicting physician sages such as Galen and Ibn Sina (Avicenna) dictating their wisdom to the text's engrossed author, whom the preface identifies as

---

[57] Eucharius Roesslin, *The Byrth of Mankynd, Otherwyse Named the Womans Booke* (London: Thomas Raynald, 1540), sig. C3r.

[58] Turner, *A New Herball*, sig. A2r. For a broader examination of the early modern physician's relationship to God, see Jones, *William Turner*, 101–102.

[59] Turner, *A New Herball*, sig. A2r.   [60] Turner, *A New Herball*, sig. A2r.

[61] Turner, *A New Herball*, sig. A2r.

a "great master" of medicine in his own right.[62] The *German Herbarius*' preface similarly highlights the way that the work is designed to demonstrate "the wonderful works of God, and His benevolence in providing natural remedies for all the ailments of mankind."[63] Such Christian devotion became conventional, particularly as Renaissance herbal authors needed to navigate increasing numbers of works of classical and Arabic authorities. What is unique to Turner's approach, however, is the way that a traditional deference to medical authority becomes explicitly religious in its commandments, synching the usual generic pieties with a clear and defined expectation for readers that conveniently aligns with the larger goals of the English medical profession: "gyue place vnto the Phiscion, as to him: whom god hath ordened."

As Turner continues his sermon on the superiority of physic, the celestial privilege afforded to doctors comes to situate ever more terrestrial concerns. After he notes that the hallowed status accorded medicine is unique among the subjects available for study, he shifts his attention from religious and historical attitudes to medicine's superior subject matter of the human form. Because "mannis body is more precious then all other creatures," "so is Phisick more noble and more worthy to be set by, then all other sciences." Turner argues that those who bring works of physic into being should be celebrated, for "howe great a benefit doth he vnto the commo[n] welth that with great study and labor promoteteth, & helpeth men to the knowledge of Phisick."[64] The printed books of physic that can be read and studied are implicit in Turner's formulation, as are the efforts of the authoring physician who makes it possible for physic to be studied to the betterment of the commonwealth. The implicit nature of the book form becomes even more explicit as Turner returns to a theme familiar from his *Libellus* of 1538. More physicians should apply themselves to authoring herbals, Turner suggests, because England's national honor is at stake:

> There haue bene in England, and there are now also certain learned men: whych haue as muche knowledge in herbes, yea, and more then diuerse Italianes and Germanes, whyche haue set furth in prynte Herballes and bokes of simples. I mean of Doctor Clement, Doctor Wendy, and Doctor Owen, Doctor Wotton, & maister Falconer. Yet hath none of al these, set furth any thyng, ether to the generall profit of hole Christendome in latin, &

[62] Joseph Frank Payne, "On the 'Herbarius' and 'Hortus Sanitatis,'" *Transactions of the Bibliographical Society* 6 (1900–1901): 63–126.

[63] Translation from Payne, "On the 'Herbarius,'" 94–95.

[64] Turner, *A New Herball* (1551), sig. A2v.

to the honor of thys realme, nether in Englysh to the proper profit of their naturall countre.[65]

Turner supplies a rationale for these men's refusals to write about plants, surmising that they do not want to risk their learned reputations by setting forth works in print in which others may find fault. Instead, Turner's own botanical efforts will serve to remedy the gap left by his fellow physicians, who are too fearful of public reproach to risk their status. Here, then, as in Turner's hunting tracts, the printed book is imagined to be a surrogate for its author, who may be made vulnerable by virtue of his works' publicity. By exaggerating the hazard to his own reputation, Turner is thus able to elevate his status as the first Englishman to author a printed herbal in any language. Turner's enthusiasm for plants can then be associated with the same nationalistic fervor that governed his reformist investment in the nascent Church of England:

> I therfore darker in name, and farr vnder these men in knowledge, for the loue that I beare vnto my countre, and at the commandeme[n]t of your grace my lord and maister, I haue set one part of a great herball more boldly then wysely and with more ieopardy of my name then with profite to my purse, as I knowe by dyuerse other bokes, whych I haue set out before this tyme, both in English and in Latin.[66]

As he thus supplicates in offering his work to Somerset, Turner's status as servant to the Lord Protector (and, by extension, to the king himself) paradoxically enhances the authority over all aspects of medicine that he claims for his profession. Turner's technique of what Erin Katherine Kelly called his "canny posture" in *Romysh Foxe* is once again deployed to authorizing effect as he positions himself as a gracious and knowledgeable public servant.

Turner's claim to authority derives from his dissemination of specialized knowledge to an otherwise-ignorant public, but this role immediately opens him up to another criticism, one that he is particularly eager to preempt: Why would a trained physician make his profession's expert understanding available to a wider audience by offering it not only in print but also *in the vernacular*? When physic manuals were written exclusively in Greek or Latin, knowledge of their contents required a modicum of humanistic training, but English works could be read by anyone literate in a populace that was ever increasing. Printing and selling books about medicine would therefore render physic public and able to be

---

[65] Turner, *A New Herball* (1551), sig. A2v.   [66] Turner, *A New Herball* (1551), sig. A3r.

practiced by everyone, a deeply unsettling prospect, because it leads, according to Turner, to *murder*:

> for now (say they) euery man with out any study of necessary artes vnto the knowledge of Phisick, will become a Phisician, to the hynderau[n]ce and minishyng of the study of liberall artes, and the tonges, & to the hurte of the comenwelth. Whilse by occasyon of thys boke euery man, nay euery old wyfe will presume not without the mordre of many, to practyse Phissick.[67]

Turner's surmised objection, that knowledge of physic printed in the vernacular would cause public harm, reaffirms his assertion of medicine's scholarly primacy, begging the question of why anyone would bother with the study of "liberall artes" at all if *not* to practice medicine.

In his response to this anticipated criticism, Turner returns to his familiar theme of bettering the English public through education, an ethos that his biographer Whitney R. D. Jones calls Turner's "Commonwealth thinking."[68] Such views involve "a completely trad-itional approach to such matters as due degree, gentility (with its cognate obligation of liberality), vocation, and economic morality" alongside a redistribution of Catholic wealth in the service of "poor relief and education."[69] Turner's English herbal of remedies is thus a public service, one which ensures that physicians, those with access to the most authori-tative, text-based information about functional medicaments, provide their medical inferiors with a comprehensive system of instruction that recognizes both their inherent intellectual limitations and the social cir-cumstances in which all medical players (including physicians) are employed. Turner's defense of printed physic is so extraordinary that it is worth repeating in full:

> I make thys answer, by a questyon, how many surgianes and apothecaries are there in England, which can vnderstande Plini in latin or Galene and Dioscorides, where as they wryte ether in greke or translated into latin, of the names descriptions and natures of herbes? And when as they haue no latin to come by the knowledge of herbes: whether all the Phisicians of England (sauyng very few) committ not [the] knowledge of herbes vnto the potecaries or no, as the potecaries do to the olde wyues, that gather herbes, & to the grossers, whylse they send all their receytes vnto the potecary, not beyng present their to se, whether the potecary putteth all that shuld be in to

[67] William Turner, *A New Herball* (1551), sig. A3v.
[68] Whitney R. D. Jones, *William Turner: Tudor Naturalist, Physician, Naturalist, and Divine* (London: Routledge, 1988), 187. See also Whitney R. D. Jones, *The Tudor Commonwealth 1529–1559* (London: Athlone Press, 1970).
[69] Jones, *William Turner*, 187–188.

the receyt or no? Then when as if the potecari for lack of knowledge of the latin tong, is ignorant in herbes: and putteth ether many a good ma[n] by ignorance in ieopardy of his life, or marreth good medicines to the great dishonestie both of the Phisician and of Goddes worthy creatures, the herbes and the medicines: when as by hauyng an herball in English all these euelles myght be auoyded: whether were it better, that many men shuld be killed, or the herball shulde be set out in Englysh? The same reason might also be made of surgeons, whether it were better [that] they should kyll men for lack of knowledge of herbes or [that] an herball shuld be set out vnto them in English, whiche for the most part vnderstand no latin at all, sauyng such as no latin eares can abyde?[70]

While surgeons remedy injuries such as wounds and broken bones them-selves, offering their patients healing medicaments where needed, phys-icians refuse such mechanic practices, instead prescribing their remedies for illnesses that patients need to take to an apothecary to be filled. As apothecaries rarely gathered their own plants but were often beholden to grocers and "old wyues, that gather herbes," the success or failure of both the surgeon and the physician's enterprise was entirely dependent on the accuracy of the plant knowledge of these inferiors all the way down the line. If England was to avoid mass death through medical error, according to Turner, medical practitioners needed a standard means to check up on the accuracy of the old wives' plant knowledge, and apothecaries needed a printed resource to guide their ministrations. Though Turner's *New Herball* is directed as much to these kinds of practitioners as it is to his fellow physicians, his massive tome nonetheless serves to benefit the physicians' authoritative interests. Once printed, Turner's herbal could become a surrogate for physicians' control over their medical subjects, a mirror of ecclesiastical dominance over an underinformed laity.

Turner's mixing of religious and medical language continued through the remainder of his career, and by the third and final volume of his herbal, published posthumously in 1568, he did not let his physician peers off lightly. In order to oversee the efforts of surgeons and apothecaries (as well as those herb gatherers and old wives that they oversaw), he claims that physicians themselves needed to become conversant in simples, for "w[ith] out [the] knowledge wherof they can not deuly exercise their office and vocation where vnto they are called / for howe can he be a good artificer that neither knoweth the names of hys toles / nether the toles themselfes when he seeth."[71] As for Turner's nonmedical or lay readers engaged in

---

[70] Turner, *A New Herball*, sig. A3v.   [71] Turner, *Thirde Parte*, sig. *3r.

a process of self-healing, a right that English men and women could claim through Henry VIII's "Quacks' Charter,"[72] Turner advises that they should not attempt medicine at all without first seeking the advice of a qualified professional. The herbal's companion volume, *The Booke of the Natures of Triacles* (1568, *STC* 24360), admonishes, "I giue warning to all men and women that wil vse these medicines, that they take the[m] not in rashly and vnaduisedly, without the aduise and counsell of a learned phisition, who may tell them, whether they be agreeing for their natures and complexions and diseases or no."[73]

A large part of Turner's defense of vernacular medical texts comes from his approval of those who self-educate only when they recognize the authority of others who claimed oversight over particular knowledge domains. The printed book therefore provided opportunities for authors to become teachers, an extension of pastoral practice. Turner's 1568 herbal was dedicated to "the right worshipfull Felowship and Companye of Surgiones of the citye of London chefely / and to all other that practyse Surgery within England," not only because its contents most readily benefited that group of medical practitioners but because this group was particularly committed to a botanical education.[74] Such approval emerges even in his address to Elizabeth, where Turner promotes the value of a humanistic education by conspicuously complementing the queen's Latin instruction, rendering his appeal for Elizabeth's patronage oddly patronizing:

> when as it pleased your grace to speake Latin vnto me: for althought I haue both in England / low and highe Germanye / and other places of my longe traueil and pilgrimage / neuer spake with any noble or gentle woman / that spake so wel and so much congrue fine & pure Latin / as your grace did vnto me so longe ago: sence whiche tyme howe muche and wounderfullye ye haue proceded in the knowledge of the Latin tonge / and also profited in the Greke / Frenche and Italian tonges and other also . . .[75]

Turner's paradoxical status as Elizabeth's medically authoritative subject is made possible through his authoring a text that, though dedicated to her majesty, is really intended for the good of her commonwealth: "my good will considered / and the profit that may come to all youre subiects by it / it is not so small as my aduersaries paraduenture will esteem it."[76]

---

[72] See 34 and 35 Henry VIII c. 8, *Statutes of the Realm*, 3:906.
[73] William Turner, *The Booke of the Natures of Triacles* (1568), sig. G1r.
[74] Turner, *Thirde Parte*, sig. *2r.   [75] Turner, *Thirde Parte*, sigs. *2r–*2v.
[76] Turner, *Thirde Parte*, sig. *2v.

Turner's endorsement of the broader benefits of education appears to have been genuinely meant and was consistent throughout his career. This "Commonwealth thinking," then, helps Turner overcome the potential collision between his sympathies as a reformer and his professional identity as a physician, and it is his bibliographic awareness that makes such a synthesis possible. Throughout his works, Turner gives his support for the widest possible dissemination of both religious and secular knowledge in print, downplaying concerns that the specialized knowledge of the professional classes is dangerous when known outside of its authorized sphere. Instead, the printed book, when properly authorized and disseminated widely, may be used for the spiritual and the physical benefits of all Englishmen.

Making Physic Public

As Turner's endorsement of physicians' biblical and social authority leads him to honor the writings of his professional forebears, he becomes vulnerable to the familiar insecurity of early modern authors concerned their would-be patrons might believe the slander of envious rivals. Turner particularly fears that he might be charged with an offense that could render his attempt at obtaining patronage null and void: "for some of them will saye / seynge that I graunte that I haue gathered this booke of so many writers / that I offer vnto you an heape of other mennis laboures / and nothinge of myne owne / and that I goo about to make me frendes with other mennis trauayles."[77] In other words, Turner worries that the very bookishness of his botanical scholarship puts him at risk for charges of plagiarism. Citing others – particularly *living* others – in his work might be viewed as theft, and Turner seems aware of the criticism that Christian Egenolff had leveled at Leonhart Fuchs a few decades earlier: despite Fuchs's pretense of authorship, his own knowledge is, to a publisher like Egenolff, just the stuff of other books. If so, anyone could engage in this craft of synthesis, particularly when it comes to depicting God's creation. To preemptively defend himself and claim the text of his herbal as his own work, Turner cites both the authority of classical authors and the early modern custom of commonplacing. His apt defense makes traditional use

---

[77] Turner, *Thirde Parte*, sig. *2v. On the common Renaissance trope of authors as bees transforming their models into honey, see G. W. Pigman III, "Versions of Imitation in the Renaissance," *Renaissance Quarterly* 33 (1980): 1–32.

of the metaphor of honeybees' collection of nectar and returns to his own
title page identification as a "gatherer":

> To whom I aunswere / that if the honye that the bees gather out of so manye
> floure of herbes / shrubbes / and trees / that are growing in other mennis
> medowes / feldes and closes: maye iustelye be called the bees honye: and
> Plinies boke *de naturali historia* maye be called his booke / allthough he haue
> gathered it oute of so manye good writers whom he vouchesaueth to name in
> the beginninge of his work: So maye I call it that I haue learned and gathered
> of manye good autoures not without great laboure and payne my booke . . .[78]

By more than a century, Turner's claim of the "laboure and payne" he took
in 1568 in composing, correcting, and compiling his herbal prefigures John
Locke's 1690 assertion in the *Two Treatises of Government* (Wing L2766)
that "every Man has a *Property* in his own *Person* . . . the *Labour* of his
Body, and the *Work* of his Hands, we may say, are properly his."[79]
Through his efforts to "learn" and "gather," Turner has synthesized what
knowledge has come before him and supplemented it with his own.
Through his labor in making his book, Turner thereby fulfills the physicians' ordained role and served the commonweal by making it possible for
the secrets of God's creation to be publicly known.

Turner's defense in his preface contains two parts. First, he echoes the
same defense used by the Frankfurt printer Christian Egenolff when
Egenolff was charged with the violation of Johannes Schott's privilege for
copying the woodcuts of the physician Otto Brunfels's *Herbarum vivae
eicones*, which I discussed in Chapter 1. Because his subject matter is the
nature of God's creation, Turner insists, only God can rightfully claim
authority over information about plants. Second, Turner claims that even
though he did examine the printed works of his predecessors, he took pains
not to rely too heavily on the work of any one of them. As Leah Knight
notes, Turner's strategy is paradoxical, resting "the defense of his work as
his *own* on the fact that it is compiled from so very *many* authors. By his
logic, a little plagiarism is a dangerous thing, but a lot is authorship."[80]
Turner mentions Fuchs, Tragus,[81] Dodoens, and Mattioli by name, noting
that he relied on their writings less to acquire new information than to
confirm his own experience.[82] By virtue of what Locke later understands as

---

[78] Turner, *Thirde Parte*, sig. *2v.
[79] John Locke, *The Two Treatises of Government* (London, 1690), sigs. R3r–R3v.
[80] Knight, *Of Books and Botany*, 49.
[81] Hieronymus Boch was a German botanist whose *Kreuterbuch* of 1546 was illustrated with images
based on those found in the herbals of Fuchs and Brunfels. "Tragus" was his assumed Latin name.
[82] Turner, *Thirde Parte*, sig. *3r.

the right of property through labor, Turner's gathering from others' works, coupled as it is with his own experiential evaluation, serves to enable him to claim of his book that "I haue something of *myne owne* to present and geue vnto your highness ... Wherefore it may please your graces gentelnes to take *these my labours* in good worthe."[83] Because Turner's labors include the correction of others' works, then, the availability of other printed herbals does not diminish but actually *reinforces* his claims to authority over English botany.[84]

The physician William Turner's reputation as a herbalist and a reformer remains unmarred by any charges of "plagiarism" or unoriginality that might otherwise accompany modern scholarly interpretations of his conspicuous borrowing from the works of his predecessors. That was not the case for the barber-surgeon John Gerard, however, who, in writing his herbal just half a century later, has been subject to a very different notion of the responsibilities of authorship. Despite his considerable civic prominence during his lifetime and his unremarkable use of the conventions of the herbal genre, historians have largely labeled Gerard's intellectual contributions to botany illegitimate. Even as Turner's humanistic endeavors to compare the works of the ancients with his own experience were celebrated, Gerard's authority as a textual "gatherer" was rejected. The following chapter examines the provenance of Gerard's *Herball or Generall Historie of Plantes* to show that newly developing expectations of the responsibilities of an editor-compiler, coupled with the continued elevation of physicians, have created an erroneous but lasting impression that Gerard was less an authoritative herbalist than a scheming plagiarizer.

---

[83] Turner, *Thirde Parte*, sig. *3r, emphasis added.

[84] Turner may have been particularly eager to proclaim his position as an authority because of a recent indignity he had suffered when an unknown printer offered an unauthorized version of his *Hunting of the Romish Wolfe* as *The hunting of the fox and the wolfe, because they make hauocke of the sheepe of Christ Iesus* (1565, STC 24357). The material manifestation of one of his other texts appearing without his name, literally un*authorized*, contributes to Turner's 1568 assertion of his scholarly and experiential authority over the contents of his *Herbal*.

CHAPTER 8

John Norton and the Redemption of John Gerard

In the previous chapter, I demonstrated that William Turner's "commonwealth thinking" enabled him to navigate the competing notions for textual authority that emerged in his writing. Turner's bibliographic self-consciousness, his awareness of how print could serve his professional and spiritual interests, continued to develop over the course of his careers as a physician, natural historian, and divine. For Turner, disseminated printed books could serve as surrogates for their absent author, multiplying a singular text's impact by being in many places at once. Yet printed books could also serve as nuanced opportunities for authors to display their domination over a knowledge domain that was – thanks to print – ever increasing. As more and more printed herbals emerged on the continent, herbalists like Turner needed to manage not only their own investigations into plants but also the threat of information overload.[1] Paradoxically, because it is much easier to edit and revise a printed codex than to assemble a large manuscript book from scratch, the affordances of print helped authors sort and manage these concerns, and Turner continued to revise earlier editions of his magnum opus even as he wrote new material.

By coupling his roles of natural historian and reformer, Turner's commonwealth thinking caused him to view his role within printed English botany as serving as a local authority gathering botanical knowledge on England's behalf, incorporating the work of foreign others into his native own. Though he expresses some trepidation that his synthesis may be seen as the product of other men's labor, Turner insisted that his acts of approval and correction simply brought accuracy to existing accounts of the beauty of God's creation – a creation that has only one true Author. As he sought to make herbal knowledge widely known within the English commonwealth, Turner could therefore evaluate continental herbal editions and amplify those authors whose accuracy he found worthy of

---

[1] On managing information, see Blair, *Too Much to Know*.

citation; and where other herbalists were found wanting, Turner could use his own work as an opportunity to correct their deficiencies. Turner's appeal to the English herbalist's communal role, and his bibliographic ego, would cast a long shadow upon the English herbals that followed.

In the concluding chapter of this book, I show how Turner's anthological approach to herbal authorship was widely understood to be a feature of the genre by returning to the large, illustrated herbal that was the subject of my prologue: John Gerard's *Herball, or General Historie of Plants*, first set into print by Bonham and John Norton in 1597 (Figure 8.1).[2] This commodious work of 1,392 folio pages (plus preliminaries and indexes) contained 2,190 distinct woodcuts, including the first printed illustration of the potato.[3] Gerard's *Herball* was remarkably successful: it was twice reprinted, and it remained an authoritative botanical textbook through the eighteenth century. Copies of the book were regularly bequeathed by name in wills, and as we have seen, poets such as John Milton profitably mined its descriptions for details about plants and their uses. Yet despite the evidence of Gerard's wide renown among his contemporaries, his reputation as a herbalist has suffered from accusations of plagiarism that have plagued discussions of his work since the publication of the book's revised second edition in 1633. This chapter will explain how this narrative about Gerard's 1597 *Herball* came about, paying close attention to the perspectives of the volume's publishers to reveal that the logic of the traditional account of Gerard as a plagiarist makes little sense in the context of early modern herbal publication.

Thinking Materially about *The Herball* (1597)

Because of their complex and expensive formatting, large herbals are a monumental publishing endeavor, and illustrated printed books like *The Herball* often found their genesis not in individual authors but in the publishers who would finance and profit from the sale of such books. Such conditions were foundational to the genre: in 1542, Leonhart Fuchs singled out his publisher, Michael Isingrin, as being put to "enormous expense in publishing this work," an effort that Fuchs tried to honor in the dedicatory epistle to *De historia stirpium*. The book's imperial decree was designed to protect not Fuchs's authorial rights but Isingrin's substantial

---

[2] Though his name in both the *Herball* and his will of 1612 add an ultimate letter "e" to his name, scholarship standardizes 'Gerard' as spelt without.

[3] Each copy of *The Herball* required 371 edition-sheets of paper; on its woodcuts, see Luborsky and Ingram, *Guide to English Illustrated Books*, 1:393.

Figure 8.1 John Gerard, *The Herball or General Historie of Plants* (1597). Image reproduced courtesy of the Ohio State University Libraries' Rare Books & Manuscripts Library (Shelfmark QK 41 G3).

financial investment. Unfortunately, the accuracy of images of God's creation proved hard to protect with a royal privilege, and, as I reveal in Chapter 1, the illustrations of *De historia* were soon copied by other publishers eager to market herbals of their own. Within three decades, the collaborative woodblocks of plants made by Albrecht Meyer, Heinrich Füllmaurer, and Viet Rudolf Speckle for Fuchs's herbal had been copied and recopied in books throughout Europe – including in Turner's celebrated *Herball* of 1551–1568.[4] As early modern readers' demands for illustrated herbals increased, the woodblocks that supplied these botanical images were likewise in high demand among the publishers who catered to these customers. Matched sets of botanical woodblocks became commodities that could generate rental incomes for the publishers who owned them. Accessing a suitable set of woodcuts, therefore, was a priority for any publisher who wished to invest in an illustrated new herbal but who did not have the extraordinary resources required to commission thousands of woodblocks for themself.[5]

I have argued throughout this book that historians of herbals need to "think materially" in order to better understand the way that the genre developed in early modern England from unillustrated, anonymous small-format books into the massive folio tomes authored by the "fathers" of English botany. Thinking materially involves recognizing the commercial and artisanal agents who were responsible for a book's production, and it inhibits the hasty, but common, critical instinct to credit a work's appearance in print to the author responsible for its verbal text. Attention to the ways that printed books circulated as valuable commodities reveals that this impulse to "author-ize" printed artifacts can be misleading; when reading the book as a crafted object, the complexity of the thing we call "Gerard's *Herball*" reveals that its creation was instigated not through the textual efforts of the man whose name eventually prominently appears on the

---

[4] For a vivid demonstration of how the blocks that produced Turner's woodcuts were copied from a printed edition of Fuchs's *De historia*, see Brent Elliott, "The World of the Renaissance Herbal," *Renaissance Studies* 25 (2011): 24–41.

[5] On the way that woodblocks could change their "epistemic status," as well as the mechanisms for their exchange, see Bruce T. Moran, "Preserving the Cutting Edge: Traveling Woodblocks, Material Networks, and Visualizing Plants in Early Modern Europe," in Matteo Valleriani (ed.), *The Structures of Practical Knowledge* (Cham: Springer, 2017), 393–419. On English stationers renting woodblocks from Antwerp, see Dirk Imhof, "Return My Woodblocks at Once: Dealings between the Antwerp Publisher Balthasar Moretus and the London Bookseller Richard Whitaker in the Seventeenth Century," in Lotte Hellinga, Alastair Duke, Jacob Harskamp, and Theo Hermans (eds.), *The Bookshop of the World: The Role of the Low Countries in the Book-trade, 1473–1941* (Utrecht: Hes & De Graaf Publishers, 2001), 179–190. I am grateful for Roger Gaskell's help in locating these articles.

work's engraved title page but through the investment and the skill of the book's manufacturers. In Brett Elliott's words, a volume like Gerard's *Herball* was "a publisher-led book."[6]

In order to net a profit, a printing project on the scale of *The Herball* needed to be led by someone with advanced management and marketing skills. John Norton would later become one of the most successful English stationers of his age, a figure whose systematic comprehension of the European book trade would enable him to be the primary bookseller to Sir Thomas Bodley, the founder of Oxford's Bodleian Library.[7] Like his stationer forebear John Day, Norton's aptitude for evaluating and selecting books to invest in was demonstratively superior to that of his contemporaries, a talent that served Norton well from the moment he obtained his freedom of the City in July 1586. Norton had been bound to his uncle, the bookseller William Norton, as an apprentice quite late, at the age of twenty-one, and his maturity upon his freedom seven years later allowed him immediately to locate opportunities for profit in the import trade. John Barnard identifies his skill as a "cultural broker and facilitator … Norton's business shows how far early seventeenth-century capitalism depended upon the effective utilisation of the openings provided by kinship, clientage, patronage, and government favour."[8] Key to Norton's lasting relationship to Bodley was the stationer's deep familiarity with continental and English book trends, a familiarity that allowed Norton to notice that, despite the English translations of Dodoens that occasionally reappeared in London bookshops, an Englishman had not authored an illustrated vernacular herbal since the last publication of William Turner in 1568. Such a considerable investment required careful planning, and what Norton did in response to this perceived gap in the marketplace suggests his awareness that there were requisite elements of the herbal genre that English readers expected to have satisfied if they were to lay out large sums of money for what would be a massive and expensive volume.

[6] Elliott, "Renaissance Herbal," 34. For a similar reading of the printer's role in Mattioli's herbals, and the way that that author was subject to deliberate "iconification," see Moran, "Preserving," 406.

[7] Once the book was printed, John Norton went to considerable expense to have its illustrations professionally water-colored as a gift for Bodley. His especial attachment to *The Herball* suggests that John, rather than Bonham Norton, was the figure most responsible for its publication, with Bonham's contributions being largely financial. See John Barnard, "Politics, Profit, and Idealism: John Norton, the Stationers' Company, and Sir Thomas Bodley," *Bodleian Library Record* 17 (2002): 385–408.

[8] See Barnard, "Politics," 385. Norton's career and wealth at death testify to his capacity for shrewd business dealings, including a deep knowledge of continental trends. He was a member of the livery of the Stationers' Company in 1598 and later twice became its Warden. See Ian Gadd, "Norton, John (1556/7–1612), bookseller," *ODNB*.

In order to produce an illustrated herbal, Norton needed both a text and the means to produce images, and while potential English herbalists seem to have been common enough (Turner listed several qualified Englishmen in his 1551 *New Herball*, and the community of naturalists on Lime Street was growing), complete sets of botanical woodblocks were a much more limited resource.[9] Norton therefore may have started his project by locating the means to produce botanical illustrations, reasoning that he could source both a text and (if needed) a party to reconcile image and text together, once the woodblocks were secured. Norton's connections to continental booksellers allowed him to acquire a large set of botanical woodblocks that had previously been used in a herbal published in Frankfurt in 1590: Nicolaus Basseus's edition of the *Eicones plantarum* of Tabernaemontanus (*USTC* 642288). It is also possible that Norton settled on the production of a new English herbal only after being presented with an opportunity to rent the set of woodblocks sometime after *Eicones* appeared in print. (The blocks were later returned to Basseus, who used them for subsequent editions.) Correctly anticipating that a new, illustrated English herbal would necessarily be a sizable investment, Norton persuaded his cousin Bonham Norton to share the costs – and the risks – of financing the large publication.

At 371 edition-sheets, *The Herball* was the second-largest book that Bonham and John Norton would ever finance, putting it in the top 1 percent of the largest books published during the entire *STC* period of 1475–1640. Assuming a modest print run of only 500 copies, the paper alone for *The Herball* would have cost the Nortons more than £135, an expense they would have needed to bear upfront in order to enable their hired printer to start printing. The labor costs for composition and impression would be nearly as much again. *The Herball*'s paper volume dwarfs even the Shakespeare First Folio (227 sheets), making it comparable to folio editions of the Authorized Version of the Bible (366 sheets). Even then, however, printing the first edition of the Authorized Version in 1611 was expensive – so much so that the King's Printer Robert Barker had to borrow money to finance it. (Incidentally, Barker reached out to the wealthiest stationers he could find: Bonham Norton and John Bill, John Norton's former apprentice and agent in continental affairs.)[10]

<hr />

[9] For a detailed "thick description" of the community of Lime Street naturalists, see Harkness, *The Jewel House*, esp. chap. 1.

[10] In 1605, Bill, along with Bonham and John Norton, founded the conglomerate Officina Nortoniana, which served as an imprint. See B. J. McMullin, "The Bible Trade," in John Barnard, D. F. McKenzie,

Publishing large books like the Bible was expensive enough, but illustrated books posed additional problems. *The Herball*'s large size and its thousands of woodcut illustrations meant that it was an unusually complicated book to produce, requiring production skills of the highest order. For its printing, the Nortons hired Edmund Bollifant, a partner in the syndicate of Eliot's Court Press, thereby ensuring that the text would be accompanied not only by the botanical woodcuts Norton had rented but also by the syndicate's impressive suite of ornamental capitals. More importantly, Bollifant was familiar with the challenges of the genre: he had recently printed an illustrated herbal of his own, a "corrected and emended" third edition of Henry Lyte's English translation of Rembert Dodoens's *Cruydeboeck* (1595; *STC* 6986). *The Herball* was such a monumental undertaking that it accounted for more than half of the Eliot's Court Press's output in 1596 and 1597. John Norton entered the rights to the title "sett forthe in folio and in all other volumes with pictures and without" on June 6, 1597.[11]

Yet how – and when – did John Gerard get attached to John Norton's herbal project? Most explanations of the provenance of *The Herball*'s textual content derive not from the evidence of the 1597 text itself but from the preface to the second edition of 1633, another "publisher-led enterprise," published at the behest of John Norton's widow Joyce and her business partner Richard Whitaker.[12] On its title page, Joyce Norton and Whitaker's 1633 edition was marketed as being "very much enlarged and amended" by the London apothecary Thomas Johnson, whom Norton and Whitaker hired to carry on the accretive herbal tradition by updating Gerard's earlier text and annotating it with his own observations. The 1633 edition was just as described: despite Johnson's efforts to streamline the text, its bulk increased to a whopping 431 edition-sheets per copy, straining the limits of what could be bound in a single codex. (When Robert Cotes would enter the rights to John Parkinson's *Theatrum botanicum* into the Stationers' Registers two years later, he would highlight its size, calling it "an herball of a Large extent."[13] When it was finally published in 1640, Parkinson's book was even slightly larger than the revised Gerard, requiring 442 edition-sheets per copy.)

Johnson's many additions and emendations in 1633 to the earlier text included a new address to the reader that was designed, in his words, to

and Maureen Bell (eds.), *The Cambridge History of the Book in Britain*, vol. 4 (Cambridge: Cambridge University Press, 2002), 455–473; and Gadd, "Norton."
[11] Arber, *Transcript*, 3:85.   [12] Elliott, "Renaissance Herbal," 35.   [13] Arber, *Transcript*, 4:307.

"acquaint you from what Fountaines this Knowledge may be drawne, by shewing what Authours haue deliuered to vs the Historie of Plants, and after what manner they have done it; and this will be a meanes that many controuersies may be the more easily vnderstood by the lesse learned and judicious Reader."[14] Johnson's musings on the history of botanical study begin with King Solomon and pass through a variety of classical authors including Aristotle, Galen, and "The Arabians" before turning to more recent authors like Ruel, Brunfels, and Fuchs, whose publications he lists by both date and format. Johnson's survey offers a useful expression of the breadth of botanical books, many published only on the continent, that were available to an urban professional in London in the 1630s, thereby confirming what Leah Knight calls "the bookishness of early modern botanical culture."[15] Like Turner, Johnson evaluates the work of his predecessors: authors are praised for their innovations, but he also occasionally offers reproofs for errors or for deceitful practice. Both Mattioli and Amatus Lusitanus are found wanting, "for as the one deceiued the world with counterfeit figures, so the other by feined cures to strengthen his opinion."[16] When he comes to Tabernaemontanus, Johnson notes that the woodcuts used in his book were "these same Figures was this Worke of our Author [i.e., Gerard] formerly printed."[17]

Upon arriving at Gerard, Johnson's comprehensive botanical history slows to include a brief biography of the authoritative figure whom Johnson's editorial efforts are designed to serve. Yet, when approaching the more recent history of Gerard's life, Johnson becomes less careful. He claims that Gerard died in 1607, "some ten years after the publishing of this worke," when Gerard actually lived until 1612 and continued to be a figure of considerable status in the Barber-Surgeon's Company after his term as Master in 1607. As Johnson was an apothecary, his lack of familiarity with the history of the Barber-Surgeons is understandable, but his biography of Gerard reveals that tensions among London's three types of authorized medical practitioners of physicians, surgeons, and apothecaries also carried over into the herbals of the seventeenth century. After the Society of Apothecaries had finally broken free of the powerful Grocers' Company in 1617 only with the assistance of the Royal College of Physicians, the Apothecaries' professional loyalties were clear, and evidence of them can be seen in Johnson's attitudes towards the barber-surgeon Gerard. Johnson

---

[14] Johnson, "To the Reader," in Gerard, *Herball* (1633), sig. ¶¶2v.
[15] Knight, *Of Books and Botany*, 133.   [16] Gerard, *Herball* (1633), sig. ¶¶5v.
[17] Johnson, "To the Reader," in Gerard, *Herball* (1633), sig. ¶¶6v.

commends Gerard's efforts in extending herbal knowledge on behalf of the nation but finds his expertise wanting: "His chiefe commendation is, that he out of a propense good will to the publique aduancement of this knowledge, endeauoured to perfome therein more than he would well accomplish; which was partly through want of sufficient learning."[18] Just as the physician Turner suggested that contemporary apothecaries were ignorant of their subjects, so does the apothecary Johnson suggest that the barber-surgeon Gerard lacked a proper education. He criticizes Gerard for being insufficiently "conuersant in the writings of the Antients," and takes Gerard to task for having "diuided the titles of honour from the name of the person whereto they did belong," errors that might better be ascribed to one of Bollifant's compositors than to the text's author.[19] That Johnson's indignation finds its source in professional jealousy soon becomes clearer as Johnson explains that his caviling was prompted by Gerard's *Herball* having generated a fame outstripping what Johnson feels is deserved: "I haue met with some that haue too much admired him, as the only learned and iudicious writer."[20] In the three decades since its publication, Gerard's massive *Herball* had dominated English herbalism, blocking other herbalists from view. For Johnson, then, Gerard's *Herball* met with its success because it proved insufficiently intertextual, misleading the "lesse learned and judicious" readers that he addresses in his own preface. By the end of the address, Johnson's narrative of the herbal genre may be read retrospectively, when it becomes less an informative chronicle than a defensive intertextual correction designed to remedy what he sees as Gerard's profound anthological failure. For all Renaissance botanists, including Johnson, the solution to a problematic book was always another book.

Johnson's indignant professional position also helps to explain what comes next, an account of Gerard's authorship of *The Herball* that builds on these earlier charges of insufficient learning by charging Gerard with the more serious accusation of plagiarism. In their discussions of plagiarism, Christopher Ricks and Peter Shaw have maintained that the offense doesn't consist merely in using the work of another author but in doing so "with the intent to deceive."[21] While copying another's work for one's

---

[18] Johnson, "To the Reader," in Gerard, *Herball* (1633), sig. ¶¶¶IV.
[19] Johnson, "To the Reader," in Gerard, *Herball* (1633), sig. ¶¶¶IV.
[20] Johnson, "To the Reader," in Gerard, *Herball* (1633), sig. ¶¶¶IV.
[21] Peter Shaw, "Plagiary," *The American Scholar* 51 (1982), 325–337; 327; Christopher Ricks, "Plagiarism," in Paulina Kewes (ed.), *Plagiarism in Early Modern England* (New York: Palgrave, 2003), 21–40; 22.

own use is widely acceptable in the early modern practice of commonplacing, allowing for the publication of such work *as one's own* deceives readers
who might be unable to locate their original source.[22] In this way, plagiarism is distinguished from more acceptable uses of others' work such as
quotation, imitation, repetition, and allusion, all of which are, by virtue of
the accuracy of their attribution, ethically acceptable. The offense of
plagiarism is thus a moral one, an attempt at dishonesty. As we saw in
Chapter 1, herbalists and physicians writing for print publication had long
accused each other of illicit copying – such accounts regularly appear in the
pages of Fuchs and the other herbalists that Johnson mentions as they
updated old works. Despite (or perhaps *because* of) the humanist Republic
of Letters that saw naturalists sharing samples, woodcut images, and plant
descriptions throughout the sixteenth and seventeenth centuries, the field
of herbalism also saw incidents of acrimony, accusations, and disdain.[23]
Some herbalists, like Mattioli and L'Obel, were notoriously embittered by
other naturalists' success, itemizing their failures and finding fault with any
work that inadequately commended their own. Calling out contemporaries for their insufficient citation and acknowledgment was thus wholly
conventional in herbals, especially by the early 1630s, when Johnson was
invited by Norton and Whitaker to edit Gerard's *Herball*. His indignation
is at once opportune (provided by the occasion of a new reprint of an old
edition) and entirely orthodox.

In his account of "how this Work was made vp," Johnson carries on
herbals' tradition of paratextual recrimination by asserting that Gerard's 1597
text derived from a lost translation of Rembert Dodoens's *Stirpium historiae
pemptades sex* (USTC 401987) that had been begun by a "Dr Priest," probably Robert Priest, then a member of the College of Physicians of London.
Dodoens's *Pemptades* had been published in Antwerp by Christopher
Plantin in 1583 and Johnson reports that "shortly after" Priest had been
hired to translate the work from Latin into English "at the charges of
Mr. Norton,"[24] confirming that the creation of what later became known
as "Gerard's *Herball*" was prompted not by an originating author but by an
originating stationer. Though Johnson's goal with this summary is to
undermine Gerard's authority, the story that Johnson tells of *The Herball*'s
provenance is the tale of how an expensive and specialized edition of a book
eventually came to be produced. Priest, however, died "either immediately

[22] On the contingencies of plagiarism in commonplace books, see Harold Love, "Originality and the Puritan Sermon" in Kewes, *Plagiarism*, 149–165.

[23] Olgilvie, *Science of Describing*, 74–82; see also Moran, "Preserving."

[24] Johnson, "To the Reader," in Gerard, *Herball* (1633), sig. ¶¶¶1v. Henrey, *British Botanical*, 1:9.

before or after the finishing of this translation," and Priest's manuscript translation of *Pemptades* then found its way into Gerard's hands, according to an unnamed someone "who knew Dr. *Priest* and Mr. *Gerard*."[25]

What was eventually published in 1597 as *The Herball* was ultimately not just a translation of Dodoens but a much larger, and decidedly more English, volume. Gerard drew on his extensive knowledge of English flora as well as his firsthand knowledge of how exotic foreign plants would fare when transported into the English climate. Johnson explains this discrepancy between Dodoens's and Gerard's texts by noting that Gerard reorganized his volume to fit the botanist Matthias de L'Obel's new system of classification that ordered plants not by pharmacological use value but by their morphological characteristics. In Gerard's *Herball*, plants are grouped together according to their kinds, enabling readers to examine what makes one species of basil or wolfsbane distinct from another. Johnson claims that Gerard's primary goal in adopting L'Obel's classification scheme was to disguise evidence of his use of Priest's translation: "Now this translation became the ground-worke whereupon Mr. *Gerard* built vp this Worke: but that it might not appeare a translation, he changes the generall method of *Dodonaeus*, into that of *Lobel*, and therein almost all ouer followes his *Icones* both in method and names, as you may plainly see in the Grasses and *Orchides*."[26] Johnson's moral position is clear and damning: "I cannot commend my Author for endeauouring to hide this thing from us."[27]

Johnson's indignation on Priest's behalf is largely baseless. Gerard could read (and write) in Latin, and he could easily have accessed Dodoens's *Pemptades* without Priest's intervention simply by acquiring a copy of Plantin's 1583 edition. What's more, as Robert Jeffers has noted, Gerard's *Herball* included not only those plants suitable for medical use but also those with culinary and aesthetic applications as well as new exotics, and as a result, "Dodoens' classifications would not have answered his purpose fully."[28] Further, because Gerard was taking his own botanical notes through the 1570s, his organizational structure would have been determined long before *Pemptades* was first published, and it reasonably bears evidence of influence from Pena and L'Obel's *Stirpium aduerseria noua* (1570–1571; *STC* 19595).[29]

---

[25] Johnson, "To the Reader," in Gerard, *Herball* (1633), sig. ¶¶¶1r.
[26] Johnson, "To the Reader," in Gerard, *Herball* (1633), sig. ¶¶¶1v.
[27] Johnson, "To the Reader," in Gerard, *Herball* (1633), sig. ¶¶¶1r.
[28] Jeffers, *Friends*, 49; see also Henrey, *British Botanical*, 1:47.
[29] Jeffers, *Friends*, 48. L'Obel's *Plantarum seu stirpium icones* (*USTC* 401886), referenced by Johnson, was published in Antwerp by Christopher Plantin in 1581 but contained unsold sheets of the 1570–1571 edition of *Stirpium aduerseria noua*.

As Gerard approached the task of reconfiguring his work to suit Norton's commission, he continued to use the classification method with which he was most familiar. Gerard's use of L'Obel's method of organizing his subject matter had little to do with Priest's translation of Dodoens, but because Johnson's goal is less to defend Priest than to demonstrate Gerard's inadequacy as a herbalist and as a botanist, his critique rests in finding fault with Gerard's technical capacity. Johnson suggests that Gerard was stymied by the woodblocks Norton presented him:

> this fell crosse for my Author, who (as it seemes) hauing no great iudgement in them, frequently put one for another … and by this means so confounded all, that none could possibly haue set them right, vnlesse they knew this occasion of these errors. By this means, and after this manner was the Worke of my Author made vp, which was printed at the charges of Mr. Norton, An. 1597.[30]

While Johnson's account of Gerard's matching woodblocks with the wrong descriptions seems damning, these kinds of errors are as likely to result from a compositor's mistakes in a print shop, as occurred with Peter Treveris's accidental swapping of the woodblocks for bombax and borage that I discussed in Chapter 5.

A verification for Johnson's account appears to come from a book published in 1655, an edited collection of L'Obel's writings from a manuscript written shortly before L'Obel's death in 1616. In *Stirpium illustrations*, L'Obel claimed that Gerard had used his work without proper acknowledgment, and he reports that he had been hired by Norton to edit Gerard's manuscript once its inadequacies had become apparent. L'Obel and Gerard had at one time been friendly, and L'Obel had even lent his name to Gerard's writings, providing a substantial commendatory letter for the 1597 *Herball*. Shortly before *The Herball* was finished printing, however, Gerard and L'Obel had fallen out, and L'Obel's grudge against Gerard continued for the remainder of his life. If Johnson's account of the making of the original volume is correct, then L'Obel's story of Gerard's failures provides additional verification for the charges of plagiarism that were leveled against Gerard. Yet there is little reason to trust L'Obel, and his biographer, Armand Louis, is not convinced that his account of editing Gerard is true. Louis notes there are no contemporary reports testifying to L'Obel's version of the events, adding that the botanist, particularly in his old age, was often cantankerous. "It is not impossible," Louis surmises,

---

[30] Johnson, "To the Reader," in Gerard, *Herball* (1633), sig. ¶¶¶1v.

"that L'Obel's concerns and accusations were merely the ruminations of a rancorous and embittered old man who felt threatened by others' authoritative rise in his dearly-loved field."[31]

Bookish details in L'Obel's biography put additional strain on his veracity and help to explain his animus. A Flemish physician, L'Obel had first come to London as a Protestant refugee in the late 1560s, when he settled in the Flemish hub of Lime Street. In 1570–1571, L'Obel and Pena collaborated to produce *Stirpium aduersaria noua,* which was entered by Thomas Purfoot into the Stationers' Registers and later printed. Even though Purfoot obtained the license to print *Stirpium,* it was L'Obel who appears to have funded its publication. In 1603, the Flemish author wrote a letter complaining that, of the original print run of 3,000 copies, he still had 2,050 remaining.[32] That print run was double what the Stationers' Company would eventually set as the maximum for a single edition, and at 120 edition-sheets, the expense for L'Obel must have been enormous.[33] "Thank God it is all paid for," L'Obel explained to L'Ecluse, "but the booksellers haven't allowed it to make a profit." By 1576, Purfoot had sold 800 copies of *Stirpium* to Plantin to bind with copies of Plantin's edition of L'Obel's *Plantarum seu stirpium historia* (*STC* 19595.3), a deal that also included Plantin acquiring the set of botanical woodblocks that Purfoot had used in printing his London edition.[34] Outside of the bulk sale to Plantin, Pena and L'Obel's *Stirpium aduersaria noua* sold exceptionally poorly, with only about 150 copies being purchased over three decades.[35] What appears to have happened is that Pena and L'Obel, recent immigrants, radically misjudged the English marketplace for herbals when they paid to publish their own work in its original Latin rather than translating it. Familiar with the bestselling herbals of Fuchs and Mattioli on the continent, the pair overestimated the audience in England for an expensive Latin herbal, as well as interest on the continent for a Latin herbal that had been printed in London and dedicated to a Protestant queen. Writing reflectively at the end of his life, L'Obel was thus motivated as much by the failure of his Latin herbal to find readers (a failure he blamed on English

---

[31] See A. Louis, *Mathieu de L'Obel 1538–1616* (Ghent-Louvain: Story-Scientia, 1980), 274. Translation mine.

[32] Louis, *Mathieu de L'Obel,* 131n22. For an English account, see Ogilvie, *Science of Describing,* 45.

[33] See Arber, *Transcript,* 2:43, and W. W. Greg, *A Companion to Arber* (Oxford: Clarendon Press, 1967), 43.

[34] See note to *STC* 19595.

[35] The original edition was reissued in 1605 and 1618, indicating that the edition continued not to sell on its own. See Albert E. Lownes, "Persistent Remaindering (Pena and de l'Obel's Adversaria, 1570–1618)," *Publications of the Bibliographical Society of America* 52 (1958): 295–299.

booksellers), and his jealousy of Norton's support for Gerard, as he was by Gerard's textual malfeasance.[36]

Johnson's and L'Obel's case for Gerard's plagiarism has been picked up by historians and oft repeated, but Johnson's evidence for vilifying Gerard breaks down even in the telling.[37] As Johnson reports it, the book that became Gerard's *Herball* began not with Gerard at all but with a publisher's recognition of an opportunity to profit: "Mr. Norton," surveying what Christopher Plantin was doing on the continent, saw room in the marketplace for an English translation of Dodoens's *Pemptades* and sought to commission one.[38] Recognizing that successful printed herbals are illustrated, Norton also acquired a large sequence of woodblocks. These blocks corresponded to the text of a different herbal, but it seems clear that Norton reasoned he could hire someone to reconcile Tabernaemontanus's images with Dodoens's text. The anthological impulse of the early modern herbal can thus be found not simply in the textual "gathering" of the authors so identified on these books' title pages but also in the material efforts of the publishers who assembled their herbal commodities from parts.[39] This facet of herbals' material forms is revealing: if Johnson's unnamed informant was accurate, and John Norton actually *did* commission a translation of Dodoens from Priest, the stationer owned the rights to use that text in whatever form he chose thereafter – which included handing off the manuscript to someone else once Priest was unable to finish it. Stephen Bredwell, one of Gerard's commendatory verse writers in 1597, suggests that exactly such a thing happened:

> The first gatherers out of the Antients, and augmentors by their owne paines, haue alreadie spread the odour of their good names, through all the Lands of learned habitations. D. *Priest*, for his translation of so much as *Dodonæus*, hath thereby left a tombe for his honourable sepulture.

[36] Louis suggests that L'Obel was also indignant that in several cases of classification, Gerard had sided with Dodoens over him (*Mathieu de L'Obel*, 274).

[37] See Raven, *English Naturalists*, 204–217; Arber, *Herbals*, 129–130, Ogilvie, *Science of Describing*, 37; Pavord, *Naming of Names*, 334; and most recently, Vin Nardizzi, "Daphne Described: Ovidian Poetry and Speculative Natural History in Gerard's *Herball*," *Philological Quarterly* 98 (2019): 137–156. For a particularly vivid, but fictionalized, account of what L'Obel described occurring in Norton's retail bookshop, see Harkness, *The Jewel House*, 15–19.

[38] Johnson's phrasing suggests that the "Mr. Norton" who commissioned Priest around 1583 was the same figure who published the finished *Herball* in 1597; however, as John Norton was an apprentice until 1586, and was often resident in Edinburgh until 1594, it is possible that, if true, it is actually another "Mr. Norton," John Norton's uncle and master, William Norton, that had initially made the arrangement with Priest.

[39] Kusukawa, *Picturing the Book of Nature*, 49–61.

M. *Gerard* coming last, but not the least, hath many waies accommodated the whole work vnto our English nation.[40]

In saying that Gerard "accommodated" those who came before him, Bredwell not only recognizes Gerard's anthological "gathering" efforts but endorses them, celebrating Gerard's synthesis in the volume's new English presentation. In other words, the "commonwealth thinking" of William Turner was recognized and celebrated when it reappeared in the writings of his native successor.

Thus, with Priest's death and inability to finish his translation, John Norton had a problem, but it was one that was solved by a bookseller with a talent for figuring out what a public would buy. His choice to deploy Gerard as his herbal's authorial figure was a smart one: while Priest was relatively unknown, Gerard in the 1590s was a gardener of some celebrity. He had been superintendent to the gardens of Sir William Cecil, Baron Burleigh, at Burleigh's residences in the Strand and at Hertfordshire since 1577, filling the void for botanical patronage in Cecil's service following the death of William Turner in 1568. In addition to tending Burleigh's gardens, Gerard had a large garden of his own in Holborn near the River Fleet. He was of such renown that in 1586 he was appointed curator of the garden of the College of Physicians, which would otherwise have had no reason to grant such authority to a mere barber-surgeon. Through his associations with Cecil, Gerard gained many advantages, including access to the latest plant specimens from the Americas and status in the growing botanical scene of Renaissance Europe, acquainting him with the leading physicians, scientists, and botanists visiting London and the Court. In 1597, Gerard was appointed Warden of the Barber-Surgeons' Company, and after the publication of *The Herball*, his status in London only continued to increase: by August 1604, Gerard had been appointed surgeon and herbalist to James I, and he was elected Master of the Barber-Surgeons' Company on August 17, 1607.[41] Historical accounts from a variety of sources reveal that, *unlike* Priest, Gerard's fame and influence were significant enough in late Elizabethan London to have sold books on its own. In short, there is a clear rationale why a savvy stationer like Norton would have wanted Gerard's name on a book he produced. Gerard's biographer, Robert Jeffers, suggests that he had been working on a herbal project throughout his career as a surgeon, and Norton's offer would have been a welcome

---

[40] Gerard, *Herball* (1633), sig. B3v.   [41] Jeffers, *Friends*, 79.

opportunity to "accommodate" that manuscript into an expanded and revised form.[42]

In his own address to the reader, dated December 1, 1597, Gerard made the form, and the anthological nature, of his work clear. He writes,

> I haue here therefore set downe not onely the names of sundry Plants, but also their natures, their proportions and properties, their affects and effects, their increase and decrease, their flourishing and fading, their distinct varieties and seuerall qualities, as well of those which our owne Countrey yeeldeth, as of others which I haue fetched further, or drawene out by perusing diuers Herbals set forth in other languages, wherein none of my country-men hath to my knowledge taken any paines, since that excellent Worke of Master Doctor *Turner*.[43]

In admitting to "perusing diuers Herbals," Gerard both echoes and cites his English forebear William Turner, who admitted to having "learned and gathered of manye good autoures" in the writing of his own book.[44] Turner's defense, as I and others have noted, relies on the breadth and diversity of his gathering, as well as on the way that Turner justifies this synthesis as being for the good of the English nation. It is not surprising, then, that Gerard's account continues by specifically focusing on his fellow "country-men" who have contributed to the herbal genre: "After which time Master *Lyte* a Worshipfull Gentleman translated *Dodonaeus* out of French into English: and since that, Doctor *Priest*, one of our London Colledge, hath (as I heard) translated the last Edition of *Dodonaeus*, and meant to publish the same; but being preuented by death, his translation likewise perished."[45] Missing from this account is Pena and L'Obel, whose status as foreign nationals residing within England rendered their contributions to English botany unworthy of inclusion in this particular list. Gerard's account of English-language herbals written by Englishmen, then, is in keeping both with the extant evidence and with what John Norton saw in the marketplace before commissioning the book that bears Gerard's name and advertises his status as a high-ranking Londoner on its title page.[46]

Gerard's book is, like the herbals that came before it, inherently inter-textual, drawing from its predecessors and, in turn, providing its successors

---

[42] Jeffers, *Friends*, 48.   [43] Gerard, *Herball* (1597), sig. ¶¶2r.   [44] Turner, *Thirde Parte*, sig. *2v.
[45] Gerard, *Herball* (1597), sig. ¶¶2r.
[46] Joyce Norton and Richard Whitaker would mimic this detail in their title pages of 1633 and 1636 and add to it by also advertising Thomas Johnson's status as a "Citizen and Apothecarye of London."

with ample opportunities for allusion, borrowing, and correction. In using Gerard's *Herball* as a guide for his botanical exegesis, John Milton was following in the footsteps of other authors; decades earlier, in his *Poly-olbion* (1612), Michael Drayton had identified the author as "skilful Gerard."[47] Editions of Gerard or quotations taken from them appear in the libraries of John Donne, Anne Southwell, Elizabeth Freke, and Lady Anne Clifford, among many others.[48] Gerard's reputation also continued through the seventeenth and eighteenth centuries: the works of John Coakley and Sir Joseph Banks testify that Gerard's *Herball* in its various editions continued to be of use in their own naturalist studies. Gerard's *Herball* remained a reference text to students of botany through the nineteenth century; as late as 1806, Richard Weston noted that "[a]t this day the book is held in high esteem, particularly by those who are fond of searching into the medicinal virtues of plants."[49] Descriptions of copies held in rare book libraries throughout the world suggest that many copies of Gerard's *Herball* saw heavy use, bearing evidence of plants being pressed between their pages.

Yet the intertextuality of *The Herball* that makes it so valuable is not restricted to its verbal and illustrative botanical content; it can also be seen in the volume's organizational form and structure. *The Herball*'s detailed indexes indicate that the book was especially suited for use as a reference text, and the indexes' interconnectivity suggests that Gerard (and his publisher) depended upon readers' familiarity with similar finding aids from works such as Gibson's edition of *The Grete Herball* of 1539 and Wyer's innovative later editions of the little *Herball*.[50] Plants were listed in

---

[47] "Of these most helpfull herbes yet tell we but a few, / To those vnnumbred sorts of Simples here that grew. / Which iustly to set downe, euen Dodon short doth fall; / Nor skilfull Gerard, yet, shall euer find them all" (xiii). A printed marginal besides this passage reads "The Authors of two famous Herbals." See Michael Drayton, *Poly-olbion* (London: Printed by Humphrey Lownes for Matthew Lownes, 1612), sig. Vɪv, p. 218.

[48] See Laroche, *Medical Authority*, "Appendix B: Female Owners of Herbal Texts."

[49] See also Henrey, *British Botanical*, 1:53. As the above-named readers imply, the large folio text of Gerard's *Herball* was likely out of the price range for all but the wealthiest of London's book consumers; one scholar notes a bound copy of the 1633 edition of the text retailing at 48 shillings. Even allowing for inflation between 1633 and its original date of publication, the 1597 retail cost of the *Herball* would still have been prohibitive to most purchasers. See Francis R. Johnson, "Notes on English Retail Book-prices, 1550–1640," *The Library* 5th Series 5 (1950–1951): 83–112.

[50] The deposit copy of the *Herball* in the Bodleian, for example, displays "wear ... entirely due to its intensive use by early readers. The serious damage is restricted to the book's index section" (Barnard, "Politics," 387–389). See also Ann Blair, "Annotating and Indexing Natural Philosophy," in Marina Frasca-Spada and Nick Jardine (eds.), *Books and the Sciences in History* (Cambridge: Cambridge University Press, 2000), 69–89. On continuous and discontinuous reading, see Stallybrass, "Books and Scrolls."

Gerard's *Herball* by their proper names in both English and Latin, and each entry was keyed to a page reference; other indexes were organized according to the illnesses or injuries that simples distilled from the listed plants could treat or provided equivalency tables uniting proper names with their local or regional monikers. English readers of herbals had been familiar with these tables for some time, but *The Herball*'s indexes were so comprehensive that the book could be useful for both those searching for medical remedies and those who were interested in plants for their own sake. Whether they were Gerard's innovation or, more likely, Norton's, the indexes ensured that *The Herball* could serve a variety of readers. Gerard's massive and comprehensive tome was considered so useful to Stuart medical practitioners that it was specifically bequeathed in a surgeon's will of 1628, which offered to "George Peren, barber-surgeon, my yearball known by the name of 'Gerard's Yearball.'"[51] As a result of the book's extended value for Renaissance readers, editors of early modern texts still consider Gerard's *Herball* a valuable resource in explaining contemporary botanical knowledge, and for this reason the volume is cited regularly in the commendatory notes of Shakespeare's plays where botanical elements play a significant role.[52]

Johnson was correct that his author's book in 1597 had actually been initiated by its publisher, but he seemed less willing to acknowledge that he, too, in 1632, had been subjected to the same commercial bibliographic impulses. Though Johnson complains to his readers that he was forced to work quickly, he tries to obscure who the commissioning agent was that set the clock ticking: "But I thinke I shall best satisfie you if I briefly specifie what is done in each particular, hauing first acquainted you with what my generall intention was: I determined, as wel as the shortnesse of my time would giue me leaue, to reetaine and set forth whatsoeuer was formerly in the booke described, or figured without descriptions."[53] As he lists his numerous mechanisms for "enlarging" and "amending" the 1597 *Herball*, Johnson positions himself as an authoritative and active subject, even though the book he corrects does not actually recognize him as its author. An inattentive reader might be forgiven for thinking that it was Johnson's initiative alone that necessitated Gerard's text being updated and reprinted for sale in 1630s London.

[51] Jeffers, *Friends*, 94.
[52] See Ann Thompson and Neil Taylor's notes on Ophelia distributing flowers to the court at 4.5.169–178 in their edition of *Hamlet*, Arden Third Series (London: Bloomsbury, 2006); and R. A. Foakes's notes on *King Lear*, 4.4.6 (Cordelia describes Lear's crown of weeds). See also Chapter 3, Note 31.
[53] Johnson, "To the Reader," in Gerard, *Herball* (1633), sig. ¶¶3v.

Yet, of course, in commercial terms, it wasn't really Johnson's project at all. The impetus for the creation of the second edition of *The Herball* was its publishers, and it derived from their noticing the appearance of a competing English volume: John Parkinson's *Paradisi in sole paradisus terrestris. Or A Garden of all sorts of pleasant flowers which our English ayre will permit to be noursed vp: with A Kitchen garden of all manner of herbes, rootes, & fruites, for meate or sause vsed with vs, and An an Orchard of all sorte of fruit-bearing Trees and shrubbes fit for our Land together With the right ordering planting & preseruing of them and their vses & vertues* (1629, *STC* 19300). Though Parkinson's book did not list plants' medical virtues and was not technically a herbal but a horticultural treatise, *Paradisi* borrowed many of the genre's elements in its account of English kitchen gardens, floral gardens, and orchards.[54] Moreover, Parkinson's composition of *Paradisi* was, as is traditional with herbals, anthological and derived from his perusing the work of others, particularly the herbals of his fellow Englishmen. Having surveyed the bibliographic field, Parkinson found space for his elevation of flowers because the topic had been little approached:

> In English likewise we haue some extant, as Turner and Dodonaeus translated, who have said little of Flowers, Gerard who is last, hath no doubt giuen vs the knowledge of as many as he attained vnto in his time, but since his dates we haue had many more varieties, then he or they euer heard of, as may be perceiued by the store I haue here produced.[55]

To stationers like Joyce Norton and Richard Whitaker, who happened to hold the rights to copy Gerard's text, Parkinson's *Paradisi* was a wake-up call that a market for English herbals not only continued to exist but needed an update;[56] and Parkinson himself promised soon to provide one:

> I haue beene in some places more copious and ample then at the first I had intended, the occasion drawing on my desire to informe others with what I thought was fit to be known, reseruing what else might be said to another time & worke; wherein (God willing) I will inlarge my selfe, the subiect matter requiring it at my hands, in what my small ability can effect.[57]

Recreating what her late husband had done over three decades earlier, Joyce Norton and her business partner Richard Whitaker sprang into

---

[54] On the distinction, see Henrey, *British Botanical.*   [55] Parkinson, *Paradisi*, sig. **4r.

[56] John Bill had died in 1630 and in his will designated a number of titles to Joyce Norton and Whitaker. The pair were assigned the rights to "Gerrards herbal with Pictures and without" on August 26, 1632. See Arber, *Transcripts*, 4:283.

[57] Parkinson, *Paradisi*, sig. **4r.

action. The first thing they needed was a set of botanical woodblocks, and Whitaker knew just where to turn. By the 1630s, the Plantin Press in Antwerp had assembled a comprehensive collection of botanical wood-blocks that numbered in the thousands. In 1632, Christopher Plantin's grandson, Balthasar Moretus I, managed the shop and Whitaker turned to Moretus to supply the woodblocks that were needed to reprint an edition of Gerard's *Herball*.[58] Whitaker requested the blocks in July of 1632 and, a month later, they were on their way to England. Another set followed in September. All told, Norton and Whitaker rented almost 3,000 woodcuts, comprising images that had appeared in the most recent works of Dodoens, L'Obel, and Carolus Clusius. These found their way to Johnson: "Now come I to particulars, and first of figures: I haue, as I said, made vse of those wherewith the Workes of *Dodonaeus*, *Lobel*, and *Clusius* were formerly printed, which, though some of them be not so sightly, yet are they generally as truly exprest, and sometimes more."[59] Yet time, the bane of Johnson's editorial efforts, was of the essence, as Moretus wanted his blocks back as soon as possible, for without them he could not publish any new botanical treatises at all, and his printing house was in high demand. Both in England and in continental Europe, the technical and financial constraints upon publishers and printers limited the activities of authors and authorial figures like Thomas Johnson.

Johnson did work very, very quickly: his letter to the reader is dated October 22, 1633, and it must have been written after most of the volume had been printed by Adam Islip, who may also have shared in the publication costs of the edition. In just over a year, Norton and Whitaker had commis-sioned and produced a formidable tome that enabled them to continue to profit from Gerard's name and reputation while simultaneously offering for sale the latest and best botanical images offered anywhere in Europe (Figure 8.2). Their investment paid off: the 1633 edition sold well and sold fast – so much so that, despite an increasingly irate sequence of letters from Moretus desperate for the return of his woodblocks, Norton, Whitaker, and Islip kept them long enough to reprint another revised edition of the herbal in 1636 (*STC* 11752).[60] Extremely protective of their investment, Norton, Whitaker, and Islip even went so far as to petition King Charles to have their work protected by royal decree, lest anyone try to publish an epitomized, or shortened, version of it. On March 1, 1633, a letter was brought to the

[58] Whitaker and Moretus's correspondence is found in Imhof, "Return My Woodblocks."
[59] Johnson, "To the Reader," in Gerard, *Herball* (1633), sig. ¶¶¶3v.
[60] This third edition was clearly a plan early on: Norton and Whitaker assigned "one full third part of the Copy called Gerrards Herball" to Islip on July 13, 1634 (Arber, *Transcript*, 4:323).

Figure 8.2 John Gerard, *The Herball or General Historie of Plants* (1633). Image reproduced courtesy of the Ohio State University Libraries' Rare Books & Manuscripts Library (Shelfmark QK 41 G35).

Stationers' Company wardens from the king "that none pr[e]sume to imprint any Abridgment or Abstract of their Copie called Gerards Herball."[61] For forty years after its initial publication, Gerard's *Herball* dominated the marketplace for English herbals thanks not to the efforts of its putative author but because of the strategic maneuvering of its publishers.

Redefining Textual Authority

As I have shown, Gerard's agency had little to do in organizing the publication of the book that bears his name, though his efforts to gather and to supplement what became *The Herball*'s text were central to its success. What is curious about the censure of Gerard in botanical histories is the singling out of this early modern botanist above all others as guilty of the complex and anachronistic crime of plagiarism. The previous chapters of this book reveal that the majority of sixteenth-century English herbalists and publishers of herbals drew material from the works of their predecessors, taking what information they thought relevant and discarding or dismissing the rest; furthermore, especially in the case of the accompanying woodcut illustrations, copying was the norm rather than the exception. Stationers, acutely aware of competition from other publishers, sought to differentiate their texts by adding the name of an established authority or supplemental material based upon an editor's personal experience. Later, stationers added detailed indexes to their herbals to make their texts more user-friendly, simultaneously justifying the higher costs of their illustrated editions by suggesting that owners of their texts would be able to self-medicate and no longer require the services of physicians and apothecaries. An examination of herbal literature printed in England between the little *Herball* of 1525 and the publication of Gerard's *Herball* in 1597 indicates that, rather than being guilty of plagiarism, Gerard was writing and compiling his text in accordance with the norms and customs of printing herbals in England during the Tudor period.

---

[61] Jackson, *Records*, 255. The trio seems to have started a trend: two years later, on July 14, 1635, another royal letter would arrive to be read to the Stationers' Company wardens "concerning one Mr Parkinson an Apothecary about printing his works" (Jackson, *Records*, 265). Though Parkinson's *Theatrum botanicum* was eventually published "by the Kings Majestyes especiall privilege" in 1640, its delay in being printed seems to have caused its author no small distress: "The disastrous times, but much more wretched and perverse men have so farre prevailed against my intended purpose, and promise, in exhibiting this work to the public view of all; that their extreame covetousnesse had well nigh deprived my country of the fruition" (Parkinson, *Theatrum botanicum*, sig. A3v). See also Arber, *Bibliography*, 1:80.

It is evident from examining the printing history of early modern herbals that not only were woodcut illustrations and paratextual materials borrowed and copied from one botanical text to another but the written works of earlier herbalists provided a starting point for later ones. In some cases, herbals began as translations of an earlier work in a different language, but a translator's incorporation of their own commentary into the text was in keeping with the anthological approach to botanical study that had begun with the *German Herbarius* of 1485. Thus sixteenth-century English herbals became more collaborative as the century progressed – not only were herbalists directly referencing each other but they were often aiding each other's publications by trading illustrations and plant specimens.[62] Alternatively, they were also denigrating each other's work and citing multiple inaccuracies in order to justify their own updated or corrected works. A modern scholar of herbal literature of this period can view this conflation of texts either as an incidence of mass plagiarism and unscrupulous scientific citation or as evidence of a rapidly developing science practiced by an expanding circle of recognized experts who circulated their work in print.[63] By the time Gerard entered the botanical scene at the end of the century, more than half a dozen large volumes of plant lore had been on the market for decades. Expecting Gerard to author a completely original text in such an environment would be unreasonable, and, as John Norton and later Joyce Norton knew, publishing such a wholly original work would likely have been unprofitable.

Most of the sixteenth-century herbalists in England and on the continent took material from the works of their predecessors to confirm or to refute their own observations. As the Frankfurt printer Christian Egenolff pointed out in his disputes with Johannes Schott and Leonhart Fuchs in the 1530s and 1540s, this borrowing is reasonable: there is a limit to the originality that natural historians can claim in their accounts of God-created nature. Copying was the norm rather than the exception as early botanists sought to organize the rapidly increasing printed information available about plants into a comprehensive system. While they circulated through the channels of the book trade, herbals were locations for plant investigators to publish theories that could later be assessed by fellow and competing botanists in their own herbal publications – and to do this they needed to quote, borrow, and build upon each other's work.

Yet botanists did not use herbals only as occasions for disagreements about the particulars of plant characteristics and classifications. Because

---

[62] See Eisenstein, *Printing Press*, 266–267.   [63] See Eisenstein, *Printing Revolution*, 209–231.

plants are by their nature rooted in place, a comprehensive understanding of them across ecosystems was necessarily dependent on an observer's ability to travel to gather specimens. One reason for the infamous tulip craze in Europe in the seventeenth century was the bulbs' capacity for traveling very long distances while suffering little damage. Tulip bulbs are easily transported, while other plants are more firmly rooted in their geographies: it is more difficult to bring a tree or a shrub from overseas and guarantee its survival in transit, let alone nurture it through its lifespan in a hostile new climate. Herbalists like Gerard therefore itemized the exotic plants that they could raise in their gardens to demonstrate what plants could survive the London winters.[64] Herbals authored in other regions could solve the problem of geographical deficiency for landlocked botanists by enabling them to acquire information about species that were outside of their own climates of reference. One of *The Herball*'s commendatory letter writers, the surgeon Thomas Thorney, notes that, by bringing his private expertise into the public sphere, Gerard's *Herball* makes his work a public service. Thorney celebrates the ways that the work is a representation of Gerard's Holborn garden, but Thorney also hints that books make plants accessible to those who cannot travel to them:

> Of simples here we do behold
> Within our English soyle,
> More store than ere afore we did,
> Through this thy learned toyle:
> And each thing so methodicall,
> So aptly coucht in place,
> As I much muse, how such a worke
> Could framed be in such space.
> For in well viewing of the same
> We neede not far to rome,
> But may behold dame Natures store
> By sitting still at home.[65]

Thorney's advocacy for Gerard celebrates both Gerard's book learning and his hands-on botanical experience, but his poem also suggests that books themselves serve the needs of readers by bringing the outside indoors. The mechanical process of illustrative and textual reproduction extends the reach of a single plant specimen and individually prolongs the life of an individual flower. The celebration of "well-cut" herbals prescribed by

---

[64] Gerard's first catalogue of plants was published in Latin in 1596 (*STC* 11748); John Norton published a second edition that added the English names in 1599 (*STC* 11749).
[65] Gerard, *Herball* (1597), sig. B2v.

Robert Burton in 1621 thus finds its seed in the preliminaries of earlier illustrated works. Yet the capacity for herbals to serve as surrogates for visits to local places also led to their adaptation in the service of colonial enterprise. As Christopher M. Parsons has shown, the description of plants in the travel accounts authored by American explorers embedded travelogue readers in landscapes that allowed them to imagine inhabiting and settling such spaces themselves.[66] It is not difficult to see how both the content and the forms of sixteenth- and seventeenth-century herbals could later serve the imperial needs of eighteenth-century colonial botany.

For his part, Gerard knew that his anthological labor was by no means finished. In his dedication to Cecil, Gerard explains that, through his participation in the collaborative effort of Renaissance botany, he expects others to find errors in his opus. He insists that by gathering together the text he has "ministered matter for riper wits, and men of deeper iudgment to polish; and to adde to my large additions where any thing is defectiue, that in time the worke may be perfect."[67] Gerard repeats these sentiments later in his address to his readers; he has presented "a worke, I confesse, for greater clerks to vndertake, yet may my blunt attempt serue as a whetstone to set and edge vpon some sharper wits, by whome I wish this my course discourse might be both fined and refined."[68] Since 1633, John Gerard has endured little from history but scorn. His "course discourse" was not perfect, and the anthological means by which it came to be is no longer fashionable. Yet was John Gerard a thief, a plagiarist? Time and botanical scholarship have often told us so; but more time and more investigation into the agents who made and sold herbals in early modern London seem to tell us otherwise.

Gerard's later status as an "authoritative English herbalist" was not simply the result of Gerard's own activity; it was a marketing strategy first produced by John Norton in 1597 that was later reinforced by Joyce Norton and Richard Whitaker in 1633 and 1636. The famous gardener would soon be Master of the company of Barber-Surgeons and he was known to many at court through his service to William Cecil – putting Gerard's name on a book about plants in 1597 was simply good business. Recognizing the preeminence of stationers in the production of English herbals helps scholars recognize the ways that scientific authorship and scientific expertise were necessarily limited by commercial concerns. Before botanists could emerge to "authorize" herbals, the genre first needed to

[66] Parsons, *A Not-So-New World*, 57. See also Nicosia, "Milton's Banana."
[67] Gerard, *Herball* (1597), sig. A3r.   [68] Gerard, *Herball* (1597), sig. B6r.

become a vendible print commodity. Early anonymous works like the little *Herball* and *The Grete Herball* demonstrated to printers and booksellers that they could make money manufacturing books about plants in the English vernacular; and as the reading public grew and demand for these texts increased, medical practitioners like physicians soon realized that print offered them a venue for professional advancement. By asserting their authority over this new genre of the printed English herbal, physicians like Thomas Gibson and William Turner could likewise proclaim their authority over the professional sphere of vernacular healing, mimicking the ways that print was used to encourage Protestant reform. The decisions that John Norton made when he chose to publish a new English herbal in 1597 show that he was fully cognizant of the genre's history and that he recognized what could make these books so popular and so profitable. Thirty years later, when preparing Gerard's *Herball* for its second edition, Joyce Norton and Richard Whitaker recognized that professional apothecaries like Thomas Johnson and John Parkinson also had a vested interest in promoting and authorizing the herbal genre. Attending to the "stationer-function" therefore helps to demonstrate how herbal authors devised their texts in response to printers' and booksellers' material and financial concerns. It was through the commodification of English herbals as occasions and locations for botanical knowledge that the "fathers of English botany" became authorized experts.

Bibliography

English Herbals Cited

Books are ordered by date of publication as established by the *STC* except where noted.

Anonymous Herbals (Listed in Order of Publication)

1525. *Here begynnyth a newe mater / the whiche sheweth and treateth of [the] vertues & proprytes of herbes / the whiche is called an Herball* (London: Richard Bankes). *STC* 13175.1

1526. *Here begynneth a newe marer / [the] whiche sheweth and treateth of the vertues & propertes of herbes / the whiche is callyd an Herball* (London: Richard Bankes). *STC* 13175.2

1526. *The grete herball whiche geueth parfyt knowlege and vnderstandyng of all maner of herbes & there gracyous vertues whiche god hath ordeyned for our prosperous welfare and helth/for they hele & cure all maner of dyseases and sekenesses that fall or mysfortune to all maner of creatoures of god created/practysed by many expert and wyse maysters/as Auicenna & other. &c. Also it geueth full parfyte vnderstandynge of the booke lately prentyd by me (Peter treueris) named the noble experiens of the vertuous handwarke of surgery* (London: Peter Treveris). *STC* 13176

1529. *The grete herball whiche gyueth parfyt knowledge and vnderstanding of all maner of herbes & there gracyous vertues whiche god hath ordeyned for our prosperous welfare and helth, for they hele & cure all maner of dyseases and sekenesses that fall or mysfortune to all maner of creatures of god created practysed by many expert and wyse maysters, as Auicenna & other. &c. Also it gyueth full parfyte vnderstandynge of the booke lately prentyd by me (Peter treueris) named the noble experie[n]ce of the vertuous handwarke of surgery.* (London: Peter Treveris and Lawrence Andrewe). *STC* 13177/*STC* 13177.5

1537[c.?]. *A Boke of the propertyes of herbes the which is called an Herball.* (London: John Skot). *STC* 13175.4

1539[?]. *A boke of the propertyes of herbes the whiche is called an Herbal.* (London: Robert Redman). *STC* 13175.5

1539. *The great herball newly corrected. The contentes of this boke. A table after the latyn names of all herbes, a table after the Englysshe names of all herbes. The*

*propertees and qualytes of all thynges in this booke. The descrypcyon of vrynes, how
a man shall haue trewe knoweledge of all sekenesses. An exposycyon of the wordes
obscure and not well knowen. A table, quyckly to fynde remedyes for all dyseases, God
saue the Kynge* (London: Thomas Gibson). *STC* 13178

1541. *Hereafter foloweth the knowledge, properties, and the vertues of Herbes.*
(London: Robert Wyer). *STC* 13175.6 (Note: See Tracy, *Robert Wyer.*)

1541. *A boke of the propertyes of herbes the whiche is called an Harbal* (London:
Thomas Petyt). *STC* 13175.8

1541[?]. *A boke of the propertyes of herbes the whiche is called an Herbal*
(London: Elizabeth Pickering Redman). *STC* 13175.7

1544. *A newe Herball of Macer. Translated out of Laten in to Englysshe* (London:
Robert Wyer). *STC* 13175.8c (Note: See Tracy, *Robert Wyer.*)

1545[?]. *A boke of the propertyes of herbes the which is called an herball* (London: Robert
Copland). *STC* 13175.11 (Note: Conjectured date supplied by Blayney, *Stationers'
Company,* 1,046.)

1546. *A boke of the propertyes of herbes the whiche is called an Herbal* (London:
William Middleton). *STC* 13175.10

1548[?]. *A boke of the propertes of herbes the which is called an herball* (London: John
Rastell for John Walley). *STC* 13175.12 (Note: See Blayney, *Stationers' Company,*
1,046.)

1550. *A lytel herball of the properties of herbes newely amended and corrected, with
certayne addicions at the end of the boke [as] appointed in the almanacke, made in
M.D.L. the xii. day of February by A. Askham* (London: William Powell). *STC*
13175.13

1552[c.]. *Macers herbal. Practysyd by doctor Lynacro. Translated out of laten, in to
Englysshe, whiche shewynge theyr Operacyons & Vertues, set in the margent of this
Boke, to the entent you might know theyr Vertues* (London: Robert Wyer). *STC*
13175.13c

1552[?]. *A boke of the propreties of Herbes called an herball, wherunto is added the time
[the] herbes, floures and Sedes shold be gathered to be kept the whole yere, with the
virtue of [the] Herbes when they are stilled. Also a generall rule of all maner of
Herbes drawen out of an auncyent booke of Phisyck by W.C.* (London: William
Copland for John Wight/Richard Kele). *STC* 13175.15/*STC* 13175.15A

1555[?]. *A boke of the propreties of Herbes called an herball, whereunto is added the
time [the] herbes, floures and Sedes shold be gathered to be kept the whole yere, with
the virtue of [the] Herbes when they are stilled. Also a general rule of al maner of
Herbes drawen out of an auncient boke of Phisyck by W.C.* (London: John King
for John Walley/Antony Veale). *STC* 13175.16/*STC* 13175.17

1559[?]. *A boke of the propreties of Herbes called an herbal, whereunto is added the
tyme [the] herbes, floures and Sedes shoulde be gathered to be kept the whole yere,
with the virtue of [the]Herbes whe[n] they are stylled. Also a generall rule of al
manner of Herbes drawen out of an auncient boke of Physycke by W.C.* (London:
William Copland). *STC* 13176.18

1561. *A little Herball of the properties of Herbes, newly amended & corrected, wyth
certayn Additions at the ende of the boke, declaring what Herbes hath influence of*

certain Sterres and constellations, wherby maye be chosen the best and most lucky tymes and days of their ministraction, according to the Moone being in the signes of heaue[n] the which is daily appoi[n]ted in the Almanacke, made and gathered in the yeare of our Lorde God, M.D.L. the .xxi. daye of February, by Anthony Askha[m], Physycyon (London: John King). *STC* 13175.19

1561. *The greate Herball, which geueth parfyte knowledge & understanding of al maner of herbes, and theyr gracious vertues, whiche GOD hath ordeyned for our prosperous welfare and health, for they heale and cure all maner of disases and sekenesses, that fall or misfortune too all maner of creatures of GOD created, practysed by many expert and wyse maysters, as Auicenna, Pandecta, and more other, &c. Newlye corrected and diligently ouersene. In the yeare of our Lord God. M. CCCCC.LXI* (London: John King). *STC* 13179

1567[c]. *A booke of the properties of herbes, called an herbal. Whereunto is added the tyme that herbes, floures and seedes should bee gathered to bee kept the whole yeare, wyth the virtue of the herbes when they are stylled. Also a generall rule of all maner of herbes, drawen out of an auncient booke of physycke by W.C.* (London: John Awdely for Anthony Kitson). *STC* 13175.19c

Authored and/or Epitomized English Herbals (Listed in Order of Publication)

1538. William Turner. *Libellus de re Herbaria novus in quo Herbarum aliquot nomina greca, latina & anglica habes, vna cum nominibus officinarum* (London: John Byddell). *STC* 24358

1548. William Turner. *The Names of Herbes in Greke, Latin, Englishe Duche & Frenche. Gathered by William Turner* (London: Steven Mierdman for John Day and William Seres). *STC* 24359

1551. William Turner. *A New Herball, wherein are conteyned the names of Herbes in Greke, Latin, Englysh, Duch Frenche, and in the Potecaries and Herbaries Latin, with the properties degrees and natural places of the same, gathered and made by Wylliam Turner, Physicion vnto the Duke of Somersettes Grace* (London: Steven Mierdman). *STC* 24365

1562. William Turner. *The seconde part of Vuilliam Turners herball wherein are conteyned the names of herbes in Greke, Latin, Duche, Frenche, and in the apothecaries Latin, and somtyme in Italiane, wyth the vertues of the same herbes wyth diuerse confutationes of no small errours, that men of no small learning haue committed in the intreatinge of herbes of late yeares. Here vnto is ioyned also a booke of the bath of Baeth in Englande, and of the vertues of the same wyth diuerse other bathes moste holsum and effectuall, both in Almany and Englande, set furth by William Turner Doctor of Physik* (Cologne: Arnold Birckman). *STC* 24366

1568. William Turner. *The first and seconde partes of the Herbal of William Turner Doctor in Phisick lately ouersene/ corrected and enlarged with the Thirde parte/ lately gathered/and nowe set oute with the names of the herbes/in Greke Latin/ English/Duche/Frenche/ and in the Apothecaries and Herbaries Latin/with the properties/degrees/and natural places of the same. Here vnto is ionned also a Booke of the bath of Baeth in England/. and of the vertues of the same with diuerse other bathes/ moste holsom and effectuall/both in Almaye and England/set furth by William Turner Doctor in Phsick* (Cologne: Heirs of Arnold Birckman). *STC* 24367

1570–1571. Pierre Pena and Matthias de L'Obel. *Stirpium aduerseria noua, perfacilis vestigatio* (London: Thomas Purfoot). *STC* 19595 (Note: *STC* 19595.3, *STC* 19595.5, and *STC* 19595.7 are reissues of the 1st ed.)

1578. Rembert Dodoens. *A Niewe Herball, or Historie of Plantes: Wherin is contayned the whole discourse and perfect description of all sorts of Herbes and Plants: their diuers and sundry kindes: their straunge Figures, Fashions, and Shapes: their Names / Natures / Operations, and Vertues: and that not onely of those whiche are here growyng in this our Countrie of Englande/ but of all others also of forrayne Realmes /commonly vsed in Physicke. First set foorth in the Doutche or Almaigne tongue, by that learned D. Rembert Dodoens, Physition to the Emperour: And now first translated out of French into English, by Henrie Lyte Esquier* (London [Antwerp]: Printed by Hendrik van der Loe for Garrat Dewes). *STC* 6984

1586. Rembert Dodoens. *A New Herball, or Historie of Plants: Wherin is contained the whole discourse and perfect description of all sorts of Herbes and Plants: their diuers and sundrie kindes: their Names, Natures, Operations, & Vertues: and that not only of those which are heere growing in this our Countrie of England, but of all others also of foraine Realms commonly vsed in Physicke. First set foorth in the Douch or Almaigne toong, by that learned D. Rembert Dodoens, Phisition to the Emperor: And now first translated out of French into English, by Henrie Lyte Esquier* (London: Ninian Newton). *STC* 6985

1595. Rembert Dodoens. *A New Herball, or Historie of Plants: Wherin is contained the whole discourse and perfect description of all sorts of Herbes and Plants: their diuers and sundrie kindes: their Names, Natures, Operations, & Vertues: and that not only of those which are heer growing in this our Countrie of England, but of al others also of foraine Realms commonly vsed in Physicke. First set foorth in the Dutch or Almaigne toong, by that learned D. Rembert Dodoens, Phisition to the Emperor: And now first translated out of French into English, by Henrie Lyte Esquier. Corrected and amended* (London: Edmund Bollifant). *STC* 6986

1597. John Gerard. *The Herball or Generall Historie of Plantes. Gathered by John Gerarde of London Master in Chirvrgerie* (London: Edmund Bollifant for Bonham and John Norton). *STC* 11750

1606. William Ram. *Rams Little Dodeon* (London: Simon Stafford). *STC* 6988

1619. Rembert Dodoens. *A New Herbal, or Historie of Plants: Wherin is contained the whole discourse and perfect description of all sorts of Herbes and Plants: their diuers and sundrie Kindes, their Names, Natures, Operations, and Vertues: and that not onely of those which are here growing in this our Country of Engalnd [sic], but of all others also of forraine Realmes commonly vsed in Physicke. First set forth in the Dutch or Almaigne tongue, by that learned D. Rembert Dodoens, Physition to the Emperor: And now first translated out of French into English, by Henrie Lyte Esquier. Corrected and amended* (London: Edward Griffin). *STC* 6987

1629. John Parkinson. *Paradisi in sole paradisus terrestris. Or A Garden of all sorts of pleasant flowers which our English ayre will permit to be noursed vp: with A Kitchen garden of all manner of herbes, rootes, & fruites, for meate or sause vsed with vs, and An an Orchard of all sorte of fruit-bearing Trees and shrubbes fit for our Land together With the right ordering planting & preseruing of them and their vses & vertues* (London: Humphrey Lownes and Robert Young). *STC* 19300

1633. John Gerard. *The Herball or Generall Historie of Plantes. Gathered by John Gerarde of London Master in Chirvrgerie Very much Enlarged and Amended by Thomas Johnson Citizen and Apothecarye of London* (London: Adam Islip for Joyce Norton and Richard Whitaker). *STC* 11751

1636. John Gerard. *The Herball or Generall Historie of Plantes. Gathered by John Gerarde of London Master in Chirvrgerie Very much Enlarged and Amended by Thomas Johnson Citizen and Apothecarye of London* (London: Adam Islip for Joyce Norton and Richard Whitaker). *STC* 11752

1640. John Parkinson. *Theatrum Botanicum. The Theater of Plantes. Or, An Universall and Compleate Herball* (London: Thomas Cotes). *STC* 19302

Other Works Cited

Ackerman, James S., "Scientific Illustration," in Allan Ellenius (ed.), *The Natural Sciences and the Arts* (Uppsala: Almqvist & Wiksell International, 1985), 1–17.

Adams, Michael, Caroline Berset, Michael Kessler, and Matthias Hamburger, "Medicinal Herbs for the Treatment of Rheumatic Disorders: A Survey of European Herbals from the 16th and 17th Century," *Journal of Ethnopharmacology* 121 (2009): 343–359.

Adams, Michael, Wandana Alther, Michael Kessler, Martin Kluge, and Matthias Hamburger, "Malaria in the Renaissance: Remedies from European Herbals from the 16th and 17th Century," *Journal of Ethnopharmacology* 133 (2011): 278–288.

Adams, Michael, Sarah-Vanessa Schneider, Martin Kluge, Michael Kessler, and Matthias Hamburger, "Epilepsy in the Renaissance: A Survey of Remedies from 16th and 17th Century German Herbals," *Journal of Ethnopharmacology* 143 (2012): 1–13.

Adlington, Hugh, "Seven More Books from the Library of John Donne," *The Book Collector* 67 (2018): 528–533.

Agnus castus, ed. Gösta Brodin (Cambridge, MA: Harvard University Press, 1950).

Aiken, Pauline, "Arcite's Illness and Vincent of Beauvais," *Publications of the Modern Language Association* 51 (1936): 361–369.

Arber, Agnes, *Herbals, Their Origin and Evolution: A Chapter in the History of Botany 1470–1670*, 3rd ed. (Cambridge: Cambridge University Press, 1986).

Arber, Edward (ed.), *A Transcript of the Registers of the Company of Stationers of London, 1554–1640 A.D.*, 5 vols. (London: Privately Printed, 1875–1894).

Archer, Ian, "Responses to Alien Immigrants in London, c. 1400–1650," in Simonetta Cavaciocchi (ed.), *Le migrazioni in Europa secc. XIII–XVIII: Atti della "venticinquesima settimana di studi"* (Florence: Le Monnier, 1994), 755–774.

Bacon, Francis, *Advancement of Learning*, ed. William Aldis Wright (Oxford: Clarendon Press, 1869).

Barker, Nicolas, *Hortus Eystettensis: The Bishop's Garden and Bessler's Magnificent Book* (London: British Library, 1994).

Barker, Nicolas, "The Old English Letter Foundries," in John Barnard, D. F. McKenzie, and Maureen Bell (eds.), *The Cambridge History of the Book in Britain*, vol. 4 (Cambridge: Cambridge University Press, 2002), 602–619.

Barlowe, H. M., "Old English Herbals, 1525–1640," *Journal of the Royal Society of Medicine* 6 (1913): 108–149.

Barnard, John, "Politics, Profit, and Idealism: John Norton, the Stationers' Company, and Sir Thomas Bodley," *Bodleian Library Record* 17 (2002): 385–408.

Barnard, John, D. F. McKenzie, and Maureen Bell (eds.), *The Cambridge History of the Book in Britain*, vol. 4 (Cambridge: Cambridge University Press, 2002).

Barrett, C. R. B., *The History of the Society of Apothecaries of London* (London: Elliot Stock, 1905).

Bartholomaeus Anglicus, *Liber de proprietatibus rerum* (Westminster: Wynkyn de Worde, 1495). *STC* 1536

Bartholomaeus Anglicus, *Liber de proprietatibus rerum* (London: Thomas Berthelet, 1535). *STC* 1537

Bartholomaeus Anglicus, *Batman vppon Barholome, his booke Liber de proprietatibus rerum enlarged and amended* (London: Thomas East, 1582). *STC* 1538

Beal, Peter (ed.), *Catalogue of English Literary Manuscripts 1450–1700*, www.celm-ms.org.uk

Beaumont, Francis, *The Knight of the Burning Pestle*, in Arthur F. Kinney (ed.), *Renaissance Drama* (Oxford: Blackwell, 1999), 383–431.

Bennett, H. S., *English Books and Readers, 1475–1557*, 2nd ed. (Cambridge: Cambridge University Press, 1969).

Bennett, Stuart, *Trade Bookbinding in the British Isles, 1660–1800* (New Castle, DE: Oak Knoll Press, 2004).

Best, Michael, "Medical Use of a Sixteenth-Century Herbal: Gervase Markham and the Bankes Herbal," *Bulletin of the History of Medicine* 53 (1979): 449–458.

Bicks, Caroline, *Midwiving Subjects in Shakespeare's England* (Burlington, VT: Ashgate, 2003).

Bidwell, John, "French Paper in English Books," in John Barnard, D. F. McKenzie, and Maureen Bell (eds.), *The Cambridge History of the Book in Britain*, vol. 4 (Cambridge: Cambridge University Press, 2002), 583–601.

Binns, J. W., *Intellectual Culture in Elizabethan and Jacobean England: The Latin Writings of the Age* (Leeds: Francis Cairns Press, 1990).

Blagden, Cyprian, *The Stationers' Company: A History 1403–1959* (London: George Allen & Unwin, 1960).

Blair, Ann, "Annotating and Indexing Natural Philosophy," in Marina Frasca-Spada and Nick Jardine (eds.), *Books and the Sciences in History* (Cambridge: Cambridge University Press, 2000), 69–89.

Blair, Ann, "An Early Modernist's Perspective," *Isis* 95 (2004): 420–430.

Blair, Ann, "Errata Lists and the Reader As Corrector," in Sabrina Alcorn Baron, Eric N. Lindquist, and Eleanor F. Shevlin (eds.), *Agent of Change: Print Culture Studies after Elizabeth L. Eisenstein* (Boston: University of Massachusetts Press, 2007), 21–41.

Blair, Ann M., *Too Much to Know: Managing Scholarly Information before the Modern Age* (New Haven, CT: Yale University Press, 2010).

Blayney, Peter W. M., *The Texts of King Lear and Their Origins* (Cambridge: Cambridge University Press, 1982).

Blayney, Peter W. M., "The Publication of Playbooks," in David Scott Kastan and John D. Cox (eds.), *A New History of Early English Drama* (New York: Columbia University Press, 1997), 384–422.

Blayney, Peter W. M., "William Cecil and the Stationers," in Robin Myers and Michael Harris (eds.), *The Stationers' Company and the Book Trade 1550–1990* (New Castle, DE: Oak Knoll Press, 1997), 11–34.

Blayney, Peter W. M., "John Day and the Bookshop That Never Was," in Lena Cowen Orlin (ed.), *Material London, ca. 1600* (Philadelphia: University of Pennsylvania Press, 2000), 322–343.

Blayney, Peter W. M., *The Stationers' Company Before the Charter, 1403–1557* (Cambridge: The Worshipful Company of Stationers & Newspapermakers, 2003).

Blayney, Peter W. M., *The Stationers' Company and the Printers of London, 1501–1557*, 2 vols. (Cambridge: Cambridge University Press, 2013).

Blayney, Peter W. M., "If It Looks Like a Register . . .," *The Library* 20 (2019): 230–242.

Bolens, Guillemette and Lukas Erne (eds.), *Medieval and Early Modern Authorship* (Tübingen: Narr Verlag, 2011).

Bowers, Fredson, "Authorial Intention and Editorial Problems," *Text* 5 (1991): 49–62.

Bradshaw, John (ed.), *The Poetical Works of John Milton* (London: William Allen, 1878).

Brayman Hackel, Heidi, *Reading Material in Early Modern England: Print, Gender, and Literacy* (Cambridge: Cambridge University Press, 2005).

Brunfels, Otto, *Herbarum vivae eicones ad naturae imitationem* (Strasbourg: John Scott, 1530–1536). *USTC* 662096

Bullman, James C. (ed.) *King Henry IV, Part II*, Arden Shakespeare Third Series (London: Bloomsbury, 2016).

Burton, Robert, *The Anatomy of Melancholy* (Oxford: John Lichfield and James Short for Henry Cripps, 1621). *STC* 4159

Cairncross, A. S. (ed.), *The Third Part of King Henry VI*, Arden Shakespeare Second Series (London: Bloomsbury, 1964).

Carlson, Eric Josef, "The Marriage of William Turner," *Historical Research* 65 (1992): 336–339.

Chartier, Roger, *The Order of Books: Readers, Authors and Libraries in Europe between the Fourteenth and Eighteenth Centuries*, trans. Lydia G. Cochrane (Cambridge: Polity Press, 1994).

Clark, George, *A History of the Royal College of Physicians of London* (Oxford: Clarendon, 1964).

Clegg, Cyndia Susan, *Press Censorship in Elizabethan England* (Cambridge: Cambridge University Press, 1997).

Cook, Harold, *The Decline of the Old Medical Regime in Stuart London* (Ithaca, NY: Cornell University Press, 1986).

Cooper, Alix, *Inventing the Indigenous: Local Knowledge and Natural History in Early Modern Europe* (Cambridge: Cambridge University Press, 2007).

Darnton, Robert, "What Is the History of Books?" *Daedalus* 111 (1982): 65–83.

Daston, Lorraine, "Taking Note(s)" *Isis* 95 (2004): 443–448.

Daston, Lorraine and Katharine Park, *Wonders and the Order of Nature, 1150–1750* (New York: Zone Books, 2001).

Dee, John, *The Private Diary of Dr. John Dee*, ed. J. O. Halliwell-Phillipps (London: Camden Society, 1842).

De Grazia, Margreta and Peter Stallybrass, "The Materiality of the Shakespearean Text," *Shakespeare Quarterly* 44 (1993): 255–83.

Dillman, Jefferson. *Colonizing Paradise: Landscape and Empire in the British West Indies* (Tuscaloosa: University of Alabama Press, 2015).

Dioscorides. Pedantius, *De medicinali materia*, trans. Jean Ruel (Paris: Henri Estienne, 1516). *USTC* 144550

Dioscorides. Pedantius, *De medicinali materia libri sex*, trans. Jean Ruel, ed. Walther Ryff (Marburg: Christian Egenolff, 1543). *USTC* 683351

Dolan, Frances E., "Compost/Composition," in Hillary Eklund (ed.), *Ground-Work: English Renaissance Literature and Soil Science* (Pittsburgh: Duquesne University Press, 2015), 21–39.

Doran, Madeline, "On Elizabethan 'Credulity': With Some Questions Concerning the Use of the Marvelous in Literature," *Journal of the History of Ideas* 1 (1940): 151–176.

Drayton, Michael, *Poly-olbion* (London: Printed by Humphrey Lownes for Matthew Lownes, 1612). *STC* 7226

Driver, Martha, "Christine de Pisan and Robert Wyer: *The C.Hystoryes of Troye, or L'Epistre d'Othea* Englished," *Gutenberg-Jahrbuch* 72 (1997): 125–139.

Duff, E. Gordon, *A Century of the English Book Trade* (London: Bibliographical Society, 1905).

Duff, E. Gordon, *The Printers, Stationers and Bookbinders of Westminster and London,* 1906 (New York: Arno Press, 1977).

Duff, E. Gordon, "Notes on Stationers from the Lay Subsidy Rolls of 1523–4," *The Library*, Series 2, 35 (1908): 257–266.

Edwards, Karen L. *Milton and the Natural World: Science and Poetry in Paradise Lost* (Cambridge: Cambridge University Press, 1999).

Egenolff, Christian, *Adversum illiberales Leonhardi Fuchsij, medici Tubingensis, … calumnias, responsio* (Frankfurt: Christian Egenolff, 1544). *USTC* 609318

Eisenstein, Elizabeth, *The Printing Press As an Agent of Change* (Cambridge: Cambridge University Press, 1979).

Eisenstein, Elizabeth, "An Unacknowledged Revolution Revisited," *American Historical Review* 107 (2002): 87–105.

Eisenstein, Elizabeth, *The Printing Revolution in Early Modern Europe*, 2nd ed. (Cambridge: Cambridge University Press, 2005).

Eisenstein, Elizabeth, *Divine Art, Infernal Machine: The Reception of Printing in the West from First Impressions to the Sense of an Ending* (Philadelphia: University of Pennsylvania Press, 2011).

Elliott, Brent, "The World of the Renaissance Herbal," *Renaissance Studies* 25 (2011): 24–41.

Erler, Mary C., "Wynkyn de Worde's Will: Legatees and Bequests," *The Library* 6th Series 10 (1988): 107–121.

Evenden, Elizabeth, *Patents, Pictures and Patronage: John Day and the Tudor Book Trade* (Burlington, VT: Ashgate, 2008).

Ezell, Margaret J. M., "Elizabeth Isham's Books of Remembrance and Forgetting," *Modern Philology* 109 (2011): 71–84.

Farmer, Alan B., "Shakespeare and the New Textualism," in W. R. Elton and John M. Mucciolo (eds.), *The Shakespearean International Yearbook 2: Where Are We Now in Shakespearean Studies?* (Burlington, VT: Ashgate, 2002), 158–179.

Farmer, Alan B., "Playbooks and the Question of Ephemerality," in Heidi Brayman, Jesse M. Lander, and Zachary Lesser (eds.), *The Book in History, The Book As History: New Intersections of the Material Text: Essays in Honor of David Scott Kastan* (New Haven, CT: Beinecke Rare Book and Manuscript Library and Yale University, 2016), 87–125.

Farmer, Alan B. and Zachary Lesser, "What Is Print Popularity? A Map of the Elizabethan Book Trade," in Andy Kesson and Emma Smith (eds.), *The Elizabethan Top Ten: Defining Print Popularity in Early Modern England* (Burlington, VT: Ashgate, 2013), 19–54.

Feather, John, "The Book Trade in Politics: The Making of the Copyright Act of 1710," *Publishing History* 8 (1980): 19–44.

Feather, John, "English Book Trade and the Law," *Publishing History* 12 (1982): 51–76.

Fehrenbach, R. J. (ed.), *Private Libraries in Renaissance England: A Collection and Catalogue of Tudor and Early Stuart Book-Lists* (Binghamton, NY: Medieval and Renaissance Texts and Studies, 1992–2004).

Ferguson, Meraud Grant, "Grafton, Richard (c.1511–1573)," *ODNB*, 2004.

Foucault, Michel, "What Is an Author?," in Paul Rabinow (ed.), *The Foucault Reader*, trans. Josué V. Harari (New York: Random House, 1984), 101–120.

Frye, Susan, *Pens and Needles: Women's Textualities in Early Modern England* (Philadelphia: University of Pennsylvania Press, 2010).

Fuchs, Leonhart, *De historia stirpium commentarii insignes* (Basel: Michael Isingrin, 1542). *USTC* 602520

Fuchs, Leonhart, *Apologia … qua refellit malitiosas Gualtheri Ryffi veteratoris pessimi reprehensiones* (Basel: Michael Isingrin, 1544). *USTC* 602518

Fuchs, Leonhart, *Adversus mendaces et Christiano homine indignas Christiani Egenolphi typographi Francofortani suique architecti calumnias responsio* (Basel: Erasmus Zimmermann, 1545). *USTC* 602515

Fuchs, Leonhart, *Primi De stirpium historia commentariorum tomi viuae imagines, in exiguam augustiorem formam contractae* (Basel: Michael Isingrin, 1545). *USTC* 602522

Gadd, Ian, "Gibson, Thomas (d. 1562)," *ODNB*, 2004.

Gadd, Ian, "Norton, John (1556/7–1612), Bookseller," *ODNB*, 2004.

Gee, John Archer, "John Byddell and the First Publication of Erasmus," *ELH* 4 (1937): 43–59.

Getz, Faye, "Medical Education in Later Medieval England," in Vivian Nutton and Roy Porter (eds.), *The History of Medical Education in Britain* (Amsterdam: Rodopi, 1995), 76–93.

Gibson, Strickland, "Fragments from Bindings at the Queen's College Oxford," *The Library*, 4th Series, 12 (1932): 429–433.

Gillespie, Alexandra, *Print Culture and the Medieval Author: Chaucer, Lydgate, and their Books 1473–1557* (Oxford: Oxford University Press, 2006).

Gilmor, John, *British Botanists* (London: William Collins, 1944).

Givens, Jean A., "Reading and Writing the Illustrated *Tractatus de herbis*, 1280–1526," in Jean Ann Givens, Karen Reeds, and Alain Touwaide (eds.), *Visualizing Medieval Medicine and Natural History, 1200–1550* (Burlington, VT: Ashgate, 2006), 136–145.

Goldgar, Anne, *Tulipmaina: Money, Honor, and Knowledge in the Dutch Golden Age* (Chicago: Chicago University Press, 2007).

Goode, Jeanne, "[Untitled Review]," *Brittonia* 40 (1988): 47.

Greg, W. W., and Eleanore Boswell (eds.), *Records of the Court of the Stationers' Company 1576–1602 from Register B* (London: The Bibliographical Society, 1930).

Greg, W. W., *A Companion to Arber* (Oxford: Clarendon Press, 1967).

Grendler, Paul F., *The Universities of the Italian Renaissance* (Baltimore, MD: Johns Hopkins University Press, 2004).

Gunther, R. T., *Early Botanists and their Gardens: Based on the Unpublished Writings of Goodyer, Tradescant, and Others* (Oxford: Oxford University Press, 1922).

Hamilton, A. C. (ed.), *Spenser: The Faerie Queene*, 2nd ed. (Toronto: Pearson, 2007).

Harari, Jousé V., *Textual Strategies: Perspectives in Post-Structuralist Criticism* (Ithaca, NY: Cornell University Press, 1979).

Harkness, Deborah E., *The Jewel House: Elizabethan London and the Scientific Revolution* (New Haven, CT: Yale University Press, 2007).

Henslowe, Philip, *Henslowe's Diary*, ed. R. A. Foakes, 2nd ed. (Cambridge: Cambridge University Press, 2002).

Herbert, George, *A Priest to the Temple* (London: T. Maxey for T. Garthwait, 1652). Wing H1512

Henrey, Blanche, *British Botanical and Horticultural Literature before 1800*, 3 vols. (Oxford: Oxford University Press, 1975).

Heywood, Thomas, *The Wise Woman of Hoxton*, ed. Sonia Massai, Globe Quartos (New York: Routledge, 2002).

Hill, Alexandra, *Lost Books and Printing in London, 1557–1640: An Analysis of the Stationers' Company Register* (Leiden: Brill, 2018).

Hoby, Margaret, *The Private Life of an Elizabethan Lady: The Diary of Lady Margaret Hoby, 1599–1605*, ed. Joanna Moody (Stroud: Sutton Publishing, 1998).

Hodgson, John, *Memoirs of the Lives of Thomas Gibson . . . Jonathan Harle . . . John Horsley . . . William Turner* (Newcastle upon Tyne: Charles Henry Cook, 1831).

Hodnett, Edward, *English Woodcuts 1480–1535* (London: Bibliographical Society, 1973).

Hooks, Adam G., "Book Trade" in Arthur F. Kinney (ed.), *The Oxford Handbook of Shakespeare* (Oxford: Oxford University Press, 2012), 126–142.

Howard, Jean E., *The Stage and Social Struggle in Early Modern England* (London: Routledge, 1994).

Hughes, Paul L. and James F. Larkin (eds.), *Tudor Royal Proclamations*, 3 vols. (New Haven, CT: Yale University Press, 1964–1969).

Hulvey, Monique, "Not So Marginal: Manuscript Annotations in the Folger Incunabula," *Papers of the Bibliographical Society of America* 92 (1998): 159–176.

Hunter, Lynette, "Cankers in *Romeo and Juliet*: Sixteenth-Century Medicine at a Figural/Literal Cusp" in Stephanie Moss and Kaara L. Peterson (eds.), *Disease, Diagnosis, and Cure on the Early Modern Stage*, (Aldershot: Ashgate, 2004), 171–185.

Imhof, Dirk, "Return My Woodblocks at Once: Dealings between the Antwerp Publisher Balthasar Moretus and the London Bookseller Richard Whitaker in the Seventeenth Century," in Lotte Hellinga, Alastair Duke, Jacob Harskamp, and Theo Hermans (eds.), *The Bookshop of the World: The Role of the Low Countries in the Book-Trade, 1473–1941* (Utrecht: Hes & De Graaf Publishers, 2001), 179–190.

Iyengar, Sujata, *Shakespeare's Medical Language: A Dictionary* (London: Bloomsbury, 2011).

Jackson, Benjamin Daydon, *William Turner: Libellus de Re Herbaria 1538, The Names of Herbes 1548* (London: privately printed, 1877; reprint. London: The Ray Society, 1965).

Jackson, William A., "Variant Entry Fees of the Stationers' Company," *Papers of the Bibliographical Society of America* 51 (1957): 103–110.

Jeffers, Robert F., *The Friends of John Gerard (1545–1612), Surgeon and Botanist* (Falls Village, CT: The Herb Grower Press, 1967).

Johns, Adrian, *The Nature of the Book: Print and Knowledge in the Making* (Chicago: University of Chicago Press, 1998).

Johns, Adrian, *Piracy: The Intellectual Property Wars from Gutenberg to Gates* (Chicago: University of Chicago Press, 2009).

Johnson, Francis R., "*A New Herball of Macer* and Bankes's *Herball*: Notes on Robert Wyer and the Printing of Cheap Handbooks of Science in the Sixteenth Century," *Bulletin of the History of Medicine* 15 (1944): 246–260.

Johnson, Francis R. "Notes on English Retail Book-prices, 1550–1640," *The Library* 5th Series, 5 (1950–1951): 83–112.

Jones, Ann Rosalind and Peter Stallybrass, *Renaissance Clothing and the Materials of Memory* (Cambridge: Cambridge University Press, 2000).

Jones, Whitney R. D., *The Tudor Commonwealth 1529–1559* (London: Athlone Press, 1970).

Jones, Whitney R. D., *William Turner: Tudor Naturalist, Physician, and Divine* (London: Routledge, 1988).

Jones, Whitney R. D. "Turner, William (1509/10–1568), *Naturalist and Religious Controversialist,*" *ODNB*, 2004.

Jonson, Benjamin, *Volpone, or, The Fox*, in David Bevington, ed., *English Renaissance Drama* (New York: W. W. Norton, 2002), 673–773.

Jordanova, Ludmilla, "The Social Construction of Medical Knowledge," *Social History of Medicine* 8 (1995): 361–381.

Kerrigan, John, "Revision, Adaptation, and the Fool in *King Lear*," in Gary Taylor and Michael Warren (eds.), *The Division of the Kingdoms: Shakespeare's Two Versions of King Lear* (Oxford: Clarendon Press, 1986), 195–245.

Katritzky, M. A., *Women, Medicine and Theatre, 1500–1750: Literary Mountebanks and Performing Quacks* (Burlington, VT: Ashgate, 2007).

Keiser, George R., "Vernacular Herbals: A Growth Industry in Late Medieval England," in Margaret Connolly and Linne R. Mooney (eds.), *Design and Distribution of Late Medieval Manuscripts in England* (York: York Medieval Press, 2008), 292–308.

Kelly, Erin Katherine, "Chasing the Fox and the Wolf: Hunting in the Religious Polemic of William Turner," *Reformation* 20 (2015): 113–129.

Kerwin, William, "'Physicians are Like Kings': Medical Politics and *The Duchess of Malfi*," *English Literary Renaissance* 28 (1998): 95–117.

Kesson, Andy and Emma Smith (eds.), *The Elizabethan Top Ten: Defining Print Popularity in Early Modern England* (Burlington, VT: Ashgate, 2013).

Kewes, Paulina (ed.), *Plagiarism in Early Modern England* (New York: Palgrave, 2003).

Knappen, M. M. (ed.), *Two Elizabethan Puritan Diaries* (Chicago: American Society of Church History, 1933).

Knight, Jeffrey Todd, *Bound to Read: Compilations, Collections, and the Making of Renaissance Literature* (Philadelphia: University of Pennsylvania Press, 2013).

Knight, Leah, *Of Books and Botany in Early Modern England: Sixteenth-Century Plants and Print Culture* (Burlington, VT: Ashgate, 2009).

Knight, Leah, *Reading Green in Early Modern England* (Burlington, VT: Ashgate, 2014).

Knighton, C. S. (ed.), *Calendar of State Papers, Domestic Series of the reigns of Edward VI, 1547–1553; Mary I, 1553–1558*, 2 vols. (London, 1992–1998).

Kusukawa, Sachiko, "Leonard Fuchs on the Importance of Pictures," *Journal of the History of Ideas* 58 (1997): 403–427.

Kusukawa, Sachiko, "Illustrating Nature," in Marina Frasca-Spada and Nick Jardine (eds.), *Books and the Sciences in History* (Cambridge: Cambridge University Press, 2000), 90–113.

Kusukawa, Sachiko, *Picturing the Book of Nature: Image, Text, and Argument in Sixteenth-Century Human Anatomy and Medical Botany* (Chicago: University of Chicago Press, 2012).

Lake, D. J., "Three Seventeenth-Century Revisions: *Thomas of Woodstock*, *The Jew of Malta*, and *Faustus B*," *Notes and Queries* 30 (1983): 133–143.

Lamb, Mary Ellen, "The Agency of the Split Subject: Lady Anne Clifford and the Uses of Reading," *English Literary Renaissance* 22 (1992): 347–368.

Larkey, Sanford V. and Thomas Pyles (eds.), *An Herbal [1525]* (Battleboro, VT: New York Botanical Garden, 1941).

Laroche, Rebecca, *Medical Authority and Englishwomen's Herbal Texts, 1550–1650* (Burlington, VT: Ashgate, 2009).

Lathrop, H. B., "Some Rogueries of Robert Wyer," *The Library* 3rd series, 5 (1914): 349–364.

Lawrence, George H. M., *History of Botany: Two Papers Presented at a Symposium held at the William Andrews Clark Memorial Library December 7, 1963* (Los Angeles and Pittsburgh: The Clark Memorial Library and The Hunt Botanical Library, 1965).

Lecky, Katarzyna, "The Strange and Practical Beauty of Small-Format Herbals," *The Collation,* Folger Shakespeare Library, March 15, 2018. https://collation .folger.edu/2018/03/small-format-herbals/

Leedham-Green, E. S., *Books in Cambridge Inventories: Book-lists from Vice Chancellor's Court Probate Inventories in the Tudor and Stuart Periods*, 2 vols. (Cambridge: Cambridge University Press, 1986).

Leher, Seth, "Errata: Print, Politics, and Poetry in Early Modern England," in Kevin Sharpe and Steven N. Zwicker (eds.), *Reading, Society, and Politics in Early Modern England* (Cambridge: Cambridge University Press, 2003), 41–71.

Lemon, R. (ed.), *Calendar of State Papers, Domestic Series, of the Reigns of Edward VI, Mary, Elizabeth 1547-(-1603), Preserved in the State Paper Department of Her Majesty's Public Record Office, vol. 1: 1547–1580* (London, 1856).

Lesser, Zachary, *Renaissance Drama and the Politics of Publication: Readings in the English Book Trade* (Cambridge: Cambridge University Press, 2004).

Lewis, Wayne, "Six Doctors in Literature: Number 5: the Doctor from *King Lear*, by William Shakespeare," *The British Journal of General Practice* 49 (May 1999): 416.

Locke, John, *The Two Treatises of Government* (London, 1690). Wing L2766

Louis, A., *Mathieu de L'Obel 1538–1616* (Ghent-Louvain: Story-Scientia, 1980).

Love, Harold, "Originality and the Puritan Sermon," in Paulina Kewes (ed.), *Plagiarism in Early Modern England* (New York: Palgrave, 2003), 149–165.

Lovejoy, Arthur O., "Milton and the Paradox of the Fortunate Fall," *ELH* 4 (1937): 161–179.

Lowenstein, Joseph, "The Script in the Marketplace," *Representations* 12 (1985): 101–114.

Lownes, Albert E., "Persistent Remaindering (Pena and de l'Obel's *Adversaria*, 1570–1618)," *Publications of the Bibliographical Society of America* 52 (1958): 295–299.

Luborsky, Ruth Samson and Elizabeth Morley Ingram, *A Guide to English Illustrated Books 1536–1603*, 2 vols. (Tempe, AZ: Medieval & Renaissance Texts & Studies, 1998).

Markham, Gervase, *The English Housewife*, ed. Michael Best (McGill-Queen's University Press, 1986).

Marlowe, Christopher, *The Jew of Malta*, in David Bevington (ed.), *English Renaissance Drama* (New York: W. W. Norton, 2002), 287–349.

McGann, Jerome, *A Critique of Modern Textual Criticism* (Charlottesville: University Press of Virginia, 1983).

McGann, Jerome, *The Textual Condition* (Princeton, NJ: Princeton University Press, 1991).

McKenzie, D. F., *Bibliography and the Sociology of Texts: The Panizzi Lectures* (London: British Library, 1985).

McKerrow, R. B. and F. S. Ferguson, *Title-Page Borders Used in England and Scotland 1485–1640* (London: Bibliographical Society, 1932).

McMullin, B. J., "The Bible Trade," in John, Barnard, D. F. McKenzie, and Maureen Bell (eds.), *The Cambridge History of the Book in Britain*, vol. 4 (Cambridge: Cambridge University Press, 2002), 455–473.

McSheffrey, Shannon, "Stranger Artisans and the London Sanctuary of St. Martin le Grand in the Reign of Henry VIII," *Journal of Medieval and Early Modern Studies* 43 (2013): 545–571.

Melnikoff, Kirk, *Elizabethan Publishing and the Makings of Literary Culture* (Toronto: University of Toronto Press, 2018).

Meyer, Frederick G., Emily Emmart Trueblood, and John L. Heller (eds.), *The Great Herbal of Leonhart Fuchs*, 2 vols. (Stanford, CA: Stanford University Press, 1999).

Milton, John, *Paradise Lost*, ed. A. W. Verity (Cambridge: Cambridge University Press, 1929).

Milton, John, *Paradise Lost*, ed. David Scott Kastan (Indianapolis, IN: Hackett Publishing, 2005).

Monroe, Jennifer, *Gender and the Garden in Early Modern English Literature* (Burlington, VT: Ashgate, 2008).

Moran, Bruce T., "Preserving the Cutting Edge: Traveling Woodblocks, Material Networks, and Visualizing Plants in Early Modern Europe," in Matteo Valleriani (ed.), *The Structures of Practical Knowledge* (Cham: Springer, 2017), 393–419.

Morton, A. G., *History of Botanical Science: An Account of the Development of Botany from its Ancient Times to the Present Day* (London: Academic Press, 1981).

Moxon, Joseph, *Mechanick Exercises on the Whole Art of Printing*, ed. Herbert Davis and Harry Carter (Oxford: Oxford University Press, 1958).

Munk, William, *The Roll of the Royal College of Physicians of London*, 3 vols., 2nd ed. (London: Royal College of Physicians, 1878).

Munro, John H., "The Coinages of Renaissance Europe, ca. 1500," in Thomas A. Brady (ed.), *Handbook of European History, 1400–1600: Late Middle Ages, Renaissance, and Reformation*, Vol. 1 (Leiden: Brill, 1994), 671–678.

Murphy, Hannah, "Common Places and Private Spaces: Libraries, Record-Keeping and Orders of Information in Sixteenth-Century Medicine," *Past and Present* Supplement 11 (2016): 253–268.

Nardizzi, Vin. "Daphne Described: Ovidian Poetry and Speculative Natural History in Gerard's *Herball*," *Philological Quarterly* 98 (2019): 137–156.

Needham, Paul, "The Customs Rolls As Documents for the Printed-book Trade in England," in Lotte Hellinga and J. B. Trapp (eds.), *The Cambridge History of the Book in Britain, Vol. 3: 1400–1557* (Cambridge: Cambridge University Press, 1999), 148–163.

Neville, Sarah, "*Nihil biblicum a me alienem puto*: W.W. Greg, Bibliography, and the Sociology of Texts," *Variants* 11 (2014): 91–112.

Neville, Sarah, "Referencing Pliny's *Naturalis Historia* in Early Modern England," *Notes & Queries* 64 (2017): 321–325.

Neville, Sarah, "The 'Dead Body Problem': The Dramaturgy of Coffins on the Renaissance Stage," in Annalisa Castaldo and Rhonda Knight, *Stage Matters: Props, Bodies, and Space in Shakespearean Performance* (Madison, NJ: Farleigh Dickinson University Press, 2018), 127–141.

Neville, Sarah, "Female Stationers and Their 'Second-Plus' Husbands," in Valerie Wayne (ed.), *Women's Labour and the History of the Book in Early Modern England* (London: Bloomsbury, 2020), 75–93.

Nicosia, Marissa, "Milton's Banana: *Paradise Lost* and Colonial Botany," *Milton Studies* 58 (2017): 49–66.

Nutton, Vivian, "Linacre, Thomas (c. 1460–1524), Humanist Scholar and Physician," *ODNB*, 2004.

Oastler, C. L., *John Day, the Elizabethan Printer* (Oxford: Oxford Bibliographical Society, 1975).

Ogilvie, Brian W., *The Science of Describing: Natural History in Renaissance Europe* (Chicago: University of Chicago Press, 2006).

Osler, William, "The Library of Robert Burton," *Proceedings and Papers of the Oxford Bibliographical Society* (Oxford: Oxford University Press: 1922–1926), 182–190.

Parsons, Christopher M., *A Not-So-New World: Empire and Environment in French Colonial North America* (Philadelphia: University of Pennsylvania Press, 2018).

Patterson, Annabel, *Censorship and Interpretation: the Conditions of Writing and Reading in Early Modern England* (Madison: University of Wisconsin Press, 1984).

Pavord, Anna, *The Naming of Names: The Search for Order in the World of Plants* (London: Bloomsbury, 2005).

Payne, Joseph Frank. "On the 'Herbarius' and 'Hortus Sanitatis,'" *Transactions of the Bibliographical Society* 6 (1900–1901): 63–126.

Peck, Linda Levy, *Costuming Splendor: Society and Culture in Seventeenth-Century England* (Cambridge: Cambridge University Press, 2005).

Pelling, Margaret, "Appearance and Reality: Barber-Surgeons, the Body and Disease," in A. L. Beier and Roger Finlay (eds.), *London 1500–1700: The Making of the Metropolis* (London and New York: Longman, 1986), 82–112.

Pelling, Margaret, "Compromised by Gender: The Role of the Male Medical Practitioner in Early Modern England," in Hilary Marland and Margaret Pelling (eds.), *The Task of Healing: Medicine, Religion and Gender in England and the Netherlands 1450–1800* (Rotterdam: Erasmus Publishing, 1996), 101–33.

Pelling, Margaret, *Medical Conflicts in Early Modern London: Patronage, Physicians, and Irregular Practitioners 1550–1640* (Oxford: Oxford University Press, 2003).

Pelling, Margaret, "Recorde and *The Vrinal of Physick*: Context, Uroscopy and the Practice of Medicine," in Gareth Roberts and Fenny Smith (eds.), *Robert Recorde: The Life and Times of a Tudor Mathematician* (Cardiff: University of Wales Press, 2012), 39–56.

Pelling, Margaret and Charles Webster, "Medical Practitioners," in Charles Webster (ed.), *Health, Medicine and Morality in the Sixteenth Century* (Cambridge: Cambridge University Press, 1979), 165–235.

Pérez-Ramos, Antonio, *Francis Bacon's Idea of Science and the Maker's Knowledge Tradition* (Oxford: Oxford University Press, 1988).

Pettegree, Andrew, *The Book in the Renaissance* (New Haven, CT: Yale University Press, 2010).

Picciotto, Joanna, *Labors of Innocence in Early Modern England* (Cambridge, MA: Harvard University Press, 2010).

Pigman, G. W., III, "Versions of Imitation in the Renaissance," *Renaissance Quarterly* 33 (1980): 1–32.

Pineas, Rainer, "William Turner and Reformation Politics," *Bibliothèque D'Humanisme et Renaissance* 37 (1975): 193–200.

Pineas, Rainer, "William Turner's Polemical Use of Ecclesiastical History and His Controversy with Stephen Gardiner," *Renaissance Quarterly* 33 (1980): 599–608.

Pineas, Rainer, "William Turner's *Spiritual Physik*," *The Sixteenth Century Journal* 14 (1983): 387–398.

Pliny the Elder, *The Natural History*, trans. John Bostock and H. T. Riley (London: Taylor and Francis, 1855).

Plomer, Henry R., *Robert Wyer, Printer and Bookseller* (London: Bibliographical Society, 1897).

Plomer, Henry R., "Notices of English Stationers in the Archives of the City of London," *Transactions of the Bibliographical Society* 6 (1901): 13–27.

Plomer, Henry R., "The Importation of Books into England in the Fifteenth and Sixteenth Centuries: An Examination of Some Customs Rolls." *The Library* 4th Series, 2 (1923): 146–150.

Pollard, A. W., *Shakespeare's Fight with the Pirates and the Problems of the Transmission of his Texts* (London: Alexander Moring, 1917).

Pollard, Graham, "The Company of Stationers Before 1557," *The Library*, 4th Series, 18 (1937): 1–38.

Pollard, Graham, "The Early Constitution of the Stationers' Company," *The Library*, 4th Series, 18 (1937): 235–60.

Pollard, Tanya, "'No Faith in Physic': Masquerades of Medicine Onstage and Off," in Stephanie Moss and Kaara L. Peterson (eds.), *Disease, Diagnosis and Cure on the Early Modern Stage* (Burlington, VT: Ashgate, 2004), 29–41.

Pollard, Tanya, *Drugs and Theater in Early Modern England* (Oxford: Oxford University Press, 2005).

Pollock, Linda, *With Faith and Physic: The Life of a Tudor Gentlewoman Lady Grace Mildmay, 1552–1620* (New York: St. Martin's Press, 1993).

Poovey, Mary, *A History of the Modern Fact: Problems of Knowledge in the Sciences of Wealth and Society* (Chicago: University of Chicago Press, 1998).

A Proclamation . . . to Avoice Suche Englishe Bookes, as Containe Heresies (London: Thomas Berthelet, 1546). *STC* 7809

Raleigh, Walter, *The History of the World* (London: William Stansby for Walter Burre, 1614). *STC* 20637

Rappaport, Steve, *Worlds within Worlds: Structures of Life in Sixteenth-Century London* (Cambridge: Cambridge University Press, 1989).

Raven, Charles E., *English Naturalists from Neckham to Ray: A Study of the Making of the Modern World* (Cambridge: Cambridge University Press, 1947).

Reed, A. W., "The Regulation of the Book Trade before the Proclamation of 1538," *Transactions of the Bibliographical Society* 15 (1917–1919): 157–184.

Reeds, Karen, "[Untitled Review]," *Isis* 79 (1998): 288–289.

Richards, Jennifer, "Reading and Hearing *The Womans Booke* in Early Modern England," *Bulletin of the History of Medicine* 89 (2015): 434–462.

Richardson, Lisa, "Plagiarism and Imitation in Renaissance Historiography," in Paulina Kewes (ed.), *Plagiarism in Early Modern England* (New York: Palgrave, 2003), 106–118.

Richlin, A. "Pliny's Brassiere," in Laura K. McClure (ed.), *Sexuality and Gender in the Classical World* (Oxford: Blackwell, 2002), 225–255.

Ricks, Christopher, "Plagiarism," in Paulina Kewes (ed.), *Plagiarism in Early Modern England* (New York: Palgrave, 2003), 21–40.

Riddle, John M., "[Untitled Review]," *Systemic Botany* 13 (1988): 473.

Roesslin, Eucharius, *The Byrth of Mankinde* (London: Thomas Raynald, 1540). *STC* 21153

Roesslin, Eucharius, *The Byrth of Mankynde, Otherwyse Named the Womans Booke* (London: Thomas Raynald, 1545). *STC* 21154

Rohde, Eleanour Sinclair, *The Old English Herbals* (London: Longmans, Green and Co., 1922).

Rose, Mark, "The Author as Proprietor: *Donaldson v. Becket* and the Genealogy of Modern Authorship," *Representations* 23 (1988): 51–85.

Rose, Mark, *Authors and Owners: The Invention of Copyright* (Cambridge, MA: Harvard University Press, 1993).

Ryrie, Alec, "Marshall, William (d. 1540?), Printer and Translator," *ODNB*, 2004.

Saenger, Paul and Michael Heinlen, "Incunable Description and Its Implication for the Analysis of Fifteenth-Century Reading Habits," in Sandra Hindman (ed.), *Printing the Written Word: The Social History of Books circa 1450–1520* (Ithaca, NY: Cornell University Press, 1991), 225–258.

Salaman, Redcliffe N., *The History and Social Influence of the Potato* (Cambridge: Cambridge University Press, 1949).

Schroder, H. J. (ed.), *Disciplinary Decrees of the General Councils* (London: B. Herder Book Company, 1937).

Secord, Anne, "Botany on a Plate: Pleasure and the Power of Pictures in Promoting Early Nineteenth-Century Scientific Knowledge," *Isis* 93 (2002): 28–57.

Shakespeare, William, *King Lear*, ed. Kenneth Muir, Arden Second Series (London: Routledge, 1972).

Shakespeare, William, *All's Well That Ends Well*, ed. Susan Snyder (Oxford: Oxford University Press, 1993).

Shakespeare, William, *King Lear*, ed. R. A. Foakes, Arden Third Series (London: Bloomsbury, 1997).

Shakespeare, William, *Hamlet*, ed. Ann Thompson and Neil Taylor, Arden Third Series (London: Bloomsbury, 2006).

Shakespeare, William, *The New Oxford Shakespeare: The Complete Works, Modern Critical Edition*, ed. Gary Taylor, John Jowett, Terri Bourus, and Gabriel Egan (Oxford: Oxford University Press, 2016).

Shapin, Steven, *A Social History of Truth: Civility and Science in Seventeenth-Century England* (Chicago: University of Chicago Press, 1994).

Shaw, Peter, "Plagiary," *The American Scholar* 51 (1982): 325–337.

Sherman, William H., "What Did Renaissance Readers Write in Their Books?" in Jennifer Andersen and Elizabeth Sauer (eds.), *Books and Readers in Early Modern England: Material Studies* (Philadelphia: University of Pennsylvania Press, 2002), 119–137.

Sherman, William H., *Used Books: Marking Readers in Renaissance England* (Philadelphia: University of Pennsylvania Press, 2008).

Shevlin, Eleanor F., "'To Reconcile Book and Title, and Make 'Em Kin to One Another': The Evolution of the Title's Contractual Functions," *Book History* 2 (1999): 42–77.

Slack, Paul, "Mirrors of Health and Treasures of Poor Men: The Uses of the Vernacular Medical Literature of Tudor England," in Hilary Marland and Margaret Pelling (eds.), *The Task of Healing: Medicine, Religion and Gender in England and the Netherlands* (Rotterdam: Erasmus Publishing, 1996), 239–273.

Smith, Pamela, *The Body of the Artisan: Art and Experience in the Scientific Revolution* (Chicago: University of Chicago Press, 2004).

Sofer, Andrew, *The Stage Life of Props* (Ann Arbor: University of Michigan Press, 2003).

Stallybrass, Peter, "Books and Scrolls: Navigating the Bible," in Jennifer Andersen and Elizabeth Sauer (eds.), *Books and Readers in Early Modern England* (Philadelphia: University of Pennsylvania Press, 2002), 42–79.

Stannard, Jerry, "Dioscorides and Renaissance Material Medica," in *Materia Medica in the XVI Century: Proceedings of a Symposium at the International Academy of the History of Medicine* (London: Pergamon Press, 1966), 1–21

Tanselle, G. Thomas, "Historicism and Critical Editing," *Studies in Bibliography* 39 (1986): 1–46.

Tanselle, G. Thomas, *A Rationale of Textual Criticism* (Philadelphia: University of Pennsylvania Press, 1989).

Tanselle, G. Thomas, "Textual Instability and Editorial Idealism," *Studies in Bibliography* 49 (1996): 1–60.

Taylor, Gary, "The War in *King Lear*," *Shakespeare Survey* 33 (1980): 27–34.

Taylor, Gary and Michael Warren (eds.), *The Division of the Kingdoms: Shakespeare's Two Versions of King Lear* (Oxford: Clarendon Press, 1986).

Thomas, A. H. (ed.), *Calendar of Plea and Memoranda Rolls Preserved among the Archives of the Corporation of the City of London at the Guildhall*, 6 vols. (London: 1929–1961).

Tomlins, Thomas E. and John Raithby (eds.), *The Statutes at Large, of England and of Great Britain: From Magna Carta to the Union of the Kingdoms of Great Britain and Ireland*, 20 vols. (London: G. Eyre and A. Strahan, 1811).

Topham, Jonathan R, "A View from the Industrial Age," *Isis* 95 (2004): 431–442.

Tracy, P. B., "Robert Wyer: A Brief Analysis of His Types and a Suggested Chronology for the Output of His Press," *The Library* 6th series, 2 (1980): 293–303.

Traister, Barbara Howard, *The Notorious Astrological Physician of London: Works and Days of Simon Forman* (Chicago: University of Chicago Press, 2001).

Traister, Barbara Howard, "'Note Her a Little Farther': Doctors and Healers in the Drama of Shakespeare," in Stephanie Moss and Kaara L. Peterson (eds.), *Disease, Diagnosis, and Cure on the Early Modern Stage* (Burlington, VT: Ashgate, 2004), 43–52.

Turner, William, *The Huntyng of the Romyshe Vuolpe* (Emden: Egidius van der Erve, 1555). *STC* 24356

Turner, William, *Turner on Birds: A Short and Succinct History of the Principal Birds Noticed by Pliny and Aristotle*. ed. and trans. A. H. Evans (Cambridge: Cambridge University Press, 1903).

Turner, William, *William Turner: Libellus de Re Herbaria 1538, The Names of Herbes 1548*, ed. William T. Stern (London: Ray Society, 1965).

Twyning, John, "Dekker, Thomas (c. 1572–1632), Playwright and Pamphleteer," *ODNB*, 2008.

Unwin, George, *Industrial Organization in the Sixteenth and Seventeenth Centuries* (Oxford: Clarendon Press, 1904).

Unwin, George, *The Gilds and Companies of London*, 3rd ed. (London: Allen & Unwin, 1938).

Viswanathan, S., "Milton and Purchas' Linschoten: An Additional Source for Milton's Indian Figtree," *Milton Newsletter* 2 (1968): 43–45.

Wabuda, Susan, "Crome, Edward (d. 1562), Church of England Clergyman and Religious Controversialist," *ODNB*, 2008.

Wall, Wendy, *The Imprint of Gender: Authorship and Publication in the English Renaissance* (Ithaca, NY: Cornell University Press, 1993).

Wall, Wendy, "Reading the Home: *The Case of The English Housewife*," in Helen Smith and Louise Wilson (eds.), *Renaissance Paratexts* (Cambridge: Cambridge University Press, 2011), 165–184.

Wall, Wendy. *Recipes for Thought: Knowledge and Taste in the Early Modern English Kitchen* (Philadelphia: University of Pennsylvania Press, 2016).

Watt, Diane, "Barton, Elizabeth (c.1506–1534)," *ODNB*, 2004.

Webster, John, *The Duchess of Malfi*, ed. Elizabeth M. Brennan, New Mermaids (London: Ernest Benn, 1964).

Webster, Charles, "Alchemical and Paracelsian Medicine," in Charles Webster (ed.), *Health, Medicine and Morality in the Sixteenth Century* (Cambridge: Cambridge University Press, 1979), 301–334.

Wogan-Browne, J., *Saints' Lives and Women's Literary Culture: Virginity and Its Authorizations* (Oxford: Oxford University Press, 2001).

Xavier, Angela Barreto and Ines G. Županov, *Catholic Orientalism: Portuguese Empire, Indian Knowledge (16th–18th Centuries)* (Oxford: Oxford University Press, 2014).

Yale, Elizabeth, *Sociable Knowledge: Natural History and the Nation in Early Modern Britain* (Philadelphia: University of Pennsylvania Press, 2016).

Young, Sidney, *The Annals of the Barber-Surgeons of London* (New York: AMS Press, 1978).

Index